Dan Appleman's Win32 API Puzzle Book and Tutorial for Visual Basic Programmers

DANIEL APPLEMAN

Apress™

Dan Appleman's Win32 API Puzzle Book and Tutorial for Visual Basic
Programmers Copyright ©1999 by Daniel Appleman

Printed in the United States of America

1 2 3 4 5 6 7 8 9 10—02 01 00 99

Trademarked names are used throughout this book. Rather than use a trademark
symbol with every occurrence of a trademarked name, we are using the names
only in an editorial fashion and to the benefit of the trademark owner, with no
intention of infringement of the trademark.

Project Editor: Carol Carreon Lombardi
Cover, Interior Design, and Composition: Derek Yee Design
Copy Editor: Lunaea Hougland
Proofreader: Christine Sabooni
Production Assistance: Lori Ash
Indexer: Nancy Humphreys
Technical Reviewer: Franky Wong

Distributed to the book trade worldwide by Springer-Verlag New York, Inc.,
175 Fifth Avenue, New York, NY 10010, USA
In the United States: phone: 1-800-SPRINGER; orders@springer-ny.com;
http://www.springer-ny.com/

For information on translations, please contact APress directly:
APress, 555 De Haro Street, Suite 250, San Francisco, CA 94107
phone: 415-552-0445; fax: 415-863-9950; info@apress.com; www.apress.com

ISBN 1-893115-0-11 (alk. paper)

Contents

Preface

WHEN GARY CORNELL AND I STARTED APress, we each committed to writing a book for the new company. I wanted my book to be something special. I wanted to take full advantage of the freedom that comes from having total control and the final say on editorial content and style. I wanted to write a book that would make it possible for every Visual Basic programmer to answer every Win32 API question for themselves. I wanted to write a book that would help VB programmers really learn and understand how to handle even the most complicated API calls. And I wanted to write a book that was fun. Fun to read. Fun to write.

Most books (including my previous books) resemble lectures. They start out by presenting information. They demonstrate how to perform various tasks. They explain sample code. Maybe they ask a few questions or offer suggestions on how to proceed. And most of them double as excellent cures for insomnia.

Now, don't get me wrong. I'm very proud of my previous books. In fact, you'll probably need to refer to my API book (*Dan Appleman's Visual Basic Programmer's Guide to the Win32 API*) in order to get the most out of this book. As a lecturer, I've tried to be a responsible one, providing information that is accurate and useful and providing it in as entertaining a manner as possible. Lectures are an efficient way to get information across and can serve as valuable references for knowledge. But they're still lectures, and lectures just aren't the best way to truly learn something.

This book is not a lecture.

What it is, I'm not quite sure. Perhaps it is a game. Or maybe a toy. Certainly I intend it to be a challenge. I hope you'll find parts of it intriguing, compelling, entertaining, frustrating, and mind-boggling. I hope you'll find yourself learning a lot—not just information and techniques, but also approaches and attitudes. Above all, I hope you'll have fun.

Acknowledgments

Writing your first book for a new publisher is always interesting. Sometimes it is frustrating. Sometimes it is a "learning experience" (which is usually a nice way of saying that you never want to go through that experience again). When Gary, Bill, and I started APress, we wanted to create an author-friendly company. And that included making sure that the production process was designed as much as possible to serve the needs of the author. And as the first author for APress, I got to be the guinea pig.

I must say that Bill Pollock, the publisher, put together one amazing team. I've grown somewhat choosy in terms of what I want from a copy editor—someone who can fix my grammar, spelling, and language, yet with a light touch that does not interfere with the style I've adopted for a given chapter. Lunaea Hougland did a great job in this respect and was backstopped nicely by Chris Sabooni, the proofreader. Thanks also to Lori Ash, who worked on the initial phase of the project. Carol Lombardi was the project manager and my primary contact. Her eye for quality and polite way in which she encouraged me to keep to the schedule made her everything I could ask for in a project manager. Derek Yee handled the composition and rendered my graphics, managing to make them look nice while keeping the precision necessary to maintain accuracy.

One of our highest priorities for APress was to achieve the highest possible quality. While Bill and his crew watched the production quality, maintaining the quality of the content is even more important. Franky Wong, a good friend and co-worker at Desaware, served as technical editor on this book. To say that he did a great job would be an understatement.

Finally, I'd like to thank the many of you who are reading this book and have read my previous works or purchased Desaware's products. Without your support, this book would not exist.

Daniel Appleman
January 1999
dan@desaware.com

Shall We Play a Game?

HAVE YOU EVER WATCHED KIDS PLAY?

It's amazing how intense they can get. Fun is serious business when you're a kid.

It's also interesting that most child development specialists say that when kids are playing they're also learning—a lot.

It seems we lose that somewhere along the way. Learning becomes homework—something we do, at first, because we want to get a good grade and, later, because we have to stay current if we want to stay relevant in this industry. Gradually, the fun is drained out of learning. Play is replaced by long, boring lectures and dry, lifeless textbooks. Who said that information must come in lecture format? Who said that technical books must be serious and dry? I reject that assumption!

And I reject the idea that learning must be hard work!

In a way, we programmers are lucky. Most of us sneak in some time to experiment with new technologies, even if we can't really justify the effort for a given project or bill a customer for the work. We'll spend hours trying to figure out how something works or find a cool new way to do something, even if we'll never use what we learned. We may call it "study" or "research" or "evaluation," but just between you and me, we know it's playing around. It's fun. And it's when we do some of our best learning.

So let's learn something.

Let's play.

How This Book Is Structured

The structure of this book is unlike any other book I've written. In fact, I can't recall seeing anything quite like it. It consists of three parts, each with a different purpose. What's more, it is specifically designed *not* to be read sequentially from cover to cover.

Part I: The Puzzles

Each "chapter" in Part I consists of a short puzzle. The first puzzles (in Section 1 of the book) should prove only mildly frustrating even for beginning VB programmers who have limited experience with API programming. The puzzles increase in difficulty, and the puzzles toward the end—in Sections 4 and 5— should prove challenging even for experts. Although most of the puzzles consist primarily of a code sample that doesn't work and needs to be fixed, expect some surprises along the way.

If you run into trouble, check out Appendix A, "Hints" (also see hint information below).

Part II: The Solutions

Here's where you'll find the solutions to the puzzles in Part I. Each solution includes not only the corrected code, but also an in-depth explanation of why the problem exists and how and why the correction works. Although I realize you may be tempted to jump straight to the solution, I encourage you to spend some time on the puzzle before checking the answer. You'll learn more that way, and the knowledge will stick better.

Part III: The Tutorials

These detailed tutorials cover subjects that relate to calling API functions from Visual Basic. Some of them are intended to fill in gaps that are often found in the education of Visual Basic programmers. Some of them are intended to offer examples that don't lend themselves to a simple puzzle/solution approach for advanced programmers. Some of them contain information or techniques for which I couldn't find a better place.

The Appendixes

Appendix A: Hints

The solutions obviously contain all of the information you need to solve the puzzles in this book. But since you're reading this book in the first place, you are probably well aware that you will run into many cases where a solution to your programming questions is not conveniently available in a book. You'll need to search through other resources to find the answers, and this book is empathetically *not* designed to be a reference that you can go to for questions relating to specific API functions.

If you don't know the solution to a problem, I encourage you to use Appendix A, "Hints," to help locate the information you need in other resources.

There are several resources you should always consider:

The Win32 SDK or MSDN (Microsoft Developer's Network Library or *http://www.microsoft.com*). These are places where you can find the actual

C/C++ documentation for the API in question or the latest bug lists. Visual Basic comes with a limited version of the MSDN library, which includes the Win32 SDK documentation, so you already have the information you need.

The C header files. These are the C header files used by C++ Windows developers and represent the final authority on correct function descriptions. The entire set of Win32 SDK header files is included on the CD-ROM for this book, courtesy of Microsoft.

The Visual Basic documentation. This includes some information on calling API functions.

Chapters 1–4 of my book *Dan Appleman's Visual Basic Programmer's Guide to the Win32 API* (SAMS, ISBN 0-672-31590-4). These chapters include fundamental information on Windows and calling API functions that you must know to solve the puzzles in this book.

In addition, the hints in Appendix A may contain one or more of the following explicit references to resources that can help you solve the puzzles:

My API book (see above). To make life a bit easier, in many cases I've identified the specific chapter in my API book that relates to the API covered by the puzzle. Whereas the chapter might help you solve the puzzle, it will often be more useful for providing background information on the functions in question and will serve as a resource for further reference.

API "Ten Commandment" references. This refers to one of the commandments in my "Ten Commandments for Safe API Programming" (which follow). These commandments can be used as guides to solving almost every API problem.

Tutorials. This refers you to the tutorial (in Part III of this book) that teaches the fundamental concepts necessary to solve the puzzle. These hints will be most useful to beginning programmers, especially for the early puzzles.

My other book: *Dan Appleman's Developing COM/ActiveX Components with Visual Basic 6.0: A Guide to the Perplexed* (SAMS, ISBN 1-56276-576-0). What does an ActiveX book have to do with the Win32 API? A great deal, if you consider that Microsoft's OLE (or ActiveX) technology is implemented using DLLs that export literally hundreds of functions.

Appendix B: Frequently Asked Questions

This book presents a large number of techniques for calling API functions from Visual Basic. But because of the nature of the book, these techniques are scattered among the different puzzles and tutorials. It occurred to me that it would be helpful to provide a cross-reference to help readers find all of the places where particular techniques are covered in the book.

Like most technical books, this one contains an index to help you find information on subjects of interest. But indexes are really nothing more than a keyword search system, and anyone who has spent time using a Web search engine knows that keyword searches have their limits.

This appendix supplements the Index by providing a list of frequently asked questions that are, in effect, a directory of API techniques that are organized into categories.

Appendix C: The APIGID32.DLL Library

This appendix contains documentation for apigid32.dll, a dynamic link library included with this book that contains functions useful for working with API functions from Visual Basic. The source code for this DLL is provided for those interested in writing C++ DLLs for use with Visual Basic.

Navigating the CD-ROM

The most important file on the CD that comes with this book is the file pzl1.hlp in the root directory. Just double-click on this file to launch the Help screen. This Help file includes the following:

- The very latest installation notes and last minute corrections—the equivalent to the traditional "readme" file

- Links to the installation program, which will install any necessary controls and DLLs to run the sample programs

- A half-hour video presentation

- A list of the major directories on the CD-ROM and their contents

- Desaware's online catalog

The sample code can be found in the SourceVB6 and SourceVB5 directories. The SourceVB6 directory contains the VB6 source, which is the reference source code for the book. The SourceVB5 directory contains VB5 versions of the sample programs; however, all of the behavior of the code (as described in the puzzles and solutions) is based on VB6. The VB5 versions are provided as a courtesy and should exhibit the same behavior, but I won't guarantee it.

Under the SourceVB6 directory, you will find three subdirectories: Puzzles, Solved, and Tutorial. Each of these directories contains additional subdirectories for each individual puzzle or tutorial. The Puzzles subdirectory contains the sample code that exhibits the problem described in the puzzle. The Solved directory contains the final solution to each puzzle. The Tutorial directory contains the sample code for the tutorials.

The Cheaders directory contains the Microsoft C header files and is included here courtesy of Microsoft under their Open Tools program. Search these header files to find the values of constants and data type information.

Refer to the pzl1.hlp file for additional information on the contents of the CD.

About Operating Systems

I don't know what operating system you're running. Even if you told me, I wouldn't know what operating system you're running.

At the time this book went to press, you would most likely be running one of the following: Windows 95, Windows 98, Windows NT 3.51, Windows NT 4.0, or Windows NT 2000 beta.

That means I would need to test each puzzle against five operating systems to see if the results that I describe in the solutions actually match what you will see. But even that level of testing would not be sufficient because

- Your Windows 95 might be original, have a service pack installed, or be the OSR1 or OSR2 release.

- Your NT 3.51 could have any of five different service packs.

- Your NT 4.0 could have any of four different service packs.

Even if I knew which version of Windows 95 you installed and which NT service packs you installed, it would still not be sufficient, because every time you install a package from Microsoft—be it Visual Studio (in all of its versions and associated service packs), Internet Explorer (which changes monthly), or Microsoft Office—you may be installing new system components.

What's an author to do?

When we ship software at Desaware, we test on all the major operating system versions with both a clean install and the latest service pack. Then we use our own VersionStamper product to give our applications or components self-diagnosis capabilities so that we can track down what's wrong on a given customer's system (and, in some cases, automatically download components from our FTP site).

But a book can't be self-updating, and a printed page can't scan your system.

So this book assumes that you are running Windows NT 4.0. This is not a bad choice if you think about it—most serious professional developers work on NT instead of Windows 95/98 because NT is a robust operating system with excellent process isolation, a necessity when working at the API level—and Windows 95 and 98 are . . . well, they are operating systems. NT 2000 is likely to exhibit similar behavior to NT 4.0 for the types of applications you'll see in this book, assuming it ever ships.

Results are described for Windows 95/98 when there are differences, because professional developers do need to consider operating system differences when developing applications. As you go through the puzzles, it should become apparent that this type of development should always be done on Windows NT, if only because it detects more errors and provides better error reporting than Windows 95/98.

What Is Not in This Book

This book is about calling API and DLL functions from Visual Basic.

If you're a beginner, you may be wondering, "What's an API function?" or "What's a DLL function?" You may be concerned that you don't know anything about how Windows works. You may not know what the terms "window handle" and "device context" refer to.

Well, I'm not going to tell you.

You see, this book is not about the Win32 API itself. I already wrote that book. It's called *Dan Appleman's Visual Basic Programmer's Guide to the Win32 API*. It's one of the best-selling books for Visual Basic programmers and is available at any bookstore with a good computer book department (or you can order it from Desaware, Inc., at *http://www.desaware.com/* and other mail-order booksellers). The first four chapters of that book contain information that even beginning VB programmers will be able to follow to learn the fundamentals of API programming from Visual Basic. The rest of the book teaches the core Win32 API—how Windows works and how the API functions work. It's 1,500 pages long (plus a few more chapters on CD-ROM). If you think I can cover the information in that book in this much shorter book, you are sorely mistaken. Not only that, why should I bother?

After all, this puzzle book is not about providing reference information. It's not about teaching you the Win32 API itself. It is about teaching you how to interpret C/C++ documentation for yourself so you can create your own declarations and solve complex API-related problems. It's about helping you understand the API calling mechanism clearly so you can effectively apply the information in my API book in cases where there are no specific examples available or where you are trying to apply a function in a way that is not shown in an example.

Why is this necessary? Because the Win32 API keeps growing—new functions are added daily—and I don't have the time to keep creating mammoth books to cover these new functions. And nobody else seems to be interested in the job.

If you are able to solve all of the puzzles in this book, you won't need another mammoth API book. You'll be able to go straight to the C/C++ documentation and create your own declarations quickly and accurately. In fact, you will be qualified to write your own VB programmer's book on any of the Win32 extension libraries.

And now that I double as an occasional acquisitions editor, you're welcome to drop me a line if you are ever actually interested in doing so.

The Ten Commandments for Safe API Programming (Revised Yet Again)

I wrote the original "Ten Commandments for Safe API Programming" around 1992, and versions of it have appeared in publications, conference proceedings, Web sites, and books. I've stated that following these commandments can solve almost every API programming problem, and for some reason people seem reluctant to believe me. Perhaps I'll be able to make my point with this book, because many of the puzzles include hints that refer to the relevant commandment.

Don't worry if some (or all) of the concepts in these commandments are unclear right now. By the time you work your way through the puzzles, solutions, and tutorials, they will become second nature.

I
Remember ByVal and keep it wholly.

Correct use of the ByVal statement is the single most important factor for successful API programming from Visual Basic. Keep in mind that the ByVal keyword is sometimes used in the function call itself, not just in the declaration. For applying advanced techniques, it is essential to really understand what the ByVal keyword does and its impact on how API functions are called from Visual Basic.

II
Thou shalt check thy parameter types.

Getting parameter types correct is critical, more so under Win32 than it was under Win16. Under Win32, most parameters are passed as 32-bit values regardless of their actual size. Thus the traditional "bad DLL calling convention" error does not detect as many errors as it did under Win16. The result can be subtle bugs that are data-dependent and extremely difficult to track down. Keep in mind that many API functions can accept more than one data type for a given parameter, so it's important to understand exactly how different parameter types are passed to the functions. Also remember that Visual Basic practices a form of evil type coercion in which it will automatically convert values from one type to another without warning. This can lead to passing a parameter that you think is the correct type, but that actually contains an invalid value.

III
Thou shalt check thy return types.

Most API functions return 32-bit long results. Problems with return values usually occur when your declaration returns anything other than a Long value. The most common mistake is to forget to add a return type to the function declaration. In this case, Visual Basic defaults to a variant return type, which is sure to be incorrect and will typically cause either a "bad DLL calling convention" error or a memory exception.

IV

*Thou shalt preinitialize thy strings,
lest ye become corrupted.*

API functions that take string parameters typically see them as addresses to locations in memory that contain a string terminated by a null character. Many functions can pass string data back to the calling VB application by loading that memory location with the data. However, the API function has no way of knowing how large a space is actually available in the buffer provided. Some functions allow you to pass the buffer size as a separate parameter. Others simply require that a buffer be of a certain size. In either case, if you pass an uninitialized or empty string to a function, the memory buffer has either no space or a single character (the NULL terminating character). If the API function tries loading data into the memory address provided, it is sure to overwrite critical data in your application memory space. Bugs introduced in this manner can range from immediate memory exceptions to subtle, rare bugs that only appear once you've shipped thousands of copies of your application. Be sure to initialize string buffers if there is any chance that the API function can modify the buffer.

V

*Thou shalt not use As Any,
for it is evil.*

When you declare a parameter type As Any, you are placing the full responsibility for passing the correct data type to the code where the function is called. Visual Basic does no type checking whatsoever.

The most common use of As Any declarations is where API function parameters can take more than one data type. Fortunately, Visual Basic allows you to create multiple declarations for the same function, thanks to the Alias option in the Declare statement.

But there are cases where it's just far more convenient to leave a parameter As Any. Sometimes a function can take too many different data types, and it would be inconvenient to define and remember a different declaration for each one. Or perhaps the function has more than one parameter that can take multiple data types, in which case each new type requires multiple declarations.

Whichever approach you choose, it's important to understand As Any parameters and how they work. Besides, you never know when you'll run into some code written by someone who doesn't follow these commandments.

VI

Thou shalt specify Option Explicit.

The Require Variable Declarations editor option is one that you should always set when working with Visual Basic. If you are reworking code that was created without this option set, be sure to add the command Option Explicit to the start of each code module (including forms, UserControls, classes, and so forth).

Without this option set, any reference to a variable automatically creates an empty instance of that variable. This includes cases where you accidentally create a new variable by misspelling the name of an existing variable. Worse yet, from the perspective of an API programmer, the newly created variable will probably be a variant. No matter how you look at it, the results are unlikely to be what you intended. The extra effort involved in declaring each variable before you use it is nothing compared to the pain and suffering of finding obscure bugs caused by typographical errors.

VII
Honor thy VB integers and thy Win32 Integers, for they are not alike.

An integer is 16 bits. Or is it? Under Win32, if you are reading C or C++ documentation (which is the default language for all Windows documentation), an "int" and all references to integers actually refer to a 32-bit value. So, if a person or document refers to "integers," it is essential that you keep in mind the context of the reference.

VIII
Always recheck thy function names, for they are now case-sensitive and may have suffixes.

All API function names are case-sensitive under Win32. This differs from the Win16 API, where the case of function names did not matter. Also watch out for suffixes in situations where the function takes string parameters. There is a good chance that the actual name of the function in the DLL has the letter "A" or "W" as a suffix, indicating the ANSI or Unicode entry point for the function.

IX
Thou shalt check parameter and return values.

One of the nicest things about Visual Basic is that it is an interpreted language. This means you can stop your code at any point in the execution and examine the values of each parameter. If an API call is not working as you would expect, stop at that point and examine the actual parameter values being used in the call. Look for values that make no sense, especially parameters that should contain valid data but contain 0 instead (suggesting a failure in a previous API call). Check the return values of the functions and use the Err.LastDllError method call to obtain additional information about the failure.

X
Save thy work often.

The nice thing about using API function calls is that, once you have them declared and coded correctly, they are extremely reliable. The not-quite-as-nice thing about using API functions is that, until you have them declared and coded correctly, your errors are likely to lead to memory exceptions that crash your program, freeze Visual Basic, and on occasion even crash your system. There is nothing quite like the frustration of hitting the Run button after adding dozens of lines of new code, only to have the code vanish in a memory exception. For peace of mind, I personally save my work every time I run my code. It's an approach I strongly recommend.

Part I
THE PUZZLES

PEOPLE HAVE DIFFERENT STYLES OF EMBARKING on journeys. Some prepare extensively, pack carefully, learn some phrases in the native language, and otherwise plan all of the details of their trip as carefully as possible. Others toss a change of clothes in a backpack, grab the next flight out, and *go*. . . .

Every book can be thought of as a journey. Let's ignore for a moment the bad books, which are like tours planned by inexperienced amateurs or scam artists who go out of business after booking your tour, leaving you stranded in some deserted airport in some Third World country, where a uniformed soldier toting an AK-47 is eyeing your luggage as if it were his own--or at least about to become his own.

Even the good books (of which I hope this is an example) can vary in style. Some books let you travel first class. They are designed to be friendly and welcoming, with every step of the journey laid out to ease you, in luxurious comfort, to your next destination.

This book is more like an adventure tour or Outward Bound trip. It's intentionally designed to challenge you and occasionally to trip up even the most experienced programmer. Ultimately the idea is to build up your knowledge and experience so that you are confident in your ability to handle any challenge that comes your way.

If you are the type of traveler who likes to plan your trip ahead of time, I encourage you to delay your departure and skip forward to Part III of this book, where you can study the tutorials and become familiar with the destinations that you are soon to visit.

But if you are the type of traveler who just likes to dive in--go right ahead. The tutorials will be there when (I mean, if) you run into trouble along the way.

In the Beginning

HAVE YOU EVER BOUGHT AN INTERMEDIATE or advanced programming book, only to find that the first chapter begins with in-depth explanations of variables, simple operations, or ways to perform simple tasks, such as adding controls to a form? I have, and I've always found that type of book very frustrating. Not because there is anything fundamentally wrong with covering this kind of beginning information, but because I know that the advanced information that I want will usually be relegated to a few chapters toward the end of the book and will usually be inadequate as well.

But you have to understand that every author faces a real dilemma: If you start out at a level that is too advanced, you risk losing much of your audience and thus selling considerably fewer books.[1] If you start out at a level that is too simple, you end up frustrating the professionals, who hate reading rehashes of things that they already know. It's a fine line to walk.

Therefore, this book is targeted at the intermediate-level Visual Basic programmer who wishes to become an expert. The puzzles assume that the reader has at least some degree of experience calling API functions. Those that don't are encouraged to work through the tutorials before trying any of the puzzles. Given those assumptions, I've taken the liberty of making even the early puzzles in this section of the book just a little bit trickier[2] than you might normally expect from the "beginning" label. I suspect that even experienced programmers may have to look twice at many of these, even though most of the solutions turn out to be quite simple.

---

1. I know this sounds a bit like crass commercialism, but I think it is important that readers understand a little bit about the economics of the publishing business, because it explains a great deal about why so many lousy books are published. I actually wrote an essay on the subject called "Are you learning Visual Basic backwards?" that is available on our Web site at www.desaware.com.

2. OK, maybe a lot trickier in some cases.

Where, oh, Where Is That API Call?

IT'S A SMALL WORLD, AND YOU NEVER KNOW when you might need to adapt your software to run correctly in other parts of the world. Awkward though it may be, other countries stubbornly insist on using their own languages, currency symbols, and punctuation marks. They even arrange date and time formats in different orders.[1]

Windows uses the term "locale" to identify a locality and its characteristics. Each locale has a unique number. Fortunately, Windows makes it easy to find out the characteristics of the locale under which your application is running.

Here's a simple program you can use to obtain the number of the current locale:

```
Private Declare Function GetUserDefaultLcid Lib "User32" () As Long

Private Sub Command1_Click()
    Dim lcid&
    Dim info$
    lcid = GetUserDefaultLcid()
    MsgBox lcid, vbOKOnly, "User Default LCID"
End Sub
```

Results

Runtime error 453:

```
Can't find DLL entry point GetUserDefaultLcid in User32
```

Where, oh, where, can you find the API call? Fix the declaration to make this program work.

---

1. Lest I be accused of being U.S.–centric right from the start, allow me to point out that the above paragraph is relevant regardless of which primary language and country you are developing for.

The Last Error

ONE OF THE INTRIGUING TASKS WINDOWS programmers sometimes undertake relates to using one program to control the system or another application. The first step in many of these programs is to obtain the window handle for the other application. The FindWindow API function can be used to find a window handle, given its caption or class. The C declaration for FindWindow is as follows:

```
HWND FindWindow(
    LPCTSTR lpClassName, // pointer to class name
    LPCTSTR lpWindowName // pointer to window name
    );
```

This function is designed so that you can specify either the window class (the type of window) or its name (the caption). You can also specify both, but that's rarely necessary. Since this example wants to use the window caption, you'll just set the class name to NULL.

You could look up the declaration for FindWindow in the api32.txt file (included on the CD with this book) or the win32api.txt file that comes with Visual Basic, but why not try to figure it out first?

Since FindWindow is part of the window subsystem, it uses User32 (kernel32 contains core OS functions, and GDI32 contains graphic functions, as described in Tutorial 1, "Finding Functions," in Part III of this book). Since the function takes string parameters, you know that there are both ANSI and Unicode entry points for the function, so you'll need to use an alias to access the ANSI entry point.[1] An HWND is a handle, which under Win32 is a Long, so the return value is a Long. Both parameters are strings, which need to be passed ByVal so that they will be passed as NULL-terminated strings. The declaration is thus

```
Declare Function FindWindow Lib "User32" Alias "FindWindowA" _
(ByVal lpClassName As String, ByVal lpWindowName As Long) As Long
```

----

1. If you do not already know that API functions that take string parameters have separate entry points, or have no idea what the terms "ANSI," "Unicode," or "entry point" refer to, please take a break from this puzzle and read Tutorial 5, "The ByVal Keyword: The Solution to 90 Percent of All API Problems," in Part III of this book.

The LastErr.vbp project (on the CD that comes with this book) has a form with a text box named txtCaption into which you can type the caption of the main window of any program. The FindWindow function retrieves the handle to that window. The program then uses the PostMessage function to post a WM_CLOSE message into the message queue for the window—this is the same message that is posted when you use the close box or system menu to close a window.

```
Private Declare Function PostMessage Lib "User32" Alias _
"PostMessageA" (ByVal hWnd As Long, ByVal Message As Long, ByVal _
wParam As Long, ByVal lParam As Long) As Long
Private Const WM_CLOSE = &H10


Private Sub cmdClose_Click()
    Dim WindowHandle As Long
    WindowHandle = FindWindow("", txtCaption.Text)
    If WindowHandle = 0 Then
        MsgBox "No window: Last Error was " & Err.LastDllError
        Exit Sub
    Else
        Call PostMessage(WindowHandle, WM_CLOSE, 0, 0)
    End If
End Sub
```

Results

The default caption is "Untitled – Notepad," which is the caption of a default Notepad application window. The program fails. The message box displays the LastError code, a value provided by the operating system that explains the reason for the error.[2] Your mission is twofold:

1. Find the meaning of the last error code.

2. Fix the program so that it will work.

---

2. The LastDllError code will be 123 on Windows NT, 0 on Windows 95/98.

Poly Want a Cracker?

THE WINDOWS GRAPHICAL DEVICE INTERFACE (GDI) has far more graphics capability than is built into Visual Basic. One of the functions allows you to draw a polygon of as many lines as you wish in a single operation. The Polygon function is defined in the C documentation as follows:

```
BOOL Polygon(
HDC hdc,                  // handle to device context
CONST POINT *lpPoints,   // pointer to polygon's vertices
int nCount               // count of polygon's vertices
);
```

The hdc parameter is the device context for the window on which the polygon will be drawn. The lpPoints parameter is a pointer to the first of a series of coordinates describing the points that are to be connected. The nCount parameter is the number of points.

Can you fix the following program to display the pattern shown in Figure P3-1?

```
' Poly Example Program
' Copyright © 1998 by Desaware Inc. All Rights Reserved

Option Explicit

Private Type POINTAPI
    X As Long
    Y As Long
End Type

Private Declare Function Polygon Lib "gdi32" (hdc As Long, _
lpPoint As POINTAPI, nCount As Long) As Long

' Function loads an array of points
Private Sub LoadPointArray(ByVal Width As Long, ByVal Height _
As Long, ByVal Increment As Integer, PointArray() As POINTAPI)
    Dim curidx As Integer
    ReDim PointArray((Height \ Increment) + 2)
    Do
```

```
        curidx = curidx + 1
        PointArray(curidx).X = Width
        PointArray(curidx).Y = Height - curidx * Increment
        curidx = curidx + 1
        PointArray(curidx).X = 0
        PointArray(curidx).Y = curidx * Increment
    Loop While curidx * Increment < Height

End Sub

Private Sub Form_Paint()
    Dim points() As POINTAPI
    LoadPointArray Width, Height, 5, points()
    Call Polygon(hWnd, points(0), UBound(points) + 1)
End Sub

Private Sub Form_Resize()
    Refresh
End Sub
```

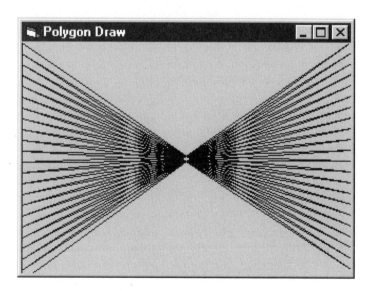

Figure P3-1: Correct display for the Poly program

Results

The code shown above displays an empty form.

    Can you make it work? It may be trickier than it looks.

It's All in the Name

WE LIKE TO NAME OUR COMPUTERS. No, this does not come from a deep-seated need to give them human characteristics. Rather, it comes from a deep need to enter some sort of a computer name when installing Windows.

Fortunately, the Win32 API makes it easy for any program to find out the name of the computer on which it is running.

The GetComputerName function is declared in C as follows:

```
BOOL GetComputerName(
LPTSTR lpBuffer,    // address of name buffer
LPDWORD nSize       // address of size of name buffer
);
```

Right off the top of your head, you can come up with the following simple program that retrieves the computer name and displays it in a label control:

```
' Computer Name
' Copyright © 1998 by Desaware Inc. All Rights Reserved

Option Explicit

Private Declare Function GetComputerName Lib "kernel32" (ByVal _
ComputerName As String, ByVal BufferSize As Long) As Long

Private Const MAX_COMPUTERNAME_LENGTH = 15

Private Sub Form_Load()
    Dim s$
    Call GetComputerName(s$, MAX_COMPUTERNAME_LENGTH + 1)
    lblName.Caption = s$
End Sub
```

Results

So much for code written off the top of your head. Care to try your hand at fixing this program?

Finding the Executable Name

YOU ALWAYS KNOW THE NAME OF your program. After all, you compiled it and probably installed it. But when you create software components, those components may be called from many different applications, and you won't necessarily know which application is using your component.

Why would you need to know this? The most common reason is if you want to license your component. You might want to detect whether it is being used from within the Visual Basic runtime environment or a compiled executable. If it's running within the VB environment, you can check to see if the license is present before allowing your component to run.

The Win32 API makes it easy to determine the name of the program that originally launched a process. The GetModuleFileName function does the trick. It is defined in the Win32 Software Development Kit (SDK) as follows:

```
DWORD GetModuleFileName(
    HMODULE hModule,      // handle to module to find filename for
    LPTSTR lpFilename,    // pointer to buffer to receive module path
    DWORD nSize  // size of buffer, in characters
    );
```

Converting these parameter types to Visual Basic is so easy as to be almost routine. The hModule parameter is a handle, so it's a 32-bit Long value. The lpFilename parameter is a string that will be loaded with the full path and name of the executable. It will need to be declared ByVal as String. The nSize parameter is another 32-bit Long value that will contain the length of the string buffer. And, because the function deals with process management, it will be in the kernel32 dynamic link library. The function can thus be declared as follows:

```
Private Declare Function GetModuleFileName Lib "kernel32" Alias _
"GetModuleFileNameA" (ByVal hModule As Long, ByVal lpFileName As _
String, ByVal nSize As Long) As Long
```

The hModule parameter deserves further discussion. A module handle under Windows contains the address at which the given module is loaded in memory.

When an application is launched, the executable is mapped into memory starting from the module address for that executable. Each DLL used by the application is mapped into a different address, which becomes the module address for that DLL.[1] The GetModuleFileName function can retrieve the file name for any module used by a process.

In this case, we take advantage of a cool trick—if you set the hModule parameter to 0, the function retrieves the name of the original application that launched the process.

The ExecutableFinder project is a simple ActiveX DLL component that contains a single-class object called Server. This object exposes a single method that allows the caller to determine if the running application is Visual Basic. When an application creates a Server object, the ExecutableFinder DLL is loaded into the process. The IsThisVB method uses the GetModuleFileName function to see if the running executable is Visual Basic. When you are running a program within the Visual Basic development environment, GetModuleFileName will indicate that the program is vb6.exe, vb5.exe, or vb32.exe depending on whether you are running VB6, VB5, or VB4. When you are running a compiled executable, it will retrieve the path of the compiled executable.

The Server class contains the following code:

```
' What's the Executable?
' Copyright © 1998 by Desaware Inc. All Rights Reserved
Option Explicit

Private Declare Function GetModuleFileName Lib "kernel32" Alias _
"GetModuleFileNameA" (ByVal hModule As Long, ByVal lpFileName As _
String, ByVal nSize As Long) As Long
Private Const MAX_PATH = 260

Public Function IsThisVB() As Boolean
    Dim ExecName As String
    Dim LastBackslashPos As Long
    ExecName = String$(MAX_PATH + 1, 0)
    Call GetModuleFileName(0, ExecName, MAX_PATH)
    ' Now strip off the path
    LastBackslashPos = InStrRev(ExecName, "\")
    If LastBackslashPos = 0 Then
        LastBackslashPos = InStrRev(ExecName, ":")
    End If
    ExecName = Mid$(ExecName, LastBackslashPos + 1)
```

---

1. Refer to Appendix B, "Frequently Asked Questions," for further resources if you wish to learn more about module handles.

```
    If LCase$(ExecName) = "vb6.exe" Or _
       LCase$(ExecName) = "vb5.exe" Or _
       LCase$(ExecName) = "vb32.exe" Then
       IsThisVB = True
    End If

End Function
```

The ExecName parameter is a string that is initialized to MAX_PATH + 1 bytes. This is long enough to contain the longest path supported by the system. The GetModuleFileName function loads the string with the full path of the executable that started the process.

In this case, you don't care about the full path—only the final executable name. The easiest way to strip off the rest of the path is to search for the last backslash character (or the colon character, in case the program is running from the root directory). Everything prior to and including the backslash is removed from the string using the Mid$ function. Finally, a case-insensitive comparison is performed against the three Visual Basic executable names. The function returns True if any of the executable names match.

Results

Add a simple project to the Visual Basic environment for testing purposes as shown in the IsThisVB group.

```
' IsThisVBTest Sample Program
' Copyright © 1998 by Desaware Inc. All Rights Reserved

Option Explicit

Private Sub Form_Load()
   Dim serverobject As New Server
   If serverobject.IsThisVB Then
      Label1.Caption = "Yes - it's VB"
   Else
      Label1.Caption = "No - it's not VB"
   End If
End Sub
```

For some reason, this program never detects that it is running within the Visual Basic environment.

Your job is to figure out why.

PUZZLE 6

Icon Fix This One

MOST PROGRAMMERS ARE FAMILIAR WITH ICONS—those cute little rectangular symbols that are used throughout Windows.[1] Icons can be stored in individual icon files (typically with the extension .ico) or as resources within Windows executables and dynamic link libraries.

The Windows system provides a number of built-in icons that can be loaded using the LoadIcon function. This function is defined as follows under the Win32 documentation:

```
HICON LoadIcon(
    HINSTANCE hInstance, // handle of application instance
    LPCTSTR lpIconName   // icon-name string or icon resource identifier
);
```

This looks quite simple. The hInstance parameter, like all handles, will be a Long and passed by value. The lpIconName parameter is a string. The type breaks down as follows:

LP   Long (far) Pointer

C   Constant, meaning that the API function does not change the contents of the string

T   Varies depending on entry point. The string will be ANSI for the ANSI entry point, Unicode for the Unicode entry point.

STR   NULL-terminated C string

The declaration is therefore

```
Private Declare Function LoadIcon Lib "user32.dll" Alias "LoadIconA" _
    ( ByVal hInstance As Long, _
    ByVal lpIconName As String) As Long
```

---

1. Rectangular, you ask? Icons are always rectangular—but portions of an icon can be made transparent, so they may seem to have many different shapes.

If you are loading an icon resource, the hInstance parameter contains the module handle of the loaded DLL. If the hInstance parameter is NULL, a system icon is loaded. The lpIconName parameter identifies the icon to load and has the following interesting description:

> *Points to a null-terminated string that contains the name of the icon resource to be loaded. Alternatively, this parameter can contain the resource identifier in the low-order word and 0 in the high-order word. Use the MAKEINTRE-SOURCE macro to create this value.*

The MAKEINTRESOURCE function is defined as follows in the winuser.h header file:

```
#define MAKEINTRESOURCEA(i) (LPSTR)((DWORD)((WORD)(i)))
#define MAKEINTRESOURCEW(i) (LPWSTR)((DWORD)((WORD)(i)))
#ifdef UNICODE
#define MAKEINTRESOURCE  MAKEINTRESOURCEW
#else
#define MAKEINTRESOURCE  MAKEINTRESOURCEA
#endif // !UNICODE
```

If the hInstance parameter is NULL, the lpIconName parameter can be one of the following predefined constants:

```
#ifdef RC_INVOKED
#define IDI_APPLICATION       32512
#define IDI_HAND              32513
#define IDI_QUESTION          32514
#define IDI_EXCLAMATION       32515
#define IDI_ASTERISK          32516
#if(WINVER >= 0x0400)
#define IDI_WINLOGO           32517
#endif /* WINVER >= 0x0400 */
#else
#define IDI_APPLICATION       MAKEINTRESOURCE(32512)
#define IDI_HAND              MAKEINTRESOURCE(32513)
#define IDI_QUESTION          MAKEINTRESOURCE(32514)
#define IDI_EXCLAMATION       MAKEINTRESOURCE(32515)
#define IDI_ASTERISK          MAKEINTRESOURCE(32516)
#if(WINVER >= 0x0400)
#define IDI_WINLOGO           MAKEINTRESOURCE(32517)
#endif /* WINVER >= 0x0400 */
#endif /* RC_INVOKED */
```

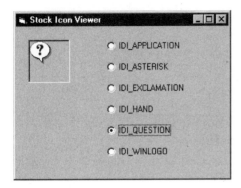

Figure P6-1: The main form of the IconView application

Figure P6-1 shows the main form of the IconView application as it should appear. Each option button selects a different predefined icon.

The m_IconID variable in the IconView project (on the CD that comes with this book) holds the constant value corresponding to the selected icon. During the picture box Paint event, the LoadIcon function is used to load the actual icon resource. The DrawIcon function is used to draw the icon onto the picture box. The DrawIcon function is described in the Win32 documentation as follows:

```
BOOL DrawIcon(
    HDC hdc, // handle to device context
    int X,    // x-coordinate of upper-left corner
    int Y,    // y-coordinate of upper-left corner
    HICON hIcon      // handle to icon to draw
    );
```

The hDC parameter is the device context of the window on which you are drawing, the X and Y parameters specify the location for the icon, and the hIcon parameter is the handle to the icon—all 32 bits, all by value.

Here's the sample program:

```
' IconView Puzzle
' Copyright © 1998 by Desaware Inc. All Rights Reserved

Option Explicit

Private Declare Function LoadIcon Lib "user32.dll" Alias _
    "LoadIconA" ( _
    ByVal hInstance As Long, _
    ByVal lpIconName As String) As Long

Private Declare Function DrawIcon Lib "user32" (ByVal hdc As Long, _
ByVal x As Long, ByVal y As Long, ByVal hIcon As Long) As Long

Private Const IDI_APPLICATION = 32512&
```

```
Private Const IDI_HAND = 32513&
Private Const IDI_QUESTION = 32514&
Private Const IDI_EXCLAMATION = 32515&
Private Const IDI_ASTERISK = 32516&
Private Const IDI_WINLOGO = 32517&


Private m_IconID As Long


Private Sub Form_Load()
   m_IconID = IDI_APPLICATION
End Sub


Private Sub optIcon_Click(Index As Integer)
   Select Case Index
Case 0
        m_IconID = IDI_APPLICATION
      Case 1
        m_IconID = IDI_ASTERISK
      Case 2
        m_IconID = IDI_EXCLAMATION
      Case 3
        m_IconID = IDI_HAND
      Case 4
        m_IconID = IDI_QUESTION
      Case 5
        m_IconID = IDI_WINLOGO   End Select
   Picture1.Refresh
End Sub


Private Sub Picture1_Paint()
   Dim iconhandle As Long
   iconhandle = LoadIcon(0, m_IconID)
   If iconhandle = 0 Then
      MsgBox GetErrorString(Err.LastDllError)
   Else
      Call DrawIcon(Picture1.hdc, 0, 0, iconhandle)
   End If
 End Sub
```

Results

No icon is displayed. Need I say more?

Supercharged Graphics

AMONG THE MOST USEFUL WIN32 API functions is a set of graphic primitives that put those offered by Visual Basic to shame. Many of the Win32 graphic functions provide not only complex drawing and filling capabilities, but also blinding speed. This is, in part, why Windows is able to delegate many drawing operations to your graphic card or printer engine instead of rendering the image on your computer.

In this example, we'll take a look at one of the more simple graphing functions—the Polyline function. This function is defined as follows in the Win32 SDK:

```
BOOL Polyline(
    HDC hdc,        // handle of device context
    CONST POINT *lppt,   // address of array containing endpoints
    int cPoints    // number of points in the array
    );
```

As you can see,

- The hdc parameter is the handle of a device context for drawing. Like most handles, this is a Long value.

- The lppt parameter is an array of POINT structures. The CONST keyword simply indicates that the values in this array are not modified by the API function.

- The nCount parameter is the number of entries in the array—the number of points in the lines. The function will draw a line from each point to the next in the array using the current color.

A POINT structure is defined in C as follows:

```
typedef struct  tagPOINT
    {
    LONG x;
    LONG y;
    } POINT;
```

The POINT structure should be declared in Visual Basic as follows:

```
Type POINTAPI
        x As Long
        y As Long
End Type
```

Why is the name changed to POINTAPI from POINT? Because "point" is a Visual Basic reserved word, and replacing it with a user-defined structure can lead to confusion both on the part of people trying to understand your program and on the part of Visual Basic itself.

The Polyline program is designed to divide a circle into a specified number of points and draw lines following a random path between all of the points on the circle as shown in Figure P7-1.

The program has a text box that allows you to specify the number of points, a Clear button that allows you to clear the form, a Draw Shape button that allows you to perform the drawing operation, and an Auto checkbox that causes the program to continuously select a random number of points and draw the line sequence based on those points. The result can be some almost-hypnotic special effects.

The example below shows the Polyline program. The SetupPoints function may be tricky to follow if you don't remember high school trigonometry. You don't really need to follow the mathematics behind the drawing to understand or

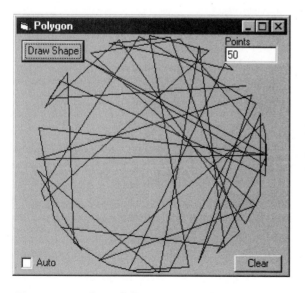

Figure P7-1: The Polyline program draws a random path of lines between points on a circle

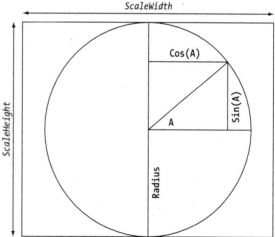

Figure P7-2: Illustration of the circle calculation

solve the puzzle, but here is a quick explanation for those who would like to make the attempt.

Figure P7-2 should help you follow the logic.

In the following example, the form is wider than it is tall. This means that the radius of the circle will be half the height, or ScaleHeight/2. For a given angle A, the horizontal distance to the center from a point on the circle will be the radius times cos(A). The vertical distance from the center to a point on the circle will be the radius times sin(A). The center of the circle is point (ScaleWidth/2, ScaleHeight/2), so these values will be added to the distance from the center to obtain the position of the point on the form. The ScaleMode parameter for the form is set to pixels because the Polyline API function expects pixel coordinate values.

```vb
' Polyline Example
' Copyright © 1998 by Desaware Inc. All Rights Reserved

Option Explicit

Private Type POINTAPI
        X As Long
        y As Long
End Type

Private Declare Function Polyline Lib "gdi32" (ByVal hdc As Long, _
lppt() As POINTAPI, ByVal nCount As Long) As Long

Private PointArray() As POINTAPI

Private CurrentColorIndex As Integer

' We need the Arccos function - arccos(0) is Pi
Private Function Arccos(X As Double)
    Arccos = Atn(-X / Sqr(-X * X + 1)) + 2 * Atn(1)
End Function

' This function divides the circle into points and mixes them up
Private Sub SetupPoints(PointCount As Long, Radius As Long, Xoffset As _
Long, Yoffset As Long)
    Dim AngleIncrement As Double
    Dim PointNumber As Long
    Dim SwapPoint As Long
    Dim TempPoint As POINTAPI
```

```
    ' Arccos(0) is Pi. 2 * Pi is the number of radians in a circle.
    ' 2 * Pi / PointCount is the angle (in radians) between points.
    AngleIncrement = 2 * Arccos(0) / PointCount
    ReDim PointArray(PointCount)
    ' The Cos and Sin functions obtain the X and Y location along a circle
    ' for a given angle.
    For PointNumber = 0 To PointCount - 1
        PointArray(PointNumber).X = Cos(PointNumber * PointCount) * _
        Radius + Xoffset
        PointArray(PointNumber).y = Sin(PointNumber * PointCount) * _
        Radius + Yoffset
    Next PointNumber
    ' Return to the original point
    LSet PointArray(PointCount) = PointArray(0)

    ' Don't move the first or last point
    For PointNumber = 1 To PointCount
        ' Swap each point with a random point
        SwapPoint = Int(Rnd() * PointCount)
        LSet TempPoint = PointArray(SwapPoint)
        LSet PointArray(SwapPoint) = PointArray(PointNumber)
        LSet PointArray(PointNumber) = TempPoint
    Next PointNumber
End Sub


Private Sub chkAuto_Click()
    Timer1.Enabled = chkAuto.Value
End Sub

Private Sub cmdClear_Click()
    ' Clear the form
    Me.Cls
End Sub

Private Sub cmdDraw_Click()
    Dim points As Long
    Dim Radius As Long

    ' The number of points is retrieved from the text box
    points = txtPoints.Text
    If points = 0 Then points = 2
    ' The radius is the smaller of half the height or width
```

```
      If ScaleWidth < ScaleHeight Then
         Radius = ScaleWidth / 2
      Else
         Radius = ScaleHeight / 2
      End If

      SetupPoints points, Radius, ScaleWidth / 2, ScaleHeight / 2
      Call Polyline(hdc, PointArray(), points)
      ' Switch to the next of the 16 standard colors
      CurrentColorIndex = (CurrentColorIndex + 1) Mod 16
      Me.ForeColor = QBColor(CurrentColorIndex)
   End Sub

Private Sub Form_Load()
   Randomize
End Sub

Private Sub Timer1_Timer()
   ' Draw using the current settings
   cmdDraw_Click
   ' And set a new point count for next time
   txtPoints.Text = Int(Rnd() * 50) + 5
End Sub
```

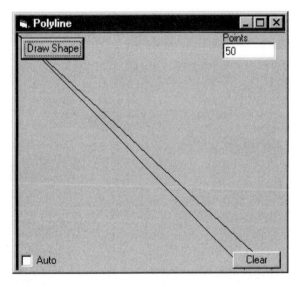

Figure P7-3: The actual image drawn by the program looks nothing like the desired result

Results

The Polyline function is very fast. You can see this by clicking on the Auto button and watching the drawing update itself.

You could, that is, except that the actual results you will see when you click the Draw Shape button may range from an empty form to something like Figure P7-3.

Can you fix the program?

PUZZLE 8

Playing Leapfrog

WINDOWS PROVIDES THE API FUNCTION GETVERSIONEX to allow your application to determine the operating system version currently running. This issue of operating system version may seem unimportant and is relatively meaningless to those using Visual Basic alone. But the system version can be a critical piece of information to programmers using the Win32 API. Why? Because Microsoft keeps adding API functions to the operating system, and the version information is your best tool to make sure a function is available before you try to call it.

A Win32 application should degrade gracefully under older operating systems. In other words, if you take advantage of functionality provided by a newer system, such as NT 5.0, your application should not attempt to use that functionality on older systems. Rather, it should disable that part of the application, use an alternate approach to providing the functionality, or terminate gracefully with a not-too-annoying suggestion that the user upgrade his system.

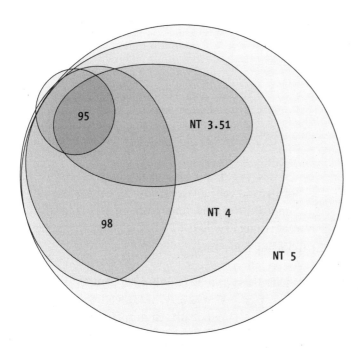

Figure P8-1: Each operating system version supports a different subset of the Win32 API

Of the major operating systems currently in use (and no, we will no longer consider 16-bit systems, even though there are many still in use), Windows 95 and NT 3.51 are the least capable. Both lack functions available under NT 4, 5, and Windows 98, and both lack functions that the other supports. Figure P8-1 shows a rough outline of the overlap of functions. As you can see, each version of Windows NT builds on the API set of earlier versions. Windows NT as of version 4.0 contains most of the functions from Windows 95 and Windows 98, but the reverse is emphatically not true. Windows 98 supports more NT functionality than Windows 95, but nowhere near all of it.

Win32 applications use the GetVersionEx function to obtain detailed version information from the operating system.

The GetVersionEx function is defined as follows in the Windows documentation:

*The **GetVersionEx** function obtains extended information about the version of the operating system that is currently running.*

```
BOOL GetVersionEx(
    LPOSVERSIONINFO lpVersionInformation    // pointer to version
                                            // information structure
);
```

The function takes as a parameter a pointer to an OSVERSIONINFO structure, which is defined as follows:

```
typedef struct _OSVERSIONINFO{
DWORD dwOSVersionInfoSize;      ' The size of the structure
DWORD dwMajorVersion;           ' The major version number
DWORD dwMinorVersion;           ' The minor version number
DWORD dwBuildNumber;            ' The build number
DWORD dwPlatformId;             ' A platform identifier
TCHAR szCSDVersion[ 128 ];      ' A string describing additional
' information
} OSVERSIONINFO;
```

The platform ID is one of the following constants:

VER_PLATFORM_WIN32_WINDOWS	Win32 on Windows 95 or Windows 98
VER_PLATFORM_WIN32_NT	Win32 on Windows NT
VER_PLATFORM_WIN32_CE	Win32 on Windows CE

The minor version number is 0 on Windows 95 and 10 on Windows 98. The major version number for both Windows 95 and Windows 98 is 4.

As a first pass, you might try the following code:

```
' WinVer Project
' Copyright © 1998 by Desaware Inc. All Rights Reserved

Private Type OSVERSIONINFO
    dwOSVersionInfoSize As Long
    dwMajorVersion As Long
    dwMinorVersion As Long
    dwBuildNumber As Long
    dwPlatformId As Long
    szCSDVersion As String * 128
End Type

Private Declare Function GetVersionEx Lib "kernel32" _
(os As OSVERSIONINFO) As Long

Private Const VER_PLATFORM_WIN32s = 0
Private Const VER_PLATFORM_WIN32_WINDOWS = 1
Private Const VER_PLATFORM_WIN32_NT = 2


Option Explicit

Private Sub Form_Load()
    Dim os As OSVERSIONINFO
    Dim res As Long
    Dim s$
    Dim nullpos&
    res = GetVersionEx(os)
    If res <> 0 Then ' success
        Select Case os.dwPlatformId
            Case VER_PLATFORM_WIN32_NT
                s$ = "Windows NT version " & os.dwMajorVersion _
                & os.dwMinorVersion
            Case VER_PLATFORM_WIN32_WINDOWS
                s$ = "Windows "
                If os.dwMinorVersion = 10 Then s$ = s$ & "98" Else _
                s$ = s$ & "95"
            Case Else
                s$ = "Unknown OS"
```

```
        End Select
        s$ = s$ & vbCrLf
        s$ = s$ & "Build: " & os.dwBuildNumber & vbCrLf
        nullpos = InStr(os.szCSDVersion, Chr$(0))
        If nullpos > 1 Then s$ = s$ & Left$(os.szCSDVersion, nullpos - 1)
    Else
        s$ = "GetVersionInfoEx failed"
    End If
    Label1.Caption = s$
End Sub
```

Results

Runtime error 453: Can't find DLL Entry Point GetVersionEx in Kernel32.
Can you fix the program?

Feeling Comfortable?

AS TRICKY AS MOST OF THE puzzles in Section 1 may have seemed, they consisted largely of combinations of relatively common and simple errors. Now that you are hopefully accustomed to the debugging process, it's time to start tackling problems that are just as common, but whose solutions demand a somewhat greater understanding of what goes on behind the scenes when an API function is called.

Here again, you may wish to review the tutorials before you proceed.

Best of luck.

PUZZLE 9

Translating DEVMODE

ONE OF THE THINGS WINDOWS DOES for programmers is make it possible to write code that has little dependency on the underlying system devices. It wasn't too many years ago that any programmer who wanted his application to print would have to create and distribute his own drivers for every printer he wanted to support. Currently, Windows hides the details of devices so well that most Visual Basic programmers need pay little attention to the type of printer or display their program will use.

But the Windows API does include many functions that allow programmers to not only find out about underlying devices, but also to configure them. For example, you've probably used the Control Panel applet to change the settings of your display card and select a new resolution or color depth. But you may not be aware that it's actually quite easy to perform this operation from any program using the ChangeDisplaySettings API.

This API function takes as a parameter a structure named DEVMODE. The DEVMODE structure is a sort of multipurpose structure used to describe many types of devices under Windows, particularly printers and display devices.

The EnumDisplaySettings function allows you to easily obtain the DEVMODE structure for every display setting your graphic card supports and is the subject of this puzzle.

The DEVMODE structure is declared in C as follows:

```
/* size of a device name string */
#define CCHDEVICENAME 32

/* size of a form name string */
#define CCHFORMNAME 32

typedef struct _devicemodeA {
    BYTE    dmDeviceName[CCHDEVICENAME];
    WORD dmSpecVersion;
    WORD dmDriverVersion;
    WORD dmSize;
    WORD dmDriverExtra;
    DWORD dmFields;
    short dmOrientation;
    short dmPaperSize;
```

```
            short dmPaperLength;
            short dmPaperWidth;
            short dmScale;
            short dmCopies;
            short dmDefaultSource;
            short dmPrintQuality;
            short dmColor;
            short dmDuplex;
            short dmYResolution;
            short dmTTOption;
            short dmCollate;
            BYTE    dmFormName[CCHFORMNAME];
            WORD    dmLogPixels;
            DWORD   dmBitsPerPel;
            DWORD   dmPelsWidth;
            DWORD   dmPelsHeight;
            DWORD   dmDisplayFlags;
            DWORD   dmDisplayFrequency;
            DWORD   dmICMMethod;
            DWORD   dmICMIntent;
            DWORD   dmMediaType;
            DWORD   dmDitherType;
            DWORD   dmICCManufacturer;
            DWORD   dmICCModel;
            DWORD   dmPanningWidth;
            DWORD   dmPanningHeight;
} DEVMODEA, *PDEVMODEA, *NPDEVMODEA, *LPDEVMODEA;

typedef struct _devicemodeW {
    WCHAR   dmDeviceName[CCHDEVICENAME];
    WORD dmSpecVersion;
    WORD dmDriverVersion;
    WORD dmSize;
    WORD dmDriverExtra;
    DWORD dmFields;
    short dmOrientation;
    short dmPaperSize;
    short dmPaperLength;
    short dmPaperWidth;
    short dmScale;
    short dmCopies;
    short dmDefaultSource;
    short dmPrintQuality;
```

```
    short  dmColor;
    short  dmDuplex;
    short  dmYResolution;
    short  dmTTOption;
    short  dmCollate;
    WCHAR  dmFormName[CCHFORMNAME];
    WORD   dmLogPixels;
    DWORD  dmBitsPerPel;
    DWORD  dmPelsWidth;
    DWORD  dmPelsHeight;
    DWORD  dmDisplayFlags;
    DWORD  dmDisplayFrequency;
    DWORD  dmICMMethod;
    DWORD  dmICMIntent;
    DWORD  dmMediaType;
    DWORD  dmDitherType;
    DWORD  dmICCManufacturer;
    DWORD  dmICCModel;
    DWORD  dmPanningWidth;
    DWORD  dmPanningHeight;
} DEVMODEW, *PDEVMODEW, *NPDEVMODEW, *LPDEVMODEW;
```

There are two versions of the structure defined, one for use with the ANSI function entry point, the other for use with the Unicode entry point. The only difference between them, as you can see, is that the strings within the structures are arrays of bytes under the ANSI version and WCHARs (16-bit integers) under the Unicode version. The EnumDisplaySettings function is described as follows in the Win32 documentation:

```
BOOL EnumDisplaySettings(
    LPCTSTR lpszDeviceName,        // specifies the display device
    DWORD iModeNum,                // specifies the graphics mode
    LPDEVMODE lpDevMode            // points to structure to receive settings
    );
```

The lpszDeviceName parameter should be NULL to use the current display device.

The iModeNum parameter refers to the number of the display mode you wish to examine. The trick for enumerating all of the display settings is to start with 0 and increment this parameter until the function returns 0, indicating that the setting is invalid.

The lpDevMode parameter is a pointer to a DEVMODE structure that will be loaded with the display setting corresponding to the iModeNum parameter.

The sample program is quite straightforward. The DEVMODE structure is converted by a simple translation of short to VB Integer, DWORD to VB Long, and BYTE to VB Byte.

```
' DisplayModes Puzzle
' Copyright © 1998 by Desaware Inc. All Rights Reserved
Option Explicit

'  size of a device name string
Private Const CCHDEVICENAME = 32

'  size of a form name string
Private Const CCHFORMNAME = 32

Private Type DEVMODE
        dmDeviceName(CCHDEVICENAME) As Byte
        dmSpecVersion As Integer
        dmDriverVersion As Integer
        dmSize As Integer
        dmDriverExtra As Integer
        dmFields As Long
        dmOrientation As Integer
        dmPaperSize As Integer
        dmPaperLength As Integer
        dmPaperWidth As Integer
        dmScale As Integer
        dmCopies As Integer
        dmDefaultSource As Integer
        dmPrintQuality As Integer
        dmColor As Integer
        dmDuplex As Integer
        dmYResolution As Integer
        dmTTOption As Integer
        dmCollate As Integer
        dmFormName(CCHFORMNAME) As Byte
        dmLogPixels As Integer
        dmBitsPerPel As Long
        dmPelsWidth As Long
        dmPelsHeight As Long
        dmDisplayFlags As Long
        dmDisplayFrequency As Long
        dmICMMethod As Long
        dmICMIntent As Long
```

```vb
            dmMediaType As Long
            dmDitherType As Long
            dmReserved1 As Long
            dmReserved2 As Long
End Type


Private Declare Function EnumDisplaySettings Lib "user32" _
    Alias "EnumDisplaySettingsA" ( _
    ByVal lpszDeviceName As String, _
    ByVal iModeNum As Long, _
    lpDevMode As DEVMODE) As Long


Private Sub AddDisplayMode(lpDevMode As DEVMODE)
    Dim s As String
    With lpDevMode
        s = .dmPelsWidth & " x " & .dmPelsHeight & " "
        s = s & .dmBitsPerPel & " Bits/Pixel "
        If .dmDisplayFrequency > 1 Then s = s & .dmDisplayFrequency & " Hz"
    End With
    List1.AddItem s
End Sub


Private Sub Form_Load()
    Dim dm As DEVMODE
    Dim ModeNumber As Long
    Dim res As Long
    Do
        res = EnumDisplaySettings(vbNullString, ModeNumber, dm)
        If res Then
            AddDisplayMode dm
        End If
        ModeNumber = ModeNumber + 1
    Loop While res
End Sub
```

Results

The results are shown in Figure P9-1.

Clearly, something is not quite right. Can you see the problem?

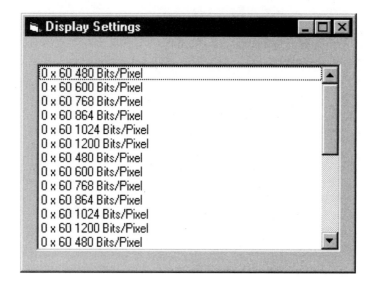

Figure P9-1: Results of the DisplayModes.vbp puzzle.

Environmentally Speaking

EVERY NOW AND THEN, YOU'LL RUN into a DLL function that returns a string whose return type is LPSTR or LPTSTR. You won't find too many of these in the core Win32 API, but some custom DLLs and extension libraries take this approach. Consider one example from the Win32 API—the GetEnvironmentStrings function. Computer programs, like all living things, live in the context of an environment. The GetEnvironmentStrings function lets you examine the environment variables for an application. This function is described in the C documentation as follows:

> *Each process has an environment block associated with it. The environment block consists of a null-terminated block of null-terminated strings (meaning there are two null bytes at the end of the block), where each string is in the following form:*
>
> name=value
>
> LPVOID GetEnvironmentStrings(VOID)
>
> *When **GetEnvironmentStrings** is called, it allocates memory for a block of environment strings. When the block is no longer needed, it should be freed by calling **FreeEnvironmentStrings**.*

Even though the declaration is LPVOID, from the explanation you can see that it is actually returning a pointer to a string. If you look at the declaration in the Win32api.txt file that comes with Visual Basic, you'll find the function declared as follows:

```
Declare Function GetEnvironmentStrings Lib "kernel32" Alias
"GetEnvironmentStringsA" () As String
```

The EnvStr.vbp project (on the CD that comes with this book) uses this function to obtain the environment strings for an application as follows:

```
Private Declare Function GetEnvironmentStrings Lib "kernel32" Alias
"GetEnvironmentStringsA" () As String
Private Sub cmdGetStrings_Click()
    Dim Environment As String
    Dim CurrentPosition As Long
    Dim NewPosition
    Environment = GetEnvironmentStrings()
    Do
        ' Look for the next null character that separates the individual
        ' environment variables
        NewPosition = InStr(CurrentPosition + 1, Environment, Chr$(0))
        If NewPosition > CurrentPosition + 1 Then
            ' Found one, add up until the null character
            List1.AddItem Mid$(Environment, CurrentPosition + 1, _
            NewPosition - CurrentPosition - 1)
            ' And start searching from the character that follows
            CurrentPosition = NewPosition
        Else
            Exit Do
        End If
    Loop While True

End Sub
```

Results

Hey, this isn't the old days. We care about the environment! And this code crashes worse than an eggshell poisoned by DDT.[1] Can you save the world, or at least this program?

---

1. That is, on Windows NT. Windows 95/98 quietly ignores the error, leaving you with an empty string and the uncertain feeling that somewhere your memory has been corrupted in a way that will be impossible to track down.

Registry Games, Part 1

READING THE SYSTEM REGISTRY IS ONE of the most common tasks that Visual Basic programmers attempt—and one of the most frustrating. The registry is a hierarchical database that looks something like a file system. File system directories correspond to registry keys. Files in a file system correspond to the values for the keys. Figure P11-1 shows a typical display from the Windows registry editor. On Windows NT 4.0, the registry has five visible roots, each of which is identified by a constant value. The highlighted entry has the following registry path:

HKEY_LOCAL_MACHINE\SYSTEM\CurrentControlSet\Control

The right pane of the figure shows that this key has three named values: CurrentUser, SystemStartOptions, and WaitToKillServiceTimeout. A key can also have a default value that does not have a name. The data type of the value appears immediately after the name—in this case, all three values are of type REG_SZ (text data). The value data follows the data type.

Your mission (should you choose to accept it) is to write a short program that enumerates all of the keys under this key and displays the values for each key. To keep things simple, the example will only look at keys that appear under the Control key—it will not scan deeper into the hierarchy. That exercise is left for the reader.

Because there are many pitfalls to reading the registry, this task is divided into several puzzles. But don't think for a minute that I am doing this just to make the examples easier to follow.

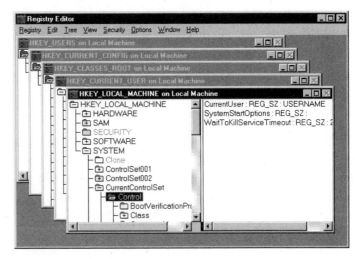

Figure P11-1: A typical display from the Windows registry editor.

This actually reflects a strategy I always use when undertaking API-based tasks: It's always best to code and test small portions of the application and eliminate bugs as you find them. That way, you gain understanding of the API subsystem you are working with early in the development cycle and can avoid propagating bugs throughout your code.

The RegOpenKeyEx function is used to open a registry key. The function is defined as follows in the API documentation:

```
LONG RegOpenKeyEx(
    HKEY hKey,                  // handle of open key
    LPCTSTR lpSubKey,           // address of name of subkey to open
    DWORD ulOptions,            // reserved
    REGSAM samDesired,          // security access mask
    PHKEY phkResult             // address of handle of open key
);
```

The HKEY parameter is a handle—a 32-bit Long value. You can find the following root constants in the api32.txt file on the CD that comes with this book:

> *Public Const HKEY_CLASSES_ROOT = &H80000000*
> *Public Const HKEY_CURRENT_USER = &H80000001*
> *Public Const HKEY_LOCAL_MACHINE = &H80000002*
> *Public Const HKEY_USERS = &H80000003*
> *Public Const HKEY_PERFORMANCE_DATA = &H80000004*
> *Public Const HKEY_CURRENT_CONFIG = &H80000005*

The lpSubKey parameter is a string that specifies the subkey you want to open. In this case, it will be \SYSTEM\CurrentControlSet\Control.

The ulOptions parameter is reserved and should be set to 0.

The samDesired parameter is a Long value that specifies which access rights you wish. For example, you can specify the constant KEY_QUERY_VALUE if you wish to be able to read the values of a key. Your request is compared to the access rights that are permitted for the account under which the program is running. If the right you request is allowed, the request is granted and you will be able to perform the requested operation.

The phkResult parameter is a Long variable that will be loaded with the open key.

A separate function, RegCloseKey, is used to close the key when it is no longer needed.

As a first step, the following program attempts to open the Control key and reports on whether it succeeds:

```
' Reading Registry Keys
' Copyright © 1998 by Desaware Inc. All Rights Reserved
```

```
Option Explicit

Private Declare Function RegCloseKey Lib "advapi32.dll" _
(ByVal hKey As Long) As Long
Private Declare Function RegOpenKeyEx Lib "advapi32.dll" _
Alias "RegOpenKeyExA" (ByVal hKey As Long, ByVal lpSubKey As String, _
ByVal ulOptions As Long, ByVal samDesired As Long, phkResult As Long) _
As Long
Private Const KEY_QUERY_VALUE = &H1
Private Const KEY_SET_VALUE = &H2
Private Const KEY_CREATE_SUB_KEY = &H4
Private Const KEY_ENUMERATE_SUB_KEYS = &H8
Private Const KEY_NOTIFY = &H10
Private Const SYNCHRONIZE = &H100000

Private Const STANDARD_RIGHTS_READ = &H20000
Private Const KEY_READ = ((STANDARD_RIGHTS_READ Or _
KEY_QUERY_VALUE Or KEY_ENUMERATE_SUB_KEYS Or KEY_NOTIFY) And _
(Not SYNCHRONIZE))

Dim controlkey As String
Private Const HKEY_LOCAL_MACHINE = &H80000002

Private Sub Form_Load()
   Dim rootkey As Long
   Dim res As Long

   controlkey = "SYSTEM/CurrentControlSet/Control"
   res = RegOpenKeyEx(HKEY_LOCAL_MACHINE, controlkey, KEY_READ, 0, rootkey)
   If res <> 0 Then
      MsgBox "Unable to open registry key: " & GetErrorString(res)
      Exit Sub
   Else
      MsgBox "Key opened successfully"
   End If
   Call RegCloseKey(rootkey)
End Sub
```

The GetErrorString function can be found in the file ErrString.bas. It uses the
FormatMessage function to convert an error code into a description of a system
error message.

Results

The message box reports that it is unable to open the registry key. The system cannot find the file specified. Can you solve the puzzle?

Registry Games, Part 2

NOW THAT YOU KNOW HOW TO open a registry key, the next step is to enumerate its subkeys and their values. The main functions for enumerating key information are the RegEnumKey and RegEnumValue functions. Win32 also supports a function called RegEnumKeyEx, which allows you to retrieve additional information about keys, such as the last modification time for the subkey, but for our purposes RegEnumKey is fine. Let's take a quick look at the C declaration for the RegEnumKey function:

```
LONG RegEnumKey(
    HKEY hKey,                  // handle of key to query
    DWORD dwIndex,              // index of subkey to query
    LPTSTR lpName,              // address of buffer for subkey name
    DWORD cbName                // size of subkey buffer
    );
```

We'll look at the VB declaration for this function in Puzzle 13. For now, consider how this function works. The hKey parameter is obvious—it's a handle to the key whose subkeys you wish to enumerate. The dwIndex parameter is the index of the subkey whose name you want to retrieve. The lpName parameter is a buffer to load with the subkey name. It will clearly be a string parameter, and since the API function loads the string with data, the string variable must be initialized to a length that is long enough to hold the key name.

Clearly, one way to use this function would be to call it in a loop, incrementing the dwIndex parameter each time, until an error occurs. The lpName parameter could be initialized to some very large value (the Win32 API documentation says that this parameter need never be larger than MAX_PATH + 1 characters or 261 bytes).

Another approach to this function would be to determine ahead of time the maximum key name length and how many subkeys are present. This can be accomplished using the RegQueryInfoKey function. This function is declared as follows:

```
LONG RegQueryInfoKey (
    HKEY hKey,                  // handle of key to query
    LPTSTR lpClass,             // address of buffer for class string
    LPDWORD lpcbClass,          // address of size of class string buffer
```

```
        LPDWORD lpReserved,             // reserved - Must be NULL
        LPDWORD lpcSubKeys,             // address of buffer for number of subkeys
        LPDWORD lpcbMaxSubKeyLen,       // address of buffer for longest
                                        // subkey name length
        LPDWORD lpcbMaxClassLen,        // address of buffer for longest
                                        // class string length
        LPDWORD lpcValues,              // address of buffer for number of
                                        value entries
        LPDWORD lpcbMaxValueNameLen,    // address of buffer for longest value
                                        // name length
        LPDWORD lpcbMaxValueLen,        // address of buffer for longest value
                                        // data length
        LPDWORD lpcbSecurityDescriptor, // address of buffer for security
                                        // descriptor length
        PFILETIME lpftLastWriteTime     // address of buffer for last write time
    );
```

Looks intimidating, doesn't it? Don't let the number of parameters throw you. The first one is a handle to the key you are examining. The rest of the parameters are all pointers to variables to load with information about the key. They all have the prefix LP or P (indicating a pointer). Most of them are pointers to DWORD (32-bit variables), which will use Visual Basic Long variables. Since the parameters are all pointers, they will all be declared by reference (except, of course, for the lpClass parameter, which, like most strings, is passed by value).

The Visual Basic declaration for this function is therefore

```
Private Declare Function RegQueryInfoKey Lib "advapi32.dll" Alias _
"RegQueryInfoKeyA" (ByVal hKey As Long, ByVal lpClass As String, _
lpcbClass As Long, lpReserved As Long, lpcSubKeys As Long, _
lpcbMaxSubKeyLen As Long, lpcbMaxClassLen As Long, lpcValues As _
Long, lpcbMaxValueNameLen As Long, lpcbMaxValueLen As Long, _
lpcbSecurityDescriptor As Long, lpftLastWriteTime As FILETIME) _
As Long
```

The FILETIME structure is a 64-bit structure that holds a system date. (The Win32 API provides a number of functions that work with FILETIME structures, but that is beyond the scope of this book.)

```
Private Type FILETIME
        dwLowDateTime As Long
        dwHighDateTime As Long
End Type
```

Before enumerating the subkeys, you should be able to use the RegQueryInfoKey function to obtain the number of keys and the maximum length of the subkey names using the following function:

```
Private Function GetKeyInfo(ByVal hKey As Long, NumberOfKeys _
As Long, MaxKeyNameLength As Long) As Long
    Dim cbClass As Long
    Dim cSubKeys As Long
    Dim cbMaxSubKeyLen As Long
    Dim cbMaxClassLen As Long
    Dim cValues As Long
    Dim cbMaxValueNameLen As Long
    Dim cbMaxValueLen As Long
    Dim cbSecurityDescriptor As Long
    Dim ftLastWriteTime As FILETIME
    Dim res As Long

    res = RegQueryInfoKey(hKey, vbNullString, cbClass, _
            0, cSubKeys, cbMaxSubKeyLen, cbMaxClassLen, _
            cValues, cbMaxValueNameLen, cbMaxValueLen, _
            cbSecurityDescriptor, ftLastWriteTime)
    If res <> 0 Then
        MsgBox "RegQueryInfoKey error: " & GetErrorString(res)
    Else
        NumberOfKeys = cSubKeys
        MaxKeyNameLength = cbMaxSubKeyLen
    End If
    GetKeyInfo = res
End Function
```

Note how vbNullString is passed as a parameter for the lpClass parameter. This passes a NULL pointer (pointer with a value of 0) to the API function. The RegQueryInfoKey function is designed so that you can simply pass NULL values for any parameters whose information you do not need. This also improves performance, because Windows won't calculate values you don't ask for.

The Challenge

The GetKeyInfo function shown above is large and inefficient. It forces Windows to calculate information the function does not actually need. Your challenge is to come up with a more efficient solution that uses the RegQueryInfoKey function.

Actually, while you're at it, see if you can come up with *two* solutions that are more efficient!

Oh, and I almost forgot . . . if you are using Windows NT, the above sample doesn't work at all.

Registry Games, Part 3

BEFORE MOVING ON TO ENUMERATING VALUES, let's review how to enumerate keys. The RegEnumKey function was shown earlier and appears like this in the Win32 API documentation:

```
LONG RegEnumKey(
    HKEY hKey,                  // handle of key to query
    DWORD dwIndex,              // index of subkey to query
    LPTSTR lpName,              // address of buffer for subkey name
    DWORD cbName               // size of subkey buffer
    );
```

The Visual Basic declaration is straightforward:

```
Private Declare Function RegEnumKey Lib "advapi32.dll" Alias _
"RegEnumKeyA" (ByVal hKey As Long, ByVal dwIndex As Long, ByVal _
lpName As String, ByVal cbName As Long) As Long
```

The EnumerateKeys function has been extended to perform the full enumeration. It uses the GetKeyInfo3 function to obtain the number of keys and necessary buffer length. The keybuffer variable is preinitialized to this length (plus an extra byte for the terminating NULL character) to prevent possible memory overwrites. The RegEnumKey function is called once for each subkey. On success, a new clsKeyValues object is created. This object is first loaded with the name of the subkey. The RegOpenKeyEx function is then used to open and obtain a handle to the subkey. This handle is passed to the EnumerateValues function, which returns another collection, this one containing a list of the values for the subkey. The subkey is then closed, and the clsKeyValues object added to the KeyCollection collection. This collection is returned as a result by the EnumerateKeys function, as follows:

```
' Enumerate all of the subkeys of this key, returning a collection
' containing clsKeyValues objects
Private Function EnumerateKeys(ByVal hKey As Long) As Collection
    Dim NumberOfSubKeys As Long
    Dim MaxSubKeyLength As Long
    Dim res As Long
```

```
    Dim KeyIndex As Long
    Dim keybuffer As String
    Dim KeyCollection As New Collection
    Dim currentkey As clsKeyValues
    Dim nulloffset As Long
    Dim NewKey As Long

    res = GetKeyInfo3(hKey, NumberOfSubKeys, MaxSubKeyLength)
    If res <> 0 Then
        Exit Function
    End If

    keybuffer = String$(MaxSubKeyLength + 1, 0)

    For KeyIndex = 0 To NumberOfSubKeys - 1
        res = RegEnumKey(hKey, KeyIndex, keybuffer, MaxSubKeyLength + 1)
        If res = 0 Then
            Set currentkey = New clsKeyValues
            nulloffset = InStr(keybuffer, Chr$(0))
            currentkey.KeyName = Left$(keybuffer, nulloffset - 1)
            ' Enumerate values here
            ' Open the subkey
            res = RegOpenKeyEx(hKey, currentkey.KeyName, 0, KEY_READ, NewKey)
            ' Get a collection containing the subvalues
            Set currentkey.ValueNames = EnumerateValues(NewKey)
            ' Close the subkey
            Call RegCloseKey(NewKey)
            KeyCollection.Add currentkey
        End If
    Next KeyIndex
    Set EnumerateKeys = KeyCollection
End Function
```

Enumerating the Values

The RegEnumValue function is somewhat more flexible than the RegEnumKey function, in that it is able to retrieve the data for each value during the enumeration. We won't take advantage of this feature at this time, in order to keep things simple. As with the RegQueryInfoKey function, you can simply pass a NULL pointer to this function for those parameters you do not wish to use. In this case, the lpType, lpData, and lpcbData parameters will be set to NULL. Once you've eliminated these three parameters and the lpReserved parameter, the function is almost identical to the RegEnumKey function, as shown below:

```
LONG RegEnumValue(
    HKEY hKey,                  // handle of key to query
    DWORD dwIndex,              // index of value to query
    LPTSTR lpValueName,         // address of buffer for value string
    LPDWORD lpcbValueName,      // address for size of value buffer
    LPDWORD lpReserved,         // reserved - Set to NULL
    LPDWORD lpType,             // address of buffer for type code
    LPBYTE lpData,              // address of buffer for value data
    LPDWORD lpcbData            // address for size of data buffer
    );
```

The Visual Basic declaration is as follows:

```
Private Declare Function RegEnumValue Lib "advapi32.dll" _
Alias "RegEnumValueA" (ByVal hKey As Long, ByVal dwIndex As Long, _
ByVal lpValueName As String, ByVal lpcbValueName As Long, _
ByVal lpReserved As Long, ByVal lpType As Long, ByVal lpData As Long, _
ByVal lpcbData As Long) As Long
```

Now let's proceed with the code that does the value enumeration. It is based on and almost identical to the code for enumerating keys. The GetValueInfo function is based on the GetKeyInfo3 function and retrieves the number of subvalues and the length of the buffer needed to hold the value names, as shown below:

```
' Get the number of values and maximum value length
Private Function GetValueInfo(ByVal hKey As Long, NumberOfValues, _
MaxValueNameLength) As Long
    GetValueInfo = RegQueryInfoKeyV3(hKey, vbNullString, 0, 0, 0, 0, _
    0, VarPtr(NumberOfValues), VarPtr(MaxValueNameLength), 0, 0, 0)
End Function
```

The EnumerateValues function is nearly identical to the EnumerateKeys function. The only difference is that instead of building a collection of clsKeyValues objects, it builds a collection of value names, as you can see below:

```
Private Function EnumerateValues(ByVal hKey As Long) As Collection
    Dim NumberOfSubValues As Long
    Dim MaxSubValueLength As Long
    Dim res As Long
    Dim ValueIndex As Long
```

```
Dim Valuebuffer As String
Dim ValueCollection As New Collection
Dim currentValue As clsKeyValues
Dim nulloffset As Long

res = GetValueInfo(hKey, NumberOfSubValues, MaxSubValueLength)
If res <> 0 Then
    Exit Function
End If

Valuebuffer = String$(MaxSubValueLength + 1, 0)

For ValueIndex = 0 To NumberOfSubValues - 1
    res = RegEnumValue(hKey, ValueIndex, Valuebuffer, _
    MaxSubValueLength, 0, 0, 0, 0)
    If res = 0 Then
        nulloffset = InStr(Valuebuffer, Chr$(0))
        If nulloffset<=1 Then
            ValueCollection.Add "Default"
        Else
            ValueCollection.Add Left$(Valuebuffer, nulloffset-1)
        End If
    End If
Next ValueIndex
Set EnumerateValues = ValueCollection
End Function
```

The program has been extended with a second list box. The Form_Load event has been extended to load the first list box with the list of subkey names returned by the EnumerateKeys function, using the following code:

```
Set keylist = EnumerateKeys(rootkey)

For Each currentkey In keylist
    List1.AddItem currentkey.KeyName
Next
Set GlobalKeyCollection = keylist
```

When you click on the list box, the List1_Click function is called. This function searches for the corresponding clsKeyValues object in the GlobalKeyCollection collection. When it finds the correct object, it clears the second list box and loads it with the names of the values for that subkey, using the following code:

```
Private Sub List1_Click()
    Dim thiskey As String
    Dim thisvalue As Variant
    Dim currentkey As clsKeyValues
    thiskey = List1.Text

    For Each currentkey In GlobalKeyCollection
        If currentkey.KeyName = thiskey Then
            List2.Clear
            For Each thisvalue In currentkey.ValueNames
                List2.AddItem thisvalue
            Next
        End If
    Next currentkey

End Sub
```

Results

Naturally, the sample code shown here does not work. It wouldn't be much of a puzzle if it did. Your challenge is to fix the program.

Registry Games, Part 4

ONLY ONE TASK REMAINS IN OUR registry project—reading data from the registry. The program has been modified so that the data will be displayed in a label control when you click on the list box containing the registry value names as shown in Figure P14-1.

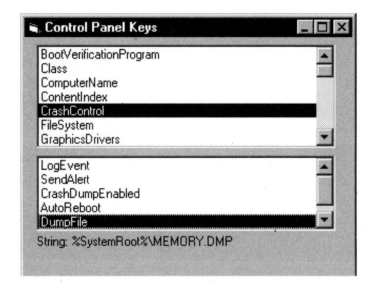

Figure P14-1: The Reg4.vbp application in action

The List2_Click event opens a key using the key name from the List1 listbox, then calls the DisplayValue function to display the value of the data, as shown below:

```
Private Sub List2_Click()
    Dim thiskey As String
    Dim KeyToCheck As Long
    Dim res As Long

    lblValue.Caption = ""    ' Clear label
```

```
    res = RegOpenKeyEx(HKEY_LOCAL_MACHINE, _
    "SYSTEM\CurrentControlSet\Control\" & List1.Text, _
    0, KEY_READ, KeyToCheck)
    ' This should always work, but we'll be cautious
    If res = 0 Then
        Call DisplayValue(KeyToCheck, List2.Text)
        Call RegCloseKey(KeyToCheck)
    End If
End Sub
```

The DisplayValue function uses the RegQueryValueEx function to read the registry value. This function is defined in the Microsoft documentation as follows:

```
LONG RegQueryValueEx(
    HKEY hKey,                // handle of key to query
    LPTSTR lpValueName,       // address of name of value to query
    LPDWORD lpReserved,       // reserved - Must be NULL
    LPDWORD lpType,           // address of buffer for value type
    LPBYTE lpData,            // address of data buffer
    LPDWORD lpcbData          // address of data buffer size
);
```

The hKey parameter is a handle to the open key, a Long value as always. The lpValueName parameter is the name of the value. The lpReserved parameter should be NULL. The lpType parameter is a pointer to a Long variable. This variable will be loaded with a constant describing the type of data in this registry entry. A partial list of variable types is presented in Table P14-1.

REG_NONE = 0	No value type
REG_SZ = 1	NULL-terminated string
EG_EXPAND_SZ = 2	NULL-terminated string with references to environment variables that have not yet been expanded.
REG_BINARY = 3	Binary data
REG_DWORD = 4	32-bit Long value
REG_MULTI_SZ = 7	Series of strings separated by NULL characters and terminated by two NULL characters.

Table P14-1: Partial list of registry data types

The string data is stored in the registry as Unicode strings, but the ANSI version of the RegQueryValueEx function retrieves ANSI strings.

The lpData parameter is an address of a buffer to load with data from the registry. The lpcbData parameter is a pointer to a Long variable that contains the size of the data buffer. If the buffer is not large enough to hold the registry data, the function returns error number 234 (ERROR_MORE_DATA) to indicate that a larger buffer is required and loads the lpcbData variable with the required buffer length. If the lpData parameter is NULL, the RegQueryValueEx function loads the lpcbData variable with the necessary buffer length (but does not report error 234). If the registry value is a string data type, the buffer length includes the NULL termination characters.

The DisplayValue function uses the RegQueryValueEx API function to read and display the data. This version of the function only handles the string, long, and binary data types, because these are the types used most often. The function is shown here:

```
Private Sub DisplayValue(ByVal hKey As Long, ByVal ValueName As String)
    ' Load the lblValue label control with the data.
    ' Can you handle string, long, and binary data types?
End Sub
```

Results

As you can see, the function works perfectly.

> TECH REVIEWER TO AUTHOR
> – *Dan, you forgot the VB declaration and code for this example. Please fill it in.*
>
> PUBLISHER TO TECH REVIEWER
> – *Can't seem to reach Dan. I think he's partying at Disney World or something. Is there anything you can do?*
>
> TECH REVIEWER TO PUBLISHER
> – *You're not paying me enough to rewrite the book. If Dan can't check his e-mail while he's on vacation, then you'll have to set the page as is. But it will look awfully careless of him.*
>
> PUBLISHER TO TECH REVIEWER
> – *I have an idea. Tell the readers that they're supposed to create the declaration and write the code. We'll get Dan to write in some working code before we go to print. Nobody will realize that this was a major screw-up.*
>
> TECH REVIEWER TO PUBLISHER
> – *This book is so strange already—I bet we'll get away with it. But be sure your Production Department deletes all annotations before we go to print.*

What Time Zone Is It?

IF YOU HAVE EVER INSTALLED WINDOWS 95/98 or NT 4.0 or later, you may recall that, in one of the final steps in the installation process, you are asked to specify the time zone for your Windows installation.[1] You may also have experienced situations where you boot up your machine only to have it notify you that it has switched to or from daylight savings time. Clearly Windows has a fairly sophisticated time sense.

The Win32 API has a number of functions that allow your applications to take advantage of the operating system's support for times and dates. In this puzzle, we'll address the simple task of determining the current time zone, time difference from UTC,[2] and whether daylight savings time is in effect. The function that retrieves this information is the GetTimeZoneInformation function, which is declared in the Win32 API documentation as follows:

```
DWORD GetTimeZoneInformation(
    LPTIME_ZONE_INFORMATION lpTimeZoneInformation  // address of time-zone
                                                   // settings
    );
```

What is LPTIME_ZONE_INFORMATION?

The first hint is in the prefix LP. LP indicates that the parameter is a pointer, specifically, a pointer to a TIME_ZONE_INFORMATION structure. The Win32 API documentation defines this structure as follows:

```
typedef struct _TIME_ZONE_INFORMATION { // tzi
    LONG       Bias;
    WCHAR      StandardName[ 32 ];
    SYSTEMTIME StandardDate;
    LONG       StandardBias;
    WCHAR      DaylightName[ 32 ];
    SYSTEMTIME DaylightDate;
```

---

1. Come to think of it, that's a rather silly question, since anyone reading this book has probably installed these operating systems more times than they would care to remember.

2. UTC means Universal Time Coordinates, which is more often called Coordinated Universal Time—unless you're old-fashioned, in which case you call it Greenwich Mean Time or GMT. UTC is the time at 0° longitude, which just happens to pass through Greenwich, England.

```
LONG        DaylightBias;
} TIME_ZONE_INFORMATION;
```

The Bias field indicates a time difference in minutes from UTC such that UTC = your local time + Bias. The StandardBias field indicates the additional bias when standard time is in effect. The DaylightBias field indicates the additional bias when daylight savings time is in effect.

The StandardDate field is the date when the system should switch from daylight savings time to standard time. The DaylightDate field is the date when the system should switch from standard time to daylight savings time. The StandardName and DaylightName fields indicate the name of the time zone when in standard time and daylight savings time, respectively.

A SYSTEMTIME is another structure, defined as follows:

```
typedef struct _SYSTEMTIME {  // st
    WORD wYear;
    WORD wMonth;
    WORD wDayOfWeek;
    WORD wDay;
    WORD wHour;
    WORD wMinute;
    WORD wSecond;
    WORD wMilliseconds;
} SYSTEMTIME;
```

A WORD parameter is a 16-bit unsigned value. We'll use the Visual Basic Integer type because it is 16 bits long, and we can always convert from signed to unsigned if necessary (it won't be with this structure).

The tz.vbp application uses the GetTimeZoneInformation function to retrieve and display information about the current time zone.

The tz.vbp program (on the CD that comes with this book) contains the following code:

```
' Get Time Zone Information
' Copyright © 1998 by Desaware Inc. All Rights Reserved

Option Explicit

Private Type SYSTEMTIME
        wYear As Integer
        wMonth As Integer
        wDayOfWeek As Integer
        wDay As Integer
```

```
                wHour As Integer
                wMinute As Integer
                wSecond As Integer
                wMilliseconds As Integer
End Type


Private Type TIME_ZONE_INFORMATION
        Bias As Long
        StandardName(32) As Integer
        StandardDate As SYSTEMTIME
        StandardBias As Long
        DaylightName(32) As Integer
        DaylightDate As SYSTEMTIME
        DaylightBias As Long
End Type
Private Declare Function GetTimeZoneInformation Lib _
"kernel32" (lpTimeZoneInformation As TIME_ZONE_INFORMATION) As Long


Private Const TIME_ZONE_ID_INVALID = &HFFFFFFFF
Private Const TIME_ZONE_ID_UNKNOWN = 0
Private Const TIME_ZONE_ID_STANDARD = 1
Private Const TIME_ZONE_ID_DAYLIGHT = 2


Private Sub Form_Load()
    Dim tz As TIME_ZONE_INFORMATION
    Dim info As String
    Dim res As Long
    res = GetTimeZoneInformation(tz)
    Select Case res
       Case TIME_ZONE_ID_INVALID
          lblTimeZone.Caption = "GetTimeZoneInformation function failed." _
          & vbCrLf
          lblTimeZone.Caption = lblTimeZone.Caption & "Error: " _
          & GetErrorString(Err.LastDllError)
       Case TIME_ZONE_ID_UNKNOWN
          lblTimeZone.Caption = "Time zone information unavailable."
       Case TIME_ZONE_ID_STANDARD
          info = "Currently on Standard Time" & vbCrLf
       Case TIME_ZONE_ID_DAYLIGHT
          info = "Currently on Daylight Savings Time" & vbCrLf
    End Select

    info = info & "Local time = UTC + " & tz.Bias / 60 & " hours" & vbCrLf
```

```
        info = info & "Standard time = UTC + " & tz.StandardBias / 60 & _
        " hours" & vbCrLf
        info = info & "Daylight time = UTC + " & tz.DaylightBias / 60 & _
        " hours" & vbCrLf
        info = info & "Standard time name: ???" & vbCrLf
        info = info & "Daylight time name: ???" & vbCrLf
        lblTimeZone.Caption = info
End Sub
```

Results

Figure P15-1 shows the results of this program on my system (located on the West Coast of the United States). The result for the local time (based on the Bias parameter) is correct—an 8-hour difference. But the StandardBias and DaylightBias results don't make sense.

Your job:

1. Fix the program so that the StandardBias and DaylightBias information is read correctly.

2. Figure out a way to read the StandardName and DaylightName fields.

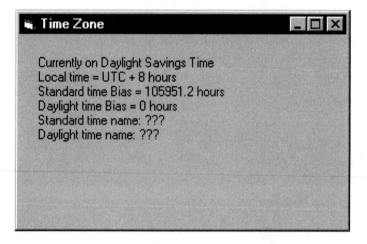

Figure P15-1: Typical results of the tz.vbp program

Serially Speaking

ONE OF THE MOST COMMON QUESTIONS I receive relates to retrieving a disk volume serial number. This can be done using the GetVolumeInformation function, which is defined in the Win32 SDK documentation as follows:

```
BOOL GetVolumeInformation(
    LPCTSTR lpRootPathName,            // address of root directory of the
                                       // file system
    LPTSTR lpVolumeNameBuffer,         // address of name of the volume
    DWORD nVolumeNameSize,             // length of lpVolumeNameBuffer
    LPDWORD lpVolumeSerialNumber,      // address of volume serial number
    LPDWORD lpMaximumComponentLength,  // address of system's maximum
                                       // filename length
    LPDWORD lpFileSystemFlags,         // address of file system flags
    LPTSTR lpFileSystemNameBuffer,     // address of name of file system
    DWORD nFileSystemNameSize          // length of lpFileSystemNameBuffer
);
```

Like many API functions, these parameters are almost self-explanatory. The lpRootPathName parameter should contain the root directory of the volume for which you want to obtain information. The following sample program has a drive control that allows you to select a drive to check. It then displays the volume name, file system name, maximum file-name length, and serial number in a list box.

```
' Volume Information
' Copyright © 1998 by Desaware Inc. All Rights Reserved

Option Explicit

Private Declare Function GetVolumeInformation Lib "kernel32" _
Alias "GetVolumeInformationA" (ByVal lpRootPathName As String, _
ByVal lpVolumeNameBuffer As String, ByVal nVolumeNameSize As Long, _
ByVal lpVolumeSerialNumber As Long, ByVal lpMaximumComponentLength _
As Long, ByVal lpFileSystemFlags As Long, ByVal _
lpFileSystemNameBuffer As String, ByVal nFileSystemNameSize As Long) As Long
```

```
Private Sub LoadVolumeInfo()
    Dim res&
    Dim VolumeName As String
    Dim FileSystem As String
    Dim SerialNumber As Long
    Dim ComponentLength As Long
    Dim FileSystemFlags As Long
    VolumeName = String$(256, Chr$(0))
    FileSystem = String$(256, Chr$(0))
    res = GetVolumeInformation(Left$(Drive1.Drive, 2) & "\", _
    VolumeName, 0, SerialNumber, ComponentLength, _
    FileSystemFlags, FileSystem, 0)
    If res = 0 Then
        MsgBox "GetVolumeInformation Error: " & _
        GetErrorString(Err.LastDllError)
        Exit Sub
    End If
    List1.Clear
    List1.AddItem "Drive " & Drive1.Drive
    List1.AddItem "Name: " & VolumeName
    List1.AddItem "Component Length: " & ComponentLength
    List1.AddItem "Serial #: " & SerialNumber
    List1.AddItem "FileSystem: " & FileSystem

End Sub

Private Sub Drive1_Change()
    LoadVolumeInfo
End Sub

Private Sub Form_Load()
    LoadVolumeInfo
End Sub
```

Results

The information provided about the function in this puzzle is sparse. You can
look up the function in the Win32 SDK documentation (or in my book *Dan
Appleman's Visual Basic Programmer's Guide to the Win32 API*), but the fact is,
you already have enough information in the declaration itself to figure out how
to correct the errors.

Once you fix the obvious problems, you should see results such as those shown in Figure P16-1. Note the serial number and compare it to the serial number returned when you use the Dir command to display a volume directory. Why are they different?

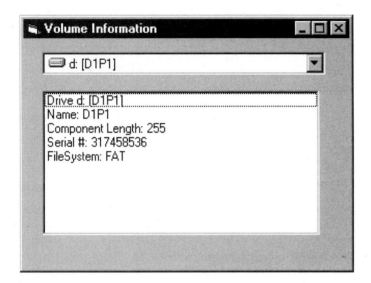

*Figure P16-1: **Result of scan operation after the first bug is fixed***

In the Groove

THIS SECTION MARKS THE HALFWAY POINT through the puzzles. I hope you've found them entertaining and challenging so far. From this point on, you could categorize most of the puzzles as somewhere between intermediate and advanced. What does this mean? It means that, even if you have a great deal of API programming experience, you will probably find many of these puzzles extremely difficult—so difficult that I expect many readers will not be able to solve all of them on their own. Those that you do solve will probably take more experimentation than the previous puzzles. Most of these cannot be solved just by looking at the sample code—you will probably need to load the puzzle and struggle with it for a while.

I encourage you not to turn too quickly to the Solutions. Even if you can't solve the puzzle, you will gain a greater understanding through the attempt than you would from a dozen more chapters of explanation.

The DEVMODE Is in the Details

THE WIN32API.TXT FILE PROVIDED WITH VISUAL STUDIO includes the following declaration for the DocumentProperties function:

```
Declare Function DocumentProperties Lib "winspool.drv" Alias _
"DocumentPropertiesA" (ByVal hwnd As Long, ByVal hPrinter As Long, _
ByVal pDeviceName As String, pDevModeOutput As DEVMODE, _
pDevModeInput As DEVMODE, ByVal fMode As Long) As Long
```

My Win32 API book defines it as follows:

```
Declare Function DocumentProperties Lib "winspool.drv" Alias _
"DocumentPropertiesA" (ByVal hwnd As Long, ByVal hPrinter As Long, _
ByVal pDeviceName As String, ByVal pDevModeOutput As Long, ByVal _
pDevModeInput As Long, ByVal fMode As Long) As Long
```

where both pDevModeOutput and pDevModeInput are defined as pointers to DEVMODE data structures.

The C declaration is as follows:

```
LONG DocumentProperties(
    HWND hWnd, // handle to window that displays dialog box
    HANDLE hPrinter, // handle to printer object
    LPTSTR pDeviceName, // pointer to device name
    PDEVMODE pDevModeOutput, // pointer to modified device mode
                            // structure
    PDEVMODE pDevModeInput, // pointer to original device mode structure
    DWORD fMode  // mode flag
    );
```

If you've read Tutorial 4, "How DLL Calls Work: Inside a Stack Frame," you know that declaring the parameter As DEVMODE (as shown in win32api.txt) will, in fact, pass a pointer to a DEVMODE structure. Why would the declaration in api32.txt advocate a more complex approach—requiring you to obtain the address of a DEVMODE structure and pass the pointer explicitly?

Was it a careless oversight on my part?

Or is it just barely possible that the declaration in the win32api.txt file is wrong—so wrong that using the declaration might lead to memory exceptions? Not just memory exceptions, but exceptions that are intermittent depending on the system configuration in use?

And if the latter, can you explain why?

Sample Program

The DocProp sample project uses the declaration from win32api.txt to show the printer setup dialog box for the current printer, then displays whether you have selected portrait or landscape mode for the printer. The code that actually performs the operation is as follows (declarations and constants are omitted from this listing):

```
Dim hPrinter&
Dim res&
Dim dmIn As DEVMODE
Dim dmOut As DEVMODE

' Non-zero on success
res = OpenPrinter(Printer.DeviceName, hPrinter, 0)
If res = 0 Then
   lblStatus.Caption = "Printer could not be opened"
   Exit Sub
End If


res = DocumentProperties(hwnd, hPrinter, Printer.DeviceName, _
dmOut, dmIn, DM_OUT_BUFFER Or DM_IN_PROMPT)
If dmOut.dmOrientation = DMORIENT_LANDSCAPE Then
      lblStatus.Caption = "Printer is in landscape mode"
   Else
      lblStatus.Caption = "Printer is in portrait mode"
   End If
' You can modify the contents of the dmout buffer, then
' call DocumentProperties with DM_IN_BUFFER to set the new values
Call ClosePrinter(hPrinter)
```

Results

Depending on your system, this sample code will either work perfectly or cause an exception. You must have a printer installed to run the DocProp example.

DT, Phone Home

*Over the past couple of years I've been known to dabble in a
rather unique form of literature—the technical humor–mystery
genre. Here is a sample.*

I DON'T GET MUCH ENTERTAINMENT BUSINESS. Frankly, my office is on the wrong side
of the tracks. No, it's not the bloodstains on the cracked windowpane, although
that might be enough to turn away many of the beautiful people. And it's not just
that I work out of Silicon Valley, which is an hour's flight from Hollywood. It's
simply that I don't do meetings. You know what I mean—I don't carry a cell
phone, and my pager battery is perpetually dead. Not that it matters; I don't give
anyone my pager number anyway. Sure, I occasionally have lunch with friends,
but I don't do meetings.

My friend DT, on the other hand, does meetings all the time. She usually
hangs out at the nearby Juice Club, the kind of place where teenagers work for
minimum wage mixing random fruits and vegetables along with mysterious
nutritional powders that don't quite promise eternal youth, vigor, and health. I
did a job once for the Food and Drug Administration—they needed an investiga-
tor to examine their systems to see if they are year 2000–compliant. I can't tell
you the results, but I'll say this: I'm sterilizing all my food starting January 2000.
And the only juice I'll be drinking is from fruit I pick myself or from cans dating
back to 1998.

Today was slow. My only client was some guy from the DOD who wanted a
complete analysis of their case against Microsoft. I photocopied the Starr report
and gave the copy to him gratis. Who can tell the difference between the two
anyway? The afternoon was dragging, so I decided to stroll down to the strip mall
and see what DT was up to.

I found her on the phone, taking a call. I could tell even from the tail end of
the conversation that it must be someone in the entertainment biz:

"Yo, babe. Good deal. Right. I'll have my computer call your computer. Ciao.
We'll do lunch." Click.

I couldn't help but smile. DT was the only person in the valley who had a cell
phone that actually went "click" when it hung up.

The fake smile she had been wearing faded faster than an Internet stock
with a bad earnings announcement.

"I hate the act, but they sure pay well," she said with a real smile.

"Interesting—but didn't they used to have their people call your people?
What's this stuff with computers calling each other?"

"It's the latest craze." She shook her head. "Now they've all discovered multi-media, so they want their computers to do everything. I'm all set up to use my modem to call out, but to do this thing right I really need to be able to add that functionality to a program I'm working on. Any ideas?"

I thought a moment. "How about RAS?"

"Yeah, I thought about that. But the Remote Access Service API is nasty stuff. I'm having trouble making it work. Take a look at this one—the RasEnumEntries API. I'm trying to get a list of the phone entries set up on the system."

I sat next to her and looked at the Win32 SDK screen she had showing:

```
DWORD RasEnumEntries (
    LPTSTR reserved, // reserved, must be NULL
    LPTSTR lpszPhonebook, // pointer to full path and file name of
                          // phone book file
    LPRASENTRYNAME lprasentryname, // buffer to receive phone
                                   // book entries
    LPDWORD lpcb, // size in bytes of buffer
    LPDWORD lpcEntries // number of entries written to buffer
    );
```

"Doesn't look too bad to me. The reserved parameter is NULL, so we'll probably make it ByVal As Long and pass 0. I see from the description below that the lpszPhonebook can also be NULL to use the default phone book. Hmm . . . now it gets tricky."

"That's right," she replied grimly. "The lprasentryname parameter is a pointer to an array of RASENTRYNAME structures. The structure looks like this:

```
typedef struct _RASENTRYNAME {
    DWORD  dwSize;
    TCHAR  szEntryName[RAS_MaxEntryName + 1];
}RASENTRYNAME;
```

where MaxEntryName is 256. We can probably pull the usual array trick and pass the first element in an array, but how big an array do we need?"

"Easy," I replied. "The lpcb parameter is a Long variable that we initialize to the size of the buffer—that is, the number of bytes in the lprasentryname array. According to the documentation, if the array isn't long enough, the function will return error 603 indicating that a larger buffer is needed. The lpcEntries parameter is a Long variable that will be loaded with the number of entries in the array."

She reviewed the comments in the documentation. "Don't forget, the dwSize parameter in the lprasentryname array structures must be set to the correct array size."

We quickly wrote up the following module to hold the public constants and declarations:

```
' RasTest #1
' Copyright © 1998 by Desaware Inc. All Rights Reserved

Option Explicit

Public Const RAS_MaxEntryName = 256
Public Const RAS_MaxEntryNameBuffer = 257

Public Type RASENTRYNAME
    dwSize As Long
    szEntryName As String * RAS_MaxEntryNameBuffer
End Type

Public Declare Function RasEnumEntries Lib "rasapi32.dll" _
Alias "RasEnumEntriesA" (ByVal reserved As Long, ByVal _
lpszPhonebook As String, lprasentryname As RASENTRYNAME, _
lpcb As Long, lpcEntries As Long) As Long
```

The RASENTRYNAME structure string is 257 bytes. The lpcb and lpcEntries parameters are both declared by reference because the function has them defined as LPDWORD—a pointer to a Long. We added a form with a list box and the following code:

```
' RasTest #1
' Copyright © 1998 by Desaware Inc. All Rights Reserved

Option Explicit

Private Sub Form_Load()
    Dim BufferSize As Long
    Dim RasEntries As Long
    Dim RasEntryBuffer() As RASENTRYNAME
    Dim RasEntrySize As Long
    Dim Res As Long
    Dim CurrentEntry As Integer
    Dim RasEntryCount As Long

    ReDim RasEntryBuffer(0)
    RasEntrySize = Len(RasEntryBuffer(0))
    RasEntryBuffer(0).dwSize = RasEntrySize
```

```
    Res = RasEnumEntries(0, vbNullString, RasEntryBuffer(0), _
    BufferSize, RasEntries)
    If Res = 603 Then
        ' Buffer is too small - Resize to selected size
        RasEntryCount = BufferSize / RasEntrySize
        ReDim RasEntryBuffer(RasEntryCount - 1)
        Res = RasEnumEntries(0, vbNullString, RasEntryBuffer(0), _
        BufferSize, RasEntries)
    End If

    If Res <> 0 Then
        MsgBox "RAS Error #" & Res, vbOKOnly, "Error"
    End If

    For CurrentEntry = 0 To RasEntries - 1
        lstEntries.AddItem RasEntryBuffer(CurrentEntry).szEntryName
    Next CurrentEntry
End Sub
```

The function has a variable named RasEntrySize, which contains the length of a RASENTRYNAME structure. We start out by creating an array with a single element and initializing its dwSize field to the RasEntrySize value. We then call the RasEnumEntries function, passing the first element of the RasEntryBuffer array, which effectively passes a pointer to the entire array. If the result is 603, we increase the size of the array so that it is large enough to hold all of the entries in the phone book and call the RasEnumEntries function again. On success, we loop through all of the entries in the array and add the names to the list box.

DT looked up at me with a wicked smile. "So you think that will work, do you? Check out the results."

Results

The first thing I noticed was that the RasEnumEntries function returned error 632. The RAS errors can be found in file Raserror.h, part of the Win32 SDK.[1] The file contains constant declarations:

```
#define RASBASE 600

#define ERROR_BUFFER_TOO_SMALL                (RASBASE+3)
```

....

1. Under Windows95/98, the first call to RasEnumEntries returns error 603, a correct result under the circumstances, suggesting that a larger buffer is needed. The second call returns error 610, indicating that the buffer is invalid (whatever that means).

```
/*
 * Caller's buffer is too small.%0
 */
#define ERROR_BUFFER_INVALID                (RASBASE+10)
/*
 * The buffer is invalid.%0
 */


#define ERROR_INVALID_SIZE                  (RASBASE+32)
/*
 * The structure size is incorrect.%0
 */
```

"Structure size incorrect? How can the structure size be incorrect?" I couldn't see it.

"I feel the same way." She frowned. "The dwSize parameter is 4 bytes and the string is 257 bytes, exactly as shown in the C declaration. That's 261 bytes— exactly what the RasEntrySize variable contains. How can the structure size be incorrect?"

I looked over the ras.h header file. The only thing that was slightly suspicious was the include statement at the top of the file:

```
#include <pshpack4.h>

Abstract:

This file turns 4-byte packing of structures on.
(That is, it disables automatic alignment of structure fields.)
An include file is needed because various compilers do this in different ways.  For
Microsoft-compatible compilers, this file uses the push option to the pack pragma
so that the poppack.h include file can restore the previous packing reliably.
```

So structures in this file use 4-byte packing instead of the usual 1-byte packing. DT and I looked at each other and reached for our juices, which had been brought to our table while we were working. We took a deep drink, then exchanged a look of shock as a sudden dizziness struck us both. Could it be poison?

> **EDITOR'S NOTE** *At this point the narrative ends. If DT's computer is going to make a call, it looks like it's going to be up to you. Be sure you have at least two entries in your dialup networking phone book before working on the problem.*

The RASDIALPARAMS Structure

THE WINDOWS REMOTE ACCESS SYSTEM IS quite flexible and sophisticated. It has a large number of API functions. Unfortunately, it can be tricky to figure out which functions work under any given environment. Some aren't available under Windows 95/98. Some require later service packs on Windows NT. The RasGetEntryDialParams function can be used to retrieve information from the last successful dial-in on a specified phone book entry. It's a way to find out if the user had to change any of the phone book entries during the previous call in order to log on. There is also a function available to read phone book entries, but it doesn't work on Windows 95/98, so I'll leave it for you to research on your own.

The RasGetEntryDialParams function is defined as follows:

```
DWORD RasGetEntryDialParams(
    LPTSTR lpszPhonebook, // pointer to the full path and file name
                          // of the phone book file
    LPRASDIALPARAMS lprasdialparams, // pointer to a structure that
                                     // receives the connection parameters
    LPBOOL lpfPassword // indicates whether the user's password
                       // was retrieved
);
```

This function is very easy to handle. The lpszPhonebook parameter will be ByVal As String, but you'll set it to vbNullString because a NULL value uses the default phone book. The lprasdialparam parameter is a pointer to a RASDIALPARAMS structure, so it will be declared by reference as the structure. The lpfPassword parameter will be a Long declared by reference and will be loaded with a flag indicating whether a stored password was retrieved into the structure. The function loads the lprasdialparams structure with any data available for the dial-in that was not in the phone book entry. The following declaration should do the trick:

```
Public Declare Function RasGetEntryDialParams Lib "rasapi32.dll" _
    Alias "RasGetEntryDialParamsA" ( _
    ByVal lpszPhonebook As String, _
    lprasdialparams As RASDIALPARAMS, _
    lpfPassword As Long) As Long
```

So all you need to do now is create a VB declaration for the RASDIALARAMS structure. It is defined in the C header file as follows:

```
typedef struct _RASDIALPARAMS {
    DWORD   dwSize;
    TCHAR   szEntryName[RAS_MaxEntryName + 1];
    TCHAR   szPhoneNumber[RAS_MaxPhoneNumber + 1];
    TCHAR   szCallbackNumber[RAS_MaxCallbackNumber + 1];
    TCHAR   szUserName[UNLEN + 1];
    TCHAR   szPassword[PWLEN + 1];
    TCHAR   szDomain[DNLEN + 1] ;
#if (WINVER >= 0x401)
    DWORD   dwSubEntry;
    DWORD   dwCallbackId;
#endif
} RASDIALPARAMS;
```

The dwSize field has to be loaded with the size of the structure before the RasGetEntryDialParams function is called.

The RasTest program from Puzzle 18 has been modified to call the RasGetEntryDialParams function for a phone book entry that appears in the application's lstEntries list box:

```
Private Sub lstEntries_Click()
    Dim rs As RASDIALPARAMS
    Dim res As Long
    Dim Password As Long
    rs.szEntryName = lstEntries.Text
    rs.dwSize = Len(rs)
    lstDetails.Clear
    res = RasGetEntryDialParams(vbNullString, rs, Password)
    If res <> 0 Then
        MsgBox "RAS error #" & res
    Else
        lstDetails.AddItem "Phone: " & rs.szPhoneNumber
        lstDetails.AddItem "User: " & rs.szUserName
        lstDetails.AddItem "Domain: " & rs.szDomain
    End If
End Sub
```

Results

The RasTest2.vbp program (on the CD that comes with this book) will either result in error 632 (incorrect structure size) or, more likely, fail with a compile time error. This isn't surprising, since the structure is defined as follows:

```
Public Type RASDIALPARAMS
    dwSize As Long
    ' Well?
End Type
```

That's right. It's your job to figure out the declaration for this structure.

But I won't abandon you completely. Here are some excerpts from the C header files that should help.

From Ras.h

```
#include <pshpack4.h>

#define RAS_MaxDeviceType      16
#define RAS_MaxPhoneNumber     128
#define RAS_MaxIpAddress       15
#define RAS_MaxIpxAddress      21

#if (WINVER >= 0x400)
#define RAS_MaxEntryName       256
#define RAS_MaxDeviceName      128
#define RAS_MaxCallbackNumber RAS_MaxPhoneNumber
#else
#define RAS_MaxEntryName       20
#define RAS_MaxDeviceName      32
#define RAS_MaxCallbackNumber 48
#endif
```

From lmcons.h

```
//
// String Lengths for various LanMan names
//
```

```
#define CNLEN         15              // Computer name length
#define LM20_CNLEN    15              // LM 2.0 Computer name length
#define DNLEN         CNLEN           // Maximum domain name length
#define LM20_DNLEN    LM20_CNLEN      // LM 2.0 Maximum domain name length

#if (CNLEN != DNLEN)
#error CNLEN and DNLEN are not equal
#endif


//
// User, Group, and Password lengths
//

#define UNLEN         256             // Maximum user name length
#define LM20_UNLEN    20              // LM 2.0 Maximum user name length

#define GNLEN         UNLEN           // Group name
#define LM20_GNLEN    LM20_UNLEN      // LM 2.0 Group name

#define PWLEN         256             // Maximum password length
#define LM20_PWLEN    14              // LM 2.0 Maximum password length
```

From raserror.h

```
#define ERROR_CANNOT_FIND_PHONEBOOK_ENTRY    (RASBASE+23)
/*
 * Cannot find the phone book entry.%0

#define ERROR_INVALID_SIZE                   (RASBASE+32)
/*
 * The structure size is incorrect.%0
 */
```

How did I find the right files to use? The File Find utility built into Windows Explorer is an easy way to search for data inside files. A good text editor is even better.

Making Connections

FIGURE P20-1 SHOWS THE FINAL VERSION of the RASTest program at design time.

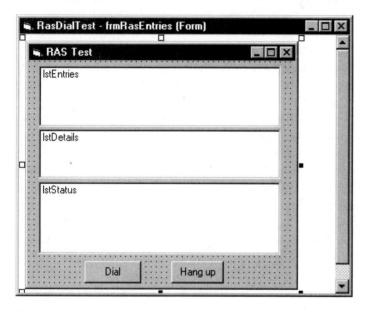

Figure P20-1: The RASTest program at design time

In Puzzles 18 and 19, you learned how to obtain a list of phone book entries and load a RASDIALPARAMS structure with information on a phone book entry. All that remains is to actually dial in and make a connection. This can be accomplished using the RasDial API function, described in the Win32 documentation as follows:

```
DWORD RasDial(
    LPRASDIALEXTENSIONS lpRasDialExtensions, // pointer to function
                                    // extensions data
    LPTSTR lpszPhonebook, // pointer to full path and file name of
                    // phone book file
    LPRASDIALPARAMS lpRasDialParams, // pointer to calling parameters data
    DWORD dwNotifierType, // specifies type of RasDial event handler
```

```
      LPVOID lpvNotifier, // specifies a handler for RasDial events
      LPHRASCONN lphRasConn // pointer to variable to receive connection
                            // handle
);
```

The LPRASDIALEXTENSIONS parameter is a structure that contains information on how to dial. The default values are fine for most situations, in which case you can pass a NULL value for this parameter or a structure with the fields set to 0.

The lpszPhonebook parameter is the same as you've seen in the previous examples and will typically be declared ByVal As String and passed the value vbNullString.

The lpRasDialParams parameter is a pointer to a RASDIALPARAMS structure loaded with information for the desired phone book entry.

The dwNotifierType parameter is a 32-bit Long that should be declared ByVal. This can have four possible values. If set to –1, the lpvNotifier parameter should contain a handle to a window that will receive WM_RASDIALEVENT messages[1] describing the progress of the dial-in operation. If the dwNotifierType parameter is set to 0 through 2, the lpvNotifier parameter should contain the address of a function that will be called with notification information during the course of the dial-in operation. When an API function calls a function address that you provide, the function you provide is called a "callback function."

The LPHRASCONN parameter is a pointer to a variable that will be loaded with the connection handle. Like all Win32 handles, this should be a 32-bit Long.

The RasHangUp function hangs up the connection for a given connection handle.

The following declarations are defined for the RASDIALEXTENSIONS structure and the RasDial and RasHangUp functions:

```
Public Type RASDIALEXTENSIONS
    dwSize As Long
    dwfOptions As Long
    hwndParent As Long
    reserved As Long
End Type

Public Declare Function RasDial Lib "rasapi32.dll" Alias "RasDialA" ( _
    lpRasDialExtensions As RASDIALEXTENSIONS, _
    ByVal lpszPhonebook As String, _
    lpRasDialParams As RASDIALPARAMS, _
```

---

1. A discussion of Windows messaging and subclassing can be found in both *Dan Appleman's Visual Basic Programmer's Guide to the Win32 API* and *Dan Appleman's Developing COM/ActiveX Components with Visual Basic 6.0*. Additional information, including a full-featured VB-authored subclasser, can be found in Desaware's SpyWorks package.

```
      ByVal dwNotifierType As Long, _
      ByVal lpvNotifier As Long, _
      lphRasConn As Long) As Long


Public Declare Function RasHangUp Lib "rasapi32.dll" Alias _
"RasHangUpA" (ByVal hRasConn As Long) As Long


Dim hRasConn As Long
```

The RasDial sample program adds a new list box called lstStatus, which is loaded
with notifications that are received by the callback function. The callback function calls a public method on the form called UpdateDialStatus, which in turn
loads the list box with the notification information as follows:

```
Public Sub UpdateDialStatus(ByVal RasConnState As Long, status As String)
    lstStatus.AddItem status
End Sub
```

The dialing process is started using the cmdDial_Click function shown here:

```
Private Sub cmdDial_Click()
    Dim dialext As RASDIALEXTENSIONS
    Dim rs As RASDIALPARAMS
    Dim res As Long
    Dim Password As Long

    If hRasConn <> 0 Then
       MsgBox "Connection already open"
       Exit Sub
    End If

    lstStatus.Clear
    dialext.dwSize = Len(dialext)

    rs.szEntryName = lstEntries.Text & Chr$(0)
    rs.dwSize = Len(rs)
    res = RasGetEntryDialParams(vbNullString, rs, Password)

    res = RasDial(dialext, vbNullString, rs, 0, AddressOf RasFunc, hRasConn)

End Sub


Private Sub cmdHangup_Click()
```

```
    If hRasConn = 0 Then
        MsgBox "No RAS connection open"
        Exit Sub
    End If
    Call RasHangUp(hRasConn)
End Sub
```

The dialext structure is a RASDIALEXTENSIONS structure. Only the dwSize field is set in order for the API function to recognize it as a valid structure. All of the structure fields are left at 0 to use the default values.

The function then clears the status list box and uses the RasGetEntryDialParams function to load the information for the specified phone book. The RasDial function sets the dwNotifierType parameter to 0 to tell the function that the lpvNotifier parameter is a function address based on a proto-type called RasDialFunc. The AddressOf operator can be used to retrieve the memory address of a function in a standard module. A RasDialFunc function is described as follows in the Win32 documentation:

```
VOID WINAPI RasDialFunc(
    UINT unMsg, // type of event that has occurred
    RASCONNSTATE rasconnstate, // connection state about to be entered
    DWORD dwError // error that may have occurred
    );
```

The unMsg parameter of this function is the message WM_RASDIALEVENT, which is defined as follows:

```
#define WM_RASDIALEVENT 0xCCCD
```

But you won't need to worry about this, because the value is passed from Windows to your function. The more important value is the rasconnstate pa-rameter, which contains a value describing the current RAS event. The RASCONNSTATE type is an enumeration—a 32-bit value. The enumeration is defined as follows:

```
#define RASCS_PAUSED 0x1000
#define RASCS_DONE   0x2000

#define RASCONNSTATE enum tagRASCONNSTATE
RASCONNSTATE
{
    RASCS_OpenPort = 0,
    RASCS_PortOpened,
```

```
    RASCS_ConnectDevice,
    RASCS_DeviceConnected,
    RASCS_AllDevicesConnected,
    RASCS_Authenticate,
    RASCS_AuthNotify,
    RASCS_AuthRetry,
    RASCS_AuthCallback,
    RASCS_AuthChangePassword,
    RASCS_AuthProject,
    RASCS_AuthLinkSpeed,
    RASCS_AuthAck,
    RASCS_ReAuthenticate,
    RASCS_Authenticated,
    RASCS_PrepareForCallback,
    RASCS_WaitForModemReset,
    RASCS_WaitForCallback,
    RASCS_Projected,

#if (WINVER >= 0x400)
    RASCS_StartAuthentication,
    RASCS_CallbackComplete,
    RASCS_LogonNetwork,
#endif
    RASCS_SubEntryConnected,
    RASCS_SubEntryDisconnected,

    RASCS_Interactive = RASCS_PAUSED,
    RASCS_RetryAuthentication,
    RASCS_CallbackSetByCaller,
    RASCS_PasswordExpired,

    RASCS_Connected = RASCS_DONE,
    RASCS_Disconnected
};


#define LPRASCONNSTATE RASCONNSTATE*
```

The RasDialFunc function's dwError parameter is a Long value whose meaning depends on the RAS event that is occurring.

You don't need to come up with a Declare statement for the RasDialFunc function. Why? Because the function is *not* in any of the Windows DLLs. It is in a standard module in your own application. Windows is calling back into your application.

You do, however, have to create a function in a standard module that can be called by Windows, and it is critical that your function's parameters match exactly what Windows uses when calling the function. The modRasTest module contains the following function:

```
Public Function RasFunc(unMsg As Long, RasConnState As Long, _
dwError As Long) As Long
   Dim result As String
   Select Case RasConnState
      Case RASCS_OpenPort
         result = "Opening port"
      Case RASCS_PortOpened
         result = "Port opened"
      Case RASCS_ConnectDevice
         result = "Connecting to device"
      Case RASCS_DeviceConnected
         result = "Device connected"
      Case RASCS_AllDevicesConnected
         result = "All devices connected"
      Case RASCS_Authenticate
         result = "Authenticating"
      Case RASCS_AuthNotify
         If dwError = 0 Then
            result = "Authentication Complete"
         Else
            result = "Authentication Failed"
         End If
      Case RASCS_AuthRetry
         result = "Authentication Retry Requested"
      Case RASCS_AuthCallback
         result = "Remote server requested a callback"
      Case RASCS_AuthChangePassword
         result = "Client requested a password change"
      Case RASCS_AuthProject
         result = "Projection phase starting"
      Case RASCS_AuthLinkSpeed
         result = "Link speed calculation"
      Case RASCS_AuthAck
         result = "Authentication phase started"
      Case RASCS_ReAuthenticate
         result = "Reauthentication started"
      Case RASCS_Authenticated
         result = "Authentication complete"
```

```
        Case RASCS_PrepareForCallback
            result = "Preparing for callback"
        Case RASCS_WaitForModemReset
            result = "Waiting for modem to reset"
        Case RASCS_WaitForCallback
            result = "Waiting for callback"
        Case RASCS_Projected
            result = "Projection results available"
        Case RASCS_StartAuthentication
            result = "Authentication starting"
        Case RASCS_CallbackComplete
            result = "Callback complete"
        Case RASCS_LogonNetwork
            result = "Logging on to network"
        Case RASCS_SubEntryConnected
            result = "Sub entry connected"
        Case RASCS_SubEntryDisconnected
            result = "Sub entry disconnected"
        Case RASCS_Interactive = RASCS_PAUSED
            result = "Connection paused"
        Case RASCS_RetryAuthentication
            result = "Retrying authentication"
        Case RASCS_CallbackSetByCaller
            result = "Callback state"
        Case RASCS_PasswordExpired
            result = "Password expired"
        Case RASCS_Connected = RASCS_DONE
            result = "Connected"
        Case RASCS_Disconnected
            result = "Disconnected"
    End Select
    Call frmRasEntries.UpdateDialStatus(RasConnState, result)
End Function
```

Results

Oh yes, I didn't mention the fact that the puzzle does not yet have Visual Basic
declarations for the enumeration, so the program won't even run. That's your
first task. Once you have the declarations, your second task will be obvious.

What Is That Mapped Drive? Part 1

IF YOU'VE USED A WINDOWS MACHINE on a network, you know that it is possible to map network drives so that they appear as local drives on your system. This can be very important to you as a programmer. For example, you might not want to use a mapped network drive to save temporary files, or you might want to know the network provider for the mapped drive. The Win32 API makes it easy to find out which local drives are actually mapped network drives. Or does it?

The Win32 API documentation defines the WNetGetConnection function as follows:

```
DWORD WNetGetConnection(
    LPCTSTR lpLocalName, // pointer to local name
    LPTSTR lpRemoteName, // pointer to buffer for remote name
    LPDWORD lpnLength  // pointer to buffer size, in characters
    );
```

It adds the following description for the lpnLength parameter:

> *lpnLength*
> *Points to a variable that specifies the size, in characters, of the buffer pointed to by the lpRemoteName parameter. If the function fails because the buffer is not big enough, this parameter returns the required buffer size.*
> *The return value of the function will be the constant ERROR_MORE_DATA if the buffer is not long enough to hold the data.*

The API declaration is fairly straightforward:

```
Private Declare Function WNetGetConnection Lib "mpr.dll" Alias _
"WNetGetConnectionA" (ByVal lpszLocalName As String, ByVal _
lpszRemoteName As String, lpnLength As Long) As Long
```

The Dynamic Link Library mpr.dll contains the network-independent API functions—those network functions that will work regardless of the network or network provider you are using. The lpszLocalName parameter is declared ByVal

As String. So is lpszRemoteName, except that, since this string will contain the return value, you have to be sure to preinitialize it to the correct length.

The lpnLength parameter is a pointer to a Long variable that contains the buffer length. Since the function expects a pointer, the parameter is passed by reference.

The sample program starts out by calling the function with an empty string and the buffer length set to 0. This allows Windows to set the correct buffer length to use on the second call.

The MapInfo1.vbp project contains the following code for the MapInfo1.frm file:

```
' MapInfo1.vbp
' Copyright © 1998 by Desaware Inc. All Rights Reserved

Option Explicit

Private Declare Function WNetGetConnection Lib "mpr.dll" Alias _
"WNetGetConnectionA" (ByVal lpszLocalName As String, ByVal _
lpszRemoteName As String, cbRemoteName As Long) As Long
Private Const ERROR_MORE_DATA = 234 '  dderror

    ' Get the source for a mapped drive
Private Function GetMappedInfo(ByVal Drive As String) As String
    Dim Buffer As String
    Dim BufferLength As Long
    Dim res As Long
    Drive = Left$(Drive, 2)

    res = WNetGetConnection(Drive, Buffer, BufferLength)
    If res = ERROR_MORE_DATA Then
        Buffer = String$(BufferLength, 0)
        res = WNetGetConnection(Drive, Buffer, BufferLength)
    End If

    If res <> 0 Then
        lblSource.Caption = GetErrorString(Err.LastDllError)
    Else
    ' Strip off the null termination character
        lblSource.Caption = Left$(Buffer, BufferLength - 1)
        GetMappedInfo = lblSource.Caption
    End If

End Function
```

```
Private Sub Drive1_Change()
   Call GetMappedInfo(Drive1.Drive)
End Sub
```

The GetErrorString function listed here uses the FormatMessage function to obtain a text description for the Err.LastDllError value retrieved when errors occur.

Results

You'll need a system connected to a network with a remote drive mapped to a local drive in order to test this example.

When the drive box selects an unmapped drive, the error message "This network connection does not exist" will be correctly displayed.

Under Windows NT, when the drive box selects a mapped drive, the error message "More data is available" will be displayed.[1]

Wait a minute—the code already retrieves the correct buffer length during the first call to WNetGetConnection. It looks like Windows is returning a buffer value that is *not* long enough to hold the lpRemoteName parameter. This contradicts the documentation shown above for the lpnLength parameter.

Is it a Windows bug? If not, why? If so, how would you work around it?

---

1. Under Windows 95/98, this puzzle works correctly. If you are not using Windows NT, I encourage you to read the puzzle and go directly to the solution, while repeating over and over in your mind, "I will test all my software on Windows NT, I will test all my software on Windows NT. . . ."

PUZZLE 22

What Is That Mapped Drive? Part 2

Now that you know how to obtain the server information for a mapped local drive, how do you obtain other information, such as the name of the network provider?

The WNetGetResourceInformation function can be used to obtain information about a network resource by loading a NETRESOURCE structure for the resource. This structure is defined in the API documentation as follows:

```
typedef struct _NETRESOURCE { // nr
DWORD dwScope;
DWORD dwType;
DWORD dwDisplayType;
DWORD dwUsage;
LPTSTR lpLocalName;
LPTSTR lpRemoteName;
LPTSTR lpComment;
LPTSTR lpProvider;
} NETRESOURCE;
```

The WNetGetResourceInformation function is defined as follows:

```
DWORD WNetGetResourceInformation (
    LPNETRESOURCE lpNetResource,  // Specifies the network resource
                                  // for which information is required
    LPVOID lpBuffer,              // Specifies a buffer to contain
                                  // the information
    LPDWORD lpcbBuffer,           // Specifies the size of the buffer
                                  // pointed to by lpBuffer
    LPTSTR *lplpSystem            // Pointer to a string in the
                                  // output buffer
);
```

The lpNetResource parameter is a pointer to a NETRESOURCE structure that defines the network resource for which to obtain information. The lpRemoteName field in the structure must be set to the name of the network resource (not the local mapped drive letter). You can set the dwType field to the constant RESOURCETYPE_DISK to improve performance somewhat (the function won't search through nondisk resource types such as printers). The lpProvider field can also be set if you know the network provider who owns the resource. The other fields in the structure are ignored.

The lpBuffer parameter takes a pointer to a memory buffer to load with a NETRESOURCE structure followed by any necessary string information. The string pointers in the returned NETRESOURCE structure will point to the strings within this buffer. The lplpSystem parameter will also be set to point to a string within this buffer.

The size of the buffer can be determined using the exact same method described in Part 1 of this puzzle—the required buffer size will be loaded into the lpcbBuffer parameter.

Confused? Here's one final thought: The win32api.txt file defines the lpLocalName, lpRemoteName, lpComment, and lpProvider fields of the NETRE-SOURCE structure as strings.

This would lead you to the following declaration and code as shown in MapInfo2.vbp project in the Puzzles subdirectory (on the CD that comes with this book):

```
Private Declare Function WNetGetResourceInformation Lib "mpr.dll" _
Alias "WNetGetResourceInformationA" ( lpNetResource As NETRESOURCE, _
lpBuffer As Byte, lpcbBuffer As Long, lplpSystem As Long) As Long
Private Type NETRESOURCE
        dwScope As Long
        dwType As Long
        dwDisplayType As Long
        dwUsage As Long
        lpLocalName As String
        lpRemoteName As String
        lpComment As String
        lpProvider As String
End Type


' Get the network provider information
Private Sub GetResourceInfo(resourcename As String)
    Dim nr As NETRESOURCE
    Dim lpSystem As Long
    Dim OutputBufferSize As Long
    Dim OutputBuffer() As Byte
    Dim res As Long
```

```
lstResource.Clear
If resourcename = "" Then Exit Sub

nr.dwType = RESOURCETYPE_DISK
nr.lpRemoteName = resourcename

' Prep the buffer
OutputBufferSize = 1024
Do
    ReDim OutputBuffer(OutputBufferSize)
    res = WNetGetResourceInformation(nr, OutputBuffer(0), _
        OutputBufferSize, lpSystem)
Loop While res = ERROR_MORE_DATA
If res <> 0 Then
    MsgBox "No Resource Information Available"
    Exit Sub
End If

' Get resulting NETRESOURCE
Call RtlMoveMemory(nr, OutputBuffer(0), Len(nr))

lstResource.AddItem "Remote Name: " & nr.lpRemoteName
lstResource.AddItem "Provider: " & nr.lpProvider

End Sub
```

Results

Everything works fine until you select a mapped drive in the drive selection box. This causes the GetResourceFunction API to be called, leading to an immediate memory exception.

Your challenge: Modify the code to allow you to retrieve the provider information for the network resource.

There Is a Question in There Somewhere

WHERE DO THESE PUZZLES COME FROM?

One of my goals for this book was to develop puzzles that are real. What do I mean by this? I've sometimes found that sample code in books is somewhat artificial. For example, object-oriented programming is demonstrated by using animals—you have a class named Animal with inherited classes that are specific types of animals, such as dog or cat. This is fine if you're running a zoo, but let's face it: Most programmers don't create software for zoos. They may work in offices that bear some resemblance to zoos, but I digress. My point is that book examples are sometimes just a bit irrelevant.

With this book, I'm fairly confident I've avoided that trap. How can I be so sure? Rather than explain, I thought I would demonstrate. Consider this, if you will, a puzzle on how to create these types of puzzles.

First, the inspiration for the puzzle.

The following is a real inquiry I received about two days ago:

Dan, you've been very helpful in the past—I'm hoping you can help with what I'm sure is actually a simple question.

I'm trying to use the user_info_2 structure with the NetAddUser function from VBA. Part of this structure is: PBYTE usri2_logon_hours; points to a 21-byte (168 bits) bit string that specifies . . .

How do I include this in my type declaration? Also, there is a constant in the C header as:

#define USER_MAXSTORAGE_UNLIMITED ((unsigned long) -1L)

Isn't this a contradiction?

Should I just declare this as a long constant with the value of 1? Thanks in advance!

Now, I don't want to give you the impression that I answer all of the questions I receive. Time does not permit me to answer more than a few. In this case, however, the question struck me as perfect for this book. I gave my correspondent a quick answer and asked permission to use his exact text in the book (without mentioning his name), which he was kind enough to grant.

The quick answer I gave him was in the form of suggestions as to how to proceed. It did not include an example of how to use the NetAddUser function. You can, if you wish, try to figure out the answer to the question now. Or you can read on as I demonstrate the process of creating a sample puzzle. To do so, I'm going to adopt a writing style that I occasionally use in articles and that I've never seen used by any other author.

This chapter is being written in real time.

What does this mean? It means that I am literally writing this chapter as I work out the problem. You get to watch over my shoulder, so to speak, as I figure out how to make this function work. In order to be effective, the writing has to be honest, so you'll get to see the mistakes I make along the way as well. Note that the chapter is written in past tense in order to maintain a consistent voice, but rest assured, I'm writing the text as I write the code.

The Function

My first step was to do a search in the Win32 SDK for the function NetAddUser. Here's where I ran into my first problem. There is no such function. So I switched to the function reference and went to the alphabetical listing of functions that begin with the word "Net." I quickly found that the function's name was NetUserAdd.

The Win32 SDK begins with a warning that the function will only work in a program that runs as a member of the Administrators group. Not surprising; after all, I'm talking about adding a user to the system. It's also a function that runs only on Windows NT. This is also not surprising, since Windows 95 doesn't provide much support when it comes to managing users. To test the program, you'll need to log on to a Windows NT workstation or server under an administrator account.

The function is declared in C as follows:

```
NET_API_STATUS NetUserAdd(
    LPWSTR servername,
    DWORD level,
    LPBYTE buf,
    LPDWORD parm_err
    );
```

What could I tell from this?

- The servername parameter is an LPWSTR (LP = Long pointer, W = Wide, STR = String). It's a pointer to a wide (Unicode) string. Since the function explicitly specifies a wide string, you can be pretty certain that there is a single entry point for the function instead of separate Unicode and ANSI entry points. This parameter can also be NULL to add the user to the local system.

- The level parameter is set to a value of 1, 2, or 3. If 1, the buf parameter points to a USER_LEVEL_1 structure; if 2, a USER_LEVEL_2 structure; and if 3, a USER_LEVEL_3 structure. These structures contain the information about the user that is being added.

- The buf parameter is a pointer to the appropriate structure. Why don't they use a specific type such as LPUSER_LEVEL_1? Because the parameter needs to point to any of the available structure types depending on the value of the level parameter. LPBYTE means pointer to a byte and is often used as a generic pointer type when a pointer has to refer to more than one type.

- The parm_err parameter is a pointer to a Long variable that is loaded with the index of the parameter in the structure that caused an error—the position of that parameter in the structure.

- The function returns a long value. According to the documentation, the value is NERR_SUCCESS if the function succeeds. A search through the header files showed that NERR_SUCCESS is equal to 0.

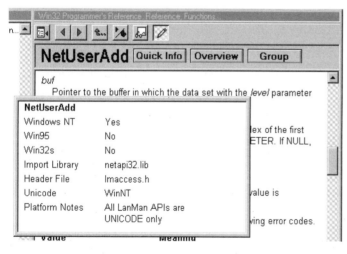

Figure P23-1: The Win32 SDK Quick Info window

I was almost ready to write the Visual Basic declaration. One question: What's the name of the DLL? I could have used the DumpInfo program (described in Tutorial 9, "Inside a DLL File: Exploring the DumpInfo Program," in Part III of this book) to search for the DLL that supports this function, but since I already had the Win32 SDK online reference open, I simply clicked on the QuickInfo button to receive summary information about the function, as shown in Figure P23-1.

The key information is the import library, which in this case is netapi32.lib. Now, the import library name is not always the same as the DLL name, so I took a quick look at the system32 directory on my NT system. Sure enough, there is a DLL named netapi32.dll. I was still not absolutely sure that this was the correct DLL, but it's a very good guess. The declaration is as follows:

```
Private Declare Function NetUserAdd Lib "netapi32.dll" ( _
    ByVal servername As Long, ByVal level As Long, _
    ByVal buf As Long, parm_err As Long) As Long
```

Why did I make these choices?

The servername parameter is a Long. If I defined it as a string, Visual Basic would convert the string to ANSI, and this needs to be a Unicode string. By specifying it ByVal As Long, I can pass an explicit address to a Unicode string. The level parameter is obviously a Long. For the buf parameter, I had several choices: I could declare it to be one of the structure types, declare it to be As Any, or use a Long again and pass the address of the structure. I chose the latter. The parm_err parameter is also a Long, but this time passed by reference because the parameter is an LPDWORD—a pointer to a 32-bit variable.

The Structure

Since the original question referred only to the USER_LEVEL_2 structure, I just dealt with that particular structure. The C declaration for the structure is as follows:

```
typedef struct _USER_INFO_2 {
    LPWSTR    usri2_name;
    LPWSTR    usri2_password;
    DWORD     usri2_password_age;
    DWORD     usri2_priv;
    LPWSTR    usri2_home_dir;
    LPWSTR    usri2_comment;
    DWORD     usri2_flags;
    LPWSTR    usri2_script_path;
    DWORD     usri2_auth_flags;
    LPWSTR    usri2_full_name;
    LPWSTR    usri2_usr_comment;
    LPWSTR    usri2_parms;
    LPWSTR    usri2_workstations;
    DWORD     usri2_last_logon;
    DWORD     usri2_last_logoff;
    DWORD     usri2_acct_expires;
    DWORD     usri2_max_storage;
```

```
DWORD      usri2_units_per_week;
PBYTE      usri2_logon_hours;
DWORD      usri2_bad_pw_count;
DWORD      usri2_num_logons;
LPWSTR     usri2_logon_server;
DWORD      usri2_country_code;
DWORD      usri2_code_page;
}
```

Is that a structure or what?

As large as the structure is, there are only three types of fields: pointers to Unicode strings, Long values, and a single PBYTE parameter. We'll get to that last one in a moment.

I won't even try to describe all of these fields—you'll have to read about them in the documentation for yourself. The important thing to know is that, in the vast majority of cases, you can simply pass NULL or 0 values in order to accept the default values. That means that, if I could define all of the fields as Long values, I would have the option of leaving the parameters at 0 to use the default values and could explicitly set the fields to an address as needed. This sounded so tempting that I defined the following VB declaration for the structure, adding a comment so I would know which fields needed to be strings:

```
Private Type USER_INFO_2
    usri2_name As Long ' Unicode string
    usri2_password As Long ' Unicode string
    usri2_password_age As Long
    usri2_priv As Long
    usri2_home_dir As Long ' Unicode string
    usri2_comment As Long ' Unicode string
    usri2_flags As Long
    usri2_script_path As Long ' Unicode string
    usri2_auth_flags As Long
    usri2_full_name As Long ' Unicode string
    usri2_usr_comment As Long ' Unicode string
    usri2_parms As Long ' Unicode string
    usri2_workstations As Long ' Unicode string
    usri2_last_logon As Long
    usri2_last_logoff As Long
    usri2_acct_expires As Long
    usri2_max_storage As Long
    usri2_units_per_week As Long
    usri2_logon_hours As Long ' Byte pointer to 168-bit number
    usri2_bad_pw_count As Long
```

```
    usri2_num_logons As Long
    usri2_logon_server As Long ' Unicode string
    usri2_country_code As Long
    usri2_code_page As Long
End Type
```

Make It Work

It was time to write some code. I wanted to find out if I was on the right track or if there were some hidden problems I had not yet seen. I started by looking at the Win32 SDK documentation to see which fields were absolutely essential.

Both usri2_Name and usri2_Password were obvious—it doesn't make much sense to create a user without a name or password.

I also needed a constant for the usri2_priv field. I found the constants in the lmaccess.h header file:

```
#define USER_PRIV_GUEST      0
#define USER_PRIV_USER       1
#define USER_PRIV_ADMIN      2
```

You might wonder how I find a specific constant when it can be hidden in any of the dozens of C header files. The truth is, I cheat. I use a text editor called Codewright (which, by the way, I highly recommend). This editor supports a feature called File Grep—a text search across multiple files. I think Visual Studio has a similar feature, at least when using the Visual C++ IDE. You can also write a text search tool like this yourself using Visual Basic. Use the VB directory functions to build a list of files, then open them one at a time in text mode. Read each line and use the instr function to see if the text you are searching for is present. It may not be the most efficient way to search through files, but it's easy to program. Of course, you can always use Windows Explorer's search capability as well. But I digress again.

The constants quickly became the following:

```
Private Const USER_PRIV_GUEST = 0
Private Const USER_PRIV_USER = 1
Private Const USER_PRIV_ADMIN = 2
```

I also needed the constant UF_NORMAL_ACCOUNT for the usri2_flags parameter:

```
#define UF_NORMAL_ACCOUNT               0x0200
```

This became the following:

```
Private Const UF_NORMAL_ACCOUNT = &H200
```

Note that the value is in hexadecimal.

A quick read of the documentation suggested that all of the other parameters could be 0. My first test used the following code:

```
Private Sub Command1_Click()
    Dim ul2 As USER_INFO_2
    Dim res As Long
    Dim parm_err As Long

    ul2.usri2_name = StrPtr("puzzle" & chr$(0))
    ul2.usri2_password = StrPtr("pass" & chr$(0))
    ul2.usri2_priv = USER_PRIV_USER

    res = NetUserAdd(0, 2, VarPtr(ul2), parm_err)
    Debug.Print "Result: " & res
    If res <> 0 Then Debug.Print "Error at index: " & parm_err
End Sub
```

What is that nasty trick I pulled with the usri2_name and usri2_password parameters? In the structure, I defined them as Longs and as requiring a pointer to a NULL-terminated Unicode string. The StrPtr operator returns a pointer to the internal string data of a Visual Basic string, and we know that Visual Basic stores data internally in Unicode. This is especially safe because these string parameters are read-only—the NetUserAdd API function never changes the data in these strings.

It was finally time to find out what would happen when I ran the program.

The result displayed by the Debug.Print statement indicated error 87, with the error at index 8.

I was curious what error 87 was. Since this is an API function, I could use the FormatMessage function to retrieve a text description of the error (as you've seen in the GetErrorString function, used in many places in this book). But in this case I was lazy, so I just did a search for ERROR_ in the api32.txt file on the CD-ROM that comes with this book. After finding the first constant in the error list, ERROR_SUCCESS, I searched down for number 87 and found the constant ERROR_INVALID_PARAMETER. I should have realized that would be the error— the SDK documentation mentioned that the parm_err parameter would only be set if a parameter was invalid. Which field is number 8? It's either usri2_script_path or usri2_auth_flags, depending on whether the first parameter is considered 0 or 1. Neither of these makes any sense. The usri2_script_path parameter is clearly documented as accepting a NULL string. The usri2_auth_flags is documented as being ignored for this function (the USER_INFO_2 structure is used by other functions as well).

Hopelessly Stuck?

At this point, I had a sudden sinking feeling. That's the trouble with writing articles in real time. What do you do when you're on a deadline, you've already invested hours in writing more than 2,000 words in a chapter, and you have no idea whether you'll be able to make it work? After a short panic break for chocolate, I took a closer look.

The documentation clearly states that the usri2_script_path parameter and usri2_auth_flags parameters may both be NULL. Yet the error clearly indicates that the problem is with one of these parameters.

When in doubt, I've found that it is always worthwhile to take a second look at the documentation—especially the parameters I was already setting. I noticed that the usri2_flags parameter had the following constant documented:

> UF_SCRIPT *The logon script executed. This value must be set for LAN Manager 2.0 or Windows NT.*

I had noticed earlier that the UF_NORMALACCOUNT constant was required, but I missed the UF_SCRIPT constant. Windows saw that the constant was missing and erroneously decided that the error was in the usri2_script_path parameter. Now, I don't know if that's a bug or just a misleading error result, but it does prove one point: When dealing with the Win32 API, never assume that something is true just because it happens to show up in the documentation. I realize that this is a scary thought, but don't get too depressed. Most of the time, the documentation is correct and Windows really is remarkably bug-free for a system of its complexity. Most Windows systems crash only once or twice a day (so much for not being depressed).

In fixing this problem, I noticed that I had left out the setting of the usri2_flags parameter completely. So I added the following code:

```
Private Const UF_SCRIPT = &H1
ul2.usri2_flags = UF_NORMAL_ACCOUNT Or UF_SCRIPT
```

The OR operator is used to combine two constants by taking the logical Or of their bit values. This is discussed further in Tutorial 3, "A Bool and Its Bitfields Are Soon Parted."

When I ran the program this time, it returned the result value 0.

But did it really work?

Yes and no. I opened the NT user manager and found that I had created a user named Pass, not one named Puzzle. How could this be?

I cheated and got caught.

You noticed that I passed Unicode strings to the structure by using the StrPtr function with a constant, as follows:

```
ul2.usri2_name = StrPtr("puzzle" & chr$(0))
```

What happens when you use the StrPtr operator on a constant? It creates a temporary variable containing the data and passes a pointer to the data. But as soon as it returns the pointer, the temporary variable ceases to exist. The next time StrPtr is called, the buffer is loaded with a different string. Frankly, I was lucky it didn't cause a system crash. The structure is holding a pointer, and you simply can't hold pointers to temporary data. I tried to get by without creating separate strings, and I got caught. This is where experience comes in handy. I had never tried using the StrPtr operator on a constant before trying it here, and I wanted to see if it would work. I was actually surprised that it did. Fortunately, I did have experience trying to hold pointers to temporary buffers and had seen similar problems, so as soon as I saw that the account was being created with the wrong name, I guessed that it was somehow related to my use of the StrPtr operator with constants. The final working code uses separate string variables whose addresses remain valid through the life of the function (as long as you don't try to change the data in the string). Here's the final version of the function:

```
Private Sub Command1_Click()
    Dim ul2 As USER_INFO_2
    Dim res As Long
    Dim parm_err As Long
    Dim username As String
    Dim userpass As String
    username = "Puzzle" & Chr$(0)
    userpass = "pass" & Chr$(0)

    ul2.usri2_name = StrPtr(username)
    ul2.usri2_password = StrPtr(userpass)
    ul2.usri2_priv = USER_PRIV_USER
    ul2.usri2_flags = UF_NORMAL_ACCOUNT Or UF_SCRIPT

    res = NetUserAdd(0, 2, VarPtr(ul2), parm_err)
    Debug.Print "Result: " & res
    If res <> 0 Then Debug.Print "Error at index: " & parm_err
End Sub
```

It turns out that the function will work even if you don't append the extra NULL character to the end of the strings. In fact, I have never seen a case where there is not a NULL character at the end of a string. So why do I explicitly add one anyway? Because there is nothing in the Windows or VB documentation that guarantees that a VB string will always have a NULL character after the string. Without that guarantee, Microsoft could change the way VB works at any time and thus break even compiled programs. By explicitly adding a NULL character, I make certain that the string will always be NULL-terminated.

The NT user manager now showed a user named Puzzle. The function worked!

The Puzzle, At Last

I hope you've enjoyed this chapter in real time. Now that you have a working test program, I leave you with the original question:

I'm trying to use the user_info_2 structure with the NetAddUser function from VBA. Part of this structure is: PBYTE usri2_logon_hours; points to a 21-byte (168 bits) bit string that specifies . . .

How do I include this in my type declaration? Also, there is a constant in the C header as:

#define USER_MAXSTORAGE_UNLIMITED ((unsigned long) -1L)

Isn't this a contradiction?

Should I just declare this as a long constant with the value of 1? Thanks in advance!

Can you answer his question?

Callback That String

FROM A READER:

In my VB5 Programmer's Guide to Win32 API, *the function EnumSystemLocales is listed, but my application keeps crashing whenever I try to implement it. I'm using the following code*
A standard module contains:

```
' Locales Puzzle
' Copyright © 1998 by Desaware Inc. All Rights Reserved

Option Explicit

Public Declare Function EnumSystemLocales Lib "kernel32" Alias _
"EnumSystemLocalesA" (ByVal lpLocaleEnumProc As Long, ByVal _
dwFlags As Long) As Long

Public Const LCID_INSTALLED = &H1   ' installed Locale ids

Public Function EnumLocalesProc(ByVal Locale As String) As Boolean
    Debug.Print Locale
    EnumLocalesProc = True
End Function
```

A form contains:

```
' Locale Example
' Copyright © 1998 by Desaware Inc. All Rights Reserved

Option Explicit

Private Sub Command1_Click()
    Dim lRet As Long
    lRet = EnumSystemLocales(AddressOf EnumLocalesProc, LCID_INSTALLED)
End Sub
```

Results

A locale defines a particular country and language combination. It is possible for a system to support more than one locale at a time. This function allows you to obtain a list of all of the locales on the system. Or it would, except that this example does crash, exactly as the reader specified, under Windows NT.[1]

---

1. Under Windows 95/98, the function does not crash, at least not immediately. But the result is not valid either.

OLE Smoke!

THERE IS THE ENTIRE WIN32 API—thousands upon thousands of functions that control virtually every aspect of Windows. And then there is OLE.

OLE, short for Object Linking and Embedding, is the old name for ActiveX, a marketing buzzword invented in the days when Microsoft was more afraid of Netscape than of the Department of Justice.[1] Nowadays, you are more likely to hear the term COM or COM+ describing those technologies that are part of or implemented by OLE.

OLE represents a large subsystem within Windows, and it comes with its own DLLs and API functions.

It is extremely important to understand the difference between API functions and object methods and properties that are part of COM. Functions and COM methods can both be implemented by dynamic link libraries, but that is where the similarity ends.

With COM, your program must first create an object. The object is implemented by the DLL (or EXE), which provides you with a pointer to the object—or, specifically, a pointer to a requested interface for an object. This pointer actually references an array of function pointers for the methods and properties of the interface to the object you have requested. Visual Basic knows how to call methods and properties for certain types of interfaces, but not every interface is compatible with VB. If you want to call methods on an interface that is not compatible with VB, you need to use another DLL to create a wrapper object, define a custom type library for the object that is compatible with VB, or use a tool such as Desaware's SpyWorks, which provides generic access to any interface.

But you can't use the Declare statement to access methods or properties of an object.

The Declare statement is used exclusively to access functions that are directly exported by a dynamic link library. The DLL contains a list of functions that can be called without creating any objects, using a mechanism that has nothing whatsoever to do with COM. These functions are said to be "exported" from the DLL.

---

1. I wouldn't even begin to hazard a guess as to who, if anyone, Microsoft will be afraid of by the time you read this.

Visual Basic DLLs can create and support COM objects, but they cannot export functions unless you use a third-party tool (such as Desaware's SpyWorks) to add that capability to Visual Basic.

This book is not about creating COM objects or about how you can call methods or properties of a COM object. (My book *Dan Appleman's Developing COM/ActiveX Components with Visual Basic 6.0* deals with that subject in depth.) But DLLs that implement COM objects do have support from the operating system to handle many of the features of OLE. That support takes the form of a large number of functions that are exported from the OLE system DLLs themselves—the OLE API. Some of these functions can be useful even when called directly by an application. This book has generally avoided focusing on any one Windows subsystem, mostly because the techniques used in one are applicable to all. However, the OLE API deserves some special attention. It is the only API that makes extensive use of objects and a data structure called a GUID (Globally Unique Identifier). Learning to deal with objects and GUIDs in API functions poses a number of interesting challenges.

And interesting challenges are, after all, what this book is about.

Universal Identifiers, Part 1

YOU'VE PROBABLY HEARD OF COM, THE Component Object Model. You may have heard of it by other terms such as ActiveX or OLE. COM is an object model—a way to create and utilize a certain type of object called a "Windows object." (An in-depth introduction to COM from the perspective of Visual Basic programmers can be found in my book *Dan Appleman's Developing COM/ActiveX Components for Visual Basic 6.0: A Guide to the Perplexed.*)

The Win32 API includes hundreds of functions that relate to COM. These functions are part of the OLE subsystem. (OLE stands for Object Linking and Embedding. It is the technology that implements COM objects. ActiveX is another name for OLE.)

Every COM object is identified by a universal identifier called a GUID, or Globally Unique Identifier. This is a 128-bit number unique to the object in question. Due to the way GUIDs are created, the odds of another object sharing the same GUID are vanishingly remote. When you read the OLE documentation, you will also see the terms UUID, CLSID, and IID, for Universally Unique Identifier, Class Identifier, and Interface Identifier, respectively. The differences among these are purely semantic. In other words, the only difference between a class identifier and an interface identifier is that one identifies a class and the other identifies an interface. They are all 128-bit numbers and can be operated on identically from the programmer's perspective.

Puzzles 25–28 will demonstrate how to work with the OLE subsystem and GUIDs. But before you can deal with a GUID, you must know how to represent it in Visual Basic. Neither Visual Basic nor C++ have a 128-bit data type.

Here's a section from the Windows header file wtypes.h that includes the C++ declarations for GUIDs, CLSIDs, and IIDs:

```
#ifndef GUID_DEFINED
#define GUID_DEFINED
typedef struct _GUID
    {
    DWORD Data1;
    WORD Data2;
    WORD Data3;
```

```
    BYTE Data4[ 8 ];
    }   GUID;

#endif // !GUID_DEFINED
#if !defined( __LPGUID_DEFINED__ )
#define __LPGUID_DEFINED__
typedef GUID __RPC_FAR *LPGUID;

#endif // !__LPGUID_DEFINED__
#ifndef __OBJECTID_DEFINED
#define __OBJECTID_DEFINED
#define _OBJECTID_DEFINED
typedef struct _OBJECTID
    {
    GUID Lineage;
    unsigned long Uniquifier;
    }   OBJECTID;

#endif // !_OBJECTID_DEFINED
#if !defined( __IID_DEFINED__ )
#define __IID_DEFINED__
typedef GUID IID;

typedef IID __RPC_FAR *LPIID;

#define IID_NULL              GUID_NULL
typedef GUID CLSID;
```

Your Challenge

Can you create a Visual Basic declaration for GUIDs, IIDs, and CLSIDs?

Note

This puzzle does not have an associated code sample on the CD that comes with this book.

PUZZLE 26

Universal Identifiers, Part 2

THE REASON FOR THE EXISTENCE OF universal identifiers is that there is no way to prevent two individuals from giving objects and interfaces the same name. For example, the default name for every Visual Basic project is Project1. The default name for the first class in such a project is Class1. If you create a quick ActiveX DLL for experimentation purposes and don't bother to change these names, you will create a server that exposes an object named Project1.Class1. How many objects named Project1.Class1 are on your system? I don't even want to count the number drifting around on mine. And if you add up the number of objects with this name on all of the systems in the world . . . well, the prospect is too terrible to contemplate.

The human-readable form of an object as described above is called a program ID, and you should strive to make each one unique. The program ID is stored in the registry so the CreateObject function can find the server that can create the object. But the developers of COM wanted to provide a way to uniquely identify objects even if they are assigned the same program ID. That's why each object is really identified by its CLSID value. The program ID in the registry only serves to find the CLSID for the object. The object is actually loaded using the CLSID, not the program ID.

For example, if you use the CreateObject function to create a Microsoft Word document, you would use the program ID "Word.Document." Windows would then look up the string "Word.Document" in the system registry and find that the CLSID for the object is {00020906-0000-0000-C000-000000000046}.

This means that there must be some way to look up the CLSID for a given program ID. You could, of course, look in the registry, but it turns out that there is an OLE function that does the work for you.

The CLSIDFromProgID function is defined in the Win32 API documentation as follows:

```
HRESULT CLSIDFromProgID(
    LPCOLESTR lpszProgID, //Pointer to the ProgID
    LPCLSID pclsid        //Pointer to the CLSID
    );
```

The lpszProgID parameter is a string that contains the program ID you are searching for. The pclsid parameter is a structure to load with the CLSID for the object.

Designing the Test Program

The test program used by this puzzle is very simple, but it is made up of four different files. Why? Because the puzzle obtains the CLSID for an object that is part of the puzzle itself.

How is this accomplished?

First, the puzzle must be an ActiveX server, because only ActiveX servers can expose objects. In this case, it is an ActiveX EXE server, because we want the program to run in stand-alone mode as well. Use the Components tab of the Project Properties dialog box to choose the Standalone start mode so that the program will run independently. Set the start-up object in the General tab to Sub Main, so that the following code from the modGUIDPuzzle module will run:

```
Sub main()
    frmShowGUID.Show
End Sub
```

The frmShowGUID form contains two label controls and implements the following code:

```
' GUID Puzzle
' Copyright © 1998 by Desaware Inc. All Rights Reserved

Option Explicit

Private Sub Form_Load()
    Dim obj As New GUIDObject
    Dim cid As CLSID
    Dim ciddesc As String
    Dim x As Long

    cid = obj.GetCLSID()

    ciddesc = Hex$(cid.Data1) & vbCrLf
    ciddesc = ciddesc & Hex$(cid.Data2) & vbCrLf
    ciddesc = ciddesc & Hex$(cid.Data3) & vbCrLf
    For x = 0 To 7
        ciddesc = ciddesc & GetDataString(VarPtr(cid.Data4(x)), 1) & " "
    Next x
```

```
   lblGUIDAsStruct.Caption = ciddesc
   lblRawData.Caption = GetDataString(VarPtr(cid), Len(cid))
End Sub
```

The form creates a GUIDObject object that exposes function GetCLSID, which is able to return the object's CLSID. The lblGUIDAsStruct label displays each field in the CLSID structure independently. The GetDataString function (which is found in the ErrString module) displays data as hexadecimal values.

The lblRawData label control displays the entire structure as it exists in memory. The reason for showing both the fields of the structure and the memory layout of the structure will become apparent later and isn't really relevant to the puzzle itself.

The GUIDObject class exposes the GUIDObject object and contains the following code:

```
' GUID Puzzle Example Class
' Copyright © 1998 by Desaware Inc. All Rights Reserved

Public Type CLSID
   Data1 As Long
   Data2 As Integer
   Data3 As Integer
   Data4(7) As Byte
End Type

Private Declare Function CLSIDFromProgID Lib "ole32.dll" _
(ByVal lpszProgId As String, lpclsid As CLSID) As Long


Option Explicit

Public Function GetCLSID() As CLSID
   Dim cid As CLSID
   Dim res As Long
   Dim MyProgramId As String

   MyProgramId = "GUIDPuzzle.GUIDObject"
   res = CLSIDFromProgID(MyProgramId, cid)
   If res = 0 Then
      GetCLSID = cid
   Else
      ' What happens when you uncomment this?
      ' Err.Raise res
   End If
```

```
      End If
   End Function
```

This class takes advantage of a new ability of Visual Basic 6 to use user-defined types as parameters and return values of class methods and properties. If you are using Visual Basic 5, you will not be able to return the CLSID value as shown here. Your easiest solution in this case is probably to have the class set the form label values directly.

Results

When you run the program, the form shown in Figure P26-1 is displayed.

Clearly, something is wrong. Your job: Fix the program so that it displays the CLSID for the object.

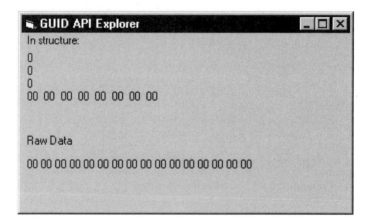

Figure P26-1: The GUIDPuzzle program results

PUZZLE 27

Universal Identifiers, Part 3

IN PUZZLE 26, "UNIVERSAL IDENTIFIERS, PART 2," you learned how to work with the CLSID structure and how the data in this structure can be represented to the user. One representation showed the individual fields of the structure; the other showed the raw data inside the structure. You also read that GUIDs are often described in string format.

The Win32 API includes the function StringFromCLSID, which can be used to obtain a string representation of GUID data. The function is defined in the Win32 documentation as follows:

```
WINOLEAPI StringFromCLSID(
REFCLSID rclsid, //CLSID to be converted
    LPOLESTR * ppsz       //Indirect pointer to the resulting string on return
  );
```

Parameters

rclsid
[in] CLSID to be converted.
ppsz
[out] Pointer to the resulting string.

The return type is WINOLEAPI, which is defined as follows in the file objbase.h:

```
#define WINOLEAPI        STDAPI
```

The STDAPI data type is defined in file basetyps.h as follows:

```
    #define STDAPI                EXTERN_C HRESULT STDAPICALLTYPE
```

EXTERN, C, and STDAPICALLTYPE are all C language terms that define the calling convention, a subject that will be discussed in Puzzle 29 and is unimportant for this puzzle. The HRESULT indicates that this function returns a 32-bit Long

HRESULT value. That means we'll define the return type as a Long and remember that the result can be raised directly as an error if it is not 0.

Now to the parameters:

The rclsid parameter is a pointer to the CLSID structure to convert into a string.

The ppsz parameter is a bit trickier. If the parameter were an LPOLESTR, it would be a pointer to an OLE string or a wide (Unicode) string. But there's an extra * character, indicating that this is a pointer to a pointer to a string. At first guess, you might consider trying to pass a string by reference, especially since you know that Visual Basic stores strings internally as Unicode data.

That would lead you to the following code:

```
' GUID Puzzle Example Class
' Copyright © 1998 by Desaware Inc. All Rights Reserved

Public Type CLSID
    Data1 As Long
    Data2 As Integer
    Data3 As Integer
    Data4(7) As Byte
End Type

Private Declare Function CLSIDFromProgID Lib "ole32.dll" _
(ByVal lpszProgId As Long, lpclsid As CLSID) As Long
Private Declare Function StringFromCLSID Lib "ole32.dll" _
(lpclsid As CLSID, lpOlestr As String) As Long

Option Explicit

Public Function GetCLSIDAsString() As String
    Dim cid As CLSID
    Dim MyString As String

    cid = GetCLSID()

    Call StringFromCLSID(cid, MyString)
    GetCLSIDAsString = MyString
End Function
```

Results

Of course, the example crashes in a spectacular memory exception on Windows NT.[1]
     Care to try your hand at it?

---

1. On Windows 95/98, the program does not crash and the data returned is garbage, but rather convincing-looking garbage.

Drawing OLE Objects

WHEN I SAW OLE 2.0 FOR the first time, I thought it was the most complicated technology I had ever seen from Microsoft. Then I chatted with a Microsoft developer. He explained that it was probably the most complicated technology yet to come from Microsoft. Now that I've been working with it for a few years, and it's called COM and ActiveX instead of OLE, I've come to realize that it is probably the most complicated technology Microsoft has ever shipped.

So I won't even begin to try to teach OLE programming from Visual Basic in this book. Puzzles 25, 26, and 27 have hopefully given you a taste. (You can learn a lot about the concepts of COM and OLE from my book *Developing COM/ActiveX Components with Visual Basic 6.0*. Without some familiarity with COM, you will find this puzzle difficult, if not incomprehensible.)

I've mentioned in several places that OLE does understand array and VB strings (BSTRs) and array parameters (SAFEARRAY). But the truth is, you will almost never run into those situations, because virtually all of the OLE functions that use these parameters duplicate functionality already provided in Visual Basic itself.

But there is one type of parameter that OLE functions understand that you will need to use extensively if you start using the OLE API: objects.

Displaying and Drawing Controls

Have you ever wanted to print out the contents of a single control? Or print or display the contents of a control that is not actually visible? Visual Basic doesn't really provide a good way to do this. You can draw or print the contents of a control by displaying it and copying the bitmap, but stretching small bitmaps to a printer usually results in poor image quality, especially for text. And it's frustrating to have to display the control before printing it.

Well, it turns out that ActiveX controls have to support an interface called IViewObject or IViewObject2. This interface describes a standard set of functions that allows an object to draw itself onto a device context (which can belong to a window or a printer). If only there was a way to directly use the IViewObject interface to force a control to draw its contents onto a device context, you would be able to display invisible controls or those that are not fully visible. You would be able to print them as well.

The OLE API has that function. It's called OLEDraw and is defined as follows in the Win32 SDK:

```
WINOLEAPI OleDraw(
    IUnknown * pUnk,        //Pointer to the view object to be drawn
    DWORD dwAspect,         //How the object is to be represented
    HDC hdcDraw,            //Device context on which to draw
    LPCRECT lprcBounds      //Pointer to the rectangle in which the object is drawn
    );
```

The pUnk parameter is defined as IUnknown *. IUnknown is the name of the interface on which all other interfaces are based. In other words, if you have a reference to a COM object, it does not matter if you are holding it in a variable declared As Object, As IUnknown, or as any other object type. It will always contain an IUnknown interface and be valid as a parameter that is declared as a pointer to an IUnknown interface.

The remaining parameters are more straightforward:

The dwAspect parameter allows you to specify a type of appearance. It will always be 1 for ActiveX controls—this value instructs the control to display its contents.

The hdcDraw parameter is a handle to a device context. This can be an API or printer device context.

The lprcBounds parameter specifies the rectangle coordinates in which to draw the contents of the control. LP indicates a Long (far) pointer to a RECT structure. The rectangle values should be specified in logical coordinates in the system used by the device context.[1]

The OLEDraw Program

Figure P28-1 illustrates the design time layout of the OLEDraw sample program. This program demonstrates the display of two controls: The first is a private UserControl that displays 16 vertical color bands; the second is Microsoft's MonthView control, which is part of the Microsoft Windows Common Controls–2 library.

---

1. Chapter 7 in my book *Visual Basic Programmer's Guide to the Win32 API* goes into almost mind-numbing detail on how to use device contexts, the meaning of coordinate systems, and the definition of logical coordinates. For now, just assume that everything is in pixel coordinates and you'll be fine.

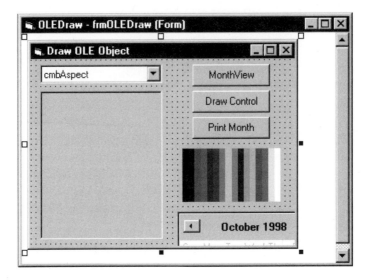

*Figure P28-1: Design time layout of the OLEDraw sample
program*

You'll notice that the MonthView control is only partially displayed on the window. Figure P28-2 shows the appearance of the program with control running after the MonthView command button is clicked. Or rather, it shows how the program will appear once you get it working.

   Before tackling the puzzle, let's take a look at the implementation of the OLEDraw program.

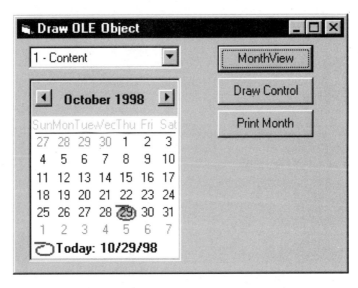

*Figure P28-2: OLEDraw program after the MonthView
command button is clicked*

The UserControl

The PrivateCtl control is a trivial control that draws 16 vertical color bars, each in a different color.

```
' OleDraw Sample
' Copyright © 1998 by Desaware Inc. All Rights Reserved
Option Explicit

Private Sub UserControl_Paint()
    Dim x As Long
    Dim bandsize As Long
bandsize = ScaleWidth / 16
    For x = 0 To 15
        Line (bandsize * x, 0)-(bandsize * (x + 1), ScaleHeight), _
        QBColor(x Mod 16), BF
    Next x
End Sub
```

The Form

The OleDraw function is declared as follows. The RECT structure contains four fields corresponding to the left, top, right, and bottom of the rectangle in which to draw. The aspects array contains the values 1, 2, 4, and 8, corresponding to the four possible Aspect values. As mentioned earlier, the only value that will not result in an error for most ActiveX controls is the number 1.

```
' OLE Drawing Puzzle
' Copyright © 1998 by Desaware Inc. All Rights Reserved
Option Explicit

Private Declare Function OleDraw Lib "ole32.dll" _
    (pUnk As Object, _
    ByVal dwAspect As Long , _
        ByVal hdcDraw As Long, _
        lprcBounds As RECT) As Long

Private Type RECT
    Left As Long
    Top As Long
    Right As Long
    Bottom As Long
```

```
End Type

Dim Aspects(3) As Long
```

The DrawTheObject and PrintTheObject functions are very similar. They only differ in that one refers to a picture control and the other to the printer object. The picture control already has its ScaleMode property set to 3 – vbPixels, so there is no need to explicitly set it, as is done in the PrintTheObject function.

```
Private Function DrawTheObject(obj As Object)
    Dim r As RECT
    Dim res As Long
    r.Right = Picture1.ScaleWidth
    r.Bottom = Picture1.ScaleHeight
    res = OLEDraw(obj, Aspects(cmbAspect.ListIndex), Picture1.hdc, r)
    If res <> 0 Then
        Err.Raise res
    End If
End Function


Private Function PrintTheObject(obj As Object)
    Dim r As RECT
    Dim res As Long
    Printer.ScaleMode = vbPixels
    r.Right = Printer.ScaleWidth
    r.Bottom = Printer.ScaleHeight
    res = OLEDraw(obj, Aspects(cmbAspect.ListIndex), Printer.hdc, r)
    If res <> 0 Then
        Err.Raise res
    End If
    Printer.EndDoc
End Function


Private Sub cmdDrawText_Click()
    DrawTheObject Privatectl1
End Sub

Private Sub cmdDrawWord_Click()
    DrawTheObject MonthView1
End Sub
```

```
Private Sub Command1_Click()
    PrintTheObject MonthView1
End Sub

Private Sub Form_Load()
    cmbAspect.ListIndex = 0
    Aspects(0) = 1
    Aspects(1) = 2
    Aspects(2) = 4
    Aspects(3) = 8
End Sub
```

Results

The results you see when you run the puzzle program will depend on the operating system you are using. In most cases, you should expect the program to vanish briefly as soon as you click on one of the drawing buttons. Shortly after it vanishes, you'll find that nothing happens. It's one of those "quiet" crashes.

Your job: Fix the program so that it not only displays the controls in the picture box, but also prints the month.

Rocket Science

AS WE APPROACH THE FINAL PUZZLES in the book, I can't help but wonder if I've set the puzzles at the right level. Are they too easy? Are they too hard? It is my hope that with the help of the tutorials (in Part III), even relative beginners will have found most of these puzzles challenging, but solvable. But I also want even the most advanced programmers to finish this book feeling that they have learned something.

This final set of four puzzles is designed to make absolutely certain that even the true API gurus have at least a few puzzles that they will find frustrating.

The term "rocket science" is historically used to describe complex technology that only really smart and educated people can understand. I'm not sure when the phrase was first used in this context, but I think you will agree, when you have finished this section, that it is well named—for these puzzles are truly nasty.

What Do You Do When It Mega Hurts?

QUICK—HOW MANY PROCESSORS ARE ON the system where your application is running? How fast is the CPU? What do you do when Intel announces a problem with a particular run of processors and you need to determine the exact type, model, and stepping number of the CPU running your application?

Intel provides a DLL that lets you obtain all this information. It's called cpuinf32.dll and can be found on their Web site at *http://developer.intel.com/vtune/cpuid/package.htm*, where you will also find instructions for downloading the package.[1]

Now, before you get too excited about this cool little DLL, I must warn you that it works reliably only with Intel processors. Nevertheless, it poses a fascinating problem.

The DLL includes a function called cpuspeed, which can be used to determine the raw and normalized speeds of the CPU.[2] The C declaration of the function is as follows:

```
struct FREQ_INFO cpuspeed(int clocks);
```

The clocks parameter should be set to 0 to use the default number of clock cycles for testing. The FREQ_INFO structure is defined as follows:

```
Type FREQ_INFO
    in_cycles As Long    ' Internal clock cycles during test
    ex_ticks As Long     ' Microseconds elapsed during test
    raw_freq As Long     ' Raw frequency of CPU in MHz
    norm_freq As Long    ' Normalized frequency of CPU in MHz
End Type
```

Care to try to come up with the correct declaration for this one?

....

1. At least, it's there at the time of publication. If it moves, you'll find the updated location at *http://www.desaware.com*—once we find it.

2. The normalized frequency is supposedly the nearest standard CPU frequency to the measured frequency. In practice, the number just seems to be the speed adjusted for rounding errors.

File Operations, Part 1

EVERY WINDOWS USER IS FAMILIAR WITH the types of file operations supported by Windows Explorer. Not Internet Explorer, mind you (though it is becoming increasingly difficult to tell the difference between them), but the main Windows interface. Windows Explorer makes it easy to drag files from one directory to another—moving them, copying them, deleting them, and so on. We've all seen the dialog boxes that prompt for confirmation, offer feedback that an operation is in progress, or report errors that occur.

There's a lot of file management functionality in Windows Explorer, and we all work with it every day. But what many Windows programmers do not realize is that most of this functionality is packed into one small function called SHFileOperation.

This simple function, with a single structure parameter, is defined as follows in the Win32 SDK:

```
WINSHELLAPI int WINAPI SHFileOperation(
    LPSHFILEOPSTRUCT lpFileOp
);
```

The Visual Basic declaration is easy:

```
Private Declare Function SHFileOperation Lib "shell32.dll" _
Alias "SHFileOperationA" (lpFileOp As SHFILEOPSTRUCT) As Long
```

How can one function perform all those file operations? Simple—all the parameters are crammed into the SHFILEOPSTRUCT structure, which is defined in the Win32 SDK as follows:

```
typedef struct _SHFILEOPSTRUCT { // shfos
    HWND         hwnd;
    UINT         wFunc;
    LPCSTR       pFrom;
    LPCSTR       pTo;
    FILEOP_FLAGS fFlags;
```

```
        BOOL        fAnyOperationsAborted;
        LPVOID      hNameMappings;
        LPCSTR      lpszProgressTitle;
} SHFILEOPSTRUCT, FAR *LPSHFILEOPSTRUCT;
```

The only parameter that is unclear here is the FILEOP_FLAGS data type, which is defined as follows:

```
typedef WORD FILEOP_FLAGS;
```

I'm in a generous mood, so rather than force you to figure out the structure declaration on your own, here is the declaration provided by Microsoft in the win32api.txt file that comes with Visual Basic:

```
Type SHFILEOPSTRUCT
        hwnd As Long
        wFunc As Long
        pFrom As String
        pTo As String
        fFlags As Integer
        fAnyOperationsAborted As Long
        hNameMappings As Long
        lpszProgressTitle As String '  only used if FOF_SIMPLEPROGRESS
End Type
```

The SHFILEOPSTRUCT Structure

This SHFILEOPSTRUCT structure uses a variety of constants to define the operation to perform. The wFunc field should be set to one of the following four values, which define the main operations:

```
Private Const FO_MOVE = &H1
Private Const FO_COPY = &H2
Private Const FO_DELETE = &H3
Private Const FO_RENAME = &H4
```

Fortunately, these constants are self-explanatory.

The fFlags field should be set to one or more of the following constants combined using the Or operator. This field modifies the operation of the function:

```
Private Const FOF_MULTIDESTFILES = &H1
Private Const FOF_CONFIRMMOUSE = &H2
```

```
Private Const FOF_SILENT = &H4     ' don't create progress/report
Private Const FOF_RENAMEONCOLLISION = &H8
Private Const FOF_NOCONFIRMATION = &H10
Private Const FOF_WANTMAPPINGHANDLE = &H20
Private Const FOF_ALLOWUNDO = &H40
Private Const FOF_FILESONLY = &H80
Private Const FOF_SIMPLEPROGRESS = &H100
Private Const FOF_NOCONFIRMMKDIR = &H200
```

Now the fun starts. The structure's pFrom and pTo fields can contain a list of one or more file or directory names.

If the FOF_MULTIDESTFILES flag is set, pFrom and pTo each contain the same number of file names. Each file in the pFrom list is copied, renamed, or moved to the file specified in the pTo list.

FOF_CONFIRMMOUSE is documented as currently not being used. FOF_SILENT prevents the SHFileOperation function from displaying any progress dialog boxes.

FOF_RENAMEONCOLLISION causes the function to create a copy of a file if one already exists in a target directory. The copy's file name takes the form "Copy of . . ."—something you have probably seen when working with Windows Explorer.

FOF_NOCONFIRMATION causes the function to automatically perform operations for which it would normally prompt for confirmation—for example, overwriting files, creating directories, and so on.

FOF_ALLOWUNDO causes deleted files and directories to be placed in the Recycle Bin.

FOF_FILESONLY causes only files to be copied during wildcard operations (such as *.*). Directories are ignored.

FOF_SIMPLEPROGRESS disables display of file names during copying. Only the message that you specify in the lpszProgressTitle field is displayed.

FOF_NOCONFIRMMKDIR causes the function to automatically create new directories as necessary to perform the operation.

FOF_WANTMAPPINGHANDLE sets the hNameMappings field to refer to an array of SHNAMEMAPPING structures containing the source and destination file names after the operation.

What makes this particular function interesting is the format of these strings. How does one string specify multiple files? Unlike Visual Basic, where the string length is kept internally for each string, Win32 API functions use the C convention, where a string is terminated by a NULL character. That's why Win32 API strings cannot contain embedded NULLs, whereas Visual Basic strings can. This function uses a common convention for passing multiple strings in a buffer, where each string is separated by a NULL character and the final string is terminated by two NULL characters.

The FileOp1 sample program contains two routines to convert string arrays to and from these double NULL-terminated string buffers. GetNullsString converts an array of strings into a buffer and is shown below:

```
Private Function GetNullsString(files() As String) As String
    Dim x&
    Dim res$
    For x = 1 To UBound(files)
        res$ = res$ & files(x) & Chr$(0)
    Next x
    ' Why do we add two nulls here? Can you guess?
    res$ = res$ & Chr$(0) & Chr$(0)
    GetNullsString = res$
End Function
```

To answer the question in the listing, consider what happens if there are no strings in the array. The reverse conversion is more complex and is shown in the GetFileArray function here:

```
' Convert a double null-terminated string
Private Function GetFileArray(NullsString As String, Optional _
ByVal SeparatorChar As Byte = 0) As Variant
    Dim nullpos&
    Dim curpos&
    Dim results() As String
    Dim itemcount&
    curpos = 1  ' Start location
    ReDim results(0)

    Do
        nullpos = InStr(curpos, NullsString, Chr$(SeparatorChar))
```

```
            If nullpos = 0 Then
                ' This should never, ever happen
                ' Just return what we have up to now
                GetFileArray = results()
                Exit Function
            End If
            If nullpos = curpos Then
                ' It's the second null, we're done
                GetFileArray = results()
                Exit Function
            End If
            itemcount = itemcount + 1
            ReDim Preserve results(itemcount)
            results(itemcount) = Mid$(NullsString, curpos, nullpos - curpos)
            curpos = nullpos + 1
        Loop While True
End Function
```

Why does this function provide for a user-defined separator character? Because
many programs allow you to enter a list of files separated by spaces in a text box.
The same function that parses strings separated by nulls can easily handle
strings separated by spaces as well.

The FileOp1 Sample Program

The program contains a single list box that has its OLEDropMode property set to
1 – Manual. The OLE events for the list box are defined so that files dragged from
Windows Explorer onto the list box are detected using the following code:

```
' This event is raised when files are dropped
Private Sub lstFiles_OLEDragDrop(Data As DataObject, Effect As Long, Button As _
Integer, Shift As Integer, x As Single, Y As Single)
    Dim count&, idx&

If (Effect And vbDropEffectCopy) <> 0 Then
        Effect = vbDropEffectCopy

        count = Data.files.count

        ReDim FileList(count)
        lstFiles.Clear
        ' Load the list of files
```

```
            For idx = 1 To count
                FileList(idx) = Data.files.Item(idx)
                ' Add them to the list box
                lstFiles.AddItem FileList(idx)
            Next idx
            lstFiles.Refresh
            ' Perform a copy operation
            DoACopy
        End If
    End Sub


    ' This event is raised when the mouse is over the list box
    Private Sub lstFiles_OLEDragOver(Data As DataObject, _
    Effect As Long, Button As Integer, Shift As Integer, x As Single, _
    Y As Single, State As Integer)
        If Data.GetFormat(vbCFFiles) Then
            ' It's a file list
            If (Effect And vbDropEffectCopy) Then
                ' We can accept a file copy operation
                Effect = vbDropEffectCopy
                Exit Sub
            End If
        End If
        ' Can't handle this data type
        Effect = vbDropEffectNone
    End Sub
```

The copy operation is started by dropping files on the list box. This causes the OLEDragDrop event to call the DoACopy function, which copies the programs to a floppy disk in your A: drive.

The reason for using a floppy disk in this example is to slow down the copy operation so you can see all of the progress dialog boxes that normally appear in these kinds of situations. The DoACopy function is defined as follows:

```
Private Sub DoACopy()
    Dim sh As SHFILEOPSTRUCT
    Dim src$, dest$
    Dim res&

    src$ = GetNullsString(FileList)
    dest$ = "A:\" & Chr$(0) & Chr$(0)

    sh.hwnd = hwnd
```

```
    sh.wFunc = FO_COPY
    sh.pFrom = src$
    sh.pTo = dest$
    sh.fFlags = FOF_RENAMEONCOLLISION Or FOF_SIMPLEPROGRESS
    sh.hNameMappings = 0
     sh.lpszProgressTitle = "Files are being copied to floppy"

    res = SHFileOperation(sh)
    If res <> 0 Then
       MsgBox "Error occurred: " & GetErrorString(Err.LastDllError)
    End If

End Sub
```

The copy operation is specified by setting the wFunc field of the structure to
FO_COPY. The FOF_RENAMEONCOLLISION forces a file rename if a file by the
same name already exists on the disk. The FOF_SIMPLEPROGRESS flag indicates
that the progress dialog box should just show the message "Files are being
copied to floppy" without displaying the individual file names.

Results

The files you drop on the list box do appear on the list box, but no copy operation occurs. What's more, when you close the application, it crashes with a
memory exception on Windows NT.

Your job is to fix the program so that it will work under Windows NT.

File Operations, Part 2

THE SHFILEOPERATION LOOKS SO INNOCENT AT first glance—only one parameter. But as you saw in the last puzzle, that parameter is a structure of nearly nightmarish complexity:

```
Type SHFILEOPSTRUCT
        hwnd As Long
        wFunc As Long
        pFrom As String
        pTo As String
        fFlags As Integer
        fAnyOperationsAborted As Long
        hNameMappings As Long
        lpszProgressTitle As String '  only used if FOF_SIMPLEPROGRESS
End Type
```

And if you thought you could sleep peacefully after solving that last puzzle, I have news for you: The nightmare has just begun.

The ShFileOperation function supports a feature you've probably seen many times when using Windows Explorer. What happens when you copy a file to the clipboard and paste it into a directory window where a file of the same name already exists? The file is automatically renamed to something along the lines of "Copy of . . .". The ShFileOperation function performs an automatic file rename if you specify the constant FOF_RENAMEONCOLLISION in the fFlags parameter.

But if a function is going to automatically rename files, there should be a way for the application to determine which files have been renamed. This is accomplished using Name Mappings. The hNameMappings field of the SHFILEOPSTRUCT is loaded with information about the files that were renamed when the FOF_WANTMAPPINGHANDLE constant is specified in the fFlags parameter.

The Win32 SDK defines the use of the FOF_WANTMAPPINGHANDLE constant as follows:

*Fills in the **hNameMappings** member. The handle must be freed by using the **SHFreeNameMappings** function.*

The structure description includes the following additional information on this parameter:

hNameMappings
> *Handle of a filename mapping object that contains an array of <u>SHNAMEMAPPING</u> structures. Each structure contains the old and new path names for each file that was moved, copied, or renamed. This member is used only if fFlags includes FOF_WANTMAPPINGHANDLE.*

A SHNAMEMAPPING structure is defined as follows in C:

```
typedef struct _SHNAMEMAPPING { // shnm
    LPSTR pszOldPath; // address of old path name
    LPSTR pszNewPath; // pointer to new path name
    int   cchOldPath; // number of characters in old path name
    int   cchNewPath; // number of characters in new path name
} SHNAMEMAPPING, FAR *LPSHNAMEMAPPING;
```

And as follows in the Win32api.txt provided by Microsoft:

```
Private Type SHNAMEMAPPING
        pszOldPath As String
        pszNewPath As String
        cchOldPath As Long
        cchNewPath As Long
End Type
```

The SHFreeNameMapping function is simple. It takes the value of the hNameMappings field from the SHFILEOPSTRUCT as a parameter and frees any data allocated for the handle.

```
Private Declare Sub SHFreeNameMappings Lib "shell32.dll" _
(ByVal hNameMappings As Long)
```

As a start, you would expect to modify the DoACopy function from the previous puzzle as shown here:

```
' Perform a copy operation
Private Sub DoACopy()
    Dim sh As SHFILEOPSTRUCT
```

```
        Dim src$, dest$
        Dim res&

        src$ = GetNullsString(FileList)
        dest$ = "A:\" & Chr$(0) & Chr$(0)

        sh.hwnd = hwnd
        sh.wFunc = FO_COPY
        sh.pFrom = src$
        sh.pTo = dest$
        sh.fFlags = FOF_RENAMEONCOLLISION Or FOF_WANTMAPPINGHANDLE
        sh.hNameMappings = 0

        res = DoTheShellCall(sh, "Files are being copied to floppy")

        If sh.hNameMappings <> 0 Then
              ' Can you read the file names here?
           Call SHFreeNameMappings(sh.hNameMappings)
        End If

End Sub
```

Removing the FOF_SIMPLEPROGRESS flag from the program allows you to see the individual file names as they are copied. The FOF_WANTMAPPINGHANDLE constant is added to enable the hNameMappings parameter. If the sh.hNameMappings is not 0, you need to free the Name Mapping object in order to prevent a memory leak.

Results

There are no results to see here yet. This is a bit more open-ended. Think you can handle it?

> **TECH REVIEWER'S COMMENT**
> – *Dan, this is totally unfair. You haven't bothered to explain what a mapping handle is or how to use it. I can't even figure out why I never see a non-zero value in the hNameMappings field. You have to give them better information than this.*
>
> **AUTHOR RESPONSE**
> – *You're right that it's a nasty one. It took me two hours to figure out how to make this work, and most people reading this are never going to get it. But it's not unfair. Believe it or not, I've included every piece of relevant*

information on this procedure that I could find in the Win32 SDK, MSDN, and Microsoft's online Knowledge Base. Frankly, the documentation on how to use this feature is terrible. But my readers are going to face situations like this on their own, and the solution (when they look at it) will help them learn how to investigate and handle these types of situations for themselves.

Animating Rectangles

ONE OF THE INTERESTING USER INTERFACE effects you can see under Windows 95 and Windows NT occurs when you minimize or maximize a window. When minimized, a window seems to collapse into the taskbar. This animated effect is provided by a cool function called DrawAnimatedRects, defined as follows in the Win32 documentation:

```
BOOL WINAPI DrawAnimatedRects(
    HWND hwnd,     // handle to clipping window
    int idAni,     // type of animation
    CONST RECT *lprcFrom, // pointer to rectangle coordinates (minimized)
    CONST RECT *lprcTo    // pointer to rectangle coordinates (restored)
    );
```

The hwnd parameter is the window in which the animation should occur. When the window handle is 0, the animation occurs on the desktop instead of within a specified window.

The idAni parameter is one of the following constants:

Private Const IDANI_OPEN = 1

Private Const IDANI_CLOSE = 2

Private Const IDANI_CAPTION = 3

IDANI_OPEN indicates that the rectangle animation should open from the minimized to the restored position. IDANI_CLOSE indicates that the rectangle animation should close from the restored to the minimized position. IDANI_CAPTION indicates that only the caption should be animated.

The lprcFrom and lprcTo parameters are pointers to RECT structures, which contain four 32-bit fields describing the left, top, width, and height of the rectangle.

The Rects.vbp sample program (on the CD that comes with this book) demonstrates the use of this function to animate a caption—which initially has a height and width of 0 at the center of the window—to fill the entire window. The ScaleMode property of the form is set to vbPixels to make sure there is no confusion between twips and pixels in the rectangle coordinates.

```
' DrawAnimatedRects Example
' Copyright © 1998 by Desaware Inc. All Rights Reserved
Option Explicit

Private Type RECT
    left As Long
    top As Long
    width As Long
    height As Long
End Type

Private Const IDANI_OPEN = 1
Private Const IDANI_CLOSE = 2
Private Const IDANI_CAPTION = 3

Private Declare Function DrawAnimatedRects Lib "user32" (ByVal hwnd _
As Long, ByVal idAni As Long, lprcFrom As RECT, lprcTo As RECT) As Long

Private Sub Command1_Click()
    Dim r1 As RECT
    Dim r2 As RECT
    ScaleMode = vbPixels
    r1.left = ScaleWidth / 2
    r1.top = ScaleHeight / 2
    r2.width = ScaleWidth
    r2.height = ScaleHeight
    Call DrawAnimatedRects(hwnd, IDANI_CAPTION, r1, r2)
End Sub
```

Results

The results of clicking the command button are odd, to say the least. The rectangle is indeed animated. But its starting and ending locations are outside the window. It is as if the coordinates in the r1 and r2 rectangles are in screen coordinates instead of relative to the window. Try passing the Command.hwnd property as a parameter to the DrawAnimatedRects function. Experimentation suggests that the function is using the hwnd parameter to determine which caption to animate instead of using the coordinates of the r1 and r2 parameters.

Your challenge is as follows:

1. Figure out how to get the function to perform the animation with the hwnd property set to 0 as described in the function documentation.

2. Come up with an example that uses the IDANI_OPEN and IDANI_CLOSE animation parameters.

3. Come up with an explanation that reconciles the behavior of the function in the example with the documentation.

Part II

THE SOLUTIONS

IN THIS PART OF THE BOOK, you will find the solutions to the puzzles presented in Part I. Before you look farther, please keep in mind that the amount you are able to learn from this book will be directly proportional to the time you spend struggling with the problems on your own.

So if you have not yet solved a puzzle, before you look at the solution, I suggest the following additional steps:

- Look at the hints provided in Appendix A.

- Read the tutorials in Part III, which can give you the tools to solve the puzzles on your own.

It will take a bit more time, but I think you will find it time well spent.

Where, oh, Where Is That API Call?

THE DECLARATION MAY HAVE LOOKED REASONABLE, but it actually had two errors. Though the function may be called GetUserDefaultLCID, locales relate to the operating system and thus are part of the kernel32 DLL, not the User32 DLL shown in the original declaration.

Next, Win32 function names are case-sensitive (unlike those in 16-bit Windows). Most API function names that contain multiple words have the first letter of each word capitalized, as you have within the function GetWindowText function. But an LCID is an acronym (for LoCale IDentifier) and thus is capitalized.

It's very easy to overlook these errors. The good news is that this error is one that Visual Basic not only detects, but also clearly identifies. If you get runtime error 453 (Can't find DLL entry point), the problem is almost certainly in the declaration—specifically, an error in the function name or the library name.

The corrected code below not only fixes the problem, but also shows you how to use the locale identifier to obtain the English name of the language in use at that locale.

```
' Where, oh, Where Is that API Call?
' Copyright © 1998 by Desaware Inc. All Rights Reserved

Option Explicit

Private Declare Function GetUserDefaultLCID Lib "kernel32" () As Long

Private Const LOCALE_SENGLANGUAGE = &H1001&
'   English name of language
Private Declare Function GetLocaleInfo Lib "kernel32" Alias _
"GetLocaleInfoA" (ByVal Locale As Long, ByVal LCType As Long, _
ByVal lpLCData As String, ByVal cchData As Long) As Long

Private Sub Command1_Click()
    Dim lcid&
    Dim info$
```

```
        lcid = GetUserDefaultLCID()
        info = String$(255, 0)
        Call GetLocaleInfo(lcid, LOCALE_SENGLANGUAGE, info, 255)
        info$ = Left$(info, InStr(info, Chr$(0)) - 1)
        MsgBox lcid & ":" & info$, vbOKOnly, "User Default LCID"
End Sub
```

SOLUTION 2

The Last Error

THE FINDWINDOW FUNCTION RETURNS either a window handle or zero. Zero is returned if no window is found or if an error occurred. How can you tell if an error occurred? That's where the LastError value comes in. Most API functions set an internal constant that indicates the meaning of an error, the value of which is only valid for functions that use the LastError capability. You can tell if a function uses the LastError value by reading the documentation for the function, which will usually say something like

To get extended error information, call GetLastError.

You can't actually call the GetLastError API function from Visual Basic, because Visual Basic clears the internal LastError value after each API call. Fortunately, Visual Basic allows you to retrieve the LastError value for the previous API call by accessing the LastDllError property of the Err object.

How can you find the meaning of the LastError values?

One way is to look in the api32.txt file or the winerror.h header file (on the CD that comes with this book) for a constant that corresponds to the value. This is not as haphazard as you might think. About halfway through the file, you'll find a long list of constants that begin with the prefix ERROR_. The list starts like this:

```
' The configuration registry database operation completed
' successfully.
Public Const ERROR_SUCCESS = 0&

'   Incorrect function.
Public Const ERROR_INVALID_FUNCTION = 1 '  dderror

'   The system cannot find the file specified.
Public Const ERROR_FILE_NOT_FOUND = 2&

'   The system cannot find the path specified.
Public Const ERROR_PATH_NOT_FOUND = 3&
```

Go down to number 123:

```
'   The filename, directory name, or volume label syntax is incorrect.
Public Const ERROR_INVALID_NAME = 123&
```

This suggests that one or both of the parameters is not correct and raises two interesting questions:

1. Why does this function return a LastError value of 123 on Windows NT, implying some sort of parameter error, and 0 on Windows 95/98?

2. Does the fact that FindWindow is returning a LastError value on NT suggest that there is a real problem with one of the parameters, or is it just that a window couldn't be found?

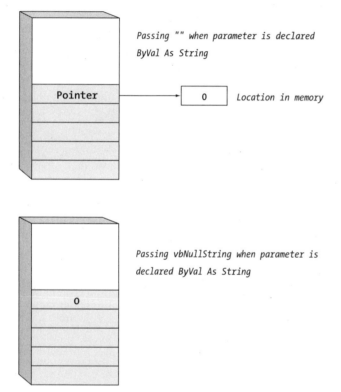

Passing "" when parameter is declared ByVal As String

Pointer → 0   *Location in memory*

Passing vbNullString when parameter is declared ByVal As String

0

Figure S2-1: Passing vbNullString and empty strings as parameters

It pays to take a closer look at the parameters in case there is a real problem. The window caption parameter type is correct, but make sure that the contents of the text box correspond to a window caption.

Which leaves the class name. The documentation for the function suggests that the class name parameter is ignored if you pass NULL.

But what exactly does NULL mean?

NULL in C++ terms always means 0—specifically, that the value 0 can be found on the stack for that parameter.[1] In the sample program, we're passing "" as the class name. Is this NULL?

No, "" is an empty string. In C terms, "" means a pointer to the terminating NULL character of a string. So, in this case, it means that a pointer will be passed as a parameter, and that pointer will appear on the stack. That is not the same thing as NULL, as shown in Figure S2-1.

Fortunately, Visual Basic provides an easy way—by using the constant vbNullString—to pass a NULL value when a parameter is declared as a string. Figure S2-1 shows the contents of the lpClassName parameter on the stack when an empty string ("") and

1. You'll find information on stacks and stack frames in Tutorial 4, "How DLL Calls Work: Inside a Stack Frame," in Part III of this book.

vbNullString are passed. The latter case corresponds to what a DLL function expects to see for a NULL value.

When the change is made, the function works correctly. If a valid window caption is specified, the window will be closed (try it with the Notepad application). If a valid window caption is not specified, you will see a message box, but the LastError value will be 0—indicating that, even though no window was found, the function did operate correctly.

What about an empty string? If you are running the program on Windows 95/98, an empty string is interpreted as a valid window class name. When the program fails to find a window belonging to that class, it returns 0 and sets the LastError value to 0 to indicate that no window was found.

If you are running the program on Windows NT, an empty string is interpreted as an invalid class name, and the LastError value is set to 123 to indicate that the parameter is incorrect.[2]

Another Way to Get the LastError Description

The FormatMessage API function is another way to obtain the string description of an error message. This function supports many different options that are beyond the scope of this discussion; all we care about is the functionality that retrieves a system message. The FormatMessage function is defined as follows:

```
Private Declare Function FormatMessage Lib "kernel32" Alias _
"FormatMessageA" (ByVal dwFlags As Long, lpSource As Any, ByVal _
dwMessageId As Long, ByVal dwLanguageId As Long, ByVal lpBuffer _
As String, ByVal nSize As Long, ByVal Arguments As Long) As Long

Private Const FORMAT_MESSAGE_FROM_SYSTEM = &H1000
```

The dwFlags parameter is set to the constant FORMAT_MESSAGE_FROM_SYSTEM. The lpSource parameter for this mode needs to be NULL. Since the declaration is specified As Any, be careful to pass a long parameter ByVal.[3] The dwMessageId parameter is the LastError value. Set the dwLanguageId parameter to 0 to use the default system language. The lpBuffer parameter is an initialized string whose maximum length is the nSize parameter. The Arguments parameter is also NULL.

---

2. Do Windows 95/98 and Windows NT differ in the way they handle an empty string parameter due to some underlying difference between operating systems? Probably not. Or because the NT programmer who implemented this function didn't talk to the Windows 95 programmer who implemented this function? Probably. And no, the difference is not documented—yet another example of why you should always test your programs under both Windows 95/98 and Windows NT.

```
' Retrieve a system error change.
Private Function GetErrorString(ByVal LastErrorValue As Long) As String
    Dim bytes&
    Dim s As String
    s = String$(129, 0)
    bytes = FormatMessage(FORMAT_MESSAGE_FROM_SYSTEM, ByVal _
    0&, LastErrorValue, 0, s$, 128, 0)
    If bytes > 0 Then
        GetErrorString = Left$(s, bytes)
    End If
End Function
```

The FormatMessage function returns the number of characters in the string, so you can simply use the Left$ function to retrieve the valid characters up to the terminating NULL character.

---

3. See Tutorial 5, "The ByVal Keyword: The Solution to 90 Percent of All API Problems," for further information on using the ByVal keyword with parameters declared As Any.

Poly Want a Cracker?

WHERE SHALL WE BEGIN?

The API declaration is an obvious place. The hdc parameter is a handle, a| 32-bit value that identifies an object. In this case, it is a handle to a device context, an object that acts as an interface between a physical device (such as a window on the screen or a printed page) and the drawing subsystem. Since you wish to pass the value of the handle as a parameter, you must specify the ByVal operator for the parameter. The same thing applies to the nCount parameter. The correct declaration is as follows:

```
Private Declare Function Polygon Lib "gdi32" (ByVal hdc As Long, _
lpPoint As POINTAPI, ByVal nCount As Long) As Long
```

This fix leads to (drum roll, please) . . . another blank screen.

The next step is to trace through and look at the result of the Polygon function. This will be easier if you change the Polygon call to use the function format as shown here:

```
Result = Polygon(hWnd, points(0), UBound(points) + 1)
```

The result is 0, which indicates that the function failed. If you examine the last error value by displaying the value of the Err.LastDllError property, you'll see the result is 6. You can use the FormatMessage function introduced in Puzzle 2 or look up the ERROR_ constants in the api32.txt or winerror.h file (on the CD that comes with this book) to find the matching error value:

```
'   The handle is invalid.
Public Const ERROR_INVALID_HANDLE = 6&
```

Take a close look at the first parameter, the handle. The function documentation defines this as a handle to a device context. But the code is using a handle to a window. Windows and device contexts are two very different things.

```
Call Polygon(hWnd, points(0), UBound(points) + 1)
```

You can use API functions to obtain a device context for a window, but it's much easier to use the hdc property of a form or picture control to obtain its device context.

```
Call Polygon(hdc, points(0), UBound(points) + 1)
```

Be careful not to make any changes to the configuration of a device context obtained in this manner—you could interfere with Visual Basic's own drawing system. Either use the SaveDC and RestoreDC API functions to save and restore the current configuration of the device context or create a separate device context using the CreateCompatibleDC function. Figure S3-1 shows the result after this fix is made.

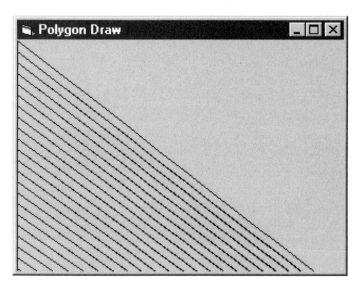

Figure S3-1: Second version of the Poly program

Clearly, something is still wrong. You could look closely at the algorithm for the LoadPointArray function, but that would be a waste of time. Not that you would be wrong to suspect it, but this is, after all, an API puzzle book. Adding an ordinary Visual Basic bug would be unfair, misleading, and something I would never dream of doing—this early in the book.

Compare Figure S3-1 with Figure P3-1. It's almost as if Figure S3-1 were a hugely magnified segment of the upper-left corner of Figure P3-1. Could we be dealing with a scaling problem?

Absolutely. The points are generated based on the form's Height and Width properties. These properties are specified in twips—1/1440 of an inch. API functions use the current logical coordinate system, which is always pixels by default. How do you convert from twips to pixels? The Screen object has a property, called TwipsPerPixelX and TwipsPerPixelY, that can be used to determine the number of twips in each pixel. Divide the height and width by the corresponding TwipsPerPixel value, as in the following code, and things are looking much better, as shown in Figure S3-2.

```
LoadPointArray Width / Screen.TwipsPerPixelX, Height / _
Screen.TwipsPerPixelY, 5, points()
```

The image does not look quite right yet. At the lower portion of the image, the vectors go off the bottom. It's almost as if the calculations are not based on the true dimensions of the window. As it turns out, that's probably because the calculations are not based on the true dimensions of the window. The Height and Width properties of a form reflect the dimensions of the entire window. The image appears only in the client area of the form (excluding the border and caption areas). The client area for a window can be obtained using an API function called GetClientRect or using the ScaleWidth and ScaleHeight properties of the form, the solution that is used here:

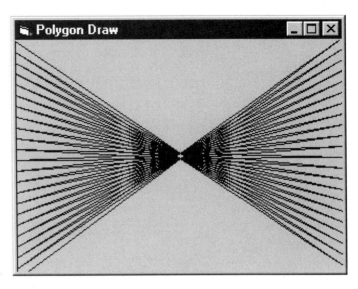

Figure S3-2: Another version of the Poly program

```
LoadPointArray ScaleWidth / Screen.TwipsPerPixelX, ScaleHeight / _
Screen.TwipsPerPixelY, 5, points()
```

And with that, the sample works perfectly.

One last question: You may note that there is a vertical line on the left side of the drawing. Can you tell where it comes from?

It's All in the Name

HOW CAN A SIMPLE LITTLE PIECE of code cause so many problems?

```
Private Declare Function GetComputerName Lib "kernel32" (ByVal _
ComputerName As String, ByVal BufferSize As Long) As Long

Private Const MAX_COMPUTERNAME_LENGTH = 15

Private Sub Form_Load()
    Dim s$
    Call GetComputerName(s$, MAX_COMPUTERNAME_LENGTH + 1)
    lblName.Caption = s$
End Sub
```

The approach for fixing a program like this is the same regardless of complexity. You try something, interpret the errors that occur, and modify the code to fix the error. Then you move on to the next error.

The DLL Entry Point

When you run this program, you get runtime error 453: Can't find DLL entry point GetComputerName in kernel32.

If you've looked at Tutorial 1, "Finding Functions" (in Part III of this book), you know that this error means that the requested API function does not exist in the specified DLL. Your first reaction might be to think that the GetComputerName function must be in a different DLL. But before you start searching, note that this function has a string parameter. In most cases, functions that take string parameters actually have two entry points: the ANSI entry point for single-byte characters and the Unicode entry point for double-byte characters.

Try changing the declaration as follows:

```
Private Declare Function GetComputerName Lib "kernel32" Alias _
"GetComputerNameA" (ByVal ComputerName As String, ByVal BufferSize _
As Long) As Long
```

This solves the problem. Runtime error 453 vanishes as the function is found.

And when you try running the program on Windows NT, it promptly crashes with a memory exception.[1]

Initialize that String!

As you see in the sample program, the function is called with a buffer length of MAX_COMPUTERNAME_LENGTH characters. Where did that number come from? It came from the function documentation, which specifies

> **Windows 95 and Windows 98: GetComputerName** *fails if the input size is less than MAX_COMPUTERNAME_LENGTH + 1.*

So the string buffer will be loaded with up to 15 characters (the value of the MAX_COMPUTERNAME_LENGTH buffer) plus the NULL termination character. When you pass the variable s$ to the API function, Visual Basic passes a pointer to a NULL-terminated string buffer to the function. How long is the buffer during the initial call? One byte—just the NULL termination character. The initial string is empty.

But the API call doesn't know that the buffer is only 1 byte long—you specifically told it that the buffer is 16 bytes long. So the API function happily loads the buffer with the computer name. In doing so, it overwrites memory that is being used by something else and thus crashes or otherwise corrupts your application's memory.

It is critical that strings always be preinitialized to the necessary length.

The following line is added before the GetComputerName function call:

```
s$ = String$(MAX_COMPUTERNAME_LENGTH + 1, 0)
```

Problem solved? Not quite—the program still crashes with an exception!

What Is that Buffer Length?

You know you're finding the correct function. And you know the string is being initialized correctly. That leaves the BufferSize variable. What could be simpler than passing the size of a buffer as a parameter?

---

1. Windows NT is quite good at detecting attempts to access invalid memory locations and raising memory exceptions as a result. Windows 95/98 does not do quite as good a job at detecting these kinds of problems, preferring to allow memory to be quietly corrupted so that your system will crash later in a spectacular manner completely unrelated to the original cause.

The nSize parameter is declared as follows:

```
LPDWORD nSize // address of size of name buffer
```

Tutorial 6, "C++ Variables Meet Visual Basic," in Part III of this book, discusses porting C++ variables to Visual Basic. A DWORD is a 32-bit variable. The LP prefix suggests that the nSize parameter is actually a pointer to the size of the buffer, not the size itself. Right now, the function is declaring the BufferSize parameter (our name for nSize) as being passed ByVal. This means we are passing the size of the buffer, not a pointer to the size. The solution is to create a Long variable to hold the size and pass a pointer to that variable, which can be accomplished easily by simply removing the ByVal keyword and passing the parameter by reference.

That brings us to the following working code:

```
' Computer Name
' Copyright © 1998 by Desaware Inc. All Rights Reserved

Option Explicit

Private Declare Function GetComputerName Lib "kernel32" Alias _
"GetComputerNameA" (ByVal ComputerName As String, BufferSize As Long) _
As Long

Private Const MAX_COMPUTERNAME_LENGTH = 15

Private Sub Form_Load()
    Dim s$
    Dim BufferLength As Long
    s$ = String$(MAX_COMPUTERNAME_LENGTH + 1, 0)
    BufferLength = MAX_COMPUTERNAME_LENGTH + 1
    Call GetComputerName(s$, BufferLength)
    lblName.Caption = s$
End Sub
```

The Missing Piece

What is actually loaded into the variable s$ buffer when this function returns? A NULL-terminated string. As a VB programmer, you don't want the NULL terminator character or anything after it. Can you come up with code to strip off the NULL terminator and the data that follows?

You saw one approach for stripping the NULL terminator from a string in Puzzle 1, "Where, oh, Where Is that API Call?," in which the Instr() function was used to find the location of the NULL-terminating character and the Left$() function was used to extract the portion of the string before that character. It may have occurred to you that it would be easier to use the Left$() function to extract the string if the API function could tell you how many characters were actually loaded into the buffer.

Seeing that this puzzle seems to be ending with a question anyway, here's another. Why did Microsoft choose to pass the BufferSize parameter by reference in this function? That would allow the function to change the value of the BufferLength variable from the value you provide during the call.[2]

What About the Result?

You may have noticed that the GetComputerName function in this example was called using the subroutine calling format in which the return value is ignored as shown here:

```
Call GetComputerName(s$, BufferLength)
```

API functions always return values indicating whether they succeed or fail. You might think that it is advisable to always check the results of API functions and write code to handle any errors that occur. The advantage of that approach is that your application will be very robust. The disadvantage is that you have to invest additional effort to write code to handle all possible errors.

Now, I would be the last person to discourage you from incorporating good error-handling into your application. But there are cases using the Win32 API when you can create code that is correct by design—in which case, additional error handling is wasted effort. This is one of those cases.

The GetComputerName function can fail if you pass invalid parameters, as you saw in this example. But once you have corrected your code so that you always pass a preinitialized string to the function with the correct BufferLength parameter, the function should always work. This is why the shorter subroutine call approach was used in this example.

---

2. You might want to take a look at the value of the BufferLength variable after the function call.

Finding the
Executable Name

DID YOU FIND IT DIFFICULT TO discover the API error in this case? I hope so—
because the declaration is perfect. In fact, the function call is just fine as well.
The problem is not in the API call, but in what we did with the result.

Let's look at the code step by step.

First, we initialize the string to 261 bytes:

```
ExecName = String$(MAX_PATH + 1, 0)
```

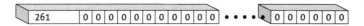

Figure S5-1: Initial contents of the ExecName string

The ExecName string now contains 261 characters, each with a 0 value. This is stored internally in BSTR format, meaning that Visual Basic stores the length of the string followed by the data, as shown in Figure S5-1. Note that the number 0 indicates that the character has the ASCII value 0, not that it contains the character "0."

Next, we load the file name using the GetModuleFileName API function:

```
Call GetModuleFileName(0, ExecName, MAX_PATH)
```

This loads the string with the full path to the application. Let's assume for this example that the program is running within the Visual Basic environment and that the program vb6.exe is located on the root directory of drive C. The string now contains the data shown in Figure S5-2.

Figure S5-2: Contents of the ExecName string after it is loaded by the GetModuleFileName function

The next step involves removing the path, since we need only the base executable name to determine if the program is Visual Basic. This is accomplished by searching from the end of the string backward for the backslash (\) character. In this example, the character is in position 3. The string is then reassigned using the Mid function to obtain the data after the \ character.

```
' Now strip off the path
LastBackslashPos = InStrRev(ExecName, "\")
If LastBackslashPos = 0 Then
    LastBackslashPos = InStrRev(ExecName, ":")
End If
ExecName = Mid$(ExecName, LastBackslashPos + 1)
```

The resulting string is shown in Figure S5-3.

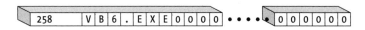

How long is the string after this operation? It depends on your point of view. If this string were passed to an API function, it would see a string containing 7 characters followed by a

Figure S5-3: Contents of the ExecName string after removing the path

NULL character. But Visual Basic sees things differently. It thinks the string is a 258-character string consisting of the file name "vb6.exe" followed by 251 NULL characters. What happens when you run the following code?

```
If LCase$(ExecName) = "vb6.exe" Or _
     LCase$(ExecName) = "vb5.exe" Or _
     LCase$(ExecName) = "vb32.exe" Then
     IsThisVB = True
   End If
```

In the comparison to "vb6.exe", Visual Basic tries to compare a 258-character string with a 7-character string. Naturally, they aren't the same. It is necessary for you to strip off all of the extra NULL characters. One way to do this is shown here:

```
NullPosition = InStr(ExecName, Chr$(0))
ExecName = Left$(ExecName, NullPosition - 1)
```

Like many API functions of this type, the GetModuleFileName function returns the number of characters that it loaded into the string. In this example, it would return 10—the length of the full path and executable name. We could have used this return value to strip off the NULL characters before removing the path. Both approaches work equally well.

I strongly encourage you to follow the example shown here for debugging your own API problems. Visualizing the contents of variables and their organization in memory can help you resolve many API-related problems.

SOLUTION 6

Icon Fix This One

PART OF THE TRICK TO SOLVING this puzzle is to step through the code. The LoadIcon function is returning 0, indicating that the icon failed to load. If you are running Windows NT, the GetErrorString function in the ErrString.bas module retrieves a description based on the LastError result retrieved from the Err.LastDllError property.

Why isn't LoadIcon working?

To understand the problem, let's walk through some of the C header code and see exactly how the icon constants are defined. Let's start with the constant definitions:

```
#ifdef RC_INVOKED
#define IDI_APPLICATION    32512
#define IDI_HAND           32513
#define IDI_QUESTION       32514
#define IDI_EXCLAMATION    32515
#define IDI_ASTERISK       32516
#if(WINVER >= 0x0400)
#define IDI_WINLOGO        32517
#endif /* WINVER >= 0x0400 */
#else
#define IDI_APPLICATION    MAKEINTRESOURCE(32512)
#define IDI_HAND           MAKEINTRESOURCE(32513)
#define IDI_QUESTION       MAKEINTRESOURCE(32514)
#define IDI_EXCLAMATION    MAKEINTRESOURCE(32515)
#define IDI_ASTERISK       MAKEINTRESOURCE(32516)
#if(WINVER >= 0x0400)
#define IDI_WINLOGO        MAKEINTRESOURCE(32517)
#endif /* WINVER >= 0x0400 */
#endif /* RC_INVOKED */
```

The #ifdef RC_INVOKED constant is true if the header file is being invoked from a resource compiler—a special compiler that combines various types of resources, such as icon and bitmap files, into a format that can be linked into an executable file. We're much more concerned with the way the constants are called from the C compiler itself, so everything within the RC_INVOKED block can be ignored. This leaves us with the following definitions:

```
#define IDI_APPLICATION      MAKEINTRESOURCE(32512)
#define IDI_HAND             MAKEINTRESOURCE(32513)
#define IDI_QUESTION         MAKEINTRESOURCE(32514)
#define IDI_EXCLAMATION      MAKEINTRESOURCE(32515)
#define IDI_ASTERISK         MAKEINTRESOURCE(32516)
#if(WINVER >= 0x0400)
#define IDI_WINLOGO          MAKEINTRESOURCE(32517)
#endif /* WINVER >= 0x0400 */
```

The IDI_WINLOGO constant describes a constant that only exists on Windows 95 and later and Windows NT and later, so we can include it.

What does the term MAKEINTRESOURCE refer to? MAKEINTRESOURCE is a precompiler macro. A macro is like a function, except that it is processed during the compilation process by the compiler. The result of the macro is text that is actually compiled. Now all we need to do is take a closer look at the MAKEIN-TRESOURCE macro:

```
#define MAKEINTRESOURCEA(i) (LPSTR)((DWORD)((WORD)(i)))
#define MAKEINTRESOURCEW(i) (LPWSTR)((DWORD)((WORD)(i)))
#ifdef UNICODE
#define MAKEINTRESOURCE   MAKEINTRESOURCEW
#else
#define MAKEINTRESOURCE   MAKEINTRESOURCEA
#endif // !UNICODE
```

We're creating an ANSI program, so the UNICODE condition does not matter to us. The MAKEINTRESOURCE macro definition reduces to the following:

```
#define MAKEINTRESOURCEA(i) (LPSTR)((DWORD)((WORD)(i)))
#define MAKEINTRESOURCE   MAKEINTRESOURCEA
```

What does this mean?

Consider what happens when you include the term IDI_WINLOGO in your program.

The term IDI_WINLOGO is replaced by MAKEINTRESOURCE(32517).

MAKEINTRESOURCE(32517) is replaced by MAKEINTRESOURCEA(32517).

MAKEINTRESOURCEA(32517) is replaced by (LPSTR)((DWORD)((WORD)32517))).

The term (LPSTR)((DWORD)((WORD)32517))) is finally compiled by the compiler.

This term is potentially confusing as well. Consider first the term ((WORD)32517). What does this mean?

When a C header has a variable type bracketed by parentheses, it means the variable that follows is coerced (or cast) into the specified type. The variables are not converted from one type to another—rather, the compiler simply treats the data as if it belongs to the new type. So ((WORD)32517) means to treat the value 32517 as an unsigned integer.

The entire macro can be interpreted as follows:

1. Take the integer value "i" and treat it as an unsigned 16-bit number.

2. Take that number and treat it as a 32-bit number (setting the high 16 bits to 0).

3. Take the 32-bit unsigned number and treat it as a pointer to a string (even though it is not a pointer at all).

You may be wondering how can you possibly pass a number that is not a pointer to an API function that expects a string parameter? The answer can be found in the somewhat cryptic description of the lpIconName parameter that you read earlier:

Points to a null-terminated string that contains the name of the icon resource to be loaded. Alternatively, this parameter can contain the resource identifier in the low-order word and 0 in the high-order word. Use the **MAKEINTRESOURCE** *macro to create this value.*

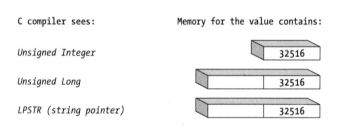

```
C compiler sees:            Memory for the value contains:

Unsigned Integer                        32516

Unsigned Long                           32516

LPSTR (string pointer)                  32516
```

Figure S6-1: Passing the IDI_ASTERISK resource identifier to the LoadIcon function

You see, the lpIconName parameter is designed to handle two types of parameters. If the LoadIcon function sees that the high 16 bits is 0, the function assumes that you are passing a numeric identifier to an icon resource. If the high 16 bits contain data, the function assumes you are passing a pointer to a NULL-terminated string. Figure S6-1 shows what gets passed to the function when the constant value is set to IDI_ASTERISK (32516). As you can see, even though the compiler is told to interpret the value of the constant as a string pointer, the value remains unchanged and is passed directly to the LoadIcon function.

What About Visual Basic?

Now you know what the API function expects to see. What are you actually passing to the function?

The lpIconParam parameter is declared ByVal As String. That means the function is always passed a NULL-terminated string. What happens when you pass a numeric constant to a parameter declared ByVal As String? Visual Basic converts it into a string before passing it to the function. This differs from the C language "cast" operator, where the data is unchanged and merely interpreted according to the new type. Visual Basic performs an actual conversion. In this case, the IDI_ASTERISK constant is converted into the string "32516" and passed, with a NULL terminator, to the function. This is illustrated in Figure S6-2.

Naturally, this is not what the function expects to see, so it returns an error result.

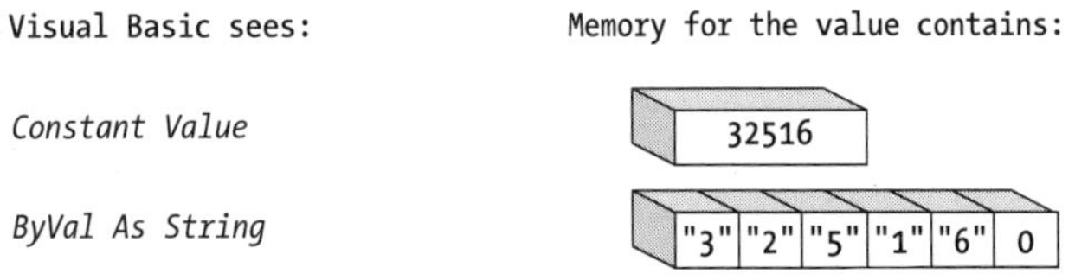

Why doesn't Visual Basic report an error when you try to pass a number to a string parameter? Most computer scientists ask this question as well—it is one area where many of us fundamentally disagree with Microsoft's approach to Visual Basic. Microsoft has built many of these automatic type conversions into Visual Basic, supposedly to make the language easier for programmers. Unfortunately, this decision has eliminated the ability of the compiler to detect many types of errors. Visual Basic happily converts parameters without so much as a hint of what it is doing, leaving you to struggle with obscure bugs. We call this "evil type coercion," and you'll find many programmers (including myself) who consider this one of the greatest flaws in what is otherwise a superb programming language.

Visual Basic sees:

Constant Value

ByVal As String

Memory for the value contains:

32516

"3" "2" "5" "1" "6" 0

Figure S6-2: Passing the IDI_ASTERISK resource identifier when a parameter is declared ByVal As String

How should you handle a situation like this? You could just change the lpIconName parameter to be ByVal As Long, but if you take that approach, the function will not be able to use string parameters. You could declare the parameter to be As Any or ByVal As Any to allow you to call the function with either a string or numeric parameter.

You can also create two separate declarations, one for Long parameters and another for string parameters. This is the approach used in the final solution for this puzzle. The Visual Basic Alias keyword allows you to define a function name for a declaration in Visual Basic that differs from the function name within the DLL file. In this case, the LoadIconBynum declaration uses a Long parameter, and the LoadIconBystring declaration uses a string parameter. Both functions use the LoadIconA entry point in the DLL.

```
' IconView Puzzle
' Copyright © 1998 by Desaware Inc. All Rights Reserved

Option Explicit

Private Declare Function LoadIconBynum Lib "user32.dll" Alias "LoadIconA" ( _
    ByVal hInstance As Long, _
    ByVal lpIconName As Long) As Long

Private Declare Function LoadIconByString Lib "user32.dll" Alias "LoadIconA" ( _
    ByVal hInstance As Long, _
    ByVal lpIconName As String) As Long

Private Declare Function DrawIcon Lib "user32" (ByVal hdc As Long, ByVal x As _
Long, ByVal y As Long, ByVal hIcon As Long) As Long

Private Const IDI_APPLICATION = 32512&
Private Const IDI_HAND = 32513&
Private Const IDI_QUESTION = 32514&
Private Const IDI_EXCLAMATION = 32515&
Private Const IDI_ASTERISK = 32516&
Private Const IDI_WINLOGO = 32517&

Private m_IconID As Long

Private Sub Form_Load()
   m_IconID = IDI_APPLICATION
End Sub

Private Sub optIcon_Click(Index As Integer)
   Select Case Index

Case 0
        m_IconID = IDI_APPLICATION
    Case 1
      m_IconID = IDI_ASTERISK
    Case 2
      m_IconID = IDI_EXCLAMATION
    Case 3
      m_IconID = IDI_HAND
    Case 4
      m_IconID = IDI_QUESTION
    Case 5
```

```
            m_IconID = IDI_WINLOGO
        End Select
        Picture1.Refresh
End Sub


Private Sub Picture1_Paint()
    Dim iconhandle As Long
    iconhandle = LoadIconBynum(0, m_IconID)
    If iconhandle = 0 Then
        MsgBox GetErrorString(Err.LastDllError)
    Else
        Call DrawIcon(Picture1.hdc, 0, 0, iconhandle)
    End If
End Sub
```

Supercharged Graphics

LIKE MOST API-RELATED PROBLEMS, THE DECLARATION is the culprit. Let's take a close look at the SDK description of the Polyline function:

```
BOOL Polyline(
    HDC hdc,        // handle of device context
    CONST POINT *lppt,    // address of array containing endpoints
    int cPoints  // number of points in the array
    );
```

```
Private Declare Function Polyline Lib "gdi32" (ByVal hdc As Long, _
lppt() As POINTAPI, ByVal nCount As Long) As Long
```

This is a function that returns a BOOL. A Win32 BOOL is a Long value, so that much is correct. The DLL is gdi32, which is also correct, since gdi32 is the DLL that holds all of the core graphics library functions.

The count is an integer, and Win32 integers are 32 bits, so the nCount parameter is also correct.

What about lpPoints?

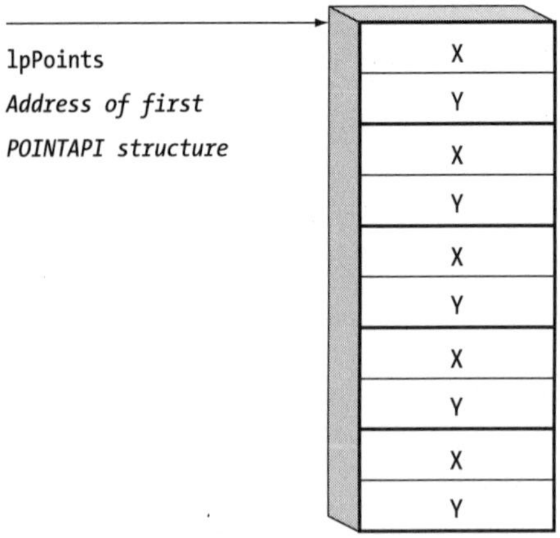

Figure S7-1 shows the lppt parameter as seen by the Polyline function. The function expects to see as a parameter a pointer to the first POINTAPI structure in an array of structures in memory.

The Visual Basic declaration defines this parameter as lppt() As POINTAPI. What is passed to an API function when you declare an array in this manner? The answer is shown in Figure S7-2.

Figure S7-2 shows that there is a lot more than meets the eye when it comes to array declarations. Visual Basic stores arrays internally using the OLE array storage mechanism. The OLE array storage system uses a structure called a SAFEARRAY to manage arrays. Each array has a SAFEARRAY structure that contains all of the information necessary to describe the array to the system. The OLE API contains a number of functions that create and manipulate SAFEARRAY structures. When you declare a variable as an array in Visual Basic, the variable actually contains a pointer to a SAFEARRAY

Figure S7-1: The lppt parameter as seen by the Polyline function

lpPoints
Address of first
POINTAPI structure

structure describing the array. The SAFEARRAY structure contains a pointer to the array data.

When you declare an API parameter as an array, Visual Basic passes a pointer to the array variable—a pointer to a pointer to a SAFEARRAY structure.

Now this is all very interesting, but what does it have to do with passing an array to the Polyline function? Nothing! The only API functions you will ever see that can work with SAFEARRAY structures are those that deal with the OLE API. The point of this discussion is that you should avoid declaring parameters as arrays when API functions specify pointers to arrays.

But how, then, can you pass a pointer to an array? Look again at Figure S7-1. An array, from the Polygon function's perspective, can be thought of as a pointer to the first element in an array. As long as all of the structures are contiguous in memory, all you need to do is make sure that the address of the first structure in the array is passed as a parameter. This suggests the following declaration:

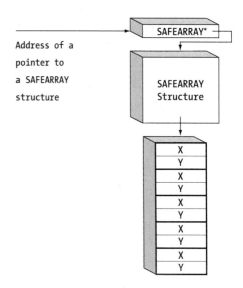

Figure S7-2: Array parameters are passed as pointers to pointers to a SAFEARRAY

```
Private Declare Function Polyline Lib "gdi32" (ByVal hdc As Long, _
lppt As POINTAPI, ByVal nCount As Long) As Long
```

Now you're passing a single POINTAPI structure—or are you? Since the parameter is passed by reference, you are passing the address of that structure. As long as it is followed in memory by the other structures in the array, you are effectively passing a pointer to the entire array—exactly the scenario shown in Figure S7-1.

But this change also requires a change in the way the function is called. If you just change the declaration, you will get a ByRef argument mismatch error. The function call must be changed from

```
Call Polyline(hdc, PointArray(), points)
```

to

```
Call Polyline(hdc, PointArray(0), points)
```

You must pass the first element in the array rather than trying to pass the entire array.

That's all you need to do to fix the program.

Playing Leapfrog

YOU PROBABLY FIGURED OUT THE FIRST problem quickly. There are two reasons why a function might not be found in a DLL: You have either the wrong DLL or the wrong function name. The operating system version number is as closely tied to the operating system as a function can get, so kernel32 is the logical DLL to hold the function. And in fact, that's where the function is. So the name must be wrong.

There are only two reasons why a system function would have a different name in the DLL than what you see in the documentation. Occasionally, the documentation describes a C macro—a name that translates into a series of C function calls. Fortunately, this is very rare, and these situations are typically described in the documentation.

Most often, the problem is that the function takes a string parameter, thus it appears in the DLL with two entry points: the ANSI entry point with an A suffix and a Unicode entry point with a W suffix.

But the GetVersionEx function doesn't take a string parameter, so how can this be the problem?

Wait a minute! Look again at the OSVERSIONINFO structure:

```
Private Type OSVERSIONINFO
    dwOSVersionInfoSize As Long
    dwMajorVersion As Long
    dwMinorVersion As Long
    dwBuildNumber As Long
    dwPlatformId As Long
    szCSDVersion As String * 128 ' Remember VB arrays are zero based!
End Type
```

Sure enough, the structure has a string. That means that the function does, indeed, need two entry points: one that can handle an ANSI string within a structure and another that can handle the Unicode string. The corrected declaration is therefore as follows:

```
Private Declare Function GetVersionEx Lib "kernel32" Alias _
"GetVersionExA" (os As OSVERSIONINFO) As Long
```

The function still fails, however, returning a 0 (invalid) result.

The C declaration for the structure suggests that the dwOSVersionInfoSize field contains the size of the structure. Does this mean that the API function loads the structure with the size or that you have to set the size before calling the function? If you followed the hint provided for this puzzle in Appendix A of this book and read the documentation for the function carefully, you will have noticed a brief comment explaining that the dwOSVersionInfoSize field must be initialized to the size of the structure before calling the function.[1]

The following simple code modification solves the problem:

```
' You have to initialize the size field
  os.dwOSVersionInfoSize = Len(os)
```

Why does Windows require you to initialize the structure size? Shouldn't it already know how big the structure is?

The answer is subtle and elegant. Windows uses the size to determine the version of the structure the calling application expects to see. Let's say the Windows developers decide that, for Windows NT 8.0, they want to add a new 128-character string that would allow you to retrieve Bill Gates's e-mail address so he could provide you with personal technical support. Older applications would still use the current OSVERSIONINFO structure, and if the system tried to write data into this new buffer, the application would almost certainly crash. This way, the system can look at the size of the buffer. The current OSVERSION-INFO structure is 148 bytes long; the new one would be 276 bytes.

Windows uses this technique extensively with structures, so if you ever find yourself with a function that uses a structure parameter and fails to work, make sure that any required fields are initialized.

---

1. My technical editor suggested that it might be unfair to expect readers to have access to my API book or the Win32 SDK online documentation. I responded that this book is useless to anyone who doesn't have access to the Win32 API documentation anyway, so of course they'll have access to it.

   He then suggested that it was unfair to offer nothing more than a hint in an appendix to point you in the right direction and especially unfair not to include the information somewhere in the puzzle itself. In this he is correct.

   My message to you is this: If the only thing you learn from this puzzle is the need to refer back to the actual API documentation and read it carefully, this puzzle has more than served its purpose.

Translating DEVMODE

WHEN YOU LOOK AT DATA WITHIN a structure and the values don't seem to make sense, chances are that there is a problem in the structure declaration in which one of the variables in your declaration has the wrong size. There is little that you can do wrong with simple numeric declarations. But strings and arrays can get tricky. For example, the dmDeviceName field is defined in C as follows:

```
#define CCHDEVICENAME 32
BYTE    dmDeviceName[CCHDEVICENAME];
```

At first glance, the following VB declaration looks correct:

```
Private Const CCHDEVICENAME = 32
dmDeviceName(CCHDEVICENAME) As Byte
```

But it isn't correct. Why? Consider: How long is the array?

The array bounds in a C++ language array define the number of elements in the array. In this case, the array holds 32 bytes. But the array bounds in a Visual Basic language array define the upper bound of the array. If the first element in the array is 0 and the upper bound is 32 (as shown here), the total number of elements is 33!

One solution is to change the VB declaration to

```
dmDeviceName(CCHDEVICENAME-1) As Byte
```

But there's an easier solution. Since this entry is designed to contain a string anyway, you can simply use a fixed-length string. Unlike dynamic strings, which are stored as BSTR pointers (32-bit pointers), a fixed-length string is stored directly within the structure. So if you declare the string as follows,

```
Dim dmDeviceName As String * CCHDEVICENAME
```

it will take up 32 bytes in the structure.

Change the dmFormName field in the same way, and the function will work flawlessly.

Environmentally Speaking

WHAT EXACTLY DOES THE GETENVIRONMENTSTRINGS function return? According to the documentation, it returns a pointer to a block of memory that contains environment variables separated by NULL characters. The final variable is terminated by two NULL characters. Let's say you had two environment variables as follows:

```
Temp=C:\TEMP
OS=NT
```

These would appear in memory as shown below:

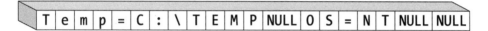

From Tutorial 6, "C++ Variables Meet Visual Basic," you know that a Visual Basic string is actually an OLE string or BSTR. A BSTR is a string that is managed (allocated and deallocated) by the OLE subsystem. A BSTR pointer points to the start of the string data. The 32 bits before that location contain the length of the string. Also, keep in mind that BSTR strings used by Visual Basic usually contain Unicode data.

How do we know that the GetEnvironmentStrings function does not return a BSTR?

- The buffer illustrated above clearly does not include any length data for the string.

- The GetEnvironmentStrings function is part of kernel32 (the core operating system DLL), not the OLE subsystem. Only the OLE subsystem knows how to handle BSTR strings.

- The documentation requires that you call the FreeEnvironmentStrings function to free the buffer. A special function would not be required for a BSTR, which could be freed by the OLE SysFreeString function.

If you declare the GetEnvironmentStrings function as returning a string, Visual Basic happily expects that the value will be a BSTR and loads it into one of its internal string variables. Unfortunately, this value is not a BSTR, so as soon as Visual Basic tries to access the data or free it, chances are pretty good you'll see a memory exception.

What to do?

The first step is to declare the resulting value as a Long. That will give you a pointer to the memory buffer, which you can then free with the FreeEnvironmentStrings function.

But what do you do with the buffer?

From the puzzle example, you already have code that can scan a string for NULL characters and add the strings into the list box. So your only problem is copying the string data from the environment buffer into a string. The RtlMoveMemory function can copy the memory, but before you can call it, you need to know the total length of the buffer up to the two NULL characters.

The FindDoubleNull function shown in the revised EnvStr.vbp project (on the CD that comes with this book) shows one way of accomplishing this:

```
' Find the number of bytes up to and including the double null
Private Function FindDoubleNull(ByVal Ptr As Long) As Long
    Dim bytebuffer(1) As Byte
    Dim offset As Long
    If Ptr = 0 Then Exit Function ' Error
    Do
        Call RtlMoveMemory(bytebuffer(0), ByVal (offset + Ptr), 2)
        If bytebuffer(0) = 0 And bytebuffer(1) = 0 Then
            FindDoubleNull = offset + 2 ' Add the two null bytes to the count
            Exit Function
        End If
        offset = offset + 1
    Loop While True
End Function
```

The function copies the data two bytes at a time into the bytebuffer array, increasing the source address by one each time. When it finds two consecutive null bytes, it exits the function and returns the total number of bytes from the start address up to (and including) the two NULL characters. The RtlMoveMemory function can now be used to copy the data from the buffer into a string that is preallocated to the desired length. Note how the destination specified in the RtlMoveMemory function passes both the string and buffer address variables ByVal. The Environment string is passed ByVal in order to handle the conversion from the VB string to a NULL-terminated C string (which is the format in the buffer). The EnvironmentBuffer variable is passed ByVal

because it contains the pointer address. If you left it out, you would be passing a pointer to the EnvironmentBuffer variable itself instead of to the address contained in the
variable. The cmdGetStrings_Click function retrieves the environment strings as follows:

```
Private Sub cmdGetStrings_Click()
    Dim Environment As String
    Dim EnvironmentBuffer As Long
    Dim BufferLength As Long
    Dim CurrentPosition As Long
    Dim NewPosition
     list1.Clear
    EnvironmentBuffer = GetEnvironmentStrings()
    ' Get the length of the buffer
    BufferLength = FindDoubleNull(EnvironmentBuffer)
    ' Allocate space for the data
    Environment = String$(BufferLength, 0)
    ' Copy the string from the buffer
    Call RtlMoveMemory(ByVal Environment, ByVal _
    EnvironmentBuffer, BufferLength)
    Do
       NewPosition = InStr(CurrentPosition + 1, Environment, Chr$(0))
       If NewPosition > CurrentPosition + 1 Then
          List1.AddItem Mid$(Environment, CurrentPosition + 1, _
          NewPosition - CurrentPosition - 1)
          CurrentPosition = NewPosition
       Else
          Exit Do
       End If
    Loop While True
    Call FreeEnvironmentStrings(EnvironmentBuffer)
End Sub
```

You might be wondering if there isn't a faster way to find the double NULL character. After all, calling a separate RtlMoveMemory function for each byte is a terribly inefficient approach. The answer, fortunately, is yes. The lstrlen API function can determine the length of a string. Since the environment buffer is nothing more than a list of NULL-terminated strings, you can loop through and call it once for each string, as follows:

```
' Find the number of bytes up to and including the double null
Private Function FindDoubleNull2(ByVal ptr As Long) As Long
```

```
        Dim offset As Long
        Dim ThisLen As Long
        If ptr = 0 Then Exit Function ' Error
        Do
            ' Find the length of this string
            ThisLen = lstrlen(offset + ptr)
            ' Set the next offset to the byte after the null character
            offset = offset + ThisLen + 1
            If ThisLen = 0 Then
                ' This will be true for two consecutive NULL characters
                FindDoubleNull2 = offset
                Exit Function
            End If
        Loop While True
End Function
```

There is an even faster way to perform this operation. The apigid32.dll DLL (on the CD that comes with this book) includes the function agGetStringFrom2NullBuffer, which is declared as follows:

```
Declare Function agGetStringFrom2NullBuffer Lib "apigid32.dll" _
(ByVal Ptr As Long) As String
```

This function takes as a parameter a pointer to a buffer containing NULL-terminated strings where the final string has two NULLs—exactly the format used by the GetEnvironmentStrings function. It returns a Visual Basic string. But wait—isn't there a problem with a DLL function returning a string? Don't worry, this function is designed specifically to return a BSTR allocated by the OLE subsystem—exactly the format Visual Basic expects. The agGetStringFrom2NullBuffer function does not include the final two NULL-terminating characters in the string that it returns, so if you take this approach you'll need to modify the loop to retrieve the final string in the buffer, since it won't be detected by the lstrlen function.

Registry Games, Part 1

IF YOU SOLVED THIS PROBLEM IN less than five minutes, congratulations! You've learned the most important part of API programming: Always double-check your code for careless and obvious mistakes.

If you didn't solve the problem quickly, you'll probably kick yourself.

First Problem

Your best hint is in the error message Unable to open the registry key: The system cannot find the file specified. Could it be that the hKey or lpSubKey parameters are wrong?

The hKey parameter is the constant from the api32.txt file. Although this certainly could be in error, it might be more efficient to check the lpSubKey parameter before spending time checking the HKEY_LOCAL_MACHINE constant against the original Microsoft header files.

The subkey is defined as follows:

```
controlkey = "SYSTEM/CurrentControlSet/Control"
```

Do you see it?

```
controlkey = "SYSTEM\CurrentControlSet\Control"
```

How about now?

Second Problem

Once you fix the string to use the correct backslash, you will receive the error message Unable to open the registry key: Access is denied if you are running on Windows NT.

That's odd. The KEY_READ constant is a logical Or combination of all of the constants that one could possibly need to open a key, read and enumerate its subkeys, and read the data values.

To solve this problem, take a closer look at the declaration for the RegOpenKeyEx function and the code that calls the function:

```
Private Declare Function RegOpenKeyEx Lib "advapi32.dll" Alias _
"RegOpenKeyExA" (ByVal hKey As Long, ByVal lpSubKey As String, _
ByVal ulOptions As Long, ByVal samDesired As Long, phkResult As _
Long) As Long

res = RegOpenKeyEx(HKEY_LOCAL_MACHINE, controlkey, KEY_READ, 0, rootkey)
```

Now look at the function parameters one at a time. We have the key, the subkey, the ... wait a minute ... are the access rights specified with the ulOptions parameter or the samDesired parameter?

You have it! The KEY_READ and 0 parameters are swapped. Change the code to

```
res = RegOpenKeyEx(HKEY_LOCAL_MACHINE, controlkey, 0, KEY_READ, rootkey)
```

It works!

By the Way . . .

You might think that both of these puzzles are artificial—that I came up with them just to confuse you and perhaps remind you that you can run into API coding bugs even when your declaration is correct.

I wish I could take the credit for such cleverness (or is it deviousness?).

The truth is, I was expecting my first registry-related puzzle to be Puzzle 12, since enumerating keys is a somewhat tricky process. But you see, I actually do follow my own advice and implement API-based code in small sections, testing each one along the way. The two problems you see here were in my original code. And although I will concede (with all due modesty) that it took me less than five minutes to solve both of them, it was clear to me that they represented real problems anyone can run into and were thus deserving of their own puzzle.

Registry Games, Part 2

FIRST, LET'S ADDRESS THE PROBLEM OF fixing the existing GetKeyInfo function so that it will work under Windows NT.[1] The error message says that a parameter is incorrect. The best approach in cases such as this is to examine the parameters one by one. The only questionable one is the lpReserved parameter, which is described as follows:

```
LPDWORD lpReserved,                 // reserved - Must be NULL
```

What does it mean when it says that the parameter must be NULL? It means that the parameter must be 0. But what are we passing as a parameter in the GetKeyInfo function? We're passing 0, right? That's a NULL, right?

Or is it?

Take a second look at the VB declaration:

```
Private Declare Function RegQueryInfoKey Lib "advapi32.dll" Alias _
 "RegQueryInfoKeyA" (ByVal hKey As Long, ByVal lpClass As String, _
lpcbClass As Long, lpReserved As Long, lpcSubKeys As Long, _
lpcbMaxSubKeyLen As Long, lpcbMaxClassLen As Long, lpcValues As Long, _
lpcbMaxValueNameLen As Long, lpcbMaxValueLen As Long, _
lpcbSecurityDescriptor As Long, lpftLastWriteTime As FILETIME) As Long
```

lpReserved is defined By Reference. What does Visual Basic do when you pass a 0 value to a parameter that is declared By Reference as Long?

It allocates a temporary Long variable, which it loads with the value 0. It then passes the address of that temporary variable to the function. And the address of a temporary variable is never 0!

If you want to pass a NULL value to a function parameter of type Long, the parameter declaration must be changed to ByVal As Long.

---

1. Curiously enough, the function works fine as shown under Windows 95 and 98, which just goes to prove how important it is that you test your applications under both operating systems. Doing your development on Windows NT will help you catch these types of errors early in the development cycle.

A Second Approach

This suggests a first solution to this puzzle's challenge for making the GetKeyInfo function more efficient. Find those parameters that are not applicable to the task at hand and change their declarations to ByVal As Long so they can accept NULL parameters. You can take advantage of the Alias command's ability to create a new declaration that calls the RegQueryInfoKey API. The following code declares a new RegQueryInfoKeyV2 function, which is designed to allow you to pass NULL parameters to all of the parameters except lpcSubKeys and lpcbMaxSubKeyLen:

```
Private Declare Function RegQueryInfoKeyV2 Lib "advapi32.dll" _
Alias "RegQueryInfoKeyA" (ByVal hKey As Long, ByVal lpClass As String, _
ByVal lpcbClass As Long, ByVal lpReserved As Long, lpcSubKeys As Long, _
lpcbMaxSubKeyLen As Long, ByVal lpcbMaxClassLen As Long, ByVal _
lpcValues As Long, ByVal lpcbMaxValueNameLen As Long, ByVal _
lpcbMaxValueLen As Long, ByVal lpcbSecurityDescriptor As Long, _
ByVal lpftLastWriteTime As Long) As Long
```

The impact on the GetKeyInfo function is impressive, as shown in the version below, named GetKeyInfo2:

```
Private Function GetKeyInfo2(ByVal hKey As Long, NumberOfKeys As _
Long, MaxKeyNameLength As Long) As Long
    Dim res As Long
    res = RegQueryInfoKeyV2(hKey, vbNullString, 0, 0, _
    NumberOfKeys, MaxKeyNameLength, 0, 0, 0, 0, 0, 0)
    If res <> 0 Then
        MsgBox "RegQueryInfoKey error: " & GetErrorString(res)
    End If
    GetKeyInfo2 = res
End Function
```

A Third Approach

The GetKeyInfo2 approach suffers from one small disadvantage: Every time you need to access a different subset of information from the RegQueryInfoKey function, you need to create a new alias. Is there a way to keep the efficiency of this approach using a single RegQueryInfoKey declaration?

Yes, you can do it by declaring parameters As Any, in which case the calling code would contain the term ByVal 0& to pass a NULL value. However, the As Any data type is dangerous and should be avoided whenever possible. In this case, it is definitely not necessary because there is a better approach that is easier to understand and support. The following declaration is used in which all of the nonstring parameters are declared ByVal As Long:

```
Private Declare Function RegQueryInfoKeyV3 Lib "advapi32.dll" _
Alias "RegQueryInfoKeyA" (ByVal hKey As Long, ByVal lpClass As String, _
ByVal lpcbClass As Long, ByVal lpReserved As Long, ByVal lpcSubKeys As _
Long, ByVal lpcbMaxSubKeyLen As Long, ByVal lpcbMaxClassLen As Long, _
ByVal lpcValues As Long, ByVal lpcbMaxValueNameLen As Long, _
ByVal lpcbMaxValueLen As Long, ByVal lpcbSecurityDescriptor As Long, _
ByVal lpftLastWriteTime As Long) As Long
```

The trick here is (1) to explicitly pass a pointer to those variables that you wish to load with information and (2) to pass 0 for the remaining parameters. The VarPtr[2] operator is used to obtain the address to the variables, and yes, it even works on stack parameters as shown here. And, as you can see, the function can now be implemented in a single line of code:

```
Private Function GetKeyInfo3(ByVal hKey As Long, NumberOfKeys _
As Long, MaxKeyNameLength As Long) As Long

  GetKeyInfo3 = RegQueryInfoKeyV3(hKey, vbNullString, 0, 0, _
VarPtr(NumberOfKeys), VarPtr(MaxKeyNameLength), 0, 0, 0, 0, 0, 0)
End Function
```

Design Notes

Even though most of the examples in this book are small, throwaway code, that's no reason to ignore software design completely. If you look closely at the Reg2 sample program (on the CD that comes with this book), you'll see some additional code that suggests where the design is going. The CD also contains a class module called clsKeyValues that contains the following code:

```
' Class clsKeyValues
' Keys and values

Option Explicit
```

----

2. The VarPtr operator is an undocumented operator. Normally, I would never advocate use of an undocumented function, but this one has been used so extensively in Microsoft's own code and samples that I think it is reasonably safe to use. The agGetAddressForObject function in the apigid32.dll included on the CD that comes with this book provides an alternate method for obtaining the address of a Visual Basic variable.

```
Public KeyName As String    ' Name of this key
Public ValueNames As Collection   ' Values of this key
```

Those of you accustomed to creating components using Visual Basic will notice the poor design of this class. The fields are accessed publicly instead of through property statements. The class exposes a pure collection object instead of a custom collection. If this were a public object exposed by an ActiveX server, this design would be just asking for trouble.

But this is not a public object exposed by an ActiveX server. It's a private object intended for use within this application. So there is no danger that some outsider might use its properties in an invalid manner. I mention this in the event that you want to expand parts of this sample application into an ActiveX object server at some point. (My book *Developing COM/ActiveX Components with Visual Basic 6.0* addresses these issues at some length.)

The EnumerateKeys function uses the GetKeyInfo function (in all its permutations) to obtain information about the subkeys. It will then do the actual enumeration and build a collection of clsKeyValues objects that it can return to the calling function, as follows:

```
' Enumerate all of the subkeys of this key, returning a collection
' containing clsKeyValues objects
Private Function EnumerateKeys(ByVal hKey As Long) _
As Collection
    Dim NumberOfSubKeys As Long
    Dim MaxSubKeyLength As LongDim res As Long

    ' First, get the number of subkeys and the buffer length we need
        res = GetKeyInfo(hKey, NumberOfSubKeys, MaxSubKeyLength)
    MsgBox "NumberOfSubKeys: " & NumberOfSubKeys & _
    "  MaxSubKeyLength: " & MaxSubKeyLength
```

```
    NumberOfSubKeys = 0
    res = GetKeyInfo2(hKey, NumberOfSubKeys, MaxSubKeyLength)
    MsgBox "NumberOfSubKeys: " & NumberOfSubKeys & _
    "  MaxSubKeyLength: " & MaxSubKeyLength

    NumberOfSubKeys = 0
    res = GetKeyInfo3(hKey, NumberOfSubKeys, MaxSubKeyLength)
    MsgBox "NumberOfSubKeys: " & NumberOfSubKeys & _
    "  MaxSubKeyLength: " & MaxSubKeyLength
End Function
```

You'll see the full implementation of this function in Puzzle 13.

SOLUTION 13

Registry Games, Part 3

YOU HAVE A LOT OF NEW code and no suggestion as to where it is failing. In cases such as this, there is no substitution for stepping through the code carefully. And I stress the word "carefully." That means not just looking at function results, but also searching for possible side effects. In this case, you will find a most perplexing situation on the following line:

```
res = GetValueInfo(hKey, NumberOfSubValues, MaxSubValueLength)
```

The function always returns a correct result (0), but never sets the NumberOfSubValues or MaxSubValueLength variables! We know from looking at the registry that many of the subkeys we are looking at do have values, so clearly there must be a problem. Let's take a closer look at the GetValueInfo function:

```
' Get the number of values and maximum value length
Private Function GetValueInfo(ByVal hKey As Long, _
NumberOfValues, MaxValueNameLength) As Long
    GetValueInfo = RegQueryInfoKeyV3(hKey, vbNullString, 0, 0, 0, 0, _
    0, VarPtr(NumberOfValues), VarPtr(MaxValueNameLength), 0, 0, 0)
End Function
```

How can the function consistently return a correct result, yet not work? The answer is, it can't. There must be a problem with this code. But what can the problem be? The function looks just like the GetKeyInfo3 function that we know works correctly. Let's take a second look at the GetKeyInfo3 function:

```
Private Function GetKeyInfo3(ByVal hKey As Long, NumberOfKeys _
As Long, MaxKeyNameLength As Long) As Long
    GetKeyInfo3 = RegQueryInfoKeyV3(hKey, vbNullString, 0, 0, _
    VarPtr(NumberOfKeys), VarPtr(MaxKeyNameLength), 0, 0, 0, 0, 0, 0)
End Function
```

Look closely now. Do you see it?

The GetKeyInfo3 function declares the NumberOfKeys parameters as Long. We neglected to specify a parameter type in the GetValueInfo function. That means that the parameters are declared as variants.

Now, if we were using the approach shown in the GetKeyInfo2 function, where an alias was created so that the RegQueryInfoKey function was called with those parameters passed by reference, this function would work. Visual Basic would take the variant parameter, create a temporary Long variable, pass the address of the Long variable to the function, then copy the Long variable back into the variant.

But we're passing the address explicitly here, and that means the VarPtr operator is returning the address of the variant. A variant is represented internally by a structure, so VarPtr returns the address of the start of the structure. And the Long value we are interested in is not stored at the start of the variant structure. The truth is, it's amazing that this bug does not crash the system by loading invalid values into the variant. In fact, it's quite possible that there are combinations of subkey counts and value name lengths that could cause this bug to trigger a memory exception instead of just failing to work.

No Boom Today—Boom Tomorrow (There's Always a Boom Tomorrow)[1]

Count yourself lucky if the preceding bug did not trigger a memory exception, because as soon as you fix it, your program will start crashing wildly (at least if you're running on NT). When you step through the code, you'll find that the crash is occurring during the RegEnumValue call. This may seem odd, considering that the function is almost identical to the RegEnumKey call.

Wait, I did say "almost" identical, didn't I? Indeed.

A close look at the declarations will show an important difference. The lpcbValueName parameter in the RegEnumValue function is an LPDWORD instead of a DWORD. This means that it must be called by reference instead of by value. The lpcbValueName variable should be set to the maximum length of the lpValueName buffer. On return, the variable will contain the actual length of the string.

What happened when we passed it ByVal? Let's say the length calculated by the GetValueInfo function was 50 bytes. When the parameter is declared ByVal, the number 50 is placed on the stack. But since the RegEnumValue function expects a pointer to the length, it interprets 50 as a memory address of a Long variable that contains the actual length. When the program tries to access memory address 50, it crashes with a memory exception. Boom![2]

....

1. This heading is shamelessly stolen from the TV show *Babylon 5*, which is, incidentally, one of the best TV shows ever made.

2. The Windows 95/98 version of this function detects that the address is invalid and returns an invalid parameter error (error 87) instead of raising a memory exception.

The revised EnumerateValues function uses the CurrentValueLength variable to handle this change. The variable is loaded with the buffer length and passed to the API function. On return, it contains the actual length of the value name. Since we have the length, there is no need to use the nulloffset variable and Instr function to determine the real string length. The CurrentValueLength variable must be reset to the maximum buffer size before each call to RegEnumValue, as follows:

```
Private Declare Function RegEnumValue Lib "advapi32.dll" _
Alias "RegEnumValueA" (ByVal hKey As Long, ByVal dwIndex As Long, _
ByVal lpValueName As String, lpcbValueName As Long, ByVal lpReserved _
As Long, ByVal lpType As Long, ByVal lpData As Long, ByVal lpcbData As _
Long) As Long


' Enumerate all of the values of this key, returning a collection
' containing the value names
Private Function EnumerateValues(ByVal hKey As Long) As Collection
    Dim NumberOfSubValues As Long
    Dim MaxSubValueLength As Long
    Dim res As Long
    Dim ValueIndex As Long
    Dim Valuebuffer As String
    Dim ValueCollection As New Collection
    Dim currentValue As clsKeyValues
    Dim CurrentValueLength As Long

    res = GetValueInfo(hKey, NumberOfSubValues, MaxSubValueLength)
    If res <> 0 Then
        Exit Function
    End If

    Valuebuffer = String$(MaxSubValueLength + 1, 0)

    For ValueIndex = 0 To NumberOfSubValues - 1
        CurrentValueLength = MaxSubValueLength + 1
        res = RegEnumValue(hKey, ValueIndex, Valuebuffer, CurrentValueLength, _
        0, 0, 0, 0)
        If res = 0 Then
            If CurrentValueLength = 0 Then
                ValueCollection.Add "Default"
            Else
                ValueCollection.Add Left$(Valuebuffer, CurrentValueLength)
```

```
        End If
      End If
    Next ValueIndex
    Set EnumerateValues = ValueCollection
End Function
```

Conclusion

The parameter-type bug shown in this puzzle is one of the most subtle bugs you'll meet when working with API functions, especially because it isn't really an API declaration bug at all. Accidentally using a variant because you forgot to declare a parameter type usually won't cause a program to fail. But it is inefficient and can lead to serious problems if you are creating public ActiveX components, because variants demand a much greater degree of error checking than do base variable types when used as component properties or parameters.

SOLUTION 14

Registry Games, Part 4

SO I'M LYING OUT BY THE pool at the Disney World resort when this blimp flies overhead with the message, "Dan, call your publisher!" What a way to interrupt a vacation. . . .

Okay, okay. Enough kidding around. You got me. The whole thing was intentional (or was it?). And if you haven't attempted to write the DisplayValue function yourself, I strongly encourage you to give it a try.

Meanwhile, it's time to get serious.

First, let's look at the VB declaration. The trick here is handling the lpData parameter. You've seen how to handle all the other situations in the preceding three puzzles. The lpData parameter is described in the documentation as follows:

```
LPBYTE lpData,                    // address of data buffer
```

The problem is that we have three different data types that can be loaded by this function: strings, Longs, and binary data. We also need to be able to pass a NULL value, since the first step will be to call the function with lpData set to NULL in order to obtain the data type and buffer size.

Let's consider all the possible ways to handle each data type, as shown in Table S14-1.

There are two general approaches you can take. You can choose the safest and easiest declaration for each data type and create multiple aliases for the RegQueryValueEx function. In this case, you would choose ByVal As Long for the null value, ByVal As String for string data, As Long for Long data, and As Byte for binary data. You can call the RegQueryValueEx function first with a NULL lpData value in order to determine the data type for the value, then call the appropriate alias for that data type.

The other approach, which is shown in our solution, is to use the As Any data type and depend on the calling routine to pass the correct variable type in the lpData parameter. The RegQueryValueEx function will thus have the following declaration:

```
Private Declare Function RegQueryValueEx Lib "advapi32.dll" Alias _
"RegQueryValueExA" (ByVal hKey As Long, ByVal lpValueName As String, _
ByVal lpReserved As Long, lpType As Long, lpData As Any, _
lpcbData As Long) As Long
```

DATA TYPE	DECLARATION	CALL
NULL	ByVal As Long	Zero or variable containing zero.
	ByVal As Any	0& or Long variable containing zero.
	As Any	ByVal 0& or ByVal with a Long variable containing zero.
String	ByVal As String	String buffer preinitialized to the necessary buffer length.
	ByVal As Any	String buffer preinitialized to the necessary buffer length.
	As Any	String buffer preinitialized to the necessary buffer length preceded by ByVal operator.
	As Byte	First byte in a byte array to load with an ANSI string. String will need to be converted to Unicode before assigning to VB string.
	ByVal As Long	Address of first byte in a byte array to load with an ANSI string obtained using the VarPtr operator. String will need to be converted to Unicode before assigning to VB string.
Long	As Long	Long variable to load with the data.
	ByVal As Long	Address of Long variable obtained using the VarPtr operator.
	As Any	Long variable to load with the data.
Binary	As Byte	First byte in a byte array to load with binary data.
	As Any	First byte in a byte array to load with binary data.
	ByVal As Long	Address of first byte in a byte array to load with binary data obtained using the VarPtr operator.

Table S14-1: How to Handle Different Data Types

STOP!

If you have come up with a code solution on your own, take a look to see which of these two approaches it uses. I encourage you to then take a break and attempt to implement the solution using the other approach. This will help you thoroughly understand the options that are available to you.

Given the approach used in this solution, the DisplayValue function becomes fairly straightforward.

When the data type is a string value, the function initializes a string buffer to the correct length and passes it to the API function with the ByVal operator. This ensures that the necessary Unicode-to-ANSI conversion takes place when the function is called. The function doesn't handle the REG_MULTI_SZ function in this example because parsing this kind of string is a straightforward Visual Basic exercise (which I encourage you to try). This kind of string contains multiple strings separated by NULL characters, with two NULL characters at the end of the final string.

When the data type is a Long value, the function passes a Long variable as a parameter. This causes the parameter to be passed by reference.

When the data type is binary, the function dimensions a byte array to the correct length, then passes the first byte of the array by reference. This effectively passes a pointer to the start of the byte array. The DisplayValue function follows:

```
Private Sub DisplayValue(ByVal hKey As Long, ByVal ValueName As String)
    Dim BufferSize As Long
    Dim DataType As Long
    Dim buffer As String
    Dim longdata As Long
    Dim binarydata() As Byte
    Dim res As Long
    Dim LabelOutput As String
    Dim x As Long
    Dim hexval As String


    ' First get the data type and buffer size
    res = RegQueryValueEx(hKey, ValueName, 0, DataType, ByVal 0&, BufferSize)
    ' This should always succeed, since we loaded the value name earlier
    If res = 0 Then
      Select Case DataType
        Case REG_SZ, REG_EXPAND_SZ, REG_MULTI_SZ
            LabelOutput = "String: "
            buffer = String$(BufferSize, 0)
            res = RegQueryValueEx(hKey, ValueName, 0, DataType, _
            ByVal buffer, BufferSize)
            LabelOutput = LabelOutput & Left$(buffer, Len(buffer) - 1)
            ' Parsing out the REG_MULTI_SZ string is left as an exercise
            ' to the reader
        Case REG_DWORD
            LabelOutput = "DWORD: "
            res = RegQueryValueEx(hKey, ValueName, 0, DataType, _
```

```
            longdata, BufferSize)
        LabelOutput = LabelOutput & Hex$(longdata)
    Case REG_BINARY
        LabelOutput = "Binary: "
        ReDim binarydata(BufferSize - 1)
        res = RegQueryValueEx(hKey, ValueName, 0, DataType, _
        binarydata(0), BufferSize)
        For x = 0 To BufferSize - 1
            hexval = Hex$(binarydata(x))
            If Len(hexval) = 1 Then hexval = "0" & hexval
            hexval = " " & hexval
            LabelOutput = LabelOutput & hexval
        Next x
    Case Else
        LabelOutput = "Unsupported data type"
    End Select
  lblValue.Caption = LabelOutput
  End If
End Sub
```

Conclusion

Sure, I could have created a buggy version of the DisplayValue routine for you to fix, but this function provides a perfect opportunity for learning to deal with parameters that handle multiple data types. If you were able to come up with solutions using either (or both) of the approaches described here, congratulations—you are now an advanced API programmer and are well on your way to guru status (if you're not already there).

What Time Zone Is It?

WHEN YOU ARE WORKING WITH A structure and you see data that seems correct near the start of the structure and meaningless data later in the structure, there is a good chance that you are dealing with an error in the structure declaration. API functions depend on all of the fields in the structure appearing in exactly the right offset in memory from the beginning of the structure. If one of the fields is declared incorrectly in your Visual Basic declaration, the location of all subsequent fields will be incorrect. In this case, the C declaration for the TIME_ZONE_INFORMATION structure is as follows:

```
typedef struct _TIME_ZONE_INFORMATION { // tzi
    LONG       Bias;
    WCHAR      StandardName[ 32 ];
    SYSTEMTIME StandardDate;
    LONG       StandardBias;
    WCHAR      DaylightName[ 32 ];
    SYSTEMTIME DaylightDate;
    LONG       DaylightBias;
} TIME_ZONE_INFORMATION;
```

We declared the StandardName field as follows:

```
StandardName(32) As Integer
```

A WCHAR is a wide 16-bit Unicode character, so, at first glance, Integer seems to be the correct type. On the other hand, you also know that many Win32 API functions have separate ANSI and Unicode entry points. When those functions have structure parameters and those structures contain strings, the string type varies depending on the entry point.

The question we have here is, which type are we dealing with? Does the GetTimeZoneInformation function have separate ANSI and Unicode entry points? If so, the StandardName and DaylightName fields of the TIME_ZONE_INFORMATION structure probably need to be changed to the Byte data type. If, however, the function has a single entry point, the StandardName and DaylightName fields probably really are 16-bit Unicode characters. Which is it?

You already know the answer. First, the StandardName and DaylightName fields are defined as the WCHAR type—indicating a 16-bit Unicode character. If the type depended on the entry point, it would have been declared as the TCHAR type, indicating a character whose size depends on the entry point. Second, the GetTimeZoneInformation function in the puzzle was declared as follows:

```
Private Declare Function GetTimeZoneInformation Lib _
"kernel32" (lpTimeZoneInformation As TIME_ZONE_INFORMATION) As Long
```

As you can see, there is no Alias term in the declaration. If the function had two entry points, you would expect to see the term `Alias "GetTimeZoneInformationA"` in the declaration. The sample program did not raise a `"Can't find DLL Entry Point"` error, so the GetTimeZoneInformation function entry point actually does exist.

So all we've done so far is prove that the Visual Basic declaration is correct. Yet the sample fails, so there is a problem.

The C++ declaration clearly shows that the StandardName and DaylightName fields are 32-character integers. The Visual Basic declaration is a 32-integer array.

Or is it?

Visual Basic array declarations are zero-based. The field

```
StandardName(32) As Integer
```

is a 33-integer array. Change the array bound to 31, and the program will work.

Reading the Names

The StandardName and DaylightName fields are loaded with the Unicode strings. How can you convert them into Visual Basic strings?

There are a number of possible solutions. One of the easiest is based on an interesting feature in Visual Basic that allows you to assign strings to and from arrays.

If you define a string

```
Dim timezonename As String
```

you can assign it directly from the array as follows:

```
timezonename = tz.StandardName
```

What about the Unicode conversion? It's automatic—or rather, irrelevant. You see, when Visual Basic does an assignment between strings and arrays, it does not perform any conversion on the data. A string contains Unicode data internally, so when you transfer the Unicode data from the array to the string via an assignment, the data will be formatted correctly in the string.

There's just one catch—you can't copy an integer array into a string.

The solution is simple. Instead of declaring the StandardName and DisplayName fields as integers, we declare them as bytes and make sure that the arrays are the same size. In this case, the arrays are 64 bytes long, so the array declaration is

```
StandardName(63) As Byte
```

Once the array has been assigned to a string, you can search for the NULL terminator character (located at the end of every C language string) and truncate the string from that point.

You can see the correct results in Figure S15-1.

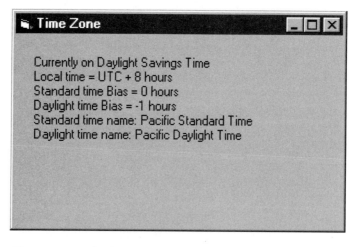

Figure S15-1: The final TimeZone program screen

The complete program follows:

```
' Get Time Zone Information
' Copyright © 1998 by Desaware Inc. All Rights Reserved

Option Explicit

Private Type SYSTEMTIME
```

```
        wYear As Integer
        wMonth As Integer
        wDayOfWeek As Integer
        wDay As Integer
        wHour As Integer
        wMinute As Integer
        wSecond As Integer
        wMilliseconds As Integer
End Type



Private Type TIME_ZONE_INFORMATION
        Bias As Long
        StandardName(63) As Byte
        StandardDate As SYSTEMTIME
        StandardBias As Long
        DaylightName(63) As Byte
        DaylightDate As SYSTEMTIME
        DaylightBias As Long
End Type

Private Declare Function GetTimeZoneInformation Lib _
"kernel32" (lpTimeZoneInformation As TIME_ZONE_INFORMATION) As Long

Private Const TIME_ZONE_ID_INVALID = &HFFFFFFFF
Private Const TIME_ZONE_ID_UNKNOWN = 0
Private Const TIME_ZONE_ID_STANDARD = 1
Private Const TIME_ZONE_ID_DAYLIGHT = 2

Private Sub Form_Load()
   Dim tz As TIME_ZONE_INFORMATION
   Dim info As String
   Dim res As Long
   Dim timezonename As String
   Dim nulloffset As Long
   res = GetTimeZoneInformation(tz)
   Select Case res
     Case TIME_ZONE_ID_INVALID
        lblTimeZone.Caption = "GetTimeZoneInformation function failed." _
        & vbCrLf
        lblTimeZone.Caption = lblTimeZone.Caption & "Error: " _
        & GetErrorString(Err.LastDllError)
     Case TIME_ZONE_ID_UNKNOWN
```

```
                lblTimeZone.Caption = "Time zone information unavailable."
            Case TIME_ZONE_ID_STANDARD
                info = "Currently on Standard Time" & vbCrLf
            Case TIME_ZONE_ID_DAYLIGHT
                info = "Currently on Daylight Savings Time" & vbCrLf
        End Select

        info = info & "Local time = UTC + " & tz.Bias / 60 & " hours" & vbCrLf
        info = info & "Standard time Bias = " & tz.StandardBias / 60 & _
        " hours" & vbCrLf
        info = info & "Daylight time Bias = " & tz.DaylightBias / 60 & _
        " hours" & vbCrLf
        timezonename = tz.StandardName
        nulloffset = InStr(timezonename, Chr$(0))
        info = info & "Standard time name: " & Left$(timezonename, _
        nulloffset - 1) & vbCrLf
        timezonename = tz.DaylightName
        nulloffset = InStr(timezonename, Chr$(0))
        info = info & "Daylight time name: " & Left$(timezonename, _
        nulloffset - 1) & vbCrLf
    lblTimeZone.Caption = info
    End Sub
```

SOLUTION 16

Serially Speaking

LET'S TAKE A CLOSER LOOK AT the SDK description for the GetVolumeInformation function:

```
BOOL GetVolumeInformation(
    LPCTSTR lpRootPathName,            // address of root directory of the
                                       // file system
    LPTSTR lpVolumeNameBuffer,         // address of name of the volume
    DWORD nVolumeNameSize,             // length of lpVolumeNameBuffer
    LPDWORD lpVolumeSerialNumber,      // address of volume serial number
    LPDWORD lpMaximumComponentLength,  // address of system's maximum
                                       // filename length
    LPDWORD lpFileSystemFlags,         // address of file system flags
    LPTSTR lpFileSystemNameBuffer,     // address of name of file system
    DWORD nFileSystemNameSize          // length of lpFileSystemNameBuffer
);
```

How much can you learn from the declaration alone without referring to the actual SDK documentation?

The only parameter you set ahead of time is the lpRootPathName parameter, which contains the root directory. The parameter type is LPCTSTR. This parses out as follows:

LP =   Long (or far) pointer

C =   Constant, meaning the parameter is not changed by the API function.

T =   ANSI when calling the ANSI entry point, Unicode when calling the Unicode entry point. The appearance of a T parameter implies that the function almost certainly has two entry points, and that you'll use the one with the A suffix, in this case GetVolumeInformationA.

STR =   String

Since you will be using the ANSI entry point, this means the function expects a pointer to a NULL-terminated ANSI string, the contents of which will not be modified by the function.

The declaration will obviously be ByVal As String.

The lpVolumeNameBuffer parameter is identical except that the C character is missing from the type definition. This means the parameter is not a constant, so the string can be modified by the API function. Since the function can modify the contents of the string, it needs to know how large a string buffer is available. This information is passed to the function using the nVolumeNameSize parameter, which is declared ByVal As Long.

In the original puzzle, the nVolumeNameSize parameter is set to 0, so the function returns an error value indicating that more information is available.[1] This parameter should be set to the length of the buffer, in this case 256 because the strings are initialized to 256 characters. In the actual solution, the nVolumeNameSize buffer is actually set to 255. Why? Because the Win32 API is often inconsistent as to whether the length includes the NULL terminating character or not. So as a matter of habit, it's always a good idea to make your buffer a byte or two larger than you need, just in case.

The same technique is used to define the lpFileSystemNameBuffer and nFileSystemNameSize parameters.

The lpVolumeSerialNumber, lpMaximumComponentLength, and lpFileSystemFlags parameters are declared as type LPDWORD. This parses out as follows:

LP = Long (far) pointer

DWORD = Unsigned double word or unsigned 32-bit value

To pass a numeric pointer to an API function, you must declare it by reference instead of ByVal. Remove the ByVal operators for each parameter.

And the Serial Number . . .

Take a look at the serial number as displayed in a DOS window in response to the Dir command:

```
D:\>dir
 Volume in drive D is D1P1
```

---

1. Under Windows 95, the error value indicates the file name is too long. The reason for this difference is a puzzle that is beyond the ability of this humble author to comprehend.

```
The volume serial number is 12EC-0868.
```

The hint in this case is the appearance of a letter between A and F in the serial number and the fact that the serial number is two four-character numbers. A four-character number in hexadecimal is 16 bits. Two four-character numbers make a 32-bit number.

The difference between the serial number as displayed in the puzzle and that displayed by a DOS window is that one is a decimal number, the other a hexadecimal number.

How do you break up a 32-bit long into two 16-bit hexadecimal numbers?

The high 32 bits can be retrieved by dividing the number by &H10000&. This shifts all of the bits in the number 16 bits to the right. You also need to mask off the high 16 bits of the number using the And operator, because the division operation will not set the high bits to 0 if the highest bit was originally 1. This can be done with the following code:

```
(SerialNumber \ &H10000) And &HFFFF&
```

The low 16 bits can be obtained using the And operator and masking with the value &HFFFF&.

The final correct result follows:

```
' Volume Information
' Copyright © 1998 by Desaware Inc. All Rights Reserved

Option Explicit

Private Declare Function GetVolumeInformation Lib "kernel32" Alias _
"GetVolumeInformationA" (ByVal lpRootPathName As String, ByVal _
lpVolumeNameBuffer As String, ByVal nVolumeNameSize As Long, _
lpVolumeSerialNumber As Long, lpMaximumComponentLength As Long, _
lpFileSystemFlags As Long, ByVal lpFileSystemNameBuffer As String, _
ByVal nFileSystemNameSize As Long) As Long

Private Sub LoadVolumeInfo()
    Dim res&
    Dim VolumeName As String
    Dim FileSystem As String
    Dim SerialNumber As Long
    Dim ComponentLength As Long
    Dim FileSystemFlags As Long
    VolumeName = String$(256, Chr$(0))
    FileSystem = String$(256, Chr$(0))
```

```
res = GetVolumeInformation(Left$(Drive1.Drive, 2) & "\",
    VolumeName, 255, SerialNumber, ComponentLength,
    FileSystemFlags, FileSystem, 255)
If res = 0 Then
    MsgBox "GetVolumeInformation Error: " & _
    GetErrorString(Err.LastDllError)
    Exit Sub
End If
List1.Clear
List1.AddItem "Drive " & Drive1.Drive
List1.AddItem "Name: " & VolumeName
List1.AddItem "Component Length: " & ComponentLength
List1.AddItem "Serial #: " & Hex$((SerialNumber \ &H10000) And &HFFFF&) _
& "-" & Hex$(SerialNumber And &HFFFF&)
List1.AddItem "FileSystem: " & FileSystem

End Sub


Private Sub Drive1_Change()
    LoadVolumeInfo
End Sub


Private Sub Form_Load()
    LoadVolumeInfo
End Sub
```

You may have noticed that the program does not bother to strip off the part of the string after the NULL termination character after the GetVolumeInformation function loads data into the FileSystem and VolumeName variables. This program can get away with this because the information is loaded directly into a list box. The list box is based on the Windows LISTBOX control. This control expects to receive NULL-terminated strings, so even though you are passing a longer string to the control using the AddItem method, the control sees only the portion of the string up to the NULL termination character.

The DEVMODE Is in the Details

ONE THING YOU'LL QUICKLY LEARN WHEN working with API functions is to read the documentation very, very carefully. Just following a tip or technique published in a magazine or on the Internet is not terribly reliable, because you never know if the author took the time to read the documentation and test the technique beyond one simple application.

In this case, you can find the secret in two places.[1]

In the description of the DocumentProperties function in my Win32 API book, you'll find the following description for the pDevModeOutput parameter:

> *Long—Pointer to a DEVMODE data structure for the device.... Note that this pointer must refer to a buffer that is large enough to include the private printer driver data as well as the standard DEVMODE structure. Use the agGetAddressForObject function (or VarPtr operator) to obtain the address of a structure or byte array, or pass the address of a memory block allocated using GlobalAlloc.*
>
> *If fMode is zero, this function returns the size of the DEVMODE structure for this device. Note that this structure may be larger than the size specified in the type definition file API32.TXT.*

If you look in the Win32 SDK, you'll find the following in the comments section:

> *If the* fMode *parameter is zero, the return value is the size of the buffer required to contain the printer driver initialization data. Note that this buffer can be larger than a* **DEVMODE** *structure if the printer driver appends private data to the structure.*
>
> *Note that the* **DEVMODE** *structure actually used by a printer driver contains the device-independent part (as defined above) followed by a driver-specific part that varies in size and content with each driver and driver*

---

1. You may think it unfair that this puzzle requires you to look in outside documentation in order to find a solution. But the intent of this book is, in part, to teach you the habits necessary to handle all of these types of problems, and you can't do serious API programming without some sort of reference. Besides, the hints for this puzzle in Appendix A clearly indicated that you would need to look elsewhere for further information.

*version. Because of this driver dependence, it is very important for applications to query the driver for the correct size of the **DEVMODE** structure before allocating a buffer for it.*

To make changes to print settings that are local to an application, an application should follow these steps:

1. *Get the number of bytes required for the full **DEVMODE** structure by calling **DocumentProperties** and specifying zero in the fMode parameter.*

2. *Allocate memory for the full **DEVMODE** structure.*

3. *Get the current printer settings by calling **DocumentProperties**. Pass a pointer to the **DEVMODE** structure allocated in Step 2 as the pDevModeOutput parameter and specify the DM_OUT_BUFFER value.*

4. *Modify the appropriate members of the returned **DEVMODE** structure and indicate which members were changed by setting the corresponding bits in the **dmFields** member of the **DEVMODE**.*

5. *Call **DocumentProperties** and pass the modified **DEVMODE** structure back as both the pDevModeInput and pDevModeOutput parameters and specify both the DM_IN_BUFFER and DM_OUT_BUFFER values (which are combined using the OR operator).*

As you can see, even though the C function declaration describes the pDevModeInput and pDevModeOutput parameters as type PDEVMODE (pointer to a DEVMODE structure), a close reading of the function description makes it clear that this is not the whole story. In fact, these parameters are pointers to memory buffers that have a DEVMODE structure at the start of the buffer, followed by additional device-specific data. From the C perspective, describing these parameters as the PDEVMODE data type is entirely correct—the parameter is, in fact, a pointer to a DEVMODE structure. It just happens to have additional data after the structure.

From the Visual Basic perspective, things are a bit more complicated. If you declare the parameter type as a DEVMODE structure, you won't be including the additional data. Some printer drivers don't use private data in the DEVMODE structure. These printers will work just fine with the code in the puzzle. But those drivers that do use the private data will attempt to access memory that is outside of the structure. In some cases, this will have no effect or will just lead to some strange printer settings. In other cases, you may get a memory exception, your application may suddenly vanish, or other bizarre behavior may appear in your application.

The sample code below shows you how to correctly handle the DEVMODE structure in the DocumentProperties call:

```
Dim hPrinter&
Dim res&
Dim dmIn As DEVMODE
Dim dmOut As DEVMODE
Dim DevmodeLength As Long
```

We allocate two dynamic byte buffers to hold the DEVMODE structure and the printer's private data:

```
Dim dmInBuf() As Byte
Dim dmOutBuf() As Byte

' Non-zero on success
res = OpenPrinter(Printer.DeviceName, hPrinter, 0)
If res = 0 Then
    lblStatus.Caption = "Printer could not be opened"
    Exit Sub
End If
```

The DocumentProperties function returns the length of the necessary buffer if you set the fMode parameter to 0. This length is used to dimension the two byte arrays:

```
' Get the length of the DEVMODE structure for this printer
    DevmodeLength = DocumentProperties(hwnd, hPrinter, _
    Printer.DeviceName, VarPtr(dmOut), VarPtr(dmIn), 0)
    lblComment.Caption = "The DEVMODE structure for this printer is " _
    & DevmodeLength & " bytes. " & _
    "The standard DEVMODE structure is " & Len(dmOut) & " bytes."
    ReDim dmInBuf(DevmodeLength)
    ReDim dmOutBuf(DevmodeLength)
```

Pass a pointer to the start of the byte arrays as the DEVMODE parameters.

```
' Load the dmOutBuf buffer with the data
    res = DocumentProperties(hwnd, hPrinter, Printer.DeviceName, _
    VarPtr(dmOutBuf(0)), VarPtr(dmInBuf(0)), DM_OUT_BUFFER Or DM_IN_PROMPT)
```

The data is in the byte array. Unfortunately, it's rather difficult to access fields of a structure when they are buried within a byte array. So we copy the byte array into a DEVMODE structure using the RtlMoveMemory function, as follows:

```
' Copy the DEVMODE portion of the buffer into
' the dmOut buffer so we can use it
Call RtlMoveMemory(dmOut, dmOutBuf(0), Len(dmOut))
If dmOut.dmOrientation = DMORIENT_LANDSCAPE Then
    lblStatus.Caption = "Printer is in landscape mode"
Else
    lblStatus.Caption = "Printer is in portrait mode"
End If
' You can modify the contents of the dmout buffer, then
' copy the data to the dmInBuf buffer and
' call DocumentProperties with DM_IN_BUFFER to set the new values
Call ClosePrinter(hPrinter)
```

This example demonstrates how you can retrieve device data. The process is reversed if you want to set the device parameters: Copy the data from the output buffer to the input buffer (all of the data, not just the DEVMODE portion). Make any modifications to the DEVMODE portion of the buffer and set the appropriate bits in the dmFieldsbits field so that the device will know which parameters you are changing. Finally, call the DocumentProperties function with the DM_IN_BUFFER flag set in the fMode parameter.

There will be any number of situations where you'll have a Visual Basic declaration for a function that someone has given you or that you have figured out for yourself, and you'll be all set to use it in your program. Next thing you know, you'll be tearing your hair out because you can't get it to work or it causes constant memory exceptions. In many cases, the solution can be found by just reading the documentation carefully, because the answer is often (as it is with the DEVMODE structure) in the details.

SOLUTION 18

DT, Phone Home

DT AND I RECOVERED QUICKLY. IT wasn't poison after all. Just brain freeze added to the story for dramatic effect. And it turned out that a quick brain freeze was just what I needed.

"It's in the packing." I showed DT.

Packing describes how variables are aligned within a structure. Most API structures have a packing of one byte, which means that each variable in the structure appears immediately after its predecessor in memory. Four-byte packing forces variables to start either on the smaller of the variable size or on the next 32-bit boundary. That means that a single byte variable can start anywhere, a 16-bit variable must start on an even byte, a 32-bit variable must start on a 32-bit boundary, and structures as a whole start on 32-bit boundaries. Visual Basic uses 4-byte packing internally, but converts structures to 1-byte packing during API function calls. The 4-byte packing required in this case has no effect on the szEntryName string, because not only does it already appear on a 32-bit boundary after the 32-bit dwSize parameter, but it is also made up of single-byte items, which can start at any address. However, it turns out that the extra padding is added even at the end of a structure so that the next structure would start at the 32-bit boundary. That's why an invalid structure size error was returned—the API function expects the structure to be padded to the next 32-bit boundary. It needs to be 264 bytes long, not 261. The easiest way to solve this problem is to change the structure declaration to this:

```
Public Type RASENTRYNAME
    dwSize As Long
    szEntryName As String * RAS_MaxEntryNameBuffer
    Padding(2) As Byte
End Type
```

"That's great!" exclaimed DT. "I'm not getting an error 632 anymore. Just an error 603 that indicates a larger buffer is needed."

I looked again at the code. After an error 603 occurs, the program calculates the number of entries it needs and resizes the RasEntryBuffer array as necessary:

```
Res = RasEnumEntries(0, vbNullString, RasEntryBuffer(0), BufferSize, _
    RasEntries)
If Res = 603 Then
```

```
      ' Buffer is too small - Resize to selected size
      RasEntryCount = BufferSize / RasEntrySize
      ReDim RasEntryBuffer(RasEntryCount - 1)
      Res = RasEnumEntries(0, vbNullString, RasEntryBuffer(0), _
      BufferSize, RasEntries)
   End If
```

I traced through the code. "Uh-oh," I said, "I'm getting an error 632 on the second call to RasEnumEntries. That doesn't make sense."

"Sure it does," laughed DT. "The dwSize parameter in the first entry in the array is initialized to the correct size, but the others are not."

"But the documentation doesn't say to initialize the dwSize fields in each entry in the structure, does it?"

"No, but it doesn't say not to, either. The documentation is vague on this."

"So how are we supposed to know to do this?"

"You guess. You try it both ways," DT grimaced. "Surely you're used to this kind of thing by now."

I quickly added some code to the function to initialize the dwSize field for each entry in the structure:

```
Res = RasEnumEntries(0, vbNullString, RasEntryBuffer(0), BufferSize, _
      RasEntries)
If Res = 603 Then
   ' Buffer is too small - Resize to selected size
   RasEntryCount = BufferSize / RasEntrySize
   ReDim RasEntryBuffer(RasEntryCount - 1)
   For CurrentEntry = 0 To RasEntryCount - 1
      RasEntryBuffer(CurrentEntry).dwSize = RasEntrySize
   Next CurrentEntry
   Res = RasEnumEntries(0, vbNullString, RasEntryBuffer(0), _
      BufferSize, RasEntries)
End If
```

It worked! The result was 0, indicating that the function worked correctly. We were about to raise our juices to toast our success when DT glanced at the screen, stunned.

"It only works for the first entry in the phone book! The second entry is empty!"

TECH EDITOR'S NOTE *The results described above may not work on your system. Read on to find out why.*

Arrays of Structures

How is it possible for the function to return a correct result, yet the structure entry to remain empty? The answer is, it isn't. The only possibility is if the structure entry you are looking at is not the same one seen by the API function.

How can this be?

Think, for a moment, about how strings are stored within Visual Basic. They are always stored as Unicode strings. Does this apply also to strings inside of structures?

Yes.

So how can a structure be passed to an API function that expects an ANSI string?

Visual Basic must convert the structure from Unicode to ANSI. To do this, it creates a temporary copy of the structure with the strings converted into ANSI as shown in Figure S18-1.

But what happens if you want to pass a pointer to an array of such structures? Normally you can pass a pointer to an array by passing a pointer to the first element in the array. But in this case Visual Basic passes a pointer to the temporary structure. Visual Basic does *not* convert all of the entries in the array—there is no reason for it to do so because, as far as VB is concerned, you are only passing the first element to the API function.

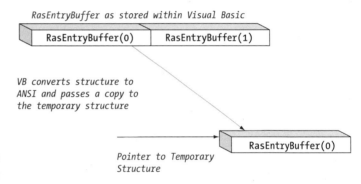

Figure S18-1: Passing structures in arrays to an API function

Which raises the question, how could the previous solution have returned a correct result? Setting the dwSize parameter for each entry in the array shouldn't have made any difference if only one entry was actually passed.

Frankly, I don't know. Perhaps it's a fluke. Perhaps the memory immediately after the temporary structure just happens to hold leftover data from a previous call that contains the record size. In other words, there's every chance that it won't work in most cases—especially if there are more than two phone book entries.

So what now?

One solution is to explicitly copy the array of structures into a memory buffer.[1]

---

1. Another solution would be to change the szEntryName field of the RASENTRYNAME structure from a fixed-length string to a byte array. This eliminates the need for Visual Basic to create a temporary structure, but does require you to perform explicit ANSI-to-Unicode string conversions for the szEntryName field.

```
Private Declare Function RasEntryToMemBuffer Lib "kernel32" Alias _
"RtlMoveMemory" (dest As Byte, source As RASENTRYNAME, _
ByVal count As Long) As Long
Private Declare Function RasEntryFromMemBuffer Lib "kernel32" _
Alias "RtlMoveMemory" (dest As RASENTRYNAME, source As Byte, _
ByVal count As Long) As Long

Dim TransferBuffer() As Byte

For CurrentEntry = 0 To RasEntryCount - 1
        RasEntryBuffer(CurrentEntry).dwSize = RasEntrySize
        Call RasEntryToMemBuffer(TransferBuffer( _
        CurrentEntry * RasEntrySize), RasEntryBuffer(CurrentEntry), _
        RasEntrySize)
Next CurrentEntry
```

Why do you need to create a separate function to do the copy instead of just using RtlMoveMemory directly? The truth is, you don't. This approach just adds some clarity and safety to the process. You could just as well have used RtlMoveMemory directly with the parameters declared As Any. But you could not have declared the parameters ByVal As Long and used the VarPtr operator. Why? Because the VarPtr operator would return the address of the structure in memory—the Visual Basic structure with its internal Unicode string.

When the RasEntryToMemBuffer function is called, the specified RasEntryBuffer entry is converted into ANSI, and a pointer to that temporary structure is passed to the RtlMoveMemory function, which then copies the data into the specified location in the TransferBuffer byte array. After the TransferBuffer byte array is completely loaded, the RasEnumEntries function can be called with the correct data, as shown in Figure S18-2.

After the RasEnumEntries loads the TransferBuffer array with the phone book entries, the process can be reversed. The RasEntryFromMemBuffer function is

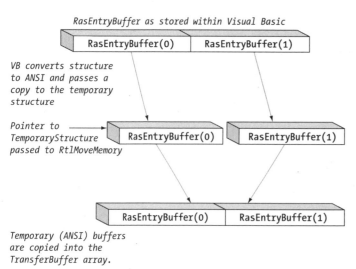

RasEntryBuffer as stored within Visual Basic

VB converts structure to ANSI and passes a copy to the temporary structure

Pointer to TemporaryStructure passed to RtlMoveMemory

Temporary (ANSI) buffers are copied into the TransferBuffer array.

Figure S18-2: Loading structures into a byte array

used to copy data back into the RasEntryBuffer array. The final program looks like this:

```
' RasTest #1
' Copyright © 1998 by Desaware Inc. All Rights Reserved

Option Explicit

Private Declare Function RasEntryToMemBuffer Lib "kernel32" Alias _
"RtlMoveMemory" (dest As Byte, source As RASENTRYNAME, _
ByVal count As Long) As Long
Private Declare Function RasEntryFromMemBuffer Lib "kernel32" _
Alias "RtlMoveMemory" (dest As RASENTRYNAME, source As Byte, _
ByVal count As Long) As Long

Private Sub Form_Load()
    Dim BufferSize As Long
    Dim RasEntries As Long
    Dim RasEntryBuffer() As RASENTRYNAME
    Dim RasEntrySize As Long
    Dim Res As Long
    Dim CurrentEntry As Integer
    Dim RasEntryCount As Long
    Dim TransferBuffer() As Byte

    ReDim RasEntryBuffer(0)
    RasEntrySize = Len(RasEntryBuffer(0))
    RasEntryBuffer(0).dwSize = RasEntrySize

    Res = RasEnumEntries(0, vbNullString, VarPtr(RasEntryBuffer(0)), _
        BufferSize, RasEntries)

    ' Now, redo based on the number of entries
    If (Res = 0 Or Res = 603) And BufferSize > 0 Then
        RasEntryCount = BufferSize / RasEntrySize
        ReDim RasEntryBuffer(RasEntryCount - 1)
        ReDim TransferBuffer(BufferSize)
        For CurrentEntry = 0 To RasEntryCount - 1
            RasEntryBuffer(CurrentEntry).dwSize = RasEntrySize
            Call RasEntryToMemBuffer(TransferBuffer(CurrentEntry * _
            RasEntrySize), RasEntryBuffer(CurrentEntry), RasEntrySize)
        Next CurrentEntry
        Res = RasEnumEntries(0, vbNullString, VarPtr(TransferBuffer(0)), _
```

```
                    BufferSize, RasEntries)
        End If

    If Res <> 0 Then
        MsgBox "RAS Error #" & Res, vbOKOnly, "Error"
    End If

    For CurrentEntry = 0 To RasEntries - 1
        Call RasEntryFromMemBuffer(RasEntryBuffer(CurrentEntry), _
        TransferBuffer(CurrentEntry * RasEntrySize), RasEntrySize)
        lstEntries.AddItem RasEntryBuffer(CurrentEntry).szEntryName
    Next CurrentEntry
End Sub
```

Conclusion

I returned to my office after sharing one last drink with DT. It had been a long tough puzzle to solve and, like so many of them, didn't arrive with a paying client I could charge at the end of the day. I checked my e-mail and smiled. It was a purchase order. DT had contacted her Hollywood client and explained to him that, with a little bit of effort, she could create a program that would let his computer not only call her computer and the computers of all his friends, but might even form the basis of a new sitcom in which families of computers all call each other, with occasional interruptions from the crazy old Atari next door. As soon as the executive heard that she was developing a program, he didn't seem to care what she had to say. He cut a P.O. on the spot, and DT was subcontracting with me to get the dialing software to work.

I guess it was a worthwhile day after all.

And I didn't even need to take a meeting.

SOLUTION 19

The RASDIALPARAMS Structure

LET'S START OUT BY LOOKING AGAIN at the structure:

```
typedef struct _RASDIALPARAMS {
    DWORD   dwSize;
    TCHAR   szEntryName[RAS_MaxEntryName + 1];
    TCHAR   szPhoneNumber[RAS_MaxPhoneNumber + 1];
    TCHAR   szCallbackNumber[RAS_MaxCallbackNumber + 1];
    TCHAR   szUserName[UNLEN + 1];
    TCHAR   szPassword[PWLEN + 1];
    TCHAR   szDomain[DNLEN + 1] ;
#if (WINVER >= 0x401)
    DWORD   dwSubEntry;
    DWORD   dwCallbackId;
#endif
} RASDIALPARAMS;
```

Two things are clear: First, we need to find the values of a number of constants. Next, we need to figure out how to deal with the dwSubEntry and dwCallbackId fields. What does the following term mean?

```
#if (WINVER >= 0x401)
    DWORD   dwSubEntry;
    DWORD   dwCallbackId;
#endif
```

The #if keyword is a conditional compilation block, similar to conditional compilation as supported by Visual Basic. It indicates that everything up to the #endif term will be included only if the compile time WINVER constant is greater than or equal to &H401. Clearly, version 4.01 of Windows added two new fields to this structure. How does the Win32 API know whether those two fields are present? It can tell based on the dwSize field! After all, those two fields add 8 bytes to the total size of the structure.

But what about the WINVER constant? What value should you assume is present when translating structures to Visual Basic? This is important to consider because, if you use a later version of the structure, it will fail to work on older-version operating systems. A C++ programmer sets the value of this constant to a value equal to the oldest operating system the application should support before compiling his application. For Visual Basic you should choose the value before creating your structure declarations.

The WINVER variable is a 2-byte number where the high byte is the major version of Windows. It will be 3 for Windows NT 3.*x*, 4 for Windows 95 and Windows NT 4, and 5 for Windows NT 5.*x*. The low byte is the minor version number.

What exactly is version 4.01 of Windows? Frankly, I have no idea. This conditional value only appears in a few places in the C header files, mostly in the RAS declarations. I suspect it applies to a service pack, or it may represent preliminary documentation for a forthcoming service pack. Either way, it seems safer under the circumstances to assume that WINVER is 0x400. This leaves out the dwSubEntry and dwCallbackID fields and ensures that the structure will be valid under Windows NT 4 and Windows 95/98.

That's an important decision to make because, as you can see from the constant declarations, they too have changed size based on the version of Windows:

```
#if (WINVER >= 0x400)
#define RAS_MaxEntryName        256
#define RAS_MaxDeviceName       128
#define RAS_MaxCallbackNumber RAS_MaxPhoneNumber
#else
#define RAS_MaxEntryName        20
#define RAS_MaxDeviceName       32
#define RAS_MaxCallbackNumber 48
#endif
```

In their case, the size is conditional on the WINVER variable being greater than or equal to 0x400. So setting WINVER to 4.0 means that the sample will not run correctly on NT 3.*x*.

Based on the header files, you can create the following constant declarations in Visual Basic. The constants with the Buffer suffix are 1 greater than the base constant, since the string declarations in the RASDIALPARAMS structure are 1 byte larger than the constant value (to allow room for the NULL terminating character).

```
Public Const RAS_MaxEntryName = 256
Public Const RAS_MaxEntryNameBuffer = 257
Public Const RAS_MaxPhoneNumber = 128
```

```
Public Const RAS_MaxPhoneNumberBuffer = 129
Public Const UNLEN = 256
Public Const UNLENBuffer = 257
Public Const PWLEN = 256
Public Const PWLENBuffer = 257
Public Const DNLEN = 15
Public Const DNLENBuffer = 16
```

The RASDIALPARAMS ends up looking like this:

```
Public Type RASDIALPARAMS
    dwSize As Long ' 4
    szEntryName As String * RAS_MaxEntryNameBuffer ' 257
    szPhoneNumber As String * RAS_MaxPhoneNumberBuffer '129
    szCallbackNumber As String * RAS_MaxPhoneNumberBuffer ' 129
    szUserName As String * UNLENBuffer ' 257
    szPassword As String * PWLENBuffer ' 257
    szDomain As String * DNLENBuffer '16
    Padding(2) As Byte
    'dwSubEntry As Long
    'dwCallbackId As Long
    '#if (WINVER >= 0x401)
    'DWORD  dwSubEntry;
    'DWORD  dwCallbackId;
    '#End If
End Type
```

What is the extra padding array at the end of the structure? This structure faces the same problem as the RASENTRYNAME structure shown in Puzzle 18. The packing is set to 4 bytes. The individual fields within the structure have no alignment problems because they all consist of arrays of single bytes, which can be located at any address. But the structure as a whole must be aligned to a 32-bit boundary. If you add up the lengths of all of the entries, you'll have 4 + 257 + 129 + 129 + 257 + 257 + 16 = 1049. The 32-bit boundary is 1052, so you need to add 3 bytes of padding.

With this structure, the function will almost work. Instead of error 632 (invalid structure size) upon startup, you'll see error 623 (invalid phone book entry) when you try to select a phone book entry. How can this be?

Consider the szEntryName field in the structure. It is a fixed-length string, which is set using the following line:

```
rs.szEntryName = lstEntries.Text
```

Let's say that the phone book entry was "MyISP." When the list box was loaded, it was set to the string "MyISP" followed by a NULL character. But that NULL character is not stored in the list box! Why? Because the list control, like most Windows controls, is written in C and uses C strings. So it stripped off the NULL termination character when the string was stored in the list box.

What happens when you assign a 5-character string to a 257-character fixed-length string? Visual Basic loads the rest of the string with spaces! When the API function tries comparing the phone book entry with a string containing the entry followed by a series of spaces, the comparison fails and the entry is not found. In order to make the function work, you must explicitly add a NULL termination character, as shown here:

```
rs.szEntryName = lstEntries.Text & Chr$(0)
```

That's all it takes.

You may find that no additional information is returned by the RasGetEntryDialParams function. That's because the function returns information from the last successful dial-in that differs from the information stored in the phone book itself. If the information is the same, the returned string will be empty.

Making Connections

ONE OF MY GOALS WITH EACH of these puzzles is to make them fair. Tough, but fair. And I'll bet some of you are thinking that this puzzle is just not fair. I've given you a block of C code (repeated below to help you avoid obsessive page-flipping), called it an enumeration, and offered absolutely no guidance on how to convert it into Visual Basic:

```
#define RASCS_PAUSED 0x1000
#define RASCS_DONE   0x2000

#define RASCONNSTATE enum tagRASCONNSTATE
RASCONNSTATE
{
    RASCS_OpenPort = 0,
    RASCS_PortOpened,
    RASCS_ConnectDevice,
    RASCS_DeviceConnected,
    RASCS_AllDevicesConnected,
    RASCS_Authenticate,
    RASCS_AuthNotify,
    RASCS_AuthRetry,
    RASCS_AuthCallback,
    RASCS_AuthChangePassword,
    RASCS_AuthProject,
    RASCS_AuthLinkSpeed,
    RASCS_AuthAck,
    RASCS_ReAuthenticate,
    RASCS_Authenticated,
    RASCS_PrepareForCallback,
    RASCS_WaitForModemReset,
    RASCS_WaitForCallback,
    RASCS_Projected,

#if (WINVER >= 0x400)
    RASCS_StartAuthentication,
    RASCS_CallbackComplete,
    RASCS_LogonNetwork,
```

```
#endif
    RASCS_SubEntryConnected,
    RASCS_SubEntryDisconnected,

    RASCS_Interactive = RASCS_PAUSED,
    RASCS_RetryAuthentication,
    RASCS_CallbackSetByCaller,
    RASCS_PasswordExpired,

    RASCS_Connected = RASCS_DONE,
    RASCS_Disconnected
};
```

It's true that I've offered no guidance on how to interpret this code, either in the puzzle or the tutorials (found in Part III). But unfair? I think not. Part of the intent of this book is to encourage, even force, you to think creatively when facing difficult problems. Since it is impossible for this book (or any other) to cover every API problem you will face with Visual Basic, it is important that you learn to apply knowledge you already have to new problems.

You may know nothing about C enumerations, but you should know quite a bit about Visual Basic enumerations created using the Enum statement. In a Visual Basic enumeration, every variable within the enumeration receives either a value that is assigned explicitly or one greater than the previous variable. The C structure you see here also uses the keyword "enum." Some of the variables are assigned explicitly, others have no assignment. Sound familiar? Take a look at the Visual Basic code that follows and compare it to the C code:

```
Private Const RASCS_PAUSED = &H1000
Private Const RASCS_DONE = &H2000

Private Enum RasConnState
    RASCS_OpenPort = 0
    RASCS_PortOpened
    RASCS_ConnectDevice
    RASCS_DeviceConnected
    RASCS_AllDevicesConnected
    RASCS_Authenticate
    RASCS_AuthNotify
    RASCS_AuthRetry
    RASCS_AuthCallback
    RASCS_AuthChangePassword
    RASCS_AuthProject
    RASCS_AuthLinkSpeed
```

```
        RASCS_AuthAck
        RASCS_ReAuthenticate
        RASCS_Authenticated
        RASCS_PrepareForCallback
        RASCS_WaitForModemReset
        RASCS_WaitForCallback
        RASCS_Projected
        RASCS_StartAuthentication
        RASCS_CallbackComplete
        RASCS_LogonNetwork
        RASCS_SubEntryConnected
        RASCS_SubEntryDisconnected
        RASCS_Interactive = RASCS_PAUSED
        RASCS_RetryAuthentication
        RASCS_CallbackSetByCaller
        RASCS_PasswordExpired
        RASCS_Connected = RASCS_DONE
        RASCS_Disconnected
End Enum
```

Do you see it? The code is virtually identical, with only minor changes due to the language syntax.

This illustrates an important point: Languages tend to fall into certain classifications. Both Visual Basic and C belong to the class of block-structured languages. They tend to have a great many similarities. One of the most important things that any Visual Basic programmer needs to learn when dealing with the Microsoft documentation is to realize that much of what you already know is directly applicable. A little bit of guesswork and experimentation can solve most API-related problems.

Which brings us to the next problem—the callback function. If you got the enumeration correct and were able to run the application, the result was probably an immediate memory exception. Why?

Let's look again at the RasDialFunc description:

```
VOID WINAPI RasDialFunc(
    UINT unMsg, // type of event that has occurred
    RASCONNSTATE rasconnstate, // connection state about to be entered
    DWORD dwError // error that may have occurred
    );
```

You may not be familiar with callback functions per se, but you should be quite familiar with what an API function would require in this case. Imagine then, for a moment, that this was an exported function. How would you declare it? The API function would expect to see the actual message, rasconnstate, and dwError values on the stack, since these parameters are not pointers. That means you would use ByVal in the declaration for all of these parameters.

```
Public Declare RasDialFunc Lib "some library" (ByVal unMsg As Long, _
ByVal rasconnstate As Long, ByVal dwError As Long) As Long
```

The C function declaration shows the function return a void, which is equivalent to no return value. You could use a Sub instead of Function declaration at this point, but it is just as valid to remain consistent and use a function declaration that returns a Long value. Just ignore the result.

How would you define a public function in a standard module so that it would take the value from the stack? In exactly the same way. The function needs to be defined as follows:

```
Public Function RasFunc(ByVal unMsg As Long, ByVal RasConnState As _
Long, ByVal dwError As Long) As Long
```

Does this mean all you need to do with a callback function is create a Declare statement and change it into a regular function? As long as you are dealing with numeric variables, yes. But this approach falls apart with strings and structures. API functions that use callbacks will pass strings or structures as pointers to a string or structure. You should define your callback function parameter ByVal As Long and interpret the variable you receive as a pointer. You can then copy the data to a local string or structure using the lstrcpy or RtlMoveMemory functions.

What Is That Mapped Drive? Part 1

WAS IT A WINDOWS BUG, a bug in the MapInfo1 project, or a documentation error? It depends on your point of view and your interpretation of the documentation.

The following code from the GetMappedInfo function in the MapInfo1.vbp project (on the CD that comes with this book) lies at the heart of the matter:

```
res = WNetGetConnection(Drive, Buffer, BufferLength)
    If res = ERROR_MORE_DATA Then
        Buffer = String$(BufferLength, 0)
        res = WNetGetConnection(Drive, Buffer, BufferLength)
    End If
```

The API documentation says this of the BufferLength parameter:

> *If the function fails because the buffer is not big enough, this parameter returns the required buffer size.*

One interpretation of this comment is that the buffer size returned will be sufficient for the function to succeed. In other words, once you call this to obtain the correct buffer size, it should not be possible for the function to return the ERROR_MORE_DATA return value. I think most reasonable people would see it this way; I certainly did.

But you could also interpret this to mean that it returns the required buffer size for the next attempt. If the buffer size was still not large enough, the function would return the ERROR_MORE_DATA result again with a new buffer size that will hopefully be large enough to hold all of the data.

Okay, maybe this second interpretation is a bit of a stretch and not particularly intuitive. However, it does match the behavior of this function. The GetMappedInfo function in the MapInfo1.vbp project can be rewritten as follows to allow multiple attempts:

```
Do
    Buffer = String$(BufferLength, 0)
    res = WNetGetConnection(Drive, Buffer, BufferLength)
Loop While res = ERROR_MORE_DATA
```

BufferLength starts at 0 with an empty Buffer string parameter. Each time the WNetGetConnection function returns ERROR_MORE_DATA, the buffer length is increased to the current estimated buffer length, and another attempt is made to call the function.

The Microsoft Win32 API documentation is the standard reference for API function calls. But even when you read it carefully, you will probably find yourself experimenting occasionally to determine exactly what the function calls do.

The Second Approach

Another common approach to handling this type of problem is potentially more efficient. Simply set the Buffer string to a very large value before calling the WNetGetConnection API function for the first time. You'll want to test for the ERROR_MORE_DATA error just in case, though if your string is set to a length of at least MAX_PATH bytes (constant MAX_PATH is 260), odds of this error occurring are slim.

If you take this approach, you'll need to find the end of the string by using the Instr function to find the NULL termination character and throwing away everything from that character to the end of the string. In the MapInfo1.vbp example, the BufferLength variable is loaded with the length of the buffer. Since the final character is the NULL termination character, the Left$ function can be used to retrieve the string to the left of that character.

What Is That Mapped Drive? Part 2

WHEN YOU STEP THROUGH THE CODE, you'll find that the crash occurs at this line:

```
Call RtlMoveMemory(nr, OutputBuffer(0), Len(nr))
```

What could cause the crash? The nr parameter is correct—it's a NETRESOURCE structure passed by reference. OutputBuffer(0) is the first byte in the byte array. Passed by reference, it will pass a pointer to the first byte of the array, which is also correct. The number of bytes being passed is the length of the NETRE-SOURCE structure. You know for a fact that the OutputBuffer array is at least as large as the NETRESOURCE structure because it is defined as containing the structure, so the WNetGetResourceInformation function should return a required size that is at least that size. If you check the OutputBufferSize variable, you will see that it is definitely larger than a NETRESOURCE structure.

That means the problem must be inside the structure.

When you copy the NETRESOURCE structure using RtlMoveMemory, the nr variable will be loaded with the exact data in the buffer. The fields that are defined as Longs won't be a problem. But what about the string variables? When defined as strings (as done in this example), Visual Basic expects each of those fields to contain a BSTR pointer to a Unicode string. However, the NETRE-SOURCE structure simply defines them as string pointers, and since we are using the ANSI version of the WNetGetResourceInformation function, those will be pointers to NULL-terminated ANSI strings.

It's not the ANSI-to-Unicode conversion that's killing us here, it's the fact that those pointers are definitely not BSTR pointers. Visual Basic will look at those values and more than likely crash right away. It will expect the length of the string to appear before the data. What values will it read in this case? Who knows? But you can be sure it will not be the actual length of the string. (See Tutorial 7, "Classes, Structures, and User-Defined Types," in Part III of this book, for more information on this problem.)

The solution is to change those parameters to the Long data type as follows:

```
Private Type NETRESOURCE
    dwScope As Long
```

```
            dwType As Long
            dwDisplayType As Long
            dwUsage As Long
            lpLocalName As Long
            lpRemoteName As Long
            lpComment As Long
            lpProvider As Long
    End Type
```

This creates two new problems.

First, before calling the WNetGetResourceInformation function, you need to set the lpRemoteName parameter to a pointer to a NULL-terminated ANSI string. That means that you must create an ANSI string buffer and obtain its address explicitly.

One of the easiest ways to create memory buffers is by using byte arrays.

Here's a code segment that can load a dynamically allocated byte array with a NULL-terminated ANSI string:

```
' Load a dynamically allocated byte array with an ANSI string.
Private Sub CreateAnsiArray(StringVar As String, ByteArray() As Byte)
    ReDim ByteArray(Len(StringVar))
    Call lstrcpy(VarPtr(ByteArray(0)), StringVar)
End Sub
```

There's a subtle technique here.

First, exactly how long is the byte array after the ReDim operation?

If the result of the Len(StringVar) operation was 5, the ByteArray parameter will be redimensioned with an index of 5. But in Visual Basic, this creates a byte array that is 6 bytes long! That extra byte will be used to hold the NULL termination character.

The lstrcpy function is defined as follows:

```
Private Declare Function lstrcpy Lib "kernel32" Alias "lstrcpyA" _
(ByVal lpString1 As Long, ByVal lpString2 As String) As Long
```

The lstrcpy function is designed to copy strings from a source pointer to a destination pointer. The destination pointer (lpString1) is specified as a Long so that we can pass the pointer that is obtained using the VarPtr operator. The lpString2 parameter is declared ByVal as a string. What happens when you pass a VB string to an API function using the ByVal operator? *It is converted into a NULL-terminated ANSI string!*—which is exactly what the lstrcpy function expects to see as a parameter.

In other words, rather than using an explicit Unicode-to-ANSI conversion, this function cheats by using the Unicode-to-ANSI conversion that Visual Basic does automatically when passing strings to API functions.

The nr.lpRemoteName field can be set using the following code, given a dynamically allocated byte array named ResourceNameArray:

```
Call CreateAnsiArray(resourcename, ResourceNameArray)
    nr.lpRemoteName = VarPtr(ResourceNameArray(0))
```

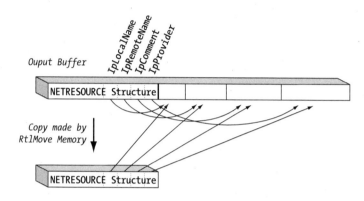

The RtlMoveMemory function will now work without crashing. You can see this in Figure S22-1, which shows the contents of the buffer loaded by the WNetGetResourceInformation function. The buffer starts with a NETRESOURCE structure and is followed by the string information. The pointers in the structure contain the addresses of those strings in the buffer as indicated by the arrows. When you copy the first part of the buffer into a NETRESOURCE-type variable, the pointers still correctly point to the string data in the original buffer.

Figure S22-1: The buffer string addresses remain valid after the RtlMoveMemory function is called

Now all that remains is to convert the string data into a form that is accessible by Visual Basic.

The following function can do the trick:

```
' Retrieve a VB string given a pointer to a null-terminated string
Private Function GetVBString(ByVal ptr As Long)
    Dim StringLength As Long
    Dim TempString As String
    If ptr = 0 Then Exit Function
    StringLength = lstrlen(ptr)
    TempString = String$(StringLength + 1, 0)
    Call lstrcpystring(TempString, ptr)
    GetVBString = Left$(TempString, StringLength)
End Function
```

Given a pointer, you can use the lstrlen function to obtain the length of the string (not including the NULL character). You can then preinitialize the string to the necessary length. This function reverses the operation shown in the CreateAnsiArray function by using the lstrcpy function and passing a Visual Basic string as the first variable and a pointer as the second variable. This requires a different declaration for lstrcpy, so we create a new alias for the function that is declared as follows:

```
Private Declare Function lstrcpystring Lib "kernel32" Alias "lstrcpyA" _
(ByVal lpString1 As String, ByVal lpString2 As Long) As Long
```

Finally, the NULL termination character is stripped from the string.

The agGetStringFromPointer function in the apigid32.dll library (included in Appendix C of this book) performs the same operation and is far more efficient, since it works with a single API call.

This leaves us with the following version of the GetResourceInfo function, which works:

```
' Get the network provider information
Private Sub GetResourceInfo(resourcename As String)
    Dim nr As NETRESOURCE
    Dim ResourceNameArray() As Byte
    Dim lpSystem As Long
    Dim OutputBufferSize As Long
    Dim OutputBuffer() As Byte
    Dim res As Long

    lstResource.Clear
    If resourcename = "" Then Exit Sub

    nr.dwType = RESOURCETYPE_DISK
    ' Create a buffer with the ANSI local name
    Call CreateAnsiArray(resourcename, ResourceNameArray)
    nr.lpRemoteName = VarPtr(ResourceNameArray(0))

    ' Prep the buffer
    OutputBufferSize = 1024
    Do
        ReDim OutputBuffer(OutputBufferSize)
        res = WNetGetResourceInformation(nr, OutputBuffer(0), _
            OutputBufferSize, lpSystem)
    Loop While res = ERROR_MORE_DATA
    If res <> 0 Then
```

```
      MsgBox "No Resource Information Available"
      Exit Sub
   End If

   ' Get resulting NETRESOURCE
   Call RtlMoveMemory(nr, OutputBuffer(0), Len(nr))

   lstResource.AddItem "Remote Name: " & GetVBString(nr.lpRemoteName)
   lstResource.AddItem "Provider: " & GetVBString(nr.lpProvider)
   lstResource.AddItem "System Name: " & GetVBString(lpSystem)

End Sub
```

There Is a Question in There Somewhere

FOR THE LAST TIME, A QUICK reminder of our original question:

I'm trying to use the user_info_2 structure with the NetAddUser function from VBA. Part of this structure is: PBYTE usri2_logon_hours; points to a 21-byte (168 bits) bit string that specifies . . .

How do I include this in my type declaration? Also, there is a constant in the C header as:

#define USER_MAXSTORAGE_UNLIMITED ((unsigned long) -1L)

Isn't this a contradiction?

Should I just declare this as a long constant with the value of 1? Thanks in advance!

Let's start with the second question. The usri2_max_storage field of the USER_INFO2 structure is a Long field that holds the maximum amount of storage the user is allowed to use on the system. The documentation suggests that you should set it to the constant value USER_MAXSTORAGE_UNLIMITED to allow the user unlimited access to the disk and defines the constant as shown in the question above.

Clearly –1 doesn't make any sense—you can't give a user access to negative disk space, so it's not surprising that the person who sent in the question was confused.

But common sense suggests that using the value 1 doesn't make much sense either, unless you wish to restrict the user to using a single byte of data on the disk.

The answer lies in an understanding of how data is stored in memory. Let's first look at how a Visual Basic Long variable stores certain numbers.

The largest possible value that a Visual Basic Long variable can hold is 2147483647. You can test this using the following code:

```
Dim l As Long
l = &H7FFFFFFF
Debug.Print l
```

I know what you're thinking: Why is &H7FFFFFFF the largest number that a Long variable can hold? What about &HFFFFFFFF?

Try it and see what happens.

The result is –1.

You see, a Visual Basic Long variable is a signed variable, which means that the high bit indicates that the number is negative. If Visual Basic supported a 32-bit unsigned variable, loading that variable with &HFFFFFFFF would result in the number 4294967294.

So, the signed value –1 corresponds to the unsigned value 4294967294. Both are stored identically in memory as &HFFFFFFFF—the only difference between them is the way the data is interpreted by the software.

When you look at the following constant definition,

```
#define USER_MAXSTORAGE_UNLIMITED ((unsigned long) -1L)
```

you'll notice that before the –1 is the term "(unsigned long)." What does this mean? It's called a "cast." When a type appears in parentheses before a number or variable in the C language, it tells the compiler to interpret the data according to that type. So, even though the number shown is –1 (the L indicates that it's a 32-bit –1), the cast tells the compiler that the programmer really intends this to be interpreted as an unsigned value, which in this case is 4294967294.

From our point of view as Visual Basic programmers, we don't really care how the data is interpreted by the C compiler. All we care about is making sure that we load the variable with the correct value. The correct value in this case is &HFFFFFFFF, and the easiest way to load a Visual Basic Long variable with that value is to set it to –1. The correct declaration is therefore

```
Private Const USER_MAXSTORAGE_UNLIMITED = -1
```

And Now the Array . . .

The usri2_logon_hours field of the USER_INFO2 structure can optionally be set to a pointer to a 21-byte (168-bit) array. In our original solution, we used Long variables for all the fields in the USER_INFO2 structure. Numeric data was handled by direct assignment of the numeric data to the Long variable. Strings were handled by loading the Long variable with the address of a Unicode string obtained using the StrPtr operator. Is it possible to set the usri2_logon_hours field to a pointer to a 21-byte array in a similar manner? Absolutely.

First, create the byte array as follows:

```
Dim HourList(20) As Byte
```

Note that this actually creates a 21-byte array with bytes numbered from 0 to 20. Next, assign a pointer to the array obtained using the VarPtr operator as shown here:

```
ul2.usri2_logon_hours = VarPtr(HourList(0))
```

All of the bytes in the array are stored in a contiguous memory block, so a pointer to the first byte in the array is the same thing as a pointer to the array.

Array Contents

The one thing I haven't discussed yet is what you would store in this array. Although not part of the original question, it is worth looking at because it illustrates some very interesting techniques that are not familiar to many Visual Basic programmers.

The array contents are defined as follows in the Win32 SDK reference:

*Points to a 21-byte (168 bits) bit string that specifies the times during which the user can log on. Each bit represents a unique hour in the week. The first bit (bit 0, word 0) is Sunday, 0:00 to 0:59; the second bit (bit 1, word 0) is Sunday, 1:00 to 1:59; and so on. A null pointer in this element for **NetUserAdd** calls means that there is no time restriction. A null pointer in this element for **NetUserSetInfo** calls means that no change is to be made.*

This is a rather interesting way of specifying times. It makes sense when you think about it. If you have 24 hours in a day and 7 days a week (as is common in most locations outside of Silicon Valley, where we routinely add hours to each day in order to have enough time to do things like writing these books), you need a total of 24 x 7 = 168 bits to allow for one bit for each hour.

How would you go about setting or clearing individual bits in the array?

Let's say, for this example, that days will be numbered 1 to 7 (Sunday through Saturday) and hours from 0 to 23. (This system uses 24-hour time. For those of you unfamiliar with this time format, all you need to know is that 13 o'clock is 1:00 PM and that you add 12 to convert after that.)

We need to convert the day and hour to an index into an array and a bit location within the indexed byte.

Fortunately, in this case, the numbers are fairly easy to calculate. Each byte holds 8 bits for 8 hours. Three bytes represents a day. We can use the following equation to figure out which byte to use:

```
ByteIndex = Int(Hour / 8) + ((Day - 1) * 3)
```

The second term, ((Day – 1) * 3), gives us the number of the first byte for a given day (each day has 3 bytes). Each byte holds 8 hours, so divide by 8 to get the byte index. You have to use the Int function to prevent rounding. For example:

```
Monday 10:00 AM is day 2, hour 10.
ByteIndex = Int(10/8) + ((2-1) * 3) = 1 + 3 = 4
```

Which bit corresponds to this time? We found the index of the byte by dividing by 8—the bit location is the remainder of this operation. The easiest way to obtain it is by using the mod operator: 10 mod 8 is 2, indicating that the correct bit is bit 2 (the third bit starting from bit 0).

But we don't really need the bit number—we actually need a byte in which the specified bit is set in order to use an AND or OR operation to clear or set the bit. Since Visual Basic does not have a shift operator, we can use its exponentiation operator as follows:

```
ByteMask = 2 ^ Int(Hour Mod 8)
```

Now, I realize that whether this makes sense to you or not depends on how far you are from your high school math. I've found that the easiest way to handle these types of problems is often to write out some sample values and see if they make sense. Use Table S23-1 as a format for your own examples.

HOUR	DAY	INT(HOUR / 8)	BYTEINDEX	HOUR MOD 8	2 ^ (HOUR MOD 8)
0	1	0	0	0	1
0	2	0	3	0	1
7	2	0	3	7	128 = &H80
8	2	1	4	0	1

Table S23-1: Trial values can help you determine if an equation is correct

To set a bit, simply use the OR operator to combine the mask value with the existing value.

To clear a bit, you actually need a mask in which all of the bits are set except for the one you want to clear. You can get this value by using the NOT operator on the mask. You can then use the AND operator to combine the mask with the original value to clear the bit.

The final function to set or clear bit values is shown here:

```
' Day is 1 - 7
' Hour is 0 - 23
```

```
Private Sub SetBitValue(HourList() As Byte, Day As Integer, Hour As _
Integer, Allow As Boolean)

    Dim ByteIndex As Integer
    Dim ByteMask As Integer
    ' Calculate the byte location
    ByteIndex = Int(Hour / 8) + ((Day - 1) * 3)
    ' Calculate the mask to use for the logical operation
    ByteMask = 2 ^ Int(Hour Mod 8)
    Debug.Print ByteIndex
    Debug.Print ByteMask
    If Allow Then
        HourList(ByteIndex) = HourList(ByteIndex) Or ByteMask
    Else
        HourList(ByteIndex) = HourList(ByteIndex) And (Not ByteMask)
    End If
End Sub
```

One Last Detail

When testing the final program, I quickly found that I could not actually log on to the account I created—I kept getting the message that the account had expired. I found that I needed to make two changes: First, I had to ask the user administrator to add the new account to a group (you can do this through API functions, but I did not do so in this case). I also needed to set the usri2_acct_expires field to the constant TIMEQ_FOREVER (also –1) so that the account would never expire.

The final function for adding a user is as follows:

```
Private Sub Command1_Click()
    Dim ul2 As USER_INFO_2
    Dim res As Long
    Dim parm_err As Long
    Dim username As String
    Dim userpass As String
    Dim HourList(20) As Byte
    username = "Puzzle" & Chr$(0)
    userpass = "pass" & Chr$(0)

    ul2.usri2_name = StrPtr(username)
    ul2.usri2_password = StrPtr(userpass)
    ul2.usri2_priv = USER_PRIV_USER
```

```
    ul2.usri2_flags = UF_NORMAL_ACCOUNT Or UF_SCRIPT
    ul2.usri2_max_storage = USER_MAXSTORAGE_UNLIMITED
    ul2.usri2_acct_expires = TIMEQ_FOREVER
    ul2.usri2_logon_hours = VarPtr(HourList(0))
    ' Allow login only on Saturday from 11:00PM to midnight!
    Call SetBitValue(HourList(), 7, 23, True)

    res = NetUserAdd(0, 2, VarPtr(ul2), parm_err)
    Debug.Print "Result: " & res
    If res <> 0 Then Debug.Print "Error at index: " & parm_err
End Sub
```

Callback That String

THE PROBLEM IS IN THE CALLBACK parameter, which is defined to be ByVal As String. When a callback parameter is declared ByVal As String, the function expects to see a pointer to a BSTR string. Because it is passed ByVal, the function assumes that the BSTR is a copy of the original string. As such, it is the function's responsibility to free the string before it returns. Unfortunately, the pointer is not a BSTR at all—it is a regular NULL-terminated C string, and an ANSI one to boot. Not only will Visual Basic interpret the string incorrectly, it will crash spectacularly as soon as it tries to free what it thinks is a BSTR.

The solution is to change the parameter to be ByVal As Long. That loads the parameter with a pointer to a NULL-terminated ANSI C string. The lstrlen function can be used to determine the length of the string, and the lstrcpy function can be used to copy the data as shown in the correct code that follows.

A standard module contains

```
' Locales Puzzle
' Copyright © 1998 by Desaware Inc. All Rights Reserved
Option Explicit

Public Declare Function EnumSystemLocales Lib "kernel32" Alias _
"EnumSystemLocalesA" (ByVal lpLocaleEnumProc As Long, ByVal dwFlags _
As Long) As Long

Public Declare Function lstrcpy Lib "kernel32" Alias "lstrcpyA" _
(ByVal dest As String, ByVal source As Long) As Long
Public Declare Function lstrlen Lib "kernel32" Alias "lstrlenA" _
(ByVal source As Long) As Long

Public Const LCID_INSTALLED = &H1  ' installed Locale ids
Public Function EnumLocalesProc(ByVal Locale As Long) As Long
    Dim LocaleName As String
    LocaleName = String$(lstrlen(Locale) + 1, Chr$(0))
    Call lstrcpy(LocaleName, Locale)
    Debug.Print LocaleName
    EnumLocalesProc = True
End Function
```

The form contains

```
' Locale Puzzle
' Copyright © 1998 by Desaware Inc. All Rights Reserved

Option Explicit

Private Sub Command1_Click()
    Dim lRet As Long
    lRet = EnumSystemLocales(AddressOf EnumLocalesProc, LCID_INSTALLED)
End Sub
```

The LocaleName variable in the EnumLocalesProc function still has a trailing
NULL termination character that you can strip off if necessary. This program will
display the results as eight hexadecimal digits. For example, U.S. English
Windows will display locale 00000409. (In-depth information on locales can be
found in the online Win32 documentation and in Chapter 6 of my *Visual Basic
Programmer's Guide to the Win32 API.*)

Universal Identifiers, Part 1

THERE ARE REALLY ONLY TWO APPROACHES to dealing with 128-bit variables in Visual Basic: You need to create either an array or a user-defined type (structure). The Windows solution is to use a structure. A large part of the trick to translating a C header file to Visual Basic is to figure out which statements are actually relevant to the task. Take another look at the listing, but this time with comments added:

```
#ifndef GUID_DEFINED        // Skip the following if the _
                            // GUID_DEFINED is already defined.
#define GUID_DEFINED        // Define the GUID_DEFINED constant - no value.
typedef struct  _GUID       // Define a structure (user-defined type)
    {
    DWORD Data1;            // 32 bit value
    WORD Data2;             // 16 bit value
    WORD Data3;             // 16 bit value
    BYTE Data4[ 8 ];        // 8 x 8 bits = 64 bits
    } GUID;                 // The GUID structure is 32+16+16+64 = 128 bits

#endif                      // !GUID_DEFINED
                            // End of the part to skip if GUID_DEFINED is
                            // already defined
```

The use of conditional compilation constants, such as the GUID_DEFINED constant above, is very common in Windows header files. The first time a program includes this header file, GUID_DEFINED will not be defined. That means that the lines up to the #endif statement will be processed by the compiler, including a line that defines the GUID_DEFINED constant. The next time the header file is included by a program, the compiler will see that the GUID_DEFINED constant is already defined and skip over the code up to the #endif statement. This will prevent the GUID structure from being defined a second time—an error in C++.

This differs from the system in Visual Basic, where you simply add modules to a project. In C++, it is possible for files to include header files. These files are treated as if they are part of the main program file. But a header file can also include additional header files. If multiple files include the same header file (as is likely in the case of the wtypes.h file used here, which includes critical data type declarations used by Windows), you run the risk of declaring functions or structures multiple times. The use of conditional compilation constants shown here serves to prevent this error:

```
// The following four lines define a new type called a LPGUID if the
// constant __LPGUID_DEFINED__ is not yet defined. An LPGUID is a
// Long Pointer to a GUID
#if !defined( __LPGUID_DEFINED__ )
#define __LPGUID_DEFINED__
typedef GUID __RPC_FAR *LPGUID;
#endif // !__LPGUID_DEFINED__
```

It's good to know what an LPGUID is, in case it is used later as a function parameter. But since it's a pointer, you know that it will be a 32-bit pointer value. The term __RPC_FAR will be described shortly.

```
// The following lines define a structure called an OBJECTID.
// It's completely irrelevant to this puzzle. In fact, I don't
// recall ever using this particular structure for anything.
#ifndef __OBJECTID_DEFINED
#define __OBJECTID_DEFINED
#define __OBJECTID_DEFINED
typedef struct _OBJECTID
    {
    GUID Lineage;
    unsigned long Uniquifier;
    } OBJECTID;
#endif // !_OBJECTID_DEFINED

#if !defined( __IID_DEFINED__ ) // If the __IID_DEFINED__ _
// constant is already defined, _
// skip the following
#define __IID_DEFINED__     // Define the __IID_DEFINED__ constant
typedef GUID IID;           // An IID is a GUID

typedef IID __RPC_FAR *LPIID;  // An LPIID is a pointer to an IID

typedef GUID CLSID;            // A CLSID is a GUID as well
#endif
```

What is the meaning of the term __RPC_FAR in the LPIID and LPGUID declarations?
    If you look in the C header file rpc.h, you'll find the following definition:

```
#define __RPC_FAR
```

But there's nothing after the word __RPC_FAR! Does that mean the term is defined as nothing? That's right. It's a constant that may be used on some platforms to instruct the compiler to generate certain types of code. But it is meaningless under Win32. So the compiler will simply discard the term during the compilation process.

The Visual Basic declaration for a GUID turns out to be the following simple structure:

```
Public Type GUID
    Data1 As Long      ' 32 bits
    Data2 As Integer   ' 16 bits
    Data3 As Integer   ' 16 bits
    Data4(7) As Byte   ' 8 x 8 bits
End Type
```

Did you define Data4 correctly? Remember that the array is zero-based. If you defined it as Data4(8) As Byte, you would have 72 bits instead of 64.

What about CLSID and IID?

You can create identical structures for these types. But why bother? Since they all refer to 128-bit values, you can simply create a single user-defined type called GUID or CLSID and use it any time you need to deal with one of these universal identifiers. Puzzles 26–28 use a structure named CLSID for this purpose.

SOLUTION 26

Universal Identifiers, Part 2

IF YOU UNCOMMENTED THE ERR.RAISE code in the GUIDObject class, the program would be as follows:

```
res = CLSIDFromProgID(MyProgramId, cid)
If res = 0 Then
    GetCLSID = cid
Else
    ' What happens when you uncomment this?
    Err.Raise res
End If
```

Since when do you raise errors with results from API functions? Normally, you would use the GetErrorString function in ErrString.bas to retrieve a text description of an error.

Let's take another look at the CLSIDFromProgID function documentation and VB declaration:

```
HRESULT CLSIDFromProgID(
    LPCOLESTR lpszProgID, //Pointer to the ProgID
    LPCLSID pclsid        //Pointer to the CLSID
    );
Private Declare Function CLSIDFromProgID Lib "ole32.dll" _
(ByVal lpszProgId As String, lpclsid As CLSID) As Long
```

What is an HRESULT? According to the declaration, it is a Long value, which is what you would expect given that API functions almost always return Long values.

If you look in the definition of HRESULT in the wtypes.h file, you'll see the following:

```
typedef LONG HRESULT;
```

So clearly an HRESULT is a Long variable. Why would I try to raise an error with an HRESULT value? How does an HRESULT differ from a normal API error code?

An HRESULT is a Long error value, but unlike regular API result codes, an HRESULT is defined by COM, the Component Object Model. COM defines a special error code format that is completely separate from the Win32 API error results that you obtain using the Err.LastDllError method. HRESULT error codes are the same values used by Visual Basic and other COM-based applications when dealing with object errors. The Err.Raise statement in the GUIDobject class raises the error "ActiveX Component Can't Create Object". This suggests that there is a problem with the program ID.

Another approach to determining the meaning of the HRESULT is to look at its value in hexadecimal. In this case, it's &H800401F3, which corresponds to the constant CO_E_CLASSSTRING found in file api32.txt. The Win32 documentation for the CLSIDFromProgID function states that one possible return value for the function is in fact CO_E_CLASSSTRING, which is described as "The registered CLSID for the ProgID is invalid."

So either the registry is hopelessly corrupt or there is something wrong with the program ID.

Let's indulge in some wishful thinking, assume that the registry is not corrupt, and examine what could be wrong with the program ID.

The first parameter to the CLSIDFromProgID function is described as an LPCOLESTR. What is an LPOLESTR? The LP indicates a pointer. The C indicates a constant value. You know that an LPSTR is a string, and an LPCSTR is a constant string—one that the API function will not modify. But what kind of string is an OLESTR?

The declaration from the wtypes.h file is

```
typedef WCHAR OLECHAR;
typedef /* [string] */ OLECHAR __RPC_FAR *LPOLESTR;
```

An LPOLESTR is a pointer to an OLESTR. An OLESTR is made of up of OLECHAR characters, which are defined as the WCHAR datatype. WCHAR is a wide character.

In other words, the string must be Unicode. This is something you might as well get used to when it comes to functions that are part of the OLE subsystem. Unlike general Win32 API functions, which have separate ANSI and Unicode entry points and generally use ANSI strings with ANSI entry points, the OLE functions almost always have a single entry point and accept Unicode string parameters.

How should you pass a Unicode string to an API function?

The lpszProgId parameter is declared ByVal As Long as shown here. The calling routine needs to pass the address of a Unicode string as a parameter.

```
Private Declare Function CLSIDFromProgID Lib "ole32.dll" _
(ByVal lpszProgId As Long, lpclsid As CLSID) As Long
```

You could define a temporary byte array and assign it from the string, then pass a pointer to the first byte of the array using code like this:

```
Dim TempBuffer() As Byte
TempBuffer() = MyProgramId
res = CLSIDFromProgID(VarPtr(TempBuffer(0)), cid)
```

But the code in the actual example takes a somewhat more efficient approach by using the StrPtr operator. This operator returns a pointer to the string data as it is actually stored within Visual Basic. Since Visual Basic stores strings in Unicode format, this provides an easy way to pass a Unicode string to a function.

```
Option Explicit

Public Function GetCLSID() As CLSID
    Dim cid As CLSID
    Dim res As Long
    Dim MyProgramId As String

    MyProgramId = "GUIDPuzzle.GUIDObject" & Chr$(0)
    res = CLSIDFromProgID(StrPtr(MyProgramId), cid)
    If res = 0 Then
        GetCLSID = cid
    End If
End Function
```

Why didn't we use VarPtr(MyProgramId) in the CLSIDFromProgID call?

Because the VarPtr operator returns the address of the MyProgramId variable. This variable contains a pointer to the BSTR string data. The difference between these two operators can be seen in Figure S26-1.

The results of this solution can be seen in Figure S26-2.

Now let's take a look at the structure data and the raw data as shown in the figures and in Table S26-1. Note that the actual values in each case will differ on your system.

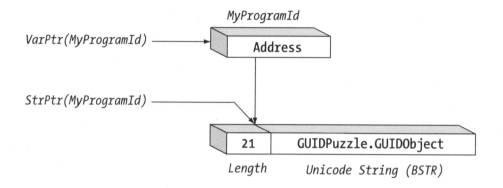

Figure S26-1: The difference between VarPtr and StrPtr

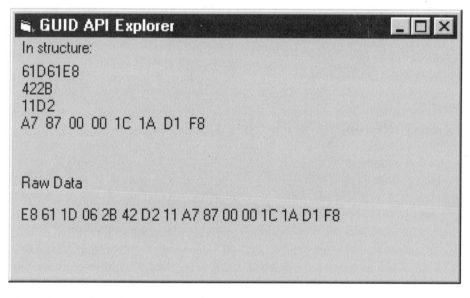

Figure S26-2: The GUIDPuzzle program now works

FIELD NAME	VALUE	RAW DATA
Data1	61D61E8	E8 61 1D 06
Data2	422B	2B 42
Data3	11D2	D2 11
Data4	A7 87 00 00 1C 1A D1 F8	A7 87 00 00 1C 1A D1 F8

Table S26-1: Representations of GUID data

Here you can see the effects of byte ordering on the way data is displayed. (You can read more about this in Tutorial 2, "Memory, Where It All Begins," found in Part III of this book.)

Why am I going to all this trouble to show you these two different ways of looking at the data? Because you may find yourself dealing with both of these representations on occasion. Even though objects are usually referred to in programs by program ID, any time you need to look under the hood in a Visual Basic project file or in the system registry, you will see the CLSID in a format that looks something like this:

```
{061D61E8-422B-11D2-A787-00001C1AD1F8}
```

As you can see, the data in this format is very similar to the value displayed in the second column of Table S26-1. The only difference is that the Data4 array is divided into a group of 2 bytes and a group of 6 bytes.

This string representation of a CLSID is used almost universally by applications and data files that display CLSID information in a format intended to be viewed by people. Where, then, might you run into the raw data? You'll see CLSIDs in the raw data format when you examine memory under a debugger, such as the Visual C++ debugger.

Given that the string format is frequently used, you might wonder if there is a function to convert between a CLSID structure and a string representation of a CLSID. There is, and that will be the subject of Puzzle 27.

Universal Identifiers, Part 3

YOU'VE ALREADY SEEN IN PREVIOUS EXAMPLES how to handle REFCLSID parameters, so you can be fairly confident that the problem does not lie with this parameter.

The fact that the solution crashes illustrates one of the most common problems in working with new or complex API functions—the tendency to jump to conclusions and create declarations without thought. The ppsz parameter is defined as an LPOLESTR * type. Believing that you can pass a Visual Basic string by reference is a nice thought, but it's wrong on many counts.

To understand why, let's review some of the possible ways to pass a string parameter to an API function and what happens behind the scenes in each case. Figure S27-1 illustrates the overall process that goes on when you pass a string to an API function. (This subject is also discussed in Tutorial 5, "The ByVal Keyword: The Solution to 90 Percent of All API Problems," in Part III of this book.)

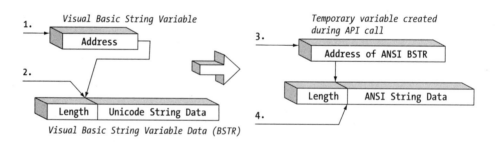

Figure S27-1: Passing strings to API functions

Visual Basic stores strings internally in BSTR format. A BSTR is an OLE string—a string that is allocated by the OLE subsystem. A Visual Basic string variable contains a BSTR, which points to the start of the BSTR string data. The 4 bytes before the start of the string data contain the length of the string. The string data in a Visual Basic string is always stored in Unicode. When Visual Basic passes a string to an API function, it creates a temporary BSTR string that contains an ANSI string. When the API function returns, the contents of that ANSI string are copied into Visual Basic's Unicode string.

The numbered arrows in Figure S27-1 represent the different pointers that one can pass to API functions:

Pointer 1 is the address of the Visual Basic String variable that contains the pointer to the Visual Basic string data (BSTR string). You can obtain this address in the same way you obtain the address of any Visual Basic variable: by using the VarPtr operator.

Pointer 2 is the value of the pointer for the string—the address of the start of the Visual Basic string data (BSTR string). You can obtain this address in Visual Basic using the StrPtr operator.

Pointer 3 is the address of the temporary variable that contains the pointer to the temporary ANSI string created by Visual Basic (BSTR string). This is the address you pass when you pass a string variable to an API function by reference.

Pointer 4 is the value of the pointer for the temporary ANSI string (BSTR string). This is the address you pass when you pass a string variable to an API function by value.

The vast majority of API functions using string pointers are declared as LPSTR, or ANSI, strings. The only pointer in the figure that points to an ANSI string is pointer 4, which explains why most string variables are passed by value.

The StringFromCLSID function requires a Unicode string, so clearly pointers 3 and 4 are out of the question. If the ppsz parameter was declared just as LPOLESTR, pointer 2 would work, since an LPOLESTR is a pointer to the actual Unicode string data. That's why you can use the StrPtr operator to obtain valid parameters for many API functions that use OLE strings. Just declare the parameter ByVal As Long and pass the value obtained using the StrPtr operator on the string. You must, of course, make sure that the string is preallocated to a length sufficient to hold any data loaded into the string by the API function.

That leaves pointer 1 as the only possible remaining solution for the StringFromCLSID function. And at first glance, it looks like it might work. Pointer 1 is a pointer to a BSTR, which contains a pointer to the string. And an LPOLESTR * parameter is a pointer to a pointer. So this should work, right?

Wrong. Why? Because an LPOLESTR is not a pointer to a BSTR. It's a pointer to a regular NULL-terminated string. A BSTR is allocated by the OLE string management system, and the string data is preceded by the length of the string. An LPOLESTR is just a generic pointer to a string. Figure S27-2 shows the ppsz parameter from the perspective of the StringFromCLSID function. The function

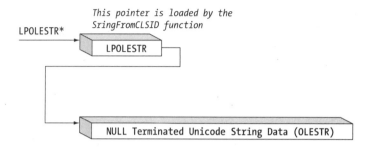

Figure S27-2: NT Performance Monitor illustrates a memory leak

receives the LPOLESTR * pointer—the address of an LPOLESTR variable that contains the address of the string data. This means that the function can modify the LPOLESTR variable. In fact, if you look at the description of this parameter, you'll see

```
LPOLESTR * ppsz  //Indirect pointer to the resulting string on return
```

This means that the LPOLESTR parameter that is referenced when the function is called is loaded by the function with a pointer to the string data.

In the original puzzle code, the StringFromCLSID does load the MyString variable with a pointer to a NULL-terminated Unicode string. But the function nevertheless fails in two ways. First, the length that precedes every BSTR is not set by this function (because it is not a BSTR). Next, the pointer is not allocated by the OLE subsystem. Under Windows NT, as soon as Visual Basic attempts to treat the pointer as a BSTR, an exception occurs. Under Windows 95, no exception occurs—at least, not right away—but the string length is incorrect, and the previous string referenced by the variable is "lost" because the pointer was overwritten.

Since Visual Basic does not provide any automatic way to handle the LPOLESTR * parameter type, it's up to you to create a declaration that gives the API function the information it wants. In this case, the function needs to see a pointer to a 32-bit variable that it can load with a pointer to a string.

The easiest way to pass a pointer to a 32-bit variable is to pass a Long variable by reference, leading to the following declaration:

```
Private Declare Function StringFromCLSID Lib "ole32.dll" _
(lpclsid As CLSID, lpOlestr As Long) As Long
```

Now all you need to do is figure out a way to retrieve the string data from the Long variable.

You might want to take a few minutes (or hours) to tackle this yourself before reading farther.

The `GetCLSIDAsString` Method

The following code can be used to convert the LPOLESTR string pointer provided by the StringFromCLSID function into a Visual Basic string:

```
Private Declare Function lstrlenW Lib "kernel32" _
(ByVal lpString As Long) As Long
Private Declare Function RtlMoveMemory Lib "kernel32" _
(dest As Any, source As Any, ByVal count As Long) As Long

Public Function GetCLSIDAsString() As String
    Dim cid As CLSID
    Dim StringBuffer() As Byte
    Dim StringLength As Long

    cid = GetCLSID()
    Dim MemoryPointer As Long

    Call StringFromCLSID(cid, MemoryPointer)
    StringLength = lstrlenW(MemoryPointer) * 2
    ReDim StringBuffer(StringLength)
    Call RtlMoveMemory(StringBuffer(0), ByVal MemoryPointer, _
    StringLength)
    GetCLSIDAsString = StringBuffer()
End Function
```

The MemoryPointer variable is a Long variable that is loaded by the StringFromCLSID function with the address of the LPOLESTR string. The first step in converting this string into a Visual Basic string is to find out how long it is. This can be accomplished using the lstrlenW function. The lstrlen API function returns the number of characters in a string. It has two entry points: lstrlenA for ANSI strings and lstrlenW for Unicode strings. Since the MemoryPointer variable will contain the address of a Unicode string, the lstrLenW function is the right one to use. The lpString parameter of the lstrlenW function is declared ByVal As Long because you are passing the address of the string data, which in this case is contained in the Long MemoryPointer variable.

The number of bytes in the string is twice the length of the string. Remember, the lstrlenW function returns the number of characters in the string, and Unicode strings use 2 bytes for each character. The function dimensions a byte array to the size necessary to hold the Unicode string data. The RtlMoveMemory function is then used to copy the text from the MemoryPointer buffer to the new StringBuffer array. Finally, the function takes advantage of Visual Basic's ability to directly assign an array to a string to copy the contents of the byte array to a Visual Basic string—in this case, the string that returns the results of the function.

One More Problem

The program shown here works perfectly.

Or does it?

Try adding the following function to the GUIDPuzzle form:

```
Private Sub cmdMemTest_Click()
    Dim obj As New GUIDObject
    Do While True
        lblGUIDString.Caption = obj.GetCLSIDAsString()
        DoEvents
    Loop
End Sub
```

When you click on the cmdMemTest button, the GetCLSIDAsString function will be called repeatedly. If you're running under Windows NT, bring up the NT performance monitor program (look in the Administrative Tools entry in your Start menu). Add a chart entry that monitors available memory. Scale the chart so that the initial memory usage line appears somewhere near the center of the window.

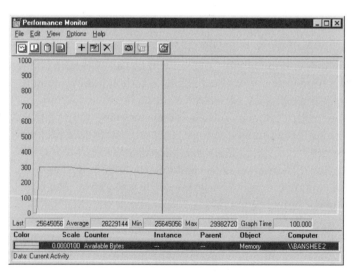

If you're using Windows 95, you can periodically check the amount of available memory by bringing up the About box for an Explorer window. The result will be similar to that shown in Figure S27-3. The amount of available memory is gradually decreasing!

This is called a memory leak, and it's a very

Figure S27-3: NT Performance Monitor illustrates a memory leak easy thing to miss. A memory leak is caused when some part of your program allocates memory but fails to release it. Where is the memory leak in this case?

Look again at Figure S27-2. The StringFromCLSID function loads the MemoryPointer variable that you passed as a parameter with a pointer to the string containing a representation of the CLSID parameter. That string occupies data in memory. Where does the data come from?

The StringFromCLSID function allocates it!

Take another look at the description of the parameters:

Parameters

rclsid
[in] CLSID to be converted.
ppsz
[out] Pointer to the resulting string.

What do the prefixes [in] and [out] mean? Remember that you are now dealing with the OLE subsystem—a part of the Win32 API that works differently in some ways from the regular Win32 API functions. You already saw in the previous puzzle that error handling in the OLE subsystem is different from that in normal Win32 API functions. It turns out that parameters work by different rules as well. Every parameter is defined as being an [in] parameter, an [out] parameter, or an [in-out] parameter.

[in] parameters are allocated and freed by the caller.
[out] parameters are allocated by the API function and must be freed by the caller using the OLE memory allocator.
[in-out] parameters are allocated by the caller and may be freed and reallocated by the API function. The caller is ultimately responsible for freeing the parameter.

In each case, you'll need to refer to the function documentation to determine how to allocate or free the memory in question. OLE actually uses several distinct memory allocation systems depending on the subsystem in use.

In this case, the string whose pointer is loaded into the MemoryPointer variable is allocated by the API function. It is your responsibility to free the buffer when it is no longer needed. Fortunately, this is very easy to accomplish.

The CoTaskMemFree API function allows you to free memory that is allocated by the OLE memory allocator. It is declared in Visual Basic as follows:

```
Private Declare Sub CoTaskMemFree Lib "ole32.dll" (ByVal ptr As Long)
```

Just add the following line of code before the end of the GetCLSIDAsString method to free the string that the MemoryPointer variable points to. The memory leak will vanish.

```
Call CoTaskMemFree(MemoryPointer)
```

SOLUTION 28

Drawing OLE Objects

WHAT IS AN OBJECT?

An object is a thing that exists somewhere in memory on either your system or another. An object variable contains a pointer to a location in local memory that contains an interface—it's actually an array of pointers to functions, but as a VB programmer you don't have to worry about those implementation details. The only way to access an object is through this pointer to an interface. A given object can support many different interfaces.

When you declare different types of object variables, all you are really doing is specifying the type of interface pointer the variable holds. For example, a variable declared As Object always contains a pointer to an IDispatch interface. If you declare a variable as a certain type of class, that variable always contains a pointer to the native interface for that class. Remember, though, every interface is based on IUnknown, so if you have an object variable declared As IUnknown, it can contain a reference to any COM object regardless of the interface you are using. Figure S28-1 illustrates how an object variable points to an interface.[1]

Now let's look again at the C declaration and Visual Basic declaration for the OleDraw function:

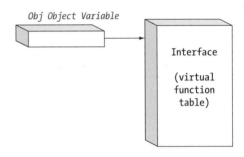

Figure S28-1: Object variables point to a block of memory that defines an interface

```
WINOLEAPI OleDraw(
    IUnknown * pUnk,          //Pointer to the view object to be drawn
    DWORD dwAspect,           //How the object is to be represented
    HDC hdcDraw,              //Device context on which to draw
    LPCRECT lprcBounds        //Pointer to the rectangle in which the
                              //object is drawn
    );
Private Declare Function OleDraw Lib "ole32.dll" _
    (pUnk As Object, ByVal dwAspect As Long , _
        ByVal hdcDraw As Long, _
        lprcBounds As RECT) As Long
```

1. Again, I must stress that, without an understanding of COM, the preceding paragraph is probably incomprehensible. My book *Developing COM/ActiveX Components with Visual Basic 6.0* will give you the necessary background.

The variable pUnk is defined as a pointer to an IUnknown interface. Will a parameter declared As Object work here? Yes, because every object interface is based on IUnknown. But what is actually passed using this declaration? Is it the object variable, or is it a pointer to the object variable?

That's right—pUnk is declared by reference, meaning that a pointer to the pUnk variable is passed to the API function, not the pointer to the interface itself (which is contained in the pUnk variable). So, even though it looks a bit odd, the correct declaration is as follows:

```
Private Declare Function OleDraw Lib "ole32.dll" _
    (ByVal pUnk As Object, _
        ByVal dwAspect As Long, _
        ByVal hdcDraw As Long, _
        lprcBounds As RECT) As Long
```

The reason this looks odd is that we usually think of ByVal as passing a "copy" of a variable. But you already know that strings are an exception. Think of objects as another exception. If an OLE function declares a parameter as IUnknown *, the object should be passed by value. If, however, the parameter is declared as IUnknown **, it indicates that the parameter is a pointer to a pointer to an interface (in other words, a pointer to a variable that contains a pointer to an interface), in which case the object should be passed by reference.

Object Relationships

Once you fix the declaration, you will start seeing error messages to the effect that the object does not support the IViewObject interface. The OleDraw function uses the IViewObject interface to draw the object, so obviously the function won't work on those objects that don't support it. Does this mean you can't use the function to draw controls?

Or does it mean you are passing the wrong object to the function?

This problem is indeed subtle. You see, when you pass a control as a parameter to a function, you are actually passing a reference to the control's extender object—an object that combines the methods and properties of the control with the methods and properties provided by Visual Basic. The Extender does not support the IViewObject interface. Instead, you must pass a reference to the control object itself. This reference can be obtained using the object property of the control, as shown in the following code:

```
Private Sub cmdDrawText_Click()
    DrawTheObject Privatectl1.object
End Sub
```

```
Private Sub cmdDrawWord_Click()
    DrawTheObject MonthView1.object
End Sub

Private Sub Command1_Click()
    PrintTheObject MonthView1.object
End Sub
```

Now, you'll find that the two drawing commands work. But the MonthView control will not print.

Telling Visual Basic to Print

Let's take another look at the PrintTheObject function:

```
Private Function PrintTheObject(obj As Object)
    Dim r As RECT
    Dim res As Long
    Printer.ScaleMode = vbPixels
    r.Right = Printer.ScaleWidth
    r.Bottom = Printer.ScaleHeight
    res = OleDraw(obj, Aspects(cmbAspect.ListIndex), Printer.hDC, r)
    If res <> 0 Then
        Err.Raise res
    End If
    Printer.EndDoc
End Function
```

How does Visual Basic know that you are actually ready to print something? Setting the ScaleMode just lets VB know what scale mode to use once you start drawing into the printer object. The OleDraw command does dump data into the printer's device context, but this bypasses Visual Basic's drawing system, so VB has no way of knowing that you actually performed a drawing operation. Thus, when the EndDoc command occurs, Visual Basic looks and sees that nothing has been drawn, so it does nothing.

It is necessary to trick Visual Basic into initializing the device context before calling the OleDraw function. This is done by changing the function to the following:

```
Private Function PrintTheObject(obj As Object)
    Dim r As RECT
    Dim res As Long
```

```
        Printer.ScaleMode = vbPixels
        Printer.PSet (0, 0)
        r.Right = Printer.ScaleWidth
        r.Bottom = Printer.ScaleHeight
        res = OleDraw(obj, Aspects(cmbAspect.ListIndex), Printer.hDC, r)
        If res <> 0 Then
            Err.Raise res
        End If
        Printer.EndDoc
End Function
```

Printing that single pixel tells Visual Basic that a printing operation has occurred, so it will correctly initialize the device context and will print the page when the EndDoc method is called. You will now see a beautiful full-page calendar page printed.[2]

Conclusion

You may have noticed that the Microsoft MonthView control is able to scale itself to print into the rectangle you provide, whereas the private control written in Visual Basic lacks this ability. This is actually one of the limitations of Visual Basic—it does not provide your control with any mechanism to determine the rectangle provided to the OleDraw function. You can use the ActiveX extension technology in version 6 of Desaware's SpyWorks to detect this rectangle and even override the IViewObject drawing operation, thus allowing your control to scale itself in the same way as the MonthView control.

Also, don't be surprised if this function does not work with every ActiveX control. Even though every ActiveX control is supposed to implement IViewObject correctly, many of them make assumptions internally that prevent them from working with arbitrary device contexts.

Although this puzzle is in the OLE section, it really belongs more in the "Rocket Science" section that follows, because all of the problems faced in solving this puzzle are subtle and require a broad understanding of Windows. Few Visual Basic programmers work extensively with the OLE API—it is indeed complex. But there are many hidden gems, such as this one, that are available to Visual Basic programmers who are willing to dig through the nearly incomprehensible documentation.

---

2. Beautiful, in this sense, does not refer to the aesthetic quality of the image drawn, which admittedly leaves something to be desired. Instead, it refers to the fact that virtually any image would look gorgeous after the frustration you probably felt trying to figure out the solution to this puzzle.

What Do You Do When It Mega Hurts?

THE FIRST STEP IN SOLVING THIS problem is to understand how a C function returns a structure. Figure S29-1 shows the stack frame for a C function that returns a structure (you might want to review Tutorial 4, "How DLL Calls Work: Inside a Stack Frame," found in Part III of this book, before continuing). In order for a function to return a structure, there must exist somewhere in memory a temporary structure to hold the data (since structure data won't fit into registers). The calling function allocates space for this temporary structure on the stack and passes a pointer to the structure as a hidden parameter.

Another way to look at this is as follows. Consider again the declaration for the cpuspeed function:

```
struct FREQ_INFO cpuspeed(int clocks);
```

This looks like a function that takes an integer parameter and returns a structure. But when a Microsoft C compiler calls this function, it interprets it as follows:

```
struct FREQ_INFO *cpuspeed(struct FREQ_INFO *hiddenstructure, int clocks);
```

The calling program knows that it must allocate extra space on the stack for the return value. The cpuspeed function knows that it will see an extra parameter to load with the result data, and that it should return the value of that parameter as a result. How do you know this? Because it is part of the calling convention implementation used by Microsoft compilers, hidden deep within the language documentation. Fortunately, understanding this calling convention is enough to allow you to figure out how to call this function from Visual Basic.

Visual Basic does not allow you to declare an API function that returns a structure. The trick for handling functions that return structures with Visual Basic is based on the fact that the temporary structure need not be on the stack. You can allocate a structure to hold the return value. Instead of having the language pass a pointer to the structure in a hidden parameter, you have to explicitly pass the pointer of the structure. This means adding a fake parameter to the function that will contain a pointer to the structure that is "returned" by the function. The actual stack frame for the cpuspeed function is shown in Figure S29-2.

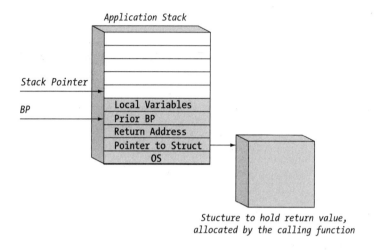

Figure S29-1: How a C function returns a structure

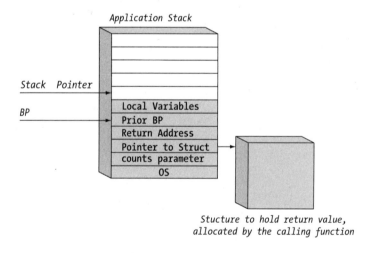

Figure S29-2: The stack frame for the cpuspeed function

```
Declare Function cpuspeed Lib "cpuinf32.dll" (HiddenStruct As _
FREQ_INFO, ByVal counts As Long) As Long
```

The cpuspeed function sees the pointer to the FREQ_INFO structure and loads the structure with the result value before the function returns. The actual return value for the function is the address of the hidden structure, but since the structure passed as a HiddenStruct parameter will be loaded with the result data by the function, you won't need to use this address.

Wait, That's Not All . . .

If you call this function, you'll find it causes a Bad DLL calling convention error. This error occurs when the called function does not restore the stack pointer to its correct location.

But why would you get a calling convention error? Aren't the parameters correct?

They are. The problem is caused by the fact that the cpuspeed function uses the C calling convention. Normally, API calls use the stdcall (standard call) calling convention, in which the calling function pushes parameters onto the stack and the called parameter pops the parameters from the stack (thus restoring the stack pointer to the location it referenced before any parameters were pushed onto the stack). Under the C calling convention, it is the responsibility of the calling function to pop parameters from the stack. The cpuspeed function does not pop the two parameters off the stack as Visual Basic expects, so the Bad DLL calling convention error occurs.

But there are two subtle points to consider:

- Visual Basic is smart enough to detect this situation and fix the stack pointer for you.

- By the time the Bad DLL calling convention error is detected, the temporary structure has already been loaded with the resulting data.

In other words, it is perfectly safe to ignore this error!

The CPUInfo project demonstrates how to use a number of the functions in the cpuinf32.dll to obtain information about an Intel processor. The ShowSpeed function obtains the speed of the CPU using the cpuspeed function and adds the information to the list box, as shown here:

```
Private Sub ShowSpeed()
    Dim freq As FREQ_INFO
    Dim res&
```

```
On Error Resume Next ' Bad DLL calling convention occurs here!
' AND WE DON'T CARE!!!
res = cpuspeed(freq, 0)  ' Always use zero here
lstDisplay.AddItem "Raw CPU Speed: " & freq.raw_freq & " Mhz"
lstDisplay.AddItem "Normalized CPU Speed: " & freq.norm_freq _
& " Mhz"
End Sub
```

Oh, By the Way . . .

This solution won't work for structures that are 8 bytes or shorter. In those cases, the C compiler is smart enough to transfer the data in registers.

How can you handle these smaller structures?

The trick is to set the Visual Basic declaration to return a Currency value. The Currency value just happens to be 8 bytes. You can then copy the data from a temporary currency value into a structure of the correct type.

Here's a short code fragment that shows how it's done:

```
Private Declare Function Test Lib "mylib" ( ) As Currency

Private Sub Command2_Click()
    Dim m As mystruct
    Dim c As Currency
    c = Test( )   ' Store the result in a temporary currency value
    ' Then copy the data from the currency variable into the structure.
    RtlMoveMemory m, c, 8
End Sub
```

File Operations, Part 1

THE OBVIOUS PLACE TO START LOOKING is with the SHFILEOPSTRUCT structure and its VB declaration. After all, what else could the problem be?

As you recall, the C declaration for the structure is as follows:

```
typedef struct _SHFILEOPSTRUCT { // shfos
    HWND           hwnd;
    UINT           wFunc;
    LPCSTR         pFrom;
    LPCSTR         pTo;
    FILEOP_FLAGS   fFlags;
    BOOL           fAnyOperationsAborted;
    LPVOID         hNameMappings;
    LPCSTR         lpszProgressTitle;
} SHFILEOPSTRUCT, FAR *LPSHFILEOPSTRUCT;
```

And the VB declaration for the structure is as follows:

```
Type SHFILEOPSTRUCT
        hwnd As Long
        wFunc As Long
        pFrom As String
        pTo As String
        fFlags As Integer
        fAnyOperationsAborted As Long
        hNameMappings As Long
        lpszProgressTitle As String '  only used if FOF_SIMPLEPROGRESS
End Type
```

Your first thought might be to suspect the strings. If you've read Tutorial 7, "Classes, Structures, and User-Defined Types" (found in Part III of this book), you know that it can be dangerous to use dynamic strings inside structures—especially if the API function modifies the contents of those fields in any way. That's because a dynamic string inside a structure holds a 32-bit BSTR value. The Win32 API does not know how to use BSTRs, so any attempt it makes to modify

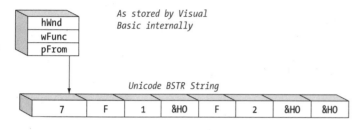

As stored by Visual Basic internally

Unicode BSTR String

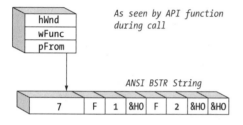

As seen by API function during call

ANSI BSTR String

Figure S30-1: Passing the SHFILEOPSTRUCT structure to an API function

the contents of those fields is likely to cause a memory exception.

What happens when a dynamic string is inside a structure that is passed as a parameter? Visual Basic creates a temporary structure and replaces the BSTR field with an ANSI BSTR string. Figure S30-1 illustrates this for the first three fields in the SHFILEOPSTRUCT structure, where the pFrom field contains two file names, F1 and F2.

As you can see from this illustration, when the function is called, the pFrom field points to an ANSI string that contains the two file names separated by NULL characters, with two NULL termination characters at the end of the string. This is exactly what the API function expects to see, so the only way that this could cause a problem is if the function were somehow modifying the contents of this structure. Is this possible?

The string in the structure is defined in the C declaration as an LPCSTR (LP = Long (far) Pointer, C = Constant, STR = String). The Constant code indicates that the API function will not change the value of the string or the field within the structure. Based on the declaration and documentation, it is safe and correct to use dynamic strings as shown in this example. Nevertheless, it fails.

Structure Alignment Revisited

Let's take a moment to look closely at how the fields in the SHFILEOPSTRUCT structure are laid out in memory. If you look at the start of the shellapi.h header file, you'll see the following line:

```
#include <pshpack1.h>
```

which turns on single-byte packing. That means that the structure will appear in memory as shown in Figure S30-2. Each field of data in the structure appears immediately after its predecessor in memory.

But Visual Basic only uses single-byte packing when writing data to disk files. When structures are passed to API functions, Visual Basic uses natural alignment rules, meaning that each field appears at a memory location divisible by the size of the field. Therefore, 32-bit variables appear at a byte address divisible by 4, and extra padding is added into the structure to enforce this alignment rule. This means the structure that Visual Basic passes to the SHFileOperation function is as shown in Figure S30-3.

The fAnyOperationsAborted, hNameMappings, and lpszProgressTitle fields appear in the wrong place in memory! To prove this, try the program again, but this time do not set the lpszProgressTitle field (delete the line where it is set to a string).

The function now works! Well, it works in the sense that the file is copied and the function does not crash when the program is closed. It still doesn't display a string.

The solution to this problem is simple in concept—you need to some-how compress the structure to eliminate the padding before it is passed to the API function, as shown in Figure S30-4.

The easiest way to do this is to use software that is designed specifically to do UDT packing (user-defined type packing), such as Desaware's SpyWorks package. With this approach, you define the structure fields for the UDT packing program and pass it the structure. The software packs it into a single-byte packed memory buffer and returns a memory buffer you can pass to the API function. It then unpacks the data back into your structure after the function call returns.

This kind of software is especially useful when you have multiple mis-alignments in a structure. When there is only one misalignment, as you have here, you can perform this operation yourself.

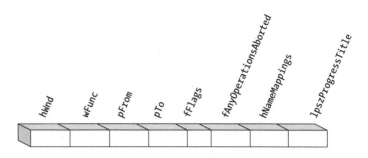

Figure S30-2: Expected layout of the SHFILEOPSTRUCT structure in memory

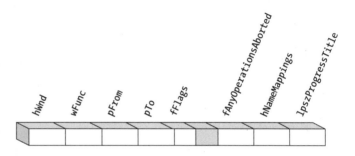

Figure S30-3: Actual layout of the SHFILEOPSTRUCT structure as passed to the SHFileOperation function

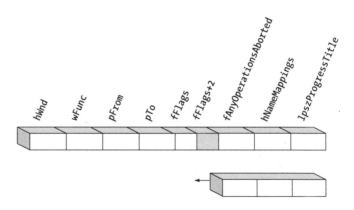

Figure S30-4: Shifting data within the SHFILEOPSTRUCT structure to achieve single-byte packing

The DoACopy function is changed as follows:

```
' Perform a copy operation
Private Sub DoACopy()
    Dim sh As SHFILEOPSTRUCT
    Dim src$, dest$
    Dim res&

    src$ = GetNullsString(FileList)
    dest$ = "A:\" & Chr$(0) & Chr$(0)

    sh.hwnd = hwnd
    sh.wFunc = FO_COPY
    sh.pFrom = src$
    sh.pTo = dest$
    sh.fFlags = FOF_RENAMEONCOLLISION Or FOF_SIMPLEPROGRESS
    sh.hNameMappings = 0

    res = DoTheShellCall(sh, "Files are being copied to floppy")

End Sub
```

We also change the SHFILEOPSTRUCT as shown here so that the lpszProgressTitle field is a Long. Why? Because the DoTheShellCall function is going to shift data within the structure, meaning that the data in the lpszProgressTitle field will change (at least from the point of view of Visual Basic). This is a sure path to a memory exception. By changing it to a Long and explicitly setting the variable to a pointer to an ANSI string, you won't have to worry about Visual Basic getting confused about the contents of that field.

```
Private Type SHFILEOPSTRUCT
        hwnd As Long
        wFunc As Long
        pFrom As String
        pTo As String
        fFlags As Integer
        fAnyOperationsAborted As Long
        hNameMappings As Long
        lpszProgressTitle As Long ' only used if FOF_SIMPLEPROGRESS
End Type
```

The DoTheShellCall function performs the SHFileOperation call and is defined as follows:

```
Private Declare Sub lstrcpy Lib "kernel32" (dest As Any, src As Any)

' Note the alignment tricks here
Private Function DoTheShellCall(sh As SHFILEOPSTRUCT, Optional _
 SimpleCaption As String) As Long
    Dim titlebuf() As Byte
    Dim res&
    ReDim titlebuf(Len(SimpleCaption) + 1)
    Call lstrcpy(titlebuf(0), ByVal SimpleCaption)
    sh.lpszProgressTitle = VarPtr(titlebuf(0))
    RtlMoveMemory ByVal (VarPtr(sh.fFlags) + 2), ByVal _
    VarPtr(sh.fAnyOperationsAborted), 12
    res = SHFileOperation(sh)
    RtlMoveMemory ByVal VarPtr(sh.fAnyOperationsAborted), ByVal _
    (VarPtr(sh.fFlags) + 2), 12
    DoTheShellCall = res
End Function
```

The function allocates a byte array to hold the ANSI string that will contain the desired caption. The lstrcpy function copies the string into the byte buffer. The lstrcpy function in this case has both parameters defined As Any. The first parameter is passed as a byte, so the lstrcpy function sees a pointer to the first byte in the array. The second parameter is passed ByVal As String (notice that ByVal must be included explicitly in the function call because it is not included in the declaration). This causes the string to be passed as a NULL-terminated ANSI string. The lstrcpy function copies that string to the byte buffer.

The lpszProgressTitle field, which is now a Long variable, is loaded with the address of the first byte in this string. The RtlMoveMemory function then compresses the structure. The destination is the address of the padding, which is 2 bytes after the fFlags field, thus the address can be calculated as the address of the fFlags field plus 2. The source is the fAnyOperationsAborted field. A total of 12 bytes are copied. This achieves the movement shown in Figure S30-4.

The memory movement is reversed after the function is called so that you can read the data in the structure correctly, in case you need to examine changes to any of the fields.

That solves the problem of copying files, but, as you will soon see, we have only begun to look at the ShFileOperation function.

File Operations, Part 2

HOW DO YOU START DEALING WITH a problem like this? Just as I did: Take it step by step. In the puzzle, I mentioned it took me about two hours to solve it. As a result, the steps I went through are still fresh in my mind.

Check the Structures

The first step is always to double-check your declarations. In this case, the only new declaration is the SHNAMEMAPPING structure, which was defined as follows in C and in Visual Basic:

```
typedef struct _SHNAMEMAPPING { // shnm
    LPSTR pszOldPath; // address of old path name
    LPSTR pszNewPath; // pointer to new path name
    int   cchOldPath; // number of characters in old path name
    int   cchNewPath; // number of characters in new path name
} SHNAMEMAPPING, FAR *LPSHNAMEMAPPING;


Private Type SHNAMEMAPPING
        pszOldPath As String
        pszNewPath As String
        cchOldPath As Long
        cchNewPath As Long
End Type
```

When you see dynamic strings inside of structures, the very first question to ask is whether there is any chance that the API function will attempt to modify those fields. If the answer is yes, you can't use dynamic strings. This is discussed at length in Tutorial 7, "Classes, Structures, and User-Defined Types" (in Part III of this book). Since the structure here is loaded by the API function itself and the pszOldPath and pszNewPath parameters are both regular NULL-terminated strings (LPSTR), it's clear that these parameters must not be defined as String.

They must be declared as Long variables. You'll have to extract the string information from the pointers using VB code.

First Code Test

My next step was to set a breakpoint at the Call SHFreeNameMappings line in the DoACopy function shown below:

```
' Perform a copy operation
Private Sub DoACopy()
    Dim sh As SHFILEOPSTRUCT
    Dim src$, dest$
    Dim res&

    src$ = GetNullsString(FileList)
    dest$ = "A:\" & Chr$(0) & Chr$(0)

    sh.hwnd = hwnd
    sh.wFunc = FO_COPY
    sh.pFrom = src$
    sh.pTo = dest$
    sh.fFlags = FOF_RENAMEONCOLLISION Or FOF_WANTMAPPINGHANDLE
    sh.hNameMappings = 0

    res = DoTheShellCall(sh, "Files are being copied to floppy")

    If sh.hNameMappings <> 0 Then
            ' Can you read the file names here?
        Call SHFreeNameMappings(sh.hNameMappings)
    End If

End Sub
```

Why did I test the code at this point before any code was written to work with the data? Curiosity, mostly. Also, I was feeling a growing distrust of the documentation. It was very vague—referring to the sh.hNameMappings field as a "handle." What does that mean? Is it a pointer to an array of structures? If so, how do you know how many structures are in the array? Perhaps the final structure is a NULL structure or a structure with empty strings? Perhaps the handle is an array of pointers to structures? I spent a good half hour scouring MSDN and Microsoft's Web site for hints before coming up dry. So I wanted to see what kind of values the field would have.

The results? The hNameMappings field was always zero, no matter what I tried or what files I copied. Zero. NULL. Nada.

I was about ready to decide that it was a Windows bug when, on a lark, I tried it on Windows 95 (most of my development is under NT 4.0). Bingo! A non-zero value appeared any time a file rename occurred.

And no, there is nothing in Microsoft's documentation to suggest that this feature is not supported under NT 4.0. It just isn't.[1]

Reading the Array

Now that I had a "handle," I had to figure out what to do with it. The documentation suggested that the handle contained an array of SHNAMEMAPPING structures. From this it was natural to conclude that the handle was a pointer to an array of these structures. So I wrote the following code:

```
' Perform a copy operation
Private Sub DoACopy()
    Dim sh As SHFILEOPSTRUCT
    Dim src$, dest$
    Dim res&
    Dim NameMapping As SHNAMEMAPPING
    Dim OriginalName As String
    Dim FinalName As String

    src$ = GetNullsString(FileList)
    dest$ = "A:\" & Chr$(0) & Chr$(0)

    sh.hwnd = hwnd
    sh.wFunc = FO_COPY
    sh.pFrom = src$
    sh.pTo = dest$
    sh.fFlags = FOF_RENAMEONCOLLISION Or FOF_WANTMAPPINGHANDLE
    sh.hNameMappings = 0


    res = DoTheShellCall(sh, "Files are being copied to floppy")

    If sh.hNameMappings <> 0 Then
        RtlMoveMemory NameMapping, ByVal sh.hNameMappings, _
        Len(NameMapping)
        If NameMapping.cchOldPath <> 0 Then
            OriginalName = String$(NameMapping.cchOldPath + 1, Chr$(0))
```

```
        Call lstrcpy(ByVal OriginalName, ByVal _
        NameMapping.pszOldPath)
    End If
    If NameMapping.cchNewPath Then
        FinalName = String$(NameMapping.cchNewPath + 1, Chr$(0))
        Call lstrcpy(ByVal FinalName, ByVal NameMapping.pszNewPath)
    End If
    lstFiles.AddItem OriginalName
    lstFiles.AddItem "- renamed to -"
    lstFiles.AddItem FinalName
    Call SHFreeNameMappings(sh.hNameMappings)
  End If

End Sub
```

I still had no idea how to determine how many structures were in the array, but I was confident that, if after running the program the hNameMappings value was non-zero, at least the first entry in the array would be valid.

The RtlMoveMemory function treats the value in the hNameMappings field as a pointer and copies it into a SHNAMEMAPPING structure named NameMapping. The cchOldPath field in the NameMapping structure contains the length of the original file name, so I initialized the OriginalName string to that length (plus 1 for the NULL terminator). The lstrcpy function in this sample program is defined as follows:

```
Private Declare Sub lstrcpy Lib "kernel32" (dest As Any, src As Any)
```

Both parameters are defined As Any, so the function call must explicitly include ByVal terms for both the string and Long parameters. This copies the string pointed to by the pszOldPath field into the OriginalName string. The operation is duplicated for the FinalName string. Finally, the strings are added into the list box.

The initial results of this on my system involved the display of garbage characters in the list box. On your system, it may even crash. When I traced through the program and looked at the actual values of the four fields, I found the following results:

---

1. Oh, you feel the hint for this chapter in Appendix A is unfair (the one that mentioned that the function is documented as running on both NT and Windows 95/98)? Well, I thought it was unfair when I discovered the documentation was wrong. That's part of the point of this puzzle—when what you see in your own experimentation does not match the documentation, there is a very real possibility that the documentation is wrong and you are right.

pszOldPath = 1

pszNewPath = &H828509FC

cchOldPath = 4

cchNewPath = 16

A bit of common sense is in order here. No valid string will have an address of 1. The source file in my test had 15 characters, not 4. Obviously, a handle in this case is not a pointer.

Researching the Handle

Tempting though it was to surrender, my project editor was putting the pressure on to get this puzzle in, and I had already invested a lot of time on the problem. So I decided to take a close look at the contents of this so-called handle. I added the following code to the DoACopy function, bringing the program to the state you'll see in the solution directory in the FileOp2.vbp project (on the CD that comes with this book). The GetDataString function is a memory-viewing function in module errstring.bas and is defined in Tutorial 2, "Memory, Where It All Begins" (in Part III of this book).

```
If sh.hNameMappings <> 0 Then
     OriginalName = GetDataString(sh.hNameMappings, 16)
     Debug.Print OriginalName
     RtlMoveMemory NameMapping, ByVal sh.hNameMappings, _
     Len(NameMapping)
     OriginalName = GetDataString(NameMapping.pszNewPath, 16)
     Debug.Print OriginalName
```

The code is based on the premise that the only field in the memory pointed to by the hNameMappings structure that looks even remotely like a pointer is the data in the pszNewPath field.

The first Debug statement showed the following data:

```
01 00 00 00 FC 09 85 82 04 00 00 00 10 00 00 00
```

The data pointed to by the pszNewPath field, which is at address &H828509FC in this case, showed the following:

```
B4 A4 94 82 CC 22 85 82 0F 00 00 00 1B 00 00 00
```

It looks a lot like a NameMapping structure. The first two 32-bit values are &H8294A4B4 and &H828522CC, which could be pointers. The next two 32-bit values are 15 and 27. The name of the source file was 15 characters, which also suggests that this could be a NameMapping structure.

So what facts did I have?

The handle in the hNameMappings field of the SHFILEOPSTRUCT structure is almost certainly a memory pointer. It points to a block of data that contains at least two 32-bit Long values. The second of those values is a pointer to an SHNAMEMAPPING structure.

What is the first value?

I tried copying two files at once, just to see what would happen. The first value in the memory buffer pointed to by the handle promptly changed to 2.

The Mystery Is Solved

The handle can be treated as a pointer to a structure of my own invention that is defined as follows in project FileOp2B.vbp (on the CD that comes with this book), which can also be found in the solution directory for this puzzle:

```
Private Type SomeSortOfHandle
    mappingcount As Long
    MappingAddress As Long
End Type
```

The DoACopy function has been rewritten as follows:

```
' Perform a copy operation
Private Sub DoACopy()
    Dim sh As SHFILEOPSTRUCT
    Dim src$, dest$
    Dim res&
    Dim NameMapping As SHNAMEMAPPING
    Dim MappingInfo As SomeSortOfHandle
    Dim mappingcounter As Long

    Dim OriginalName As String
    Dim FinalName As String
```

```
      src$ = GetNullsString(FileList)
      dest$ = "A:\" & Chr$(0) & Chr$(0)

      sh.hwnd = hwnd
      sh.wFunc = FO_COPY
      sh.pFrom = src$
      sh.pTo = dest$
      sh.fFlags = FOF_RENAMEONCOLLISION Or FOF_WANTMAPPINGHANDLE
      sh.hNameMappings = 0


      res = DoTheShellCall(sh, "Files are being copied to floppy")

      If sh.hNameMappings <> 0 Then
         ' Copy the mapping structure into a structure we made up
         RtlMoveMemory MappingInfo, ByVal sh.hNameMappings, _
         Len(MappingInfo)
         ' Look at the data for each SHNAMEMAPPING
         For mappingcounter = 1 To MappingInfo.mappingcount
            RtlMoveMemory NameMapping, ByVal _
            CLng(MappingInfo.MappingAddress + Len(NameMapping) _
            * (mappingcounter - 1)), Len(NameMapping)
            If NameMapping.cchOldPath <> 0 Then
               OriginalName = String$(NameMapping.cchOldPath + 1, Chr$(0))
               Call lstrcpy(ByVal OriginalName, ByVal _
               NameMapping.pszOldPath)
            End If
            If NameMapping.cchNewPath Then
               FinalName = String$(NameMapping.cchNewPath + 1, Chr$(0))
               Call lstrcpy(ByVal FinalName, ByVal NameMapping.pszNewPath)
            End If
            lstFiles.AddItem OriginalName
            lstFiles.AddItem "- renamed to -"
            lstFiles.AddItem FinalName
         Next mappingcounter
         Call SHFreeNameMappings(sh.hNameMappings)
      End If

End Sub
```

A structure of type SomeSortOfHandle named MappingInfo is loaded from the address pointed to by the handle using the RtlMoveMemory function. The mappingcount field of this structure contains the number of SHNAMEMAPPING structures in the array that are pointed to by the MappingAddress field. Each SHNAMEMAPPING structure is copied one at a time in a loop into the NameMapping structure.

The following line deserves special attention:

```
RtlMoveMemory NameMapping, ByVal CLng(MappingInfo.MappingAddress _
+ Len(NameMapping) * (mappingcounter - 1)), Len(NameMapping)
```

The second parameter shows a calculation of the address of each structure in the array. The MappingInfo.MappingAddress term is the address of the first structure in the array. The (mappingcounter – 1) * Len(NameMapping) terms calculate an offset to the correct structure based on the value of the mappingcounter loop variable.

The final result is similar to that shown in Figure S31-1.

Conclusion

This may be the most difficult puzzle in the book. But it best illustrates the types of problems you will face if you want to adopt the newest features in Windows. The Win32 API is vast, and sometimes Microsoft's own documentation and examples fall short. If you sometimes have trouble getting accurate answers from Microsoft's technical support, don't be too critical—they may not have the information either. In those cases, trust your own ability to experiment, explore, and ultimately figure out how to make the function work. It's quite possible that the only people who will know the solution at that point are you and the 22-year-old recent graduate Microsoft hired six months earlier, who actually wrote the code.

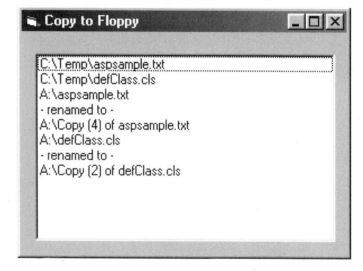

Figure S31-1: Typical display after copying files to floppy disk

SOLUTION 32

Animating Rectangles

YOUR CHALLENGE WAS THREEFOLD:

1.   Figure out how to get the function to perform the animation with the hwnd property set to 0 as described in the function documentation.

2.   Come up with an example that uses the IDANI_OPEN and IDANI_CLOSE animation parameters.

3.   Come up with an explanation that reconciles the behavior of the function in the example with the documentation.

The answers are simple.

1.   I don't know.

2.   I have not found a way to make these work on Windows 95, 98, or NT 4.

3.   My best guesses (and I stress, these are just guesses) are (a) that this is a Windows bug or (b) that the function was defined according to a certain specification but never fully implemented—and nobody bothered to tell the folks who did the documentation.

Until We Meet Again

When I wrote my book *Visual Basic Programmer's Guide to the Win32 API*, I did a fairly good job of covering the majority of API functions that might be of interest to a Visual Basic programmer. In my wildest dreams I did not expect Windows to grow in complexity as quickly as it has. The power of the Win32 API has grown immensely, well past the point where any author can translate it all for use by Visual Basic programmers.

If you have attempted to solve all of the puzzles in this book, I am confident that the scope of API functions you are able to use effectively will have grown from what it was before, even if you did not successfully solve all of the puzzles on your own.

Which brings me to this final puzzle.

I know that many of you will have tried to solve some of these puzzles—especially the later ones—and been frustrated in the process. That frustration is painful, but the knowledge and skills gained should prove worth the effort. Yet even this is only a beginning. New API functions are added daily. That some of them prove beyond my ability to solve will, I hope, increase your confidence in your own ability to tackle even the hardest puzzle and increase your willingness to distrust and take a skeptical view of what others (even Microsoft) tell you.

Finally, I invite you to visit our Web site at *http://www.desaware.com/,* where you will find any revisions and corrections that arise after publication and possibly a new puzzle or two (in fact, a sample puzzle that is not included in this book is already posted).

Oh, yes—if you happen to find the solution to this puzzle, please drop me a line.

Best wishes,
Daniel Appleman
January 1999

Part III

THE TUTORIALS

YOU MAY BE WONDERING WHY THIS part of the book is not Part I. After all, the tutorials that follow provide the fundamental knowledge that is necessary to solve the puzzles.

Well, this is a puzzle book.

I'm sure many readers will just want to dive in and try to solve the puzzles on their own without reading the tutorials. And you know what? Many of them will succeed.

But chances are that you will indeed get stuck on one or more of the puzzles. At that time, I hope you will take a break from the puzzle, curl up in front of a nice warm fire (or lay out on a blanket at a local swimming pool or beach, depending on your climate), and read these tutorials. I think even the experts among you will find them worthwhile.

And for those of you who are absolute API beginners--welcome. This is where you should start before you even look at the first puzzle in the book. By the time you are finished, you should find that the puzzles are not nearly as intimidating as they looked at first glance.

TUTORIAL 1
Finding Functions

IF YOU WERE TO COMPARE THE complexity of the Win32 API and the world's financial systems with regard to international trade, you would almost certainly find that the world's financial system is more complex.

At least for the moment.

If you were to compare the process of world trade with the way Windows manages functions, you might find that they work almost identically.[1]

Think instead, about how countries exchange goods.

A U.S. exporter might have a large supply of jumbo jet airplanes to sell. A Chinese importer might have a sudden need for these jets. A few trans-Pacific faxes later, the deal is done.

Later that day, a U.S. importer might see a great market for fried chocolate bars. He might contact his Chinese friend to see if they have any available. His friend responds that no, they aren't exporting chocolate today. The U.S. importer immediately sends e-mail to exporters around the world to see who can provide the product. If he doesn't find anyone, thousands of potential customers may have to do without their chocolate, and the importer may eventually go out of business.

A trade can occur only if the product an exporter has available exactly matches the product an importer wants to purchase.

When it comes to accessing functions in dynamic link libraries, things work exactly the same way. A DLL may make internal functions available to outside programs and other DLLs by exporting them. It does this by listing them in an internal export list that Windows knows how to examine. A Visual Basic program specifies that it wants to import a file by referencing it in a Declare statement or referencing a type library. The Declare statement contains two pieces of information to specify the function to import: the name of the DLL file and the name of the function. The function name is specified in the "alias" field of the Declare statement. If no "alias" field is present, VB assumes that the function name you specify in the statement is identical to the function name in the DLL.

For example,

```
Declare Sub myfunc Lib "mydll.dll" Alias "otherfunc" ()
```

---

1. No, I'm not referring to the fact that Microsoft finds both equally profitable.

indicates that you wish to import function "otherfunc" from mydll.dll and that you will refer to it in your VB program by the name "myfunc."

On the other hand,

```
Declare Sub myfunc Lib "mydll.dll" ()
```

indicates that you wish to import function "myfunc" from mydll.dll and refer to it in your VB program by the same name.

In the first case, the dynamic link library mydll.dll must export function "otherfunc" or the operation will fail—VB will not be able to find the function. In the second case, mydll.dll must export function "myfunc."

The Declare Statement in Depth

The Visual Basic documentation offers the following syntax for the Declare statement:

```
[Public | Private] Declare Sub name Lib "libname" [Alias "aliasname"]
[([arglist])]
```

```
[Public | Private] Declare Function name Lib "libname" [Alias "aliasname"]
[([arglist])] [As type]
```

Let's look at this one element at a time—see Table T1-1 below.

[Public | Private]	The Declare statement may be prefixed by the keyword Public or Private. The default is Public. There are two general approaches for handling Declare statements in an application. One is to make all of the Declare statements public and place them in a standard module where they can be shared by all the other modules in the application. The other is to make the statements private and place the declarations needed for each module in that module. Larger applications tend to use the former approach. Declare statements in form and class modules must be private.
Declare	The keyword that indicates that this statement is used to define access to an API or DLL function.

Sub | Function	Virtually every Win32 API function returns a Long value and should be declared as a function. You may declare the statement as a Sub if you don't need to refer to the return value. If you declare the statement as a Function, be sure to specify a return value of the correct type. The default return value (variant) will probably cause an error or memory exception.
name	The name by which the function will be called in Visual Basic. Read the notes on the Alias term for more information. This name must follow the same naming rules as any Visual Basic function. For example: the name may not match another name in the same module (regardless of case).
Lib	The term that follows this keyword is the library—the name of the DLL that contains the function.
"libname"	The name of the DLL in quotes. If you are specifying one of the three major DLLs (Kernel32, User32, or GDI32), you need not include an extension. Otherwise, be sure to include the extension (.dll in most cases). You can include a full pathname here, but in most cases you will just include the DLL name so that your application will be able to find the DLL regardless of where the application is installed. Windows will search for the DLL using the standard search rules for the operating system that you are using. The DLL will typically be placed either in the system directory (typically named *windows\\system* for Windows95/8 and *Winnt\\system32* for NT) or in the same directory as the application. Shared DLLs should be placed in the system directory.
Alias	If this term is missing, Visual Basic will assume that the "name" term also specifies the name of the function in the DLL. In this approach, note that the function name specified is case-sensitive (it must match the capitalization of the exported function exactly).
"aliasname"	If specified, this is the name of the exported function in the DLL. This term is case-sensitive.
[([arglist])]	The function parameters. This will be covered in great detail in tutorials that follow.

[As Type]	Functions should always specify a return type, typically As Long. One of the most common mistakes made with the Declare statement is to forget to specify a return type. You can also specify the function type by adding a type character to the name of the function (such as % for integer and & for long).

Table T1-1: Elements in the Declare Statement

Finding Exported Functions

The Windows operating system is made up of a great many DLLs, and figuring out which DLL contains a particular API function can be quite a challenge. Fortunately, there are a number of tools and techniques that can help.

By far the easiest way to find a DLL for a function is to look at an existing correct declaration. There are two primary sources of declarations available to you: the win32api.txt file provided with Visual Basic, and the api32.txt file included on the CD with this book. Now, I must stress the importance of finding a correct declaration, because both of these files may contain errors. The api32.txt file fixes many errors in the win32api.txt file (on which it is based) and did not contain any known errors at the time this book went to press, but I won't claim that it is perfect.

The major limitation with these two files is that they do not contain declarations for every API function. They can't—Microsoft adds new functions and DLLs almost daily.

You see, that's how Windows grows. Microsoft rarely adds new functions to existing DLLs. Instead, they create new DLLs that implement the new functionality. This suggests the next-best approach to determine the DLL that contains a function—common sense.

Table T1-2 below lists some of the most frequently used DLLs and the functionality they implement. If you know what a function does, you can often guess the DLL based on that information. For example, if you have a function that performs a graphic operation on a window, there is an excellent chance that it is in gdi32.dll, the graphic device interface library.

kernel32.dll	This DLL contains functions that implement the operating system kernel. Process management, system functionality, memory management, and most device I/O functions are found in this DLL. You need not include the .dll extension when referring to this DLL in your Visual Basic declaration.
user32.dll	This DLL contains functions that implement the windows-based user interface. Functions that create and manage

(continued)

windows, controls, and dialog boxes are found in this DLL. You need not include the .dll extension when referring to this DLL in your Visual Basic declaration.

gdi32.dll

This DLL contains the functions that implement graphic output to both windows and hard-copy devices. This includes text output. You need not include the .dll extension when referring to this DLL in your Visual Basic declaration.

mpr.dll

This DLL contains device-independent network functions, most with the prefix WNET.

version.dll

This DLL contains functions that work with version resources and obtain information included in these resources. Version resources can help you determine which version of an executable or DLL is most recent.

winmm.dll

This DLL contains a large number of functions relating to the multimedia features supported by Windows. This includes management of audio, video, and joystick devices.

winspool.drv

This DLL contains functions to manage printing and the system print spooler.

lz32.dll

This DLL contains functions to decompress files that were compressed using the Windows compress.exe utility.

shell32.dll

This DLL contains functions relating to some of the high-level user interface functionality provided by Windows. Examples include functions that implement file drag-drop operations and manage associations between files, icons, and documents.

advapi32.dll

This DLL contains functions that perform a variety of advanced tasks. Registry management functions can be found here, along with advanced process and thread management functions. NT services and security functions can be found here as well.

comdlg32.dll

This DLL implements the Windows common dialog boxes used by most Windows applications. These include the File Open, File Save, Font, and Printer Selection dialog boxes, among others.

(continued)

Comctl32.dll	This DLL implements a set of controls called the Windows common controls. These include toolbars and an image list control.
Oleaut32.dll	This DLL contains functions that implement a variety of features relating to OLE automation. These include SAFEARRAY, BSTR, and OLE Variant functions.
Ole32.dll	This DLL contains functions that implement many of the underlying features of OLE (also known as ActiveX) technology.
wsock32.dll	This DLL implements the Winsock API. These functions are used for network communication, typically over the Internet or intranets.

Table T1-2: Common DLLs

Table T1-2 is somewhat misleading. To give you an idea why, try doing a count of the dynamic link libraries (files with a .dll extension) in the system directory on your system. For NT systems, look at the system32 directory. You'll probably find that you have well over 50 of these files. Fortunately, many of them do not expose useful functions.

Ask the DLL

A final approach for finding the correct DLL for a function is to search within the DLL itself. Microsoft's DumpBin.exe program (included with Visual Studio) and the Windows Explorer "QuickView" function can be used to obtain a list of the functions exported from a DLL. The DumpInfo program (included on the CD with this book) can also be used to obtain a list of exported functions for a DLL and has the ability to search through all of the dynamic link libraries in a directory in order to find the DLL that contains a specified function. This program, which includes full source code, also demonstrates a number of advanced API programming techniques and is discussed in detail in Tutorial 9, "Inside a DLL File."

What About Type Libraries?

There is actually another method for accessing API functions from Visual Basic programs that involves use of a type library. Type libraries are written using a language called IDL (Interface Definition Language) and are compiled using a tool called midl.exe, which is included with Visual Basic. Type libraries have the following advantages over the Declare statement:

- They offer slightly better performance.

- API calls made using type libraries take less space in your VB executable.

- You can link the API declarations into a help file.

They have the following disadvantages:

- You must recompile the IDL file every time you make a change.

- Once you have created a function definition in a type library, you should not change it lest you break other applications that use the type library.

- You must learn IDL.

My book *Dan Appleman's Visual Basic Programmer's Guide to the Win32 API* includes a chapter on the creation of type libraries.[2]

This puzzle book exclusively uses the Declare approach to calling API functions. Why? Because solving these puzzles will require experimentation with declarations, and it is far easier to do this kind of experimentation using Declare statements than type libraries. I've found in my own experience that it is easier to develop and test my application using the Declare statement. Once the application is developed, I rarely have a good reason to switch to a type library.

2. The chapter on type libraries is only available in the online version of the book included on the book's CD-ROM—it does not appear in the printed version. The book also includes an API type library that covers all of the functions described in the book, along with source code. The declarations are also linked to the CD-ROM edition of the book, making it very easy to obtain help on any function call.

Memory, Where It All Begins

Warning to non-beginners:

This tutorial covers some very fundamental computer concepts. They may bore you terribly, but I include them here because I've run into a surprising number of Visual Basic programmers who do not understand them. It's not their fault—Visual Basic makes it easy to skip the fundamentals, so there are lots of VB programmers who never learned things that any computer science student learns in the first semester in college, if not earlier. Though much of this book is quite advanced, it is my responsibility to make sure that all of the necessary information is here for those who need it. If you know this material already, great—but you might want to skim through anyway. You never know what surprises I may have in store. . . .

VISUAL BASIC. A LANGUAGE THAT REVOLUTIONIZED Windows programming. A language that is so easy to use that it seems anyone can write a great VB program with almost no training. Why, there are books out there that claim to be able to teach it in a mere 21 days! A language that doesn't require you to know anything about what is going on behind the scenes, right?

So let's say you need to store the number 5 in a program. What's the difference among the following variables?

```
Dim X As Integer
Dim L As Long
Dim F As Single
Dim D As Double
Dim C As Currency
Dim B As Byte
Dim V As Variant
Dim S As String
X = 5
L = 5
```

$$F = 5$$
$$D = 5$$
$$C = 5$$
$$B = 5$$
$$V = 5$$
$$S = 5$$

The difference is that, in each case, Visual Basic stores that number in a different way. The truth is that, as a Visual Basic programmer, you may not even care which type of variable you use. Some so-called Visual Basic "experts" actually encourage people to always use variants so that they never have to worry about the type of variable they are using!

Personally, I consider this approach to be fundamentally silly. It's inefficient, harder to support in the long run, and more prone to bugs. But in many cases, it will work.

However, if you plan to call API or DLL functions from Visual Basic, ignorance of variable types and how they work will ultimately prevent you from doing more than blindly copying other people's declarations and hoping not only that the declarations are correct, but also that they are appropriate to your particular application.

We'll look at these different variable types later. First, let's take a look at the true purpose of variables.

The Inner Life of Variables

The purpose of a variable is to store data. Data is stored in memory.

But what, exactly, is memory?

When you go to your local electronics store, memory means a funny little PC card with some tiny chips on it that you can't believe costs $50, but you're grateful (because you know that it cost twice that last week) and frustrated (because you know it will cost half that next week).

You know that your system has 16MB or 32MB or 64MB or so of memory, but you may not be sure what a MB is (it's a megabyte, meaning a million bytes of data—only it's not a million bytes, it's 1,048,576 bytes—but who cares, since you're not sure what a byte is anyway?).

So I want you to forget all that. How much memory your system has may affect performance, but it means nothing to you as a VB programmer.

What you do need to know starts with a fundamental building block called a bit.

Bits

A bit forms the basis of all computer knowledge. It can have either of two values: 0 or 1.

Let's say you have one bit available to store information. Could you store the number 5 in a single bit? Certainly not—a bit can have only one of two values. But what if you wanted to use a bit to indicate if something is true or false? No problem—true and false are two values. You could also use a bit to indicate if something is on or off, or—in a black and white (monochrome) bitmap—each bit could describe a single pixel as either white or black.

Clearly bits can be useful, but they don't become really useful until you group them together.

Nibbles

The only time you will hear anyone refer to a "nibble" is in cases like this, where someone is trying to teach how binary numbers work. What's a binary number? It's a number that is made up of bits, each of which can take only one of two values (binary). We use nibbles to teach how binary numbers work because it takes up less space than using bytes. You'll see why in a moment.

You know that one bit can store only one of two values. What can you do with two bits?

Two bits can take the following possible values:

SECOND BIT	FIRST BIT
0	0
0	1
1	0
1	1

It may seem odd that I placed the second bit first, but I have an ulterior motive. Suffice it to say that I want you to get in the habit of thinking of the first bit as the one on the right.

Clearly, two bits give you four possible values. You could use them to count from 0 to 3, or from 1 to 4. You could use them to represent four different colors, for example:

SECOND BIT	FIRST BIT	
0	0	Red
0	1	Green
1	0	Blue
1	1	White

You see, the computer doesn't care what you do with those bits. It doesn't know what they mean. Giving meaning to those bits is the programmer's job. Visual Basic variables do this for you most of the time. API and DLL calls often don't. That's one of the reasons that you need to know what's going on behind the scenes.

Now let's say that you have four bits. Four bits are a nibble. Let's say that those bits each have a label indicating their position in the nibble, from Bit #0 to Bit #3. The possible values are as follows:

BIT #3	BIT #2	BIT #1	BIT #0	VALUE
0	0	0	0	0
0	0	0	1	1
0	0	1	0	2
0	0	1	1	3
0	1	0	0	4
0	1	0	1	5
0	1	1	0	6
0	1	1	1	7
1	0	0	0	8
1	0	0	1	9
1	0	1	0	10
1	0	1	1	11
1	1	0	0	12
1	1	0	1	13
1	1	1	0	14
1	1	1	1	15

Now we're getting somewhere. A nibble lets you count up to 16 values, in this case from 0 to 15. Are other values possible? What happens if we say that Bit #3 indicates whether a number is negative?

BIT #3	BIT #2	BIT #1	BIT #0	VALUE
0	0	0	0	0
0	0	0	1	1
0	0	1	0	2
0	0	1	1	3
0	1	0	0	4
0	1	0	1	5
0	1	1	0	6
0	1	1	1	7
1	0	0	0	−8
1	0	0	1	−7

(continued)

1	0	1	0	−6
1	0	1	1	−5
1	1	0	0	−4
1	1	0	1	−3
1	1	1	0	−2
1	1	1	1	−1

A nibble can show up to 16 different values, but the meanings of those values depend on how the computer language chooses to store data. When the highest bit (the one with the highest position number) is used to indicate negative numbers, the variable is considered a signed variable.[1] Otherwise, the variable is considered unsigned. Visual Basic programmers rarely worry about this, because most Visual Basic variable types are signed. But API and DLL functions can use unsigned variables.

Let's say a DLL function has a parameter that takes an unsigned nibble, and you want to pass the number 14 to it. If you have only a signed nibble variable, you could pass it the value −2. Look at the table: 14 unsigned is identical to −2 signed!

Of course, neither DLLs nor the API use nibbles. We only use them here to save us the trouble of looking at larger tables. But this is a very important reason. In fact, before we look at larger numbers of bits, let's agree that from here on we'll deal with them in groups of 4 bits. If we want to work with 16 bits, instead of 0000000000000000 for 16 bits of 0, we'll just use 0000, where each digit represents a nibble. If we want to represent binary 0011 0011 0011 0011, we'll use 3333, since each 0011 has an unsigned value of 3.

But what if we want to deal with the 16-bit binary number 1010 1011 1100 1101? The first nibble is 10, the second 11, the third 12, and the fourth 13. We could write 10111213, but that would be very confusing—it's much easier if each nibble has a single digit. This is fine from 0 to 9, but for higher numbers we need to use letters instead, as follows:

BIT #3	BIT #2	BIT #1	BIT #0	HEX DIGIT
0	0	0	0	0
0	0	0	1	1
0	0	1	0	2
0	0	1	1	3

(continued)

1. It's easy to see why the values 0–7 were assigned to the eight positive numbers, but why do the negative numbers count down from −8 to −1? This is not an accident, but the explanation is unfortunately beyond the scope of this book. The signed format used here is called 2's complement. In this format you can negate a number by complementing it (flipping the value of each of the number's bits) then adding one. This format avoids having a separate positive and negative zero value and makes arithmetic operations with negative and positive numbers work correctly.

0	1	0	0	4
0	1	0	1	5
0	1	1	0	6
0	1	1	1	7
1	0	0	0	8
1	0	0	1	9
1	0	1	0	A
1	0	1	1	B
1	1	0	0	C
1	1	0	1	D
1	1	1	0	E
1	1	1	1	F

Now the 16-bit binary number 1010 1011 1100 1101 becomes ABCD. If you have a 32-bit number to deal with, it's a lot more pleasant to write it as 049AB159 than 00000100101010101000101011001. In fact, it's so much more pleasant that no programmer in his right mind ever uses binary numbers. We use nibbles, where each digit represents four bits. Of course, we don't call it that. Since each digit represents four bits and thus 16 possible values (0–F), we call it hexadecimal (for base 16). In Visual Basic, we give it a prefix &H to indicate hexadecimal; thus we write hex AB15 as &HAB15. A C programmer would use the prefix 0x to indicate hexadecimal, so the same number would appear as 0xAB15.

Bytes

If you've followed along so far, relax—the hardest part is over. You know about bits. You know that the more bits you have, the more possible values they can take on. A single bit can have one of two values. Four bits can have a total of 16 values. Eight bits can have a total of 256 values. The number of possible values is, in fact 2^N, where N is the number of bits (in English, this means that every time you add a bit, the number of possible values doubles).

Eight bits are called a byte. Visual Basic actually has a Byte data type, which is, in fact, the only unsigned data type that Visual Basic supports natively. This means that a byte value can range from 0 to 255.

Bytes are the fundamental unit of measurement for computer memory. What does this mean?

Figure T2-1 shows how memory was organized on the first 8-bit microprocessors. Memory was divided into 65,536 bytes (64K) of memory. Each byte could be addressed individually by the microprocessor. If you wanted to check the value of a particular bit inside a byte, you had to load the entire byte and check the value of that byte to determine whether the bit was set. The process of

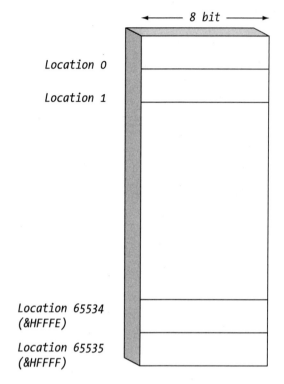

Figure T2-1: 64K of memory on an 8-bit system

checking and setting individual bits will be covered in Tutorial 3, "A Bool and Its Bitfields Are Soon Parted."

On an 8-bit system, memory is accessed by bytes. Every byte in memory has a unique address that corresponds to its location. Thus the address of the first byte of memory is 0, the second is 1, and so on until the end of memory.

Figure T2-2 shows a 32-bit system with 4.2GB of memory. Why 4.2 GB? Because with 32 bits, you can have 4.2 trillion possible values. If those values are memory addresses, you can access up to 4.2 trillion bytes. This is also referred to as a 32-bit address space. Note that the memory is organized a bit differently. Each location in memory is 32 bits wide, yet the address increases by four for each location. What does this mean? It means that the processor reads and writes memory in 32-bit blocks—four bytes at a time. But it is still capable of accessing individual bytes. Why is this important?

If a processor can move data four bytes at a time, it can move data at least four times faster than a processor that can only move data one byte at a time. It's actually even faster than that, because not only are you moving larger blocks of data, you also save all of the extra instructions needed to access the individual bytes. This is one of the main reasons that 32-bit processors are faster than 8-bit processors. What happens if you want to access a 32-bit long variable that is located at address &H100? No problem—the processor goes directly to that address and reads the data in one operation. But what if that long variable is located at address &H101? If you're running an Intel CPU, the processor actually has to perform two separate read operations. Three bytes of the variable can be found at location &H100, but one must be retrieved from location &H104. The CPU must then reassemble the data into a single long variable within the CPU in order to perform operations on the data! This is a time-consuming operation, to say the least. On some processors, the situation is even worse—the processor simply raises an invalid operation fault! This leads to a type of problem called an "alignment problem," which will be discussed in Tutorial 7, "Classes, Structures, and User-Defined Types."

As a Visual Basic programmer, you don't need to worry about these issues; they are well hidden from you. But understanding them becomes absolutely critical for advanced API and DLL calls.

Memory Space

What's this? You don't have 4.2 gigabytes of memory on your system? I confess, neither do I (though I do have that much disk space).

Now, you may know that your system has only 16MB or 64MB of memory. And you may also know that this memory is shared among all the applications running on your system and the operating system itself.

I want you to forget about that.

From now on, all you need to know is that each one of your applications has a full 32-bit address space (4.2 GB) available all to itself. True,

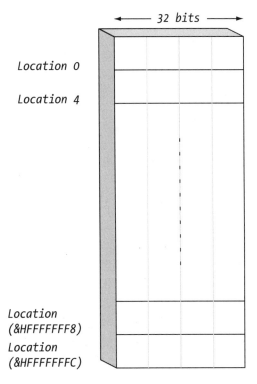

Figure T2-2: Organization of memory in a 32-bit system with 4.2GB of memory

some of that area is reserved for the operating system, and you will rarely allocate memory from this space yourself. Also, most of that memory space does not have any real memory associated with it—if you tried accessing those addresses, you would get a memory exception. The important thing is that, as far as your application is concerned, it has the entire system memory available for itself. This leads to some interesting situations, especially for those used to programming on 16-bit systems. It means that it is notoriously difficult to share memory on Win32 systems. (You can find out more about this subject in Chapter 14 of my book *Dan Appleman's Visual Basic Programmer's Guide to the Win32 API*.)

Back to Data Types

We started this tutorial with some code that stored the number 5 using different types of variables. So, exactly how are those values stored in memory? The Memory.vbp project (on the CD that comes with this book) lets you look inside the individual bytes for each variable to see what it contains. The variables are defined at the form level and set to 5 in the form's Load event. The

RtlMoveMemory API function is declared as well. This function takes two memory addresses and simply copies the number of bytes specified from the source address to the destination address.

```
' MemoryTutorial – A Quick Memory Demo Program
' Copyright © 1998 by Desaware Inc.  All Rights Reserved

Option Explicit
Private Declare Sub RtlMoveMemory Lib "kernel32" (ByVal Dest As _
Long, ByVal Source As Long, ByVal Count As Long)

Dim I As Integer
Dim L As Long
Dim F As Single
Dim D As Double
Dim C As Currency
Dim b As Byte
Dim V As Variant
Dim S As String

Private Sub Form_Load()
    I = 5
    L = 5
    F = 5
    D = 5
    C = 5
    S = 5
    b = 5
    V = 5
End Sub
```

The GetDataString function is what we use to examine the contents of memory. You pass it a memory address and a number of bytes. It starts at the address specified by the Address parameter and copies each byte in turn into a Byte variable called thisbyte.[2] The thisbyte variable is converted into a hexadecimal string using the Hex$ function. Let's say thisbyte contains &H8F. In this case, Hex$(thisbyte) would return 8F. If thisbyte contains the number 5, Hex$(thisbyte) returns 5. In order to keep things even, we add an extra zero if the first nibble of thisbyte

....

2. Purists will note that this function is possibly the least efficient way of displaying memory data. In a real application, I would have copied the data into a byte array and scanned through the bytes one at a time. But the approach shown here, although slow, does clearly illustrate the task at hand—and this is a tutorial, after all.

is zero (thus, thisbyte values of 0–F will actually appear as 00–0F). Tutorial 3 demonstrates how the AND operation is used here to test whether the high nibble is zero.

```
Private Function GetDataString(Address As Long, Bytes As Long) _
As String
    Dim thisbyte As Byte
    Dim offset As Integer
    Dim result$

    For offset = 0 To Bytes - 1
        ' We get the contents of the byte at address+offset
        Call RtlMoveMemory(VarPtr(thisbyte), Address + offset, 1)

        ' If it's 0-15, add a zero.
        If (thisbyte And &HF0) = 0 Then result$ = result$ & "0"
        result$ = result$ & Hex$(thisbyte) & " "
    Next offset

    GetDataString = result$
End Function
```

The Command1_Click routine uses the GetDataString function to retrieve the actual memory contents for each variable. The VarPtr function is a poorly documented Visual Basic function that retrieves the address of a variable in memory. You'll use this function often when working with API and DLL calls. The LenB function returns the size of the variable in memory for most types of variables. (For variants, it returns the size of the data contained in the variant rather than the size of the variant itself. For strings, it returns the length of the string.)

```
Private Sub Command1_Click()
    Dim newline As String
    Dim x&
    List1.Clear

    List1.AddItem "Integer: " & GetDataString(VarPtr(I), LenB(I))
    List1.AddItem "Long: " & GetDataString(VarPtr(L), LenB(L))
    List1.AddItem "Single (Float): " & GetDataString(VarPtr(F), LenB(F))
    List1.AddItem "Double: " & GetDataString(VarPtr(D), LenB(D))
    List1.AddItem "Currency: " & GetDataString(VarPtr(C), LenB(C))
    List1.AddItem "Byte: " & GetDataString(VarPtr(b), LenB(b))
    List1.AddItem "Variant: " & GetDataString(VarPtr(V), 16)
    List1.AddItem "String: " & GetDataString(VarPtr(S), LenB(S))
```

```
For x = 0 To List1.ListCount
    newline = newline & List1.List(x) & vbCrLf
Next x
Clipboard.Clear
Clipboard.SetText newline
End Sub
```

The results shown in the listbox are as follows:

Integer: 05 00
Long: 05 00 00 00
Single (Float): 00 00 A0 40
Double: 00 00 00 00 00 00 14 40
Currency: 50 C3 00 00 00 00 00 00
Byte: 05
Variant: 02 00 00 00 00 00 00 00 05 00 00 00 00 00 00 00
String: E4 05 18 00[3]

The most important thing to notice can be seen with the Integer and Long variables. When you assign 5 to a 16-bit integer, the value in binary will be
0000000000000101 (or &H0005). Remember the number scheme we used originally, in which the rightmost bit was Bit #0? The rightmost bit (or digit) is called
the least significant bit (or nibble) because it represents the smallest change to
the value of the overall number. As you can see in the memory display for these
variables, the least significant digit appears at the lowest address in memory (the
bytes in memory are displayed starting from the lowest memory address). Thus,
the number &H0005 will appear in a memory dump as 05 00. It looks like the
bytes are swapped! They aren't really—it's just how you arrange things on paper.

The Float, Double, and Currency values don't seem to make much sense.
That's because they don't. The internal format used by these data types is something even advanced programmers rarely worry about.

The Variant type is another one you'll rarely worry about. The 02 at the
beginning indicates that the variable contains a signed integer. A variant can
contain many types of variables, so it needs to store the type internally. The 05
appears later in the data area of the variant.

Don't worry about the string—that is definitely a subject for later.

---

3. This value will almost certainly differ on your machine.

Conclusion

This tutorial introduced some critical concepts that form the basis for computer science. Many Visual Basic programmers do quite nicely without understanding these concepts, but you need to understand them in order to work at an intermediate or advanced level.

- You need to understand that a variable is just a way of storing data in memory.

- You need to know the relationship between binary and hexadecimal and how to work with hexadecimal digits.

- You need to understand that memory is a sequence of bytes, each of which can be accessed by its address, but that on a Win32 system the data is actually transferred 32 bits at a time.

We started this tutorial by observing that the number 5 can be stored in different types of variables, and that as long as you are programming within Visual Basic, the language will usually take care of converting between the variable types so that you are always dealing with the number that you expect. But when you declare an API function, the parameter types that you specify in the Declare statement will define how the data is transferred to the API function. If the format of that data in memory does not exactly match the format expected by the API function, the function will fail or the results will be incorrect.

It will take some time to become comfortable with these concepts—at least, comfortable enough so that they become second nature. Don't worry, you'll run into many examples that are built on these concepts throughout this book. Don't hesitate to come back and review this tutorial any time you are confused. The better you grasp these basic fundamentals, the more success you'll have working with advanced techniques.

A Bool and Its Bitfields Are Soon Parted

BOOLEAN ALGEBRA

NOW, THERE'S A TERM GUARANTEED TO sow panic in the heart of almost any non-programmer. And it's amazing how many Visual Basic programmers feel the same way. Don't worry —you may not realize it, but if you've read Tutorial 2, "Memory, Where It All Begins," you already know 90 percent of what you need for even the most advanced Win32 API work.

And if you don't remember much of your high school algebra, don't worry about that either. What little you need to know will be easy to cover in this short chapter, and it will open the door for you to understand everything from combinations of flag constants to how cursors work to conversion of certain complex C data structures.

If you're looking for a mysterious meaning for the word "Bool," you won't find one: Boolean algebra was named after a mathematician named George Boole.

Simple Boolean Operations

You are probably acquainted with the Visual Basic Boolean type. This type of variable can have either of two values: True or False. Hold that thought—we'll return to it later.

Here are a couple of Boolean expressions:

Dim A As Boolean, B As Boolean
A = True
B = Not True

What is the value of B? False, of course. It's logical: Anything that is not True must be False. Boolean algebra is a lot like that—mostly common sense.

We use a special kind of table, called a truth table, to determine the results of a Boolean operation. The truth table for the NOT operation is shown below:

VARIABLE A	RESULT (NOT A)
True	False
False	True

The NOT Operation

The first column contains all of the possible values for the variable. The result is what you get after you apply the operation. Thus, Not True = False, Not False = True.

The NOT operator is the easiest one. There are three Boolean operators in Visual Basic that use two variables: the AND, OR, and XOR operators.

The truth tables for these operators are as follows:

VARIABLE A	VARIABLE B	RESULT (A AND B)
False	False	False
False	True	False
True	False	False
True	True	True

The AND Operation

VARIABLE A	VARIABLE B	RESULT (A OR B)
False	False	False
False	True	True
True	False	True
True	True	True

The OR Operation

VARIABLE A	VARIABLE B	RESULT (A XOR B)
False	False	False
False	True	True
True	False	True
True	True	False

The XOR Operation

You can verify this by running the Boolean.vbp sample project found in the Tutorial Samples directory on the CD-ROM that came with this book.

When you do, just click on the label controls to toggle A and B from True to False and back (don't uncheck the "Use Boolean Variables" checkbox for now).

Booleans and Numbers

The Boolean operations described so far operate on variables that have a True or False value. Visual Basic variables that are declared as Boolean can have only one of these two values.

Consider this simple program:

```
Dim A As Boolean
Dim B As Integer
A = 5
Debug.Print A
B = A
Debug.Print B
```

When you assign the Boolean variable A a non-zero value (5), it is set to True. The first Debug.Print statement will display "True." When you assign A to a numeric variable, the value assigned is –1.

This raises an interesting question. If any non-zero value is True, why use –1?

Believe it or not, this question is not just a narrative tool to help make this part of the book more entertaining. If you don't understand the answer to this question, there is an excellent chance that you will inadvertently add subtle bugs to many of your VB programs that use API functions, the kind of infuriating bugs that can take hours to figure out.

To answer that question, we have to back up and ask this question:

You know how Boolean operations work on Boolean variables based on the truth tables shown earlier in this tutorial. How then, do they work on numeric variables?

A numeric variable is made up of bits (as described in Tutorial 2, "Memory, Where It All Begins"). Byte variables have 8 bits, integers have 16 bits, and longs have 32 bits. Each of these bits can have a 1 or 0 value (which, in a sense, corresponds to True or False).

For example:

If you apply the NOT operator to a 16-bit variable containing the number 5, you get

```
5 = 0000000000000101 (binary)
Not 5 -> Not 0000000000000101 (binary) -> 1111111111111010 (binary) -> &HFFFA
(hex) -> -6 (decimal)
```

As you see, the NOT operation is applied to each bit.

What happens when you use an operator that acts on two variables? The operation is applied to each pair of bits on the two variables. For example:

```
5 Or 2 ->
0000000000000101 (binary) Or 0000000000000010 (binary) ->
0000000000000111 (binary) -> 7
5 Or 2 = 7
```

You can use the Boolean.vbp project (in the Tutorials section on the CD-ROM) to experiment with different numbers and Boolean operators. Just uncheck the "Use Boolean Variables" checkbox to experiment with numbers. I encourage you to enter hex values in the two text boxes for your experiments (just precede the value with &H). The results will be displayed in hexadecimal, and you should grow accustomed to using only hexadecimal when dealing with Boolean operations.

Why is this important?

Because there are many situations where API functions and structures deal with individual bits and groups of bits within a numeric variable.

Combining Bits Using the OR Operator

Let's say you want to use the SetWindowPos function to change the position of a window on the screen. This function has a number of capabilities beyond those provided by the simple Move function included in Visual Basic. For example, you can set a window to be a "topmost" window, meaning that it will appear above other windows, even when it is not active. The exact operation of the function is defined by a "flag" parameter that is partially described in the Win32 documentation as follows:

> *uFlags*
> *Specifies the window sizing and positioning flags. This parameter can be a combination of the following values:*

VALUE	MEANING
SWP_HIDEWINDOW	Hides the window.
SWP_NOACTIVATE	Does not activate the window. If this flag is not set, the window is activated and moved to the top of either the topmost or non-topmost group (depending on the setting of the hWndInsertAfter parameter).
SWP_NOCOPYBITS	Discards the entire contents of the client area. If this flag is not specified, the valid contents of the client area are saved and copied back into the client area after the window is sized or repositioned.
SWP_NOMOVE	Retains the current position (ignores the X and Y parameters).
SWP_NOSIZE	Retains the current size (ignores the cx and cy parameters).
SWP_NOZORDER	Retains the current Z order (ignores the hWndInsertAfter parameter).
SWP_SHOWWINDOW	Displays the window.

Don't worry for now if you don't understand the meanings of these parameters or the meaning of the word "flag" in this context—we'll get to that in a moment. You'll see this kind of parameter with many API functions. What does it mean when it says "a combination of the following values"? These values are names of constants defined in the api32.txt file included with this book. Let's take a look at the actual values of these constants:

```
Public Const SWP_NOSIZE = &H1
Public Const SWP_NOMOVE = &H2
Public Const SWP_NOZORDER = &H4
Public Const SWP_NOACTIVATE = &H10
Public Const SWP_SHOWWINDOW = &H40
Public Const SWP_HIDEWINDOW = &H80
Public Const SWP_NOCOPYBITS = &H100
```

Look carefully at the values themselves. They are all hex values. Picture the values in binary (you should be able to do this in your head, but feel free to look at the tables in Tutorial 2 if you need to). You should see

```
Public Const SWP_NOSIZE =     &H1 =   0000000000000001
Public Const SWP_NOMOVE =     &H2 =   0000000000000010
Public Const SWP_NOZORDER =   &H4 =   0000000000000100
Public Const SWP_NOACTIVATE = &H10 =  0000000000010000
Public Const SWP_SHOWWINDOW = &H40 =  0000000001000000
Public Const SWP_HIDEWINDOW = &H80 =  0000000010000000
Public Const SWP_NOCOPYBITS = &H100 = 0000000100000000
```

See it now? Each of the constants represents a number where a single bit is set. Not every bit has a constant in this listing, but that's because only a partial list is shown here to conserve space. A 32-bit long parameter can have up to 32 options specified in this way, one for each bit. The uFlags parameter is a 32-bit value, though only 16 bits are shown in the listing above.

Let's say you wanted to ignore the move parameters, ignore the size parameters, and hide the window without changing its position in the Z-order. To do this, you would need to combine the SWP_NOSIZE, SWP_NOMOVE, SWP_NOZORDER, and SWP_HIDEWINDOW constants.

What happens if you combine them using the AND operator?

```
&H1 And &H2 And &H4 And &H80 = 0
```

because for each pair of bits, 1 AND 0 = 0.

But if you use the OR operator, you get the following:

```
SWP_NOSIZE Or SWP_NOMOVE Or SWP_NOZORDER Or SWP_HIDEWINDOW ->
&H1 Or &H2 Or &H4 Or &H80  -> &H87 -> 000010000111 in binary.
```

Look at the binary values of each constant and the binary value of the result. The OR operator does, in effect, combine the individual bits.

Why take this approach for passing instructions to a function? Because if you used a separate parameter for each option, you would end up with functions that have dozens of parameters. And each parameter requires not only extra memory space when the function is called, but extra CPU operations to store the parameter on the stack when the function is called. Using individual bits in parameters in this manner is extremely efficient. By specifying constants that represent single bits, it is possible to precisely set any combination of bits using the OR operator. Any parameter or variable whose meaning is defined by individual bits that have separate definitions is called a flag variable, and the individual bits are called flag bits.

What about the meanings of the individual constants and use of the SetWindowPos function? The declarations and purposes of this function and other specific API functions can be found in my book *Dan Appleman's Visual Basic Programmer's Guide to the Win32 API* or other Win32 API reference. That level of detail is simply beyond the scope of this book.

Discovering Bits Using the AND Operator

Let's say you wanted to obtain information about a window in the system. Does it have a border? Is it minimized or maximized? Does it have a vertical or horizontal scrollbar? The Win32 API could define separate functions for each of these questions, but that would be very inefficient. After all, each of these questions has a simple yes or no answer, which can be represented by a single bit. In fact, this information is stored internally to the Window as a 32-bit long value called the window style. You can retrieve this value using the GetWindowLong function as follows:

```
Public Const GWL_STYLE = (-16)
Declare Function GetWindowLong Lib "user32" Alias _
"GetWindowLongA" (ByVal hwnd As Long, ByVal nIndex As Long) As Long
' Get the class info
  style& = GetWindowLong&(useHwnd&, GWL_STYLE)
```

Here are some of the available window styles:

```
Public Const WS_MINIMIZE = &H20000000
Public Const WS_VISIBLE = &H10000000
Public Const WS_DISABLED = &H8000000
Public Const WS_MAXIMIZE = &H1000000
Public Const WS_BORDER = &H800000
Public Const WS_VSCROLL = &H200000
Public Const WS_HSCROLL = &H100000
```

Let's say you determine that a window has a style of &H1A00000.

Can you determine if it has a horizontal scrollbar set?

To do this, you need to be able to determine the value of a single bit. Let's start with a simple example. Take the number 5, or 101 (binary). Define three constants as follows:

```
BIT0 = &H1
BIT1 = &H2
BIT2 = &H4
```

Now consider what happens if you use the AND operator with each of these values:

```
BIT0 And 5 -> 001 And 101 -> 001
BIT1 And 5 -> 010 And 101 -> 000
BIT2 And 5 -> 100 And 101 -> 100
```

When a bit in the constant is 0, the resulting bit is forced to be 0—that's the nature of the AND operator. When a bit in the constant is 1, the resulting bit depends on the value of the second parameter—in this case, the number 5. The constant, in effect, serves as a mask, allowing only those bits that you select in the result. In fact, constants used in this manner are often referred to as mask constants.

So, does our window have a horizontal scrollbar? To find out, we use the AND operator with the WS_HSCROLL mask constant:

```
style &And WS_HSCROLL -> &H1A00000 And &H100000 -> 0
```

You can draw out the binary values for yourself if you wish.

Does it have a vertical scrollbar?

```
style &And WS_VSCROLL -> &H1A00000 And &H200000 -> &H200000
```

The WS_VSCROLL bit is set in the style, so the window does have a vertical scrollbar. You can take advantage of the fact that the resulting number is non-zero only if the bits identified by the mask are set. The If/Then statement will interpret the &H200000 value as True, so the statement

```
If style& And WS_VSCROLL Then
```

will execute the code within the condition block if the vertical scrollbar is present.

The following excerpt from the Winview.vbp program in Chapter 5 of my Win32 API book shows how you can build a string describing the styles of a window. An introduction to window and class styles can be found in Chapter 2 of that book:

```
If style& And WS_BORDER Then
    outstring$ = outstring$ + "WS_BORDER" + crlf$
End If
If style& And WS_DISABLED Then
    outstring$ = outstring$ + "WS_DISABLED" + crlf$
End If
If style& And WS_HSCROLL Then
    outstring$ = outstring$ + "WS_HSCROLL" + crlf$
```

```
    End If
    If style& And WS_MAXIMIZE Then
        outstring$ = outstring$ + "WS_MAXIMIZE" + crlf$
    End If
    If style& And WS_MINIMIZE Then
        outstring$ = outstring$ + "WS_MINIMIZE" + crlf$
    End If
    If style& And WS_VSCROLL Then
        outstring$ = outstring$ + "WS_VSCROLL" + crlf$
    End If
```

Clearing a Bit

You know that you can set a bit using the OR operation. To set bit 1 you would use

```
Variable = Variable Or BIT1
```

How do you clear a bit? Obviously the OR operator won't do the trick.
    You could try

```
Variable = Variable And BIT1
```

Imagine the variable contained the value 6 when you performed this operation:

```
6 And BIT1 = 6 And 2 = 0110 (binary) And 0010 (binary) = 0010 = &H2.
```

This won't do. It clears every bit except for bit 1—the opposite of what you want to do. The AND operation can determine if a bit is set, but can it clear a bit?
    Yes. Remember, the AND operator can force any bit to 0. The trick is, the mask has to have a 0 for the bit you want to clear, not a 1. And it has to have a 1 for the bits you want to preserve, not a 0. Which operator changes bit values in this way? The NOT operator.
    Try this:

```
6 And (Not BIT1) = 6 And (Not 2) = 0110 And (Not 0010) = 0110 And 1101 = 0100 = &H4.
```

Bit 1 has been successfully cleared!

The Magic of XOR

The final Boolean operation we'll concern ourselves with is the XOR, or "exclusive-or" operator. It's a rather peculiar operator, and beginners usually have a hard time seeing what it might be good for. Let's take a hypothetical example where a variable has three flag bits. The bits have constants BIT0, BIT1, and BIT2, defined earlier in this tutorial.

Now let's try something a little bit different. What happens if you use the XOR operator using the BIT1 mask?

```
6 Xor BIT1 -> 0110 Xor 0010 -> 0100 = &H4
```

The XOR operator cleared the bit in one operation. What happens if you perform the same operator again on the result?

```
4 Xor BIT1 -> 0100 Xor 0010 -> 0110 -> &H6
```

The bit has been set!

To summarize:

To set a bit, use the OR operator with a bit mask.

To check a bit, use the AND operator with a bit mask.

To clear a bit, use the AND operator with the inverse bit mask (the bit mask after the NOT operator has been applied).

To toggle a bit, use the XOR operator.

The most important place where you'll toggle bits will be with graphic operations. The XOR operator is unique in that, if you apply it to a variable then apply it again to the result, you'll get the original value. If you use the XOR operator in image operations, you can apply it once to modify an image (say, by drawing a line or combining a second image with the first), then again to restore the previous image. Sprites, animation, and cursors frequently use the XOR operator in this way.

The XORLine.vbp sample program on the CD-ROM for this book illustrates this. To test it for yourself, create a form with the following properties:

BorderStyle	3 - Fixed Dialog
DrawMode	7 - Xor Pen
ForeColor	&H00FFFFFF& (white pen)

```
' XORLine Example
' Copyright © 1998 by Desaware Inc. All Rights Reserved

Option Explicit

Dim PrevX As Single
Dim PrevY As Single
Dim centerX As Single, centerY As Single

Private Sub Form_Load()
    PrevX = -1
    PrevY = -1
    centerX = Width / 2
    centerY = Height / 2
End Sub

Private Sub Form_MouseMove(Button As Integer, Shift As Integer, _
X As Single, Y As Single)
    ' If same location, leave right away
    If X = PrevX And Y = PrevY Then Exit Sub

    If PrevX >= 0 Then
        ' Erases the previous line
        Line (centerX, centerY)-(PrevX, PrevY)
    End If
    Line (centerX, centerY)-(X, Y)
    PrevX = X
    PrevY = Y
End Sub
```

You'll see that as you move your mouse over the form, a line is drawn from the center of the form to the mouse. The routine keeps track of where the current line is, so when a new MouseMove event arrives, it can erase the previous line before drawing the new one. How does it erase the previous line? By repeating the previous drawing operation. This works because the drawing mode is set to XOR mode. This means that the pen color is applied to the form color using the XOR operation. The pen color is white—all bits are set to 1, so the result is to toggle the value of the bits on the form as specified by the mouse movement.

Try changing the background color of the form and see how the actual line color changes.

Boolean Comparisons

A long time ago (toward the beginning of this tutorial), I mentioned that it is crucial to understand why Visual Basic Boolean variables always have the value –1.

To see why this is the case, let's go back to the sample code shown on page 11 for detecting if a window has a border.

```
' Get the class info
    style& = GetWindowLong&(useHwnd&, GWL_STYLE)

If style& And WS_BORDER Then
    ' This code will execute if the window has a border
End If
```

This code will work because, if the window has a border, the expression "style& And WS_BORDER" will result in the value &H800000. This value is non-zero, so the conditional statement will work.

What would happen if you wrote your code to determine if the window did not have a border?

```
If Not (style& And WS_BORDER) Then
    ' This code should execute if the window does not have a border
End If
```

If the window does not have a border, the expression "Not (style& And WS_BORDER)" will result in "Not 0", which results in –1, or True. So the conditional statement will execute.

If the window does have a border, the expression will result in "Not &H800000", which is equal to &H7FFFFF, which is also non-zero and thus True. So the conditional statement will execute.

The condition code will always execute in this case. Clearly, this is a bug. And it's one that can be very hard to discover.

That's why Visual Basic Boolean variables always use –1 for True and 0 for False. If they didn't, conditional expressions would fail.

Why is this important for API programmers? Because whereas Visual Basic consistently uses –1 for True, the Win32 API uses any non-zero value, especially the number 1, to indicate a True result.

The best way to deal with this situation is to always compare results of API functions or bit operations with zero before doing the comparison. The example shown above can be dealt with easily using the following code:

```
If Not ((style& And WS_BORDER)<>0) Then
    ' This code will execute if the window does not have a border
```

```
End If
```

or

```
If (style& And WS_BORDER)=0 Then
    ' This code will execute if the window does not have a border
End If
```

C and Booleans

Now that you understand how Visual Basic uses Boolean operators, it's time to take a quick look at how the C language differs from VB. Visual Basic Boolean variables are identical to integer variables. And because Visual Basic Boolean operators act on each bit in a variable, you must set variables to –1 for True and 0 for False in order for comparisons to work correctly.

The C language takes a radically different approach. It defines two distinct sets of Boolean operators. The first set is designed for comparisons; they base their operation on the value of the entire variable, where a 0 value indicates False and any non-zero value indicates True. These operators are as follows:

C OPERATOR	MEANING
&&	Logical AND
||	Logical OR
!	Logical NOT

For example: consider the results of the ! operator on 0, 1, and –1:

> !0 = Any value other than 0
> !1 = 0
> !-1 = 0

These operators do not work on each bit in the variable, but on the variable as a whole. The Win32 API was initially designed to be used from the C language, so it was perfectly reasonable for the designers of the Win32 API to return any non-zero value to indicate a True result. They knew that programmers would be using the C Logical Boolean comparisons, which would always work correctly with any value.

But what do C programmers do when they need to work with individual bits—combining values using the OR operation or masking them using the AND operation? The C language provides a different set of operators for these "bit-wise" Boolean operations:

C OPERATOR	MEANING
&	Bitwise AND
|	Bitwise OR
~	Bitwise NOT
^	Bitwise XOR

You will occasionally run into these operators when reading C header files.

C Bitfields

The C and C++ language occasionally makes use of a feature called a bitfield. With bitfields, individual bits in a variable in a structure are assigned a particular meaning. Consider the DCB structure shown here:

```
typedef struct _DCB { // dcb
    DWORD DCBlength;          // sizeof(DCB)
    DWORD BaudRate;           // current baud rate
    DWORD fBinary: 1;         // binary mode, no EOF check
    DWORD fParity: 1;         // enable parity checking
    DWORD fOutxCtsFlow:1;     // CTS output flow control
    DWORD fOutxDsrFlow:1;     // DSR output flow control
    DWORD fDtrControl:2;      // DTR flow control type
    DWORD fDsrSensitivity:1;  // DSR sensitivity
    DWORD fTXContinueOnXoff:1; // XOFF continues Tx
    DWORD fOutX: 1;           // XON/XOFF out flow control
    DWORD fInX: 1;            // XON/XOFF in flow control
    DWORD fErrorChar: 1;      // enable error replacement
    DWORD fNull: 1;           // enable null stripping
    DWORD fRtsControl:2;      // RTS flow control
    DWORD fAbortOnError:1;    // abort reads/writes on error
    DWORD fDummy2:17;         // reserved
    WORD wReserved;           // not currently used
    WORD XonLim;              // transmit XON threshold
    WORD XoffLim;             // transmit XOFF threshold
    BYTE ByteSize;            // number of bits/byte, 4-8
    BYTE Parity;              // 0-4=no,odd,even,mark,space
    BYTE StopBits;            // 0,1,2 = 1, 1.5, 2
    char XonChar;             // Tx and Rx XON character
    char XoffChar;            // Tx and Rx XOFF character
    char ErrorChar;           // error replacement character
    char EofChar;             // end of input character
```

```
    char EvtChar;              // received event character
    WORD wReserved1;           // reserved; do not use
}
```

Details on how different variable types are handled can be found in Tutorial 6, "C++ Variables Meet Visual Basic." For now, all you need to know is that a "struct" in C++ will become a Visual Basic user-defined type and that a DWORD refers to a 32-bit Long variable. Look only at the first three fields in this C structure.

The first is a 32-bit Long called DCBlength.

The second is a 32-bit Long called BaudRate.

The third is not a variable called fBinary. It is a 32-bit Long variable whose bits are defined as follows:

Bit 0 is fBinary
Bit 1 is fParity
Bit 2 is fOutxCtsFlow
Bit 3 is fOutxDsrFlow
Bit 4 and 5 are fDtrControl
Bit 6 is fDsrSensitivity
Bit 7 is fTXContinueOnXoff
Bit 8 is fOutX
Bit 9 is fInX
Bit 10 is fErrorChar
Bit 11 is fNull
Bit 12 and 13 are fRtsControl
Bit 14 is fAbortOnError
Bit 15–31 are not used

The : (colon) character following the variable name indicates that the variable consists of a specified number of bits. Since Visual Basic does not support the concept of bitfields, all of these bits are combined together into a single 32-bit Long variable. A VB program needs to use Boolean operations to set, clear, and determine the value of individual bits.

The actual DCB structure in Visual Basic is defined as shown here. All of the bit fields listed above are combined into the single "Bits1" field.

```
Type DCB
    DCBlength As Long
    BaudRate As Long
    Bits1 As Long
    wReserved As Integer
    XonLim As Integer
    XoffLim As Integer
```

```
    ByteSize As Byte
    Parity As Byte
    StopBits As Byte
    XonChar As Byte
    XoffChar As Byte
    ErrorChar As Byte
    EofChar As Byte
    EvtChar As Byte
        wReserved1As Integer
End Type
```

For example, if you have a DCB variable named DCB1 and want to enable parity checking, you would perform the following operation:

```
DCB1.Bits1 = DCB1.Bits1 Or &H02(set bit 1)
```

If you want to turn off parity checking, you would perform this operation:

```
DCB1.Bits1 = DCB1.Bits1 And (Not &H02&)
```

If you want to execute a block of code only if parity is enabled, you would use code like this:

```
If (DCB1.Bits1 And &H2)<>0 Then
        ' Parity is Enabled
End If
```

Now look for a moment at the field labeled fDtrControl. This field consists of two bits, because the control of the DTR line (a signal used for serial communication) is not a simple Boolean operation. This signal can have three possible modes. It takes two bits to represent three values—in this case, the values 0 through 2—described by the following constants:

Public Const DTR_CONTROL_DISABLE = &H0
Public Const DTR_CONTROL_ENABLE = &H1
Public Const DTR_CONTROL_HANDSHAKE = &H2

We know that the fDtrControl bits are located at bits 4 and 5 in the Bits1 variable. How do we extract the value so that we can read it?

The first step is to create a mask so that we are only looking at the fDtrControl bits. The mask needs to have bits 4 and 5 set. In binary, this can be seen as 0000000000110000, which is &H30.

The bits can be extracted as follows:

```
DtrBits = DCB1.Bits1 And &H30
```

Now, how do you get the two bits to the point where you can compare them with the three constants? You need to shift them so that, instead of bits 4 and 5, they will be located at bits 0 and 1. You can shift bits one value to the right by dividing the number by 2.

Want proof? Check out the table below.

NUMBER	IN BINARY	DIVIDED BY 2	IN BINARY
16	10000	8	1000
8	1000	4	100
4	100	2	10
2	10	1	1

Dividing by 2 shifts bits to the right. Multiplying by 2 shifts bits to the left. The only case you have to watch for is the high bit (bit 31 in a long variable), where you can run into an overflow situation. But that doesn't apply to this case because the high bit is not used.

For the fDtrControl bits, we need to shift the DtrBits value 4 bits to the right, as follows:

```
DtrValue = DtrBits / &H10000
```

To check whether DTR control is enabled, you can compare the value with the constant, as follows:

```
If DtrValue = DTR_CONTROL_ENABLE Then
        ' DTR_CONTROL_ENABLE is set
End If
```

Let's say you want to set the fDtrControl bits to DTR_CONTROL_HANDSHAKE. To do this, you must reverse the process, as follows:

```
DtrValue = DTR_CONTROL_HANDSHAKE          ' Set the value
DtrBits = DtrValue * &H10000              ' Shift the bits to the left
DCB1.Bits1 = DCB1.Bits1 And (Not &H30)    ' Clear the two bits
DCB1.Bits1 = DCB1.Bits 1Or DtrBits        ' Or in the desired value
```

You may want to step through this process by writing out the values on paper for several values to see how it works.

Packing Integers into Long Variables

There is one special case, very similar to bitfields, that is seen frequently when using the Win32 API. You've seen that bitfields allow you to pack groups of one or more bits into a single 32-bit Long variable. You know that a VB integer variable is 16 bits. Clearly, it is possible to pack two 16-bit integers into a 32-bit long variable. A classic example of this is when two 16-bit mouse coordinates are packed into a long value for the internal Windows mouse messages. The X mouse coordinate is kept in the lower 16-bit integer, the Y coordinate in the upper integer.

To combine integers X and Y into long variable L, do the following:

```
Dim XL As Long, YL As Long
' Both values are converted into Longs in order to prevent overflows.
' They are masked with &H7FFF to eliminate errors due to sign extension
XL = X And &H07FFF&
YL = Y And &H07FFF&
YL = YL * &H10000&
```

To divide long variable L into integers X and Y, do the following:

```
Dim XL As Long, YL As Long
XL = L And &H07FFF&          ' Extract the X value
X = XL                       ' Because of the mask we chose,
                                 there can be no overflow

YL = L And &H7FFF0000&
YL = YL / &H10000&
Y = YL
```

This example will only work with positive integer variables. With negative values, you have to take additional steps to prevent possible overflow errors. That's why this kind of packing and unpacking is often best done in a DLL support library written in C++, such as the apigid32.dll DLL included with this book. Refer to Appendix C, which describes the agDWORDto2Integers and agPOINTStoLong functions that can be used to perform these operations.

How DLL Calls Work: Inside a Stack Frame

Runtime Error 49
Bad DLL Calling Convention Error.

LOOK FAMILIAR?

This is the error message you get when your Declare statement for a DLL or API call is incorrect—if you're lucky. If you're not lucky, your declaration will have one of the many errors that Visual Basic can't detect. But that's another story.

So where does this error come from? Why does Visual Basic detect some DLL declaration errors and not others? To understand the answer, you'll have to look deep under the hood at the actual mechanism by which functions are called—and at something called a stack frame.

Stack frame? Sounds like one of those esoteric computer science terms that are designed to intimidate the uninitiated. That's probably because it is an esoteric computer science term designed to intimidate the uninitiated.

Seriously—to understand a stack frame, you must first know what a stack is.

The Stack

A stack is a data structure in memory on which two standard operations are performed. These operations are "push," which places data on the stack, and "pop," which removes data from the stack. A stack is a "Last In First Out" structure, in which the last data item placed on the stack is always the first one removed.

Figure T4-1 illustrates the push and pop operations on a simple stack that holds 32-bit Long values.

The first illustration shows the empty stack. Each stack has a stack pointer that points to the top value on the stack. This pointer can be a variable that contains a memory address, or (if the stack is implemented in an array) it can be the array index of the top data item in the array. It is not uncommon for stacks to be implemented using arrays in Visual Basic.

When a data item is pushed onto the stack, the stack pointer is moved to the next location, and the data is placed in the location referred to by the stack pointer. When the pop operation is executed, the data item referred to by the

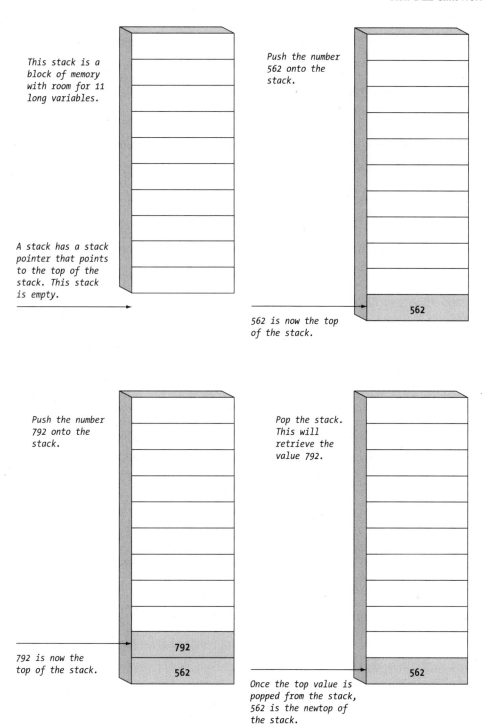

This stack is a block of memory with room for 11 long variables.

A stack has a stack pointer that points to the top of the stack. This stack is empty.

Push the number 562 onto the stack.

562 is now the top of the stack.

Push the number 792 onto the stack.

792 is now the top of the stack.

Pop the stack. This will retrieve the value 792.

Once the top value is popped from the stack, 562 is the newtop of the stack.

Figure T4-1a–d: How stacks work

stack pointer is returned (as a result of the pop function) and the stack pointer is moved to the previous location.

All it takes to implement a stack is to allocate a block of memory and operate on it using the push and pop operations. Stacks are not often used in general purpose applications, thus many Visual Basic programmers are not familiar with them. But they are an essential part of every function or subroutine call.

When an application is loaded, space is allocated in memory for a stack that will belong to the process. This is called the application stack or process stack. Your computer's CPU provides efficient hardware support for an application's stack. A CPU has a hardware register dedicated to work as a stack pointer that contains the location of the top data item on this stack. It also provides machine language push and pop instructions, along with instructions that can push and pop multiple items to and from a stack in a single operation.

There are two other facts to keep in mind when dealing with your application's stack. First, every entry in the stack is 32 bits wide. If you want to place a smaller item on the stack, the extra space is unused. If you want to place a larger item on the stack, that item must span multiple 32-bit entries. Second, under x86 systems (486, Pentium, etc.) the stack grows downward. This means that, when you push an item on the stack, the value of the stack pointer decreases. When you pop an item, it increases. In other words, the stack is upside down compared to what you might intuitively expect.

Why is it so important that the system stack be implemented efficiently in hardware? Not only is the application stack used every time a function is called, it is also used when passing parameters to functions and to allocate space for local variables. It is even sometimes used by functions to return results to the calling routine.

Calling a Simple Function

Consider a call to a function that has no parameters and no local variables. We'll define three of these functions, A, B, and C, as follows:

```
Function A() As Long
End Function

Function B() As Long
        Call A()
End Function

Sub Main()
        Call B()
End Sub
```

What happens when you run this program? First, the operating system loads the program into memory. Space is allocated for the code, for any global data, and for the application's stack. The system then transfers control to the starting point of the program, which performs some internal initialization and then calls Sub Main().

The top of the stack at this point contains a return address. What is a return address? Every time you call a function, the CPU jumps to run the code belonging to that function. When you exit the function, the processor needs a way to figure out where it came from in order to go back and run the instruction that follows the function call. The address of that instruction is the return address, which is stored on the stack when a function is called. You can see this in Figure T4-2a. When Sub Main() is called, the return address points back to a location in the application that handles initialization and cleanup and ultimately returns control to the operating system when the program terminates.

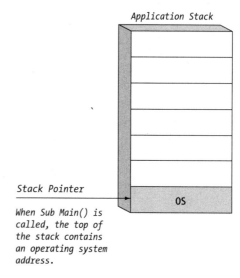

When Sub Main() is called, the top of the stack contains an operating system address.

Figure T4-2a: The process stack on initialization

Figure T4-2b shows what happens when Function B() is called during Sub Main(). The address of the location in Sub Main() after the function call is stored on the stack, and execution continues at the beginning of Function B(). The same process occurs when Function A() is called from Function B(), as shown in Figure T4-2c.

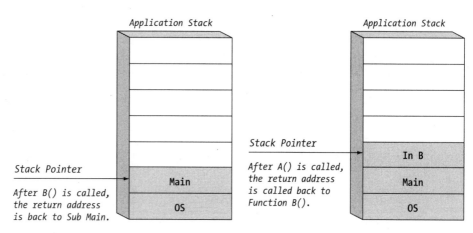

After B() is called, the return address is back to Sub Main.

After A() is called, the return address is called back to Function B().

Figures T4-2b, T4-2c: Return addresses are pushed to the stack as functions are called

When Function A() finishes executing, the return value is popped off the top of the stack, and execution continues in Function B(), as shown in Figure T4-2d.

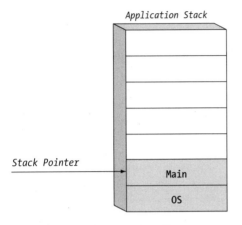

Application Stack

Stack Pointer

Main
OS

After returning from Function A(), we are back in the context of B(), and the return address is back to Sub Main.

Figure T4-2d: The return address is popped from the stack when a function exits

As you can see, a stack is an essential part of the operation of any program. It is fundamental to the way subroutine and function calls operate. But this is only the beginning.

Passing a Parameter to a Function

Now let's consider what happens when a function has a parameter. In this case, we'll use a Long parameter, since it's 32 bits wide and allows us to ignore for the moment what happens when a parameter does not fit exactly on the stack.

Function B() may be unfamiliar to some Visual Basic programmers. The first time it is called in this example, parameter L has the value of 1, so the function calls itself again, this time with the value 0. This second time through, the function sees that the value of the parameter is 0 and exits immediately. When a function calls itself in this manner, it's called a recursive function. Recursion is sometimes used for math operations and for operations on certain types of data structures. Function B() code is as follows:

```
Function B(ByVal L As Long) As Long
    Debug.Print L
    If L = 0 Then Exit Function
    B = B(L - 1)
End Function

Sub Main()
    Call B(1)
End Sub
```

Figure T4-3a illustrates the stack immediately after Function B() is called for the first time. As you can see, the parameter to the function is placed on the stack just before the return address. When the function refers to variable L, it is referring to the value on the stack. When Function B() is called a second time, parameter L is once again placed on the stack, as shown in Figure T4-3b. This time, it has the value 0. Which of the two stack locations is the real parameter L? The answer is both. The instance of parameter L with the value 1 belongs to the first call to Function B(). The instance of parameter L with the value 0 belongs to the second call to Function B(). Every time the function is called, it has its own local copy of parameter L.

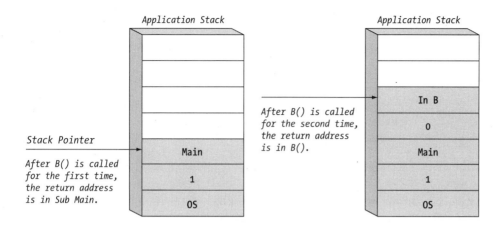

Figure T4-3a, T4-3b: Passing a single parameter to a function

When a function has multiple parameters, they are placed on the stack in order (more on this later). Even though the processor can only add and remove values at the top of the stack, it is able to read and write values anywhere on the stack. This is not surprising when you remember that the stack is really nothing more than a memory buffer.

Let's review for a moment. You've seen that the stack is essential for storing return addresses for function calls. Now you can see that it is also used for passing parameters to functions where each function has its own copy of each parameter. One can't help but ask: if the stack can hold a unique set of parameter values for each function call, could it also be used to hold other variables that are unique to each function call?

The answer is yes, and that is exactly how local variables are handled.

Local Variables

Let's take another look at Function B(). The version that follows works exactly the same way as the previous one except that it uses a local variable to hold an intermediate value which, in this case, is set to the same value as parameter L.

```
Function B(ByVal L As Long) As Long
    Debug.Print L
    Dim LocalVar As Long
```

```
    If L = 0 Then Exit Function
    LocalVar = L
    B = B(LocalVar - 1)
End Function

Sub Main()
    Call B(1)
End Sub
```

Figure T4-4a shows the stack immediately after Function B() is called for the first time. The parameters are placed on the stack first, then the return address, followed by a value called BP, and finally the local variables. This raises a new question: What is the BP value? BP stands for "base pointer." The base pointer is a register in the CPU that is used to help a function keep track of where parameters and local variables can be found on the stack. When a function begins to execute, the function pushes the existing value of the BP register onto the stack so that the register can be restored on exit. The function then loads the BP register with the current value of the stack pointer and pushes local variables onto the stack. The function can now refer to local variables as offsets to the BP register. In this example, the location of variable LocalVar can be obtained by subtracting 4 from the contents of the BP register. Local variables are above the BP register on the stack; parameters are below it.

Figure T4-4b shows the state of the stack after Function B() is called for the second time. As you can see, each time the function is called, it creates its own private copy of the local variable LocalVar. Every time a function is called, it can access its parameters, its local variables, and the return address. The segment of the stack that is used during a particular function call is called a stack frame.

You may be wondering why the BP value is pushed onto the stack only when local variables are used. The answer is simple: I lied earlier. The BP value is *always* pushed onto the stack—unless the compiler is smart enough to detect that it isn't used and skips that step. You see, the intent of this section is not to turn you into an expert on the intricacies of every detail of how stack frames are created and used. As a Visual Basic programmer, you don't need to know that. The key points you need to remember are these:

- Function parameters are passed by pushing them onto the stack before the function is called.

- Local variables are created by pushing them onto the stack after the function is called.

If you are a C++ purist, you are quite possibly still upset with me because, you see, even after adding the BP register into the equation (a fact that you are welcome to forget from here on), the description of stack frames so far is still a simplification. We need to go into just a little more detail. The reward: a real understanding of the "Bad DLL Calling Convention Error."

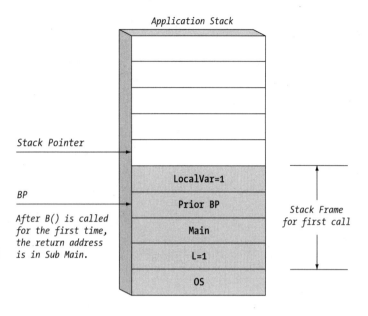

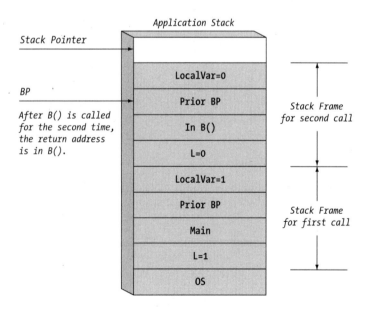

Figure T4-4a, T4-4b: The BP register keeps track of local variables

The Inner Life of Stack Frames

Let's review what we know about calling functions in DLLs. In order to call a function, an application does the following:

1. Pushes parameters onto the stack
2. Pushes the return address onto the stack
3. Allocates space on the stack for local variables

These steps are reversed when the called function returns.

This raises an interesting question: Which function is responsible for each of these steps, the calling function or the called function?

Obviously, the calling function must push parameters onto the stack. After all, the whole idea of function parameters is to allow a calling function to pass information to the called function.

But in the case of multiple parameters, which ones go on the stack first? Are parameters pushed onto the stack from right to left or left to right?

It is also plain to see that the calling function must push the return address onto the stack. In reality, this is handled by the CPU itself when it transfers control to the called function.

The called function knows what it needs in the way of local variables, so it must allocate space on the stack for these variables.

On the return side, similar issues arise. The called function must pop the local variables from the stack, since it knows how much space it allocated. But either function can pop the parameters from the stack, since both the calling function and the called function must know the function parameters.

So we're left with two questions:

- In what order are parameters pushed onto the stack?

- Which function pops the parameters from the stack?

In one sense, it does not matter—both approaches are valid. But it is absolutely critical that the calling function and the called function are compatible with each other. If one pushes function parameters left to right and the other right to left, each function will see the parameters as reversed—a sure road to a program error. If both functions try to pop the parameters from the stack, the stack will become corrupt and probably lead to an application crash when the calling function tries to return to the next higher level.

The set of standards that specifies exactly how a function is called is referred to as the "calling convention." The calling convention that is used when Visual Basic calls a DLL or Win32 API function is called the "stdcall" (for standard call) calling convention. If your DLL does not use this calling convention, you cannot call it from Visual Basic.[1] Fortunately, almost all DLL functions are exported with this calling convention.

In the stdcall calling convention, the following rules apply:

- Parameters are passed onto the stack from right to left.

- The called function pops parameters from the stack.

Why are parameters pushed onto the stack from right to left? Consider the following function:

```
Function MyFunction(Byval A as Long, ByVal B As Long) As Long
```

Now look at Figure T4-5, which shows the stack frame for the function when it is called with the line:

```
Call MyFunction ( 2, 1)
```

The leftmost parameter is pushed onto the stack last, which places it closest to the BP in the stack frame for the function. Why should this matter? The truth is that it doesn't. With some calling conventions, passing parameters from right to left makes it easier to handle situations where you have a variable number of parameters, but that doesn't apply in this case. The stdcall calling convention uses another approach, which involves passing a pointer to an array. As a Visual Basic programmer, you won't need to worry about the order.

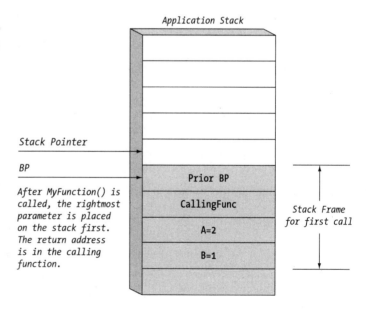

Figure T4-5: Stack frame for a function with two parameters

When Things Go Wrong

If the calling function pushes parameters onto the stack and the called function pops them from the stack, the two functions must agree on both the

---

1. Or can you? As you work your way through the puzzles, you may find a surprise or two on this score.

325

number and type of parameters. The Declare statement provides this information to your Visual Basic application. If your declaration is incorrect, you are going to run into problems.

Consider a DLL function, called MyDLLFunction, which takes two Long parameters. The correct declaration for this function would be

```
Private Declare Function MyDLLFunction Lib "mylibrary.dll" (ByVal A As _
Long, ByVal B As Long) As Long
```

What happens if you leave off the second parameter and declare the function as follows?

```
Private Declare Function MyDLLFunction Lib "mylibrary.dll" _
(ByVal A As Long) As Long
```

Figure T4-6a shows two stack frames. The one on the left shows the stack frame as it was actually called (with only one parameter). The one on the right shows the stack frame the DLL function actually expected. What happens if the DLL function uses parameter B? It tries to access the location that it believes should contain the parameter, but the calling function never pushed a value onto the stack. As a result, the DLL function sees some undetermined value. It might be a local variable from the prior stack frame. It might be another value stored on the stack. It certainly won't be what the function expects to see.

A more serious problem can be seen in Figure T4-6b. This figure shows what happens when the function returns. The DLL function is responsible for popping the parameters from the stack. It thinks that both parameters are there, so it naturally pops both of them from the stack. This means that the stack pointer is not restored to the value it had before the function was called. If this were a C program, you would be looking at an almost-certain memory exception at this point.

Visual Basic, however, has an added level of protection. Before it calls a DLL function, it stores the value of the stack pointer. When the DLL function returns, Visual Basic checks to see if the stack pointer has been restored to the original value. If it has not, it raises the following error:

Runtime Error 49
Bad DLL Calling Convention Error.

which is where this tutorial started in the first place.

This error always means that your Declare statement is incorrect and that the error was caused by a stack pointer misalignment when the DLL or API function returned.

What can cause this type of misalignment?

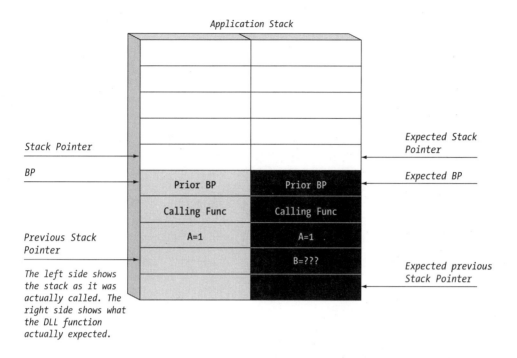

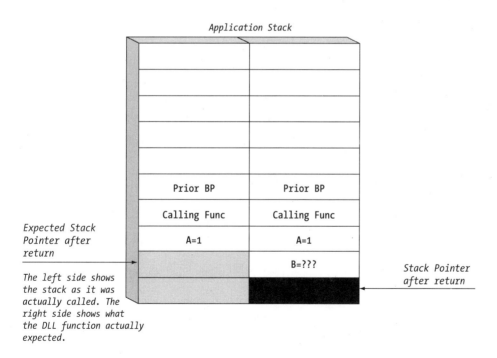

Figure T4-6: The Bad DLL Calling Convention Error illustrated

- Incorrect number of parameters

- Incorrect size of a function return value

- Incorrect size of parameters

Functions in the stdcall calling convention are almost always returned using CPU registers and thus have no impact on the stack. The exceptions to this are data types that cannot fit into a register (such as variants and user-defined structures). In order to return these data types, the calling function first allocates space on the stack within its own stack frame for the return value (just as it would allocate space for any other local variable). It then passes a pointer to that space as an extra parameter to the DLL function. The DLL function loads the space with the return value, then returns the pointer value that was passed to it as an extra parameter. You can find more information on how values are returned from DLL functions in Solution 29, "What Do You Do When It Mega Hurts?" (in Part II of this book).

The stack under 32-bit operating systems is always 32 bits wide. Those parameters that use data types larger than 32 bits actually use more than one entry in the stack. Table 4.1 shows the size of parameters as they are passed on the stack.

PARAMETER DATA TYPE	SIZE ON THE STACK
Numeric types passed ByVal (Byte, Integer, Long)	32 bits
All data types when passed By Reference (ByRef)	32 bits
User-defined types	32 bits (pointer to space on calling stack)
Double	64 bits (2 stack entries)
Currency	64 bits (2 stack entries)
Variants	128 bits (4 stack entries)

Table T4-1: Size of parameters as they are passed on the stack

Further information on passing parameters by value and by reference can be found in Tutorial 5, "The ByVal Keyword: The Solution to 90 Percent of All API Problems."

The ByVal Keyword: The Solution to 90 Percent of All API Problems

The Midnight Ride of Bugs I-Fear

*Listen, my coders, and you shall hear
Of the midnight ride of Bugs I-Fear.
Was late in a version of VB5:
Hardly a hacker is still alive
Who remembers that famous day and year.
He said to his friend, "If the program's harsh
And crashes and freezes and is a fright,
Hang a Jolt aloft in the office arch
Near the cubicle where you sleep at night—
One if ByRef and two if ByVal;
And I, though far off, will be a pal,
With ready RAS, to the Net I'll be bound,
Through every Usenet board around,
To the other hackers, their keyboards to pound."
So through the night hacked Bugs I-Fear;
And so through the Net went his cry of alarm,
To every Usenet board he found—
A cry of frustration and not of fear—
A small code fragment, with fingers so sore,
And a word that shall echo forevermore!
For, borne on the night-wind of the Net
Through all VB knowledge, you can bet,
In the hour of darkness and peril and care,
The coders awakened to listen and hear,
"Remember the ByVal in your Declare!"
was the midnight message of Bugs I-Fear.*

AFTER DEALING WITH PROBABLY THOUSANDS OF API questions over the past few years, one thing has become apparent to me. Virtually every mistake that Visual Basic programmers make when calling API functions has something to do with the ByVal keyword. Either it's there when it shouldn't be or it's missing.

It is essential that you understand exactly what this keyword does and how to use it if you are going to be able to create Visual Basic declarations for API and DLL functions.

What Does ByVal Do? The Simple Explanation

In a nutshell, the ByVal keyword tells Visual Basic that a parameter should be passed by value, meaning that the actual value of the variable should be passed to the function. When the ByVal keyword is missing, the parameter is passed as if the ByRef keyword was used, which is referred to as passing the parameter by reference. The ByValSp.vbp project (on the CD that accompanies this book) illustrates the difference between the two types of parameter passing.

```
' ByValSimple Example
' Copyright © 1998 by Desaware Inc. All Rights Reserved

Option Explicit

Private Sub Command1_Click()
    Dim myvar As Long
    myvar = 5
    Call CalledByVal(myvar)
    Debug.Print "After call ByVal: " & myvar
    Call CalledByRef(myvar)
    Debug.Print "After call ByRef: " & myvar
End Sub

Private Sub CalledByRef(x As Long)
    x = x + 1
End Sub

Private Sub CalledByVal(ByVal x As Long)
    x = x + 1
End Sub
```

The result appears as follows:

```
After call ByVal: 5
```

```
After call ByRef: 6
```

When a parameter is passed by reference, the called function receives a reference to the variable itself, so any changes made to the parameter are reflected in the value of the original variable.

But what does "a reference to the variable itself" actually mean? It means that the called function is somehow able to modify the contents of the original parameter. But how does it do this?

An in-depth look at how functions are called can be found in Tutorial 4, "How DLL Calls Work: Inside a Stack Frame." This tutorial explains how every parameter that is passed to a function is placed in a separate block of memory, called a stack. Understanding how the ByVal keyword affects the way in which a parameter is placed in the stack is key to understanding when this keyword should be used.

How ByVal Works—Numeric Variables

Every variable has two characteristics. It has a value—the data "contained" in the variable. And it has a location—the location in memory where the data is kept.

Figure T5-1 illustrates how a Long variable is passed ByVal to a function.

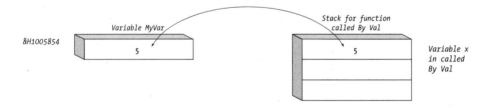

Figure T5-1: Passing a numeric variable by value

In this example, the value of the variable is 5. It is located at address &H1005654 in memory. Because ByVal was specified, the value of the variable is placed on the stack as a parameter named x. When you refer to x in the CalledByVal function, you are actually referring to the value on the stack, so any changes made to the value can't affect the original variable myvar.

Figure T5-2 illustrates how a Long variable is passed ByRef to a function.

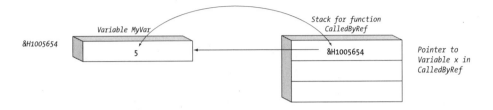

Figure T5-2: Passing a numeric variable by reference

In the previous example, the variable myvar is unchanged. But when it is passed by reference, the location (or memory address) of the variable is placed on the stack instead of the value of the variable. When the CalledByRef function refers to x, it still looks on the stack, but instead of using the value it finds there, it uses that value to determine where x is actually located. The value in the stack serves as a pointer to variable x. When the CalledByRef function attempts to read or modify the value of x, it uses the pointer to find the location of the myvar parameter and accesses that location, so changes to x serve to change variable myvar. How does the CalledByRef function know that the stack contains a pointer instead of a value? It knows this because you told it how to use the value on the stack when you declared the function.

How does a DLL or API function know that the stack contains a pointer instead of a value? The same way—the person writing the DLL or API function specified the type of parameter in the source code for the function. But Visual Basic has no automatic way of knowing what it should put on the stack for these functions. It's up to you, in the Declare statement, to tell Visual Basic exactly how to pass the parameter to the function. If you make a mistake, not only will the function call fail, it will probably lead to a memory exception. For example, say you have an API function that expects a Long value to be passed by reference, but you declare it by value. If the variable contains 0, Visual Basic will put 0 on the stack (called by value). The API function will look on the stack for the location of the variable and see that it is at location 0. When the function tries to read or write the variable itself (thinking it's at location 0), a memory exception will result.

Any 32-bit variable that contains the location of another variable instead of the value is called a pointer, and you'll soon see that there are many ways to deal with pointers when making API calls.

Where Is ByVal Used?

The ByVal keyword can appear in two places: in a function declaration or in a function call.

Consider the following two code fragments:

```
Declare Function SendMessage Lib "User32" Alias "SendMessageA" _
(ByVal Hwnd As Long, ByVal Msg As Long, ByVal wParam As Long, _
ByVal lParam As Long) As Long

Dim myvar As Long
Call SendMessage(hwnd, msg, wparam, myvar)
```

Look closely at the lParam parameter. The SendMessage function can be used in many different ways, and the lParam parameter can actually refer to many different types of data. In this declaration, the lParam parameter is always a Long value. The myvar variable is declared as a Long here, but it really wouldn't matter if it was declared as a variant or integer or even a string. Visual Basic would convert the value to a Long numeric value as part of the SendMessage call. The declaration specifies the type of the parameter and the way it should be called, so Visual Basic can force the variable to the correct type. In the following declaration, the lParam parameter is specified as the As Any type.

```
Declare Function SendMessage Lib "User32" Alias "SendMessageA" _
(ByVal Hwnd As Long, ByVal Msg As Long, ByVal wParam As Long, _
lParam As Any) As Long

Dim myvar As Long
Call SendMessage(hwnd, msg, wparam, ByVal myvar)
```

The As Any term tells Visual Basic that it should perform no type checking on the parameter that is passed. So the data passed to the SendMessage function depends on the type of the variable used in the call. In this case, it is critical that the variable be declared as a Long (if that's the type you wish to pass) because Visual Basic does no error checking or conversion. You also need to specify the ByVal keyword during the call if you wish the call to be made by value.

The As Any parameter type is extremely dangerous. You should avoid using it in your function declarations whenever possible. A far better approach is to create several aliases of a function that each take a particular parameter type. For example, the most common data types for the lParam parameter in the SendMessage function are Longs and strings. You'll find the following two declarations in the api32.txt file on the CD that comes with this book:

```
Declare Function SendMessageBynum Lib "user32" Alias "SendMessageA" _
(ByVal hwnd As Long, ByVal wMsg As Long, ByVal wParam As Long, _
ByVal lParam As Long) As Long
Declare Function SendMessageByString Lib "user32" Alias "SendMessageA" _
(ByVal hwnd As Long, ByVal wMsg As Long, ByVal wParam As Long, _
ByVal lParam As String) As Long
```

These functions provide safer ways to call the SendMessage function and reduce the likelihood of bugs due to incorrect parameter types. Using As Any in a declaration places all the responsibility for passing the correct parameter type on the person using the function instead of the person creating the declaration. Since the function is likely to be called multiple times, it's obvious that the As Any approach is more likely to result in errors than creating a type-safe declaration the first time around.

Now that you've learned that the As Any declaration is evil and should be avoided at all costs, it may surprise you to see that I use it extensively throughout this book. The reason is simple: this book is intended to teach you how to declare and call even the most complex Win32 API function given only a C declaration to work with. The As Any parameter type forces you to think carefully about the parameter each time you call the function and thus will encourage you to learn and understand how the function is called.

You'll also see that there are a few functions where you want the decision on parameter types and use of the ByVal keyword to be made each time the function is called. One good example of this is the RtlMoveMemory function.

Working with Pointers

One of the most useful functions for understanding what gets passed as a parameter is the RtlMoveMemory function. This function copies memory from a source location to a destination location. What does this mean?

A typical declaration for RtlMoveMemory is shown here:

```
Private Declare Function RtlMoveMemory Lib "kernel32" (dest As Any, _
src As Any, ByVal Count As Long) As Long
```

The function takes three parameters. The dest parameter specifies the destination for the copied memory. The src parameter specifies the source location of the data to copy. The Count parameter specifies the number of bytes to copy.

Figure T5-3 shows the contents of the stack when the RtlMoveMemory function is called. The Count parameter is passed by value, so the corresponding stack entry contains the number of bytes to transfer. The other two parameters are declared here As Any, which means you can pass anything to the function.

Because Visual Basic does not place any restrictions on the type of data you are passing, it is important that you understand exactly what needs to appear on the stack.

The stack entries for both the src and dest parameters must contain a memory address. In other words, these entries are pointers.

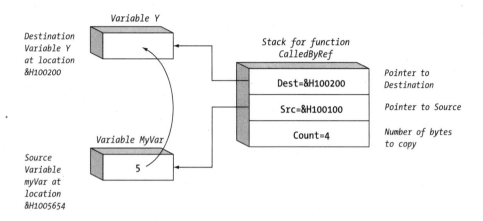

Figure T5-3: Using the RtlMoveMemory function

The obvious way to set these parameters is to pass the values by reference. The sample code in the Pointers.vbp example on your CD illustrates this:

```
Dim myVar As Long

Private Sub Form_Load()
    myVar = 5
End Sub

Private Sub Command1_Click()
    Dim Y As Long
    Call RtlMoveMemory(Y, myVar, 4)
    Debug.Print "New value of Y: " & Y
End Sub
```

In this example, the function defines a variable Y, which will be loaded with the data from the myVar variable (which was initialized to a value of 5 in the form load event). Both Y and myVar are passed by reference, which means that the stack will contain the address of the two variables. As you can see in the figure, the RtlMoveMemory function can use the pointers to copy the data from one variable to the other. Note that the addresses used in the figure are for illustrative purposes only; the actual addresses that you see will differ.

You can also use the Visual Basic VarPtr operator to obtain the address of a variable. This is shown in the following sample code:

```
Private Sub Command2_Click()
    Dim Y As Long
    Dim myVarAddress As Long
    myVarAddress = VarPtr(myVar)
    Call RtlMoveMemory(Y, ByVal myVarAddress, 4)
    Debug.Print "myVar Address is: " & Hex$(myVarAddress)
    Debug.Print "New value of Y: " & Y
End Sub
```

In this function, a new Long variable, myVarAddress, is declared. This variable is loaded with the address of the myVar variable with the help of the VarPtr function. When the myVarAddress variable is passed to the RtlMoveMemory function, it is passed with the ByVal operator. Why? Because the myVarAddress variable contains the address of the myVar variable, and we want to place that address onto the stack. When you want to place the contents of a variable on the stack, you must use the ByVal operator. This is illustrated in Figure T5-4.

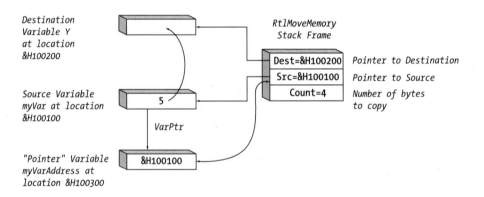

Figure T5-4: Using a pointer variable

As you can see, the end result of this approach is exactly the same as the previous one. Why would you want to take this more convoluted approach?

In this particular example, you wouldn't. But then again, you're not likely to use the RtlMoveMemory function to perform an operation that can be accomplished with a simple Y = myVar statement. But there will be many situations when you are working with API functions where you will need to deal with pointers and pointer variables. And there will be many cases where you will, in fact, use RtlMoveMemory to copy data from a block of memory to a user-defined type that will allow you to easily access the data in your Visual Basic program.

How ByVal Works (String Variables)

Everything you have read so far relating to the ByVal statement applies to almost every type of Visual Basic variable. The one glaring exception is string variables.

Forget the idea of ByVal meaning "by value"—Visual Basic always passes pointers for string parameters. The question is, pointers to what?

To understand what happens when you pass a string as a parameter to an API function, you must first know a bit about how Visual Basic stores strings internally and how Win32 API functions deal with string parameters.

Visual Basic stores strings internally using objects called BSTRs. A BSTR (short for Basic STRing) is stored in memory that is managed by the operating system, specifically the OLE subsystem. This simple statement has great significance and huge consequences on the way strings are passed to API functions.

Inside a BSTR

When you assign text to a string, you know that the text must be stored somewhere in memory. When you clear a string, you can assume that the memory used by the string can be reclaimed for use by the operating system. Every program uses memory for strings and other objects, and ultimately all memory is allocated by the operating system. But you should not conclude from this that a program goes to the operating system every time it needs memory.

It turns out that there are many different ways to manage memory, and techniques that work well to manage large blocks of memory can perform poorly when managing smaller amounts of memory. Thus it is common for different subsystems within Windows to request large blocks of memory from the operating system that are then subdivided into smaller blocks for use by that subsystem. Early versions of Visual Basic used this approach to manage string memory—Visual Basic requested a block of memory from the operating system, then used its own internal code to allocate smaller blocks for strings. As of version 4, Visual Basic switched to use the string management system built into the OLE subsystem of Windows. Strings allocated by the OLE subsystem are called BSTR strings.

Figure T5-5 shows how a BSTR looks in memory. The first thing you'll probably notice is that the data in the string is stored as Unicode. This means that each character takes two bytes in memory. In this particular example, the string "Hello", the second byte of each character is 0; however, some character sets use both bytes. BSTR strings do not have to be in Unicode, but Visual Basic uses

Unicode internally for string storage, so in most cases you can assume that a BSTR contains a Unicode string. One major exception will be discussed later in this chapter.

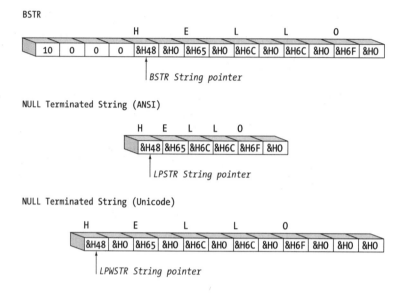

Figure T5-5: BSTR and NULL-terminated strings

The second thing you may notice is that a BSTR includes the length of the string. The length appears in the four bytes preceding the string data. When you have a pointer to a BSTR, the pointer always refers to the start of the data area.

The ByValSt.vbp example program demonstrates this with the following code:

```vb
Private Sub cmdInside_Click()
    Dim a() As Byte
    Dim x&
    Dim b$
    Dim length As Long
    b$ = "Hello"
    ' Many VB programmers are not aware that you can
    ' do dynamic assignment like this
    a() = b$
    Debug.Print "Inside Hello"
    For x = 0 To UBound(a)
        Debug.Print x, Hex$(a(x))
    Next x
```

```
   Call RtlMoveMemory(length, ByVal (StrPtr(b$) - 4), 4)
   Debug.Print "Length: " & length
End Sub
```

String b$ contains the text "Hello". We have a dynamic array a() that is loaded
with the contents of the string using the assignment a() = b$. This assignment,
which is unfamiliar to many Visual Basic programmers, is an easy way to copy
data between strings and dynamic byte arrays without any conversion process.
The dynamic array is automatically assigned to the correct length. The function
first displays the value of each byte in hexadecimal. As you can see, the data corresponds to the values shown in Figure T5-5.

Next, we use the same techniques shown earlier to copy data from memory.
In this case, the StrPtr function is used to obtain the pointer to the BSTR (VarPtr
would return a pointer to the variable that contains the pointer to the BSTR). We
subtract 4 from the pointer value to point to the string length, and copy that
value into a Long variable named length. The results are as follows:

```
Inside Hello
  0               48
  1               0
  2               65
  3               0
  4               6C
  5               0
  6               6C
  7               0
  8               6F
  9               0
Length: 10
```

Inside a C String

A C string, also referred to as a NULL-terminated string, is shown in the lower
part of Figure T5-5. This type of string is called a C string because it is the standard string format used by the C and C++ programming languages. It is called a
NULL-terminated string because the end of the string is marked by the presence
of a NULL character. Note that the end of the string is marked by a NULL character, not necessarily a 0 byte. With an ANSI string, which contains one byte per
character, the NULL character is a single byte containing the value 0 at the end
of the string. With a Unicode string, the NULL character is two bytes long, just
like any other character. Both bytes of the NULL character have a value of 0.

Because the Win32 API is written largely in C, most API functions use NULL-terminated strings. The only exceptions are those functions that are part of the OLE subsystem and specifically designed to work with BSTR strings.

You may be wondering how you can include a NULL character in a C string. The answer is simple—you can't. That's one reason why the BSTR format was developed.

How can you tell if an API function that takes a string parameter expects a Unicode or an ANSI string? The function documentation tells you. In order to provide maximum flexibility, most API functions actually consist of two separate functions, one that handles ANSI strings and another that handles Unicode strings. For example, the GetWindowText function does not actually exist. What you'll find are two functions, GetWindowTextA and GetWindowTextW. The former uses ANSI strings, the latter uses Unicode (wide) strings.

The ANSI declaration is used with Visual Basic as follows:

```
Declare Function GetWindowText Lib "user32" Alias "GetWindowTextA" _
(ByVal hwnd As Long, ByVal lpString As String, ByVal cch As Long) As Long
```

The Alias statement specifies the name of the function within the DLL. Thus, when you refer to "GetWindowText" in Visual Basic, it actually calls the GetWindowTextA function. You will almost always use the ANSI version of a function when calling it from Visual Basic. Why? Because while both Windows 95/98 and Windows NT export Unicode and ANSI versions of most functions, only the ANSI version works on Windows 95/98—the Unicode entry point may exist, but it won't do anything. This is illustrated in Figure T5-6.

You've seen that Visual Basic stores strings internally in BSTR Unicode format and that most API functions expect NULL-terminated ANSI strings. That leaves an interesting question: How do you get from here to there?

Passing Strings to DLL Functions

For most Visual Basic programmers, the following two rules are all you will ever need to know about passing strings to DLL or API functions:

- Always use ByVal when passing strings as parameters to DLL functions.

- If there is any chance that the API or DLL function will modify the string, be sure the string you pass to the function is already long enough to hold the modified string.

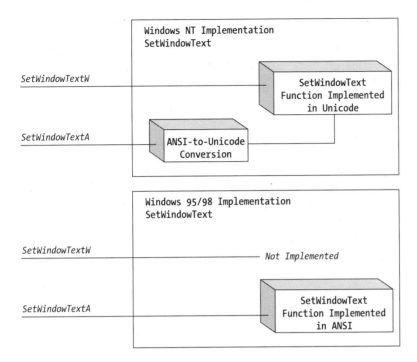

Figure T5-6: Differences between Windows 95/98 and Windows NT implementations of API functions that use strings

In the rest of this section, you'll find out why these rules exist, when it is safe to break them, what other options exist, and what's really going on behind the scenes.

When a string parameter is specified in a Declare statement, Visual Basic creates a new BSTR, which it loads with a NULL-terminated ANSI copy of the string. This is one of the rare cases where a BSTR contains an ANSI string instead of a Unicode string.

If you use the ByVal operator when passing the string, the BSTR pointer is passed to the API function. If you pass the string ByRef (the default), a pointer to a temporary pointer variable containing the BSTR pointer is passed to the API function. These cases are illustrated in Figure T5-7.

Virtually every Win32 API expects a pointer to a NULL-terminated string as a parameter. That means you must pass the strings with the ByVal keyword. You will occasionally run into situations where a custom DLL expects a pointer to a BSTR passed by Visual Basic. Those are the only cases where you will leave off the ByVal keyword.

Once the API function returns, Visual Basic copies the ANSI BSTR back into its internal Unicode format.

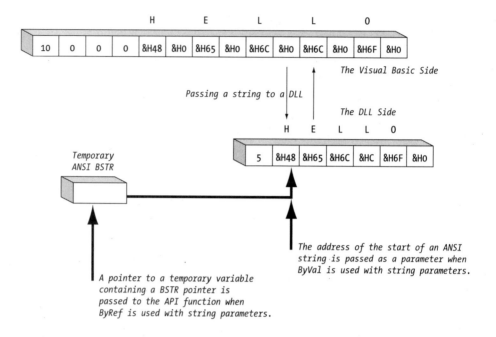

Figure T5-7: Passing strings as parameters

Calling the Unicode Entry Point

Regardless of whether you use ByVal or ByRef, Visual Basic passes a temporary ANSI string to the API functions when using the Declare statement. But what if you want to pass a pointer to a Unicode string (a pointer to a BSTR) or a pointer to a dynamic string variable that refers to a Unicode string? You might want to do this if you need to call the Unicode entry point of a function or if you are calling an OLE function that requires a Unicode string.

There are two ways to accomplish this.

- Create a type library where you actually specify the BSTR data type.

- Pass the address using a Long parameter as you saw earlier in the RtlMoveMemory examples.

For example, consider this declaration for the Unicode entry point for the SetWindowText function:

```
Declare Function SetWindowText Lib "user32" Alias "SetWindowTextW" _
(ByVal hwnd As Long, ByVal lpString As Long) As Long
```

The lpString parameter needs to be passed the address of a Unicode string. The StrPtr function can be used to obtain the address of the internal Visual Basic string, which is a Unicode string. The following code from the ByValSt.vbp example (on the CD that comes with this book) sets the form's caption using the Unicode entry point declaration for SetWindowText shown above.

```
Private Sub cmdSetWindowText_Click()
    Dim s$
    s$ = "New Text" & chr$(0)
    Call SetWindowText(hwnd, StrPtr(s$))
End Sub
```

Why do we add the NULL character at the end of the variable s$? The truth is that this may not be necessary. It is critically important that the string passed to the API function be NULL-terminated. When you use this technique, you are passing a pointer to the string as it is stored internally in Visual Basic, and as you saw earlier, a BSTR does not have a NULL termination character. In most cases, it turns out that there are a couple of NULL bytes after strings, but there is no guarantee that this will always be the case. So you should explicitly add the NULL character just to be safe.

Keep in mind also that while the SetWindowTextW entry point exists under Windows95/98, it does not do anything. Most Unicode entry points under Windows 95/98 simply return an error result.

This covers string parameters in a nutshell. Handling string parameters can be one of the more complex issues with API and DLL calls, and many of the puzzles in this book will deal with techniques for handling them.

C++ Variables Meet Visual Basic

AS A VISUAL BASIC PROGRAMMER, YOU are hopefully familiar with the Visual Basic data types. Their characteristics are shown in Table T6-1.

TYPE	BYTES	SIGN	RANGE
Byte	1	Unsigned	0 to 255
Boolean	2	NA	True or False
Integer	2	Signed	–32768 to 32767
Long	4	Signed	–2147483648 to 2147483647
Single	4	Signed	±1.4E-45 to ±3.4E38
Double	8	Signed	±4.9E-324 to ±1.7E308
Currency	8	Signed	See VB docs— not applicable to API
Decimal	14	Signed	See VB docs— not applicable to API
Date	8	NA	See VB docs— not applicable to API
Object	4	NA	
String	*	NA	Length varies by string
Variant	16	NA	Depends on contained variable
User-Defined	*		Varies depending on definition

* = Varies

Table T6-1: Characteristics of Visual Basic data types

C Data Types

When a Visual Basic programmer first looks at a C/C++ declaration, it can be more than a little bit intimidating.[1] The C language seems to have billions of different data types. How can you possibly figure out a Visual Basic equivalent for each one?

The trick to dealing with these data types is to keep two things in mind:

- It's all an illusion—C actually has very few data types.

- Each data type includes the key to decode its meaning.

Let's take a look at the C data types you will run into—see Table T6-2.

TYPE	BYTES	SIGN	RANGE
char	1	Signed	–128 to 127
unsigned char	1	Unsigned	0 to 255
short	2	Signed	–32768 to 32767
unsigned short	2	Unsigned	0 to 65535
long	4	Signed	–2147483648 to 2147483647
unsigned long	4	Unsigned	0 to 4294967295
int	4	Signed	Same as long under Win32
unsigned int	4	Unsigned	Same as unsigned long under Win32
float	4	Signed	±1.4E-45 to ±3.4E38
double	8	Signed	±4.9E-324 to ±1.7E308
class	*		Varies depending on definition
struct	*		Varies depending on definition
void	0	None	Indicates no type. A function that returns a void is like a VB Sub—it has no return value.

Table T6-2: C data types

There is also a long double data type and an __int*xx* type where *xx* is the size of the integer. These types are rarely used—in fact, I have yet to see them used in any API or DLL function.

You may be wondering, where are the string data types? What about objects and variants? What about Boolean variables?

The trick is in the way the C/C++ language allows you to derive new data types from these native types. Once you derive a new data type, the new type can be used just like those that are built into the language. You'll see how new data types are declared shortly.

---

1. The C++ language is based on the C language and is essentially identical from the point of view of a Visual Basic programmer. For this reason, C and C++ are used interchangeably in this book. As for declarations being intimidating—the complex ones can be nearly incomprehensible. In fact, this book was inspired in part by a book called *The C Puzzle Book*, which consisted largely of complex type declarations the reader had to struggle to understand.

C declarations are very similar to Visual Basic declarations, they just look reversed. Where a Visual Basic program might define a Long as follows:

```
Dim myLong As Long
```

a C program would define it as:

```
long myLong;
```

The type comes first.

Note that all of the C language native data types are in lowercase. One reason you'll want to remember this is that most C programmers use all uppercase names for constants and derived data types (data types that are defined by the programmer and not the language). Keywords, including data types, in the C language are case-sensitive. So where Visual Basic doesn't care if you type in long, Long, or LONG and force the case to match the original declaration, the C language would interpret each of these as different keywords and raise errors when you try to use one that doesn't exist.

Arrays

C language arrays are similar to Visual Basic arrays except that they are less flexible. Square brackets are used to indicate the array; thus:

```
int A[5];
```

defines an array of five integers. The valid index values for the array are A[0] through A[4]. Yes, C arrays always start at a base index of 0.

Consider the following character array:

```
char myString[4];
myString [0] = 'Y';
myString [1] = 'E';
myString [2] = 'S';
myString [3] = 0;
```

This defines an array of four characters. The final character is the NULL character (value 0). Tutorial 5, "The ByVal Keyword: The Solution to 90 Percent of All API Problems," describes a C language string as an array of characters with a NULL termination character. Sound familiar? This is exactly how C programs deal with strings—as arrays of characters.

This applies to ANSI strings where each character is one byte. What about Unicode strings where each character is two bytes? An array intended to hold a Unicode string might be defined as follows:

```
unsigned short UnicodeString[4];
```

Pointers

The C language is very big on pointers. The asterisk (*) character indicates a pointer. For example:

```
short *pIntVariable;
```

means that variable pIntVariable is a pointer to a short. Variable pIntVariable itself is 32 bits long. The data it points to is a short that is 16 bits long.

You've seen that an ANSI C language string is an array of char variables. But if you want to pass a string as a function parameter, you would not pass the entire array. Instead, you would pass a pointer to the string. What is a pointer to a string? It's a pointer that specifies the location of the first character in the array. The first character in the array is of type char, so a pointer to a string must be a pointer to a variable of type char. A pointer to a char variable is defined as follows:

```
char *pString;
```

What if you wanted to set the string pointer to the myString array defined earlier? A C programmer could do it like this:

```
pString = &myString[0];
```

The & operator means the address of the variable. In this case, it's exactly like the VarPtr operator a Visual Basic programmer would use to obtain the address of a VB variable.

References

A reference is a declaration that works just like a pointer, except it uses a different syntax. It uses the & character in a slightly different way. For example:

```
int myVariable;
int &ReferenceToVariable = myVariable;
```

Variable ReferenceToVariable is a pointer to myVariable.

The only place where references are regularly used is with certain types of structures in the OLE subsystem. When you see a reference data type, just treat it as if it were a pointer, and you'll do fine.

Classes and Structures

These terms are used to define user-defined types in the C language. You'll find out a lot more about how to handle classes and structures as you proceed through this book. From a Visual Basic programmer's perspective, there is no difference between a class and a structure. They are defined as follows:

```
class myClass {
        Define variables within the structure here
        };
```

Derived Data Types

So far you've seen that the C language actually specifies the following keywords for data types: char, short, int, long, float, and double, as well as the following modifiers:

- unsigned: Indicates the data is unsigned. There is also a signed keyword, but it is rarely used because the default is signed.

- [ ]: Indicate an array of a fundamental data type.

- *: Indicates a pointer to a data type.

- &: Indicates the address of a variable or a reference to a variable.

Despite the shortness of this list, any API or DLL documentation you see will have dozens of additional data types. Where do they come from?

The answer lies in the fact that the C language allows you to derive new data types from existing data types. This is done using a statement called "typedef." For example, consider the statement:

```
typedef  unsigned char BYTE;
```

Once this line appears in a C program or header file, it is thereafter possible to declare variables of type unsigned char by using the new type definition BYTE. Thus, the following two statements are identical:

```
unsigned char myChar;
BYTE myChar;
```

The declaration:

```
typedef char *LPSTR;
```

defines LPSTR as a pointer to a character—which, as you may recall, is how C also refers to strings. That's why LPSTR often appears as a parameter in an API declaration to indicate a string parameter. The parameter is a pointer to a string, which is the same thing as a pointer to a char if the character that is pointed to is the first character in a NULL-terminated string.

By convention, derived data types use all uppercase characters.

The typedef statement can also be used to define pointers to functions. A pointer to a function is like any other pointer in that it contains the address of a location in memory. The only difference is that a pointer to a function points to memory that contains executable code rather than data. The Visual Basic AddressOf operator can be used to obtain a pointer to a function in a standard module.

A typedef statement that defines a pointer to a function looks like this:

```
typedef void (*MYFUNCTIONTYPE)();
```

This defines MYFUNCTIONTYPE as a data type that points to a function that has no parameters and no return value.

```
typedef long (*MYFUNCTIONTYPE)(short a, char *b);
```

This defines MYFUNCTIONTYPE as a data type that points to a function that takes two parameters, a 16-bit integer and a 32-bit pointer to a character array, and returns a long value.

Macros

The C language also has a macro capability in which you can define a keyword to be replaced by other text at compile time. These definitions are specified using the #define statement. Thus, the line:

```
#define VOID void
```

means that the word "VOID" will be replaced by the word "void" during the compilation process. Macros can take parameters as well. Thus, the macro:

```
#define DECLARE_HANDLE(name) typedef HANDLE name
```

defines a macro called DECLARE_HANDLE that takes a parameter.
If the following code appeared:

```
DECLARE_HANDLE(HWND);
```

the following code would be substituted:

```
typedef HANDLE HWND;
```

Decoding Type Notation

The ability of the C language to let programmers define their own data types explains why you'll see hundreds of different data types in Windows. Microsoft didn't do this to confuse you—they did it to help programmers create more reliable programs. The type definitions help both you and the C compiler make sure you are passing the correct parameters to functions and not assigning variables with incompatible types of data.

The programmers who wrote Windows helped make data types self-describing by using a consistent notation for data type names. Each data type has a base name that describes the data. For example, CHAR is used to indicate a character data type. For ANSI characters, this would be based on the char data type. For Unicode characters, this would be based on the unsigned short data type.

The name then has one or more prefix characters, as shown in Table T6-3.

PREFIX	MEANING
P	Type is a pointer. Thus, PCHAR is a pointer to a CHAR.
LP	Type is a pointer. On 16-bit Windows, there is a difference between near and far memory pointers. Thus, LPCHAR would be a far pointer to a CHAR, and a PCHAR or NPCHAR would be a near pointer to a CHAR. On Win32 these are identical—all pointers are 32 bits, so you can treat NP, P, and LP identically.
NP	Type is a pointer. See LP.
C	Type refers to constant data. Thus, LPCCHAR might be a char acter that is not allowed to change once the program starts running. Visual Basic programmers can ignore the C prefix or use it to identify parameters that will not be changed by the

(continued)

API function. Thus, LPCSTR is a pointer to a string that will not be modified when passed to a function.

W   Used to indicate wide (Unicode) data. Thus, LPWCHAR is a pointer to a wide character. Note that a wide character is based on the unsigned short data type.

T   C programmers can create applications that default to use Unicode or ANSI internally. The T prefix indicates a character data type that is Unicode in native Unicode applications, ANSI in native ANSI applications. Thus, LPTSTR will be LPSTR for an ANSI function entry point, LPWSTR for a Unicode function entry point.

Table T6-3: Common data type prefixes

Exploring the Common Windows Data Types

To help you become familiar with the most common Windows data types, let's take a close look at the first part of the header file called winnt.h, distributed with the Win32 Software Development Kit (SDK) and other developers' tools.[2] Only the typedef statements are shown in Table T6-4.

typedef void *PVOID;	The void data type is used for untyped data. You can't actually create a variable with type void. But you can create a pointer to a void. Such a pointer is considered a pointer to any type of data. PVOID is thus a pointer to any type of data.
typedef char CHAR; typedef short SHORT; typedef long LONG;	The simple explanation is that these three type defs are simple substitutions for those programmers who wish to use only uppercase data type[3] names. *(continued)*

2. Another good file to look at for base data types is the file winbase.h. Thanks to Microsoft's Open Tools program, all of the Win32 Software Development Kit header files are included on the CD that comes with this book.

3. The complex explanation is that these type declarations help a programmer create portable applications. Let's say you need a variable to be 16 bits. A short may be 16 bits under Win32, but the C language actually defines it as any size smaller or equal in size to an int, and larger or equal in size to a char. If you tried to compile your program on a version of C that defined short as 8 bits, you could run into trouble and have to change your variable types throughout your program. By using the SHORT typedef, all you would need to do is redefine it to a 16-bit type under the new compiler, and all of your variables and parameters defined as SHORT would compile correctly.

typedef unsigned short wchar_t; typedef wchar_t WCHAR;	This wide character definition actually appears in file basetyps.h. Wide (or Unicode) characters are 16 bits. Note how one typedef can be based on another. WCHAR derives from wchar_t, which in turn derives from short.
typedef WCHAR *PWCHAR; typedef WCHAR *LPWCH, *PWCH; NWPSTR, LPW typedef WCHAR *NWPSTR; typedef WCHAR *LPWSTR, *PWSTR;	PWCHAR points to a Unicode character, which can also be the start of a Unicode string. LPWCH and PWCH are the same. STR and PWSTR are identical—they just suggest the idea of a string (STR) instead of a character. Why so many different ways of describing a pointer to a Unicode string? I would say for the convenience of programmers, though this does seem to be overkill.
typedef const WCHAR *LPCWSTR, *PCWSTR;	These two declarations include the const specifier that says the type points to constant data—data that is not expected to change. Visual Basic programmers can ignore the const keyword because const data types are treated the same as those that are not constant.
typedef CHAR *PCHAR; typedef CHAR *LPCH, *PCH; typedef CONST CHAR *LPCCH, *PCCH; typedef CHAR *NPSTR; typedef CHAR *LPSTR, *PSTR; typedef CONST CHAR *LPCSTR, *PCSTR;	CHAR was defined earlier as a char. PCHAR, LPCH, PCH, LPCCH, PCCH, NPSTR, LPSTR, PSTR, LPCSTR, and PCSTR are all exactly the same thing—pointers to a variable with the char data type. As you now know, this is the same as a pointer to a NULL-terminated string.
typedef SHORT *PSHORT; typedef LONG *PLONG;	Pointers to short data or long data. The numeric cases are considerably simpler than characters.
typedef void *HANDLE; typedef HANDLE *PHANDLE;	A HANDLE is defined as a pointer to any data type. This may seem odd, since VB programmers are used to dealing with handles as 32-bit long values. There is no conflict—a pointer is 32 bits wide, so

(continued)

handles are stored in long variables. You will almost never actually access the data a HANDLE points to; that data is almost always used internally by Windows.[4]

```
typedef unsigned short WORD;
typedef unsigned long DWORD;
typedef WORD far *LPWORD;
typedef DWORD far *LPDWORD;
```

A WORD is a 16-bit unsigned short variable. An LPWORD points to a WORD.
    A DWORD is a 32-bit unsigned long variable. An LPDWORD points to a DWORD.

```
typedef DWORD LCID;
typedef PDWORD PLCID;
```

LCID stands for locale identifier, a number that indicates a particular language and country. An LCID is also a 32-bit long value, but by using LCID instead of long, the data type becomes more clear to programmers trying to read the code. A PLCID is a pointer to an LCID.

Table T6-4: Common Windows data types

Back to Visual Basic

Now that you have a good understanding of how C defines different types of data, let's take a quick look at how you might convert data from C to Visual Basic. The key thing to remember is the only thing you really have to know is the length of the data variable. Don't get confused with the complex notation of various C data types. The goal of showing them in the preceding section was to give you the tools to figure out what fundamental data type the derived type is based on. Table T6-5 shows the Visual Basic data types that most closely correspond to the built-in C data types.

C DATA TYPE	VISUAL BASIC EQUIVALENT
char	Byte
short	Integer

(continued)

4. If the data that a HANDLE points to is never used by an application, why is a HANDLE defined as a pointer instead of a Long? Actually, in earlier versions of Windows, it was a Long value. But by changing it to a pointer, Microsoft was able to define many different types of handles as pointers to different structures. The C compiler could detect attempts to pass one type of handle to functions expecting a different type of handle. This helped eliminate careless programming errors such as passing device context handles to functions expecting window handles.

long	Long
float	Single
double	Double
class, struct	User-defined type

Table T6-5: VB equivalents to the base C data types

Handling Signed and Unsigned Types

The C char data type is 8 bits wide, thus you would use the Visual Basic Byte data type for both signed and unsigned chars. The trick to handling these data types is to recognize the range limitations that occur during the conversion process.

Let's say you had a C structure defined that included a signed char, and you needed to set it to –50.

```
struct myStruct {
char myChar;
}
```

The Visual Basic equivalent structure is:

```
Type myStruct
myChar As Byte
End Type
```

If you tried to assign:

```
Dim S As myStruct
S.myChar = -50
```

you would get a range overflow error, because the Byte variable is unsigned and cannot be set to a negative number.

If you look at Tutorial 2, "Memory, Where It All Begins," you'll see that the only difference between a signed and an unsigned variable is the placement of the range. Signed bytes range from –128 to 127, unsigned bytes from 0 to 255. All you need to do to convert an out of range number from one to another is to subtract 256 using the following expression:

```
SignedValue = UnsignedValue - 256
UnsignedValue = SignedValue + 256
```

So to set the mChar value, just add 256 to –50 to obtain 206.

```
S.myChar = 206
```

Integers are handled similarly:

```
SignedValue = UnsignedValue - &H10000
UnsignedValue = SignedValue + &H10000
```

Note that you'll have to use long variables to do the calculations in order to prevent overflows. The same technique works with long variables, except that you'll need to use doubles to handle the intermediate results to prevent overflows (and risk losing some precision along the way).

Currency and Dates

Neither the Currency nor Date data types are used by Win32 API functions. Refer to the source code for the apigid32.dll project (in C++) for examples of how these parameters can be used with custom dynamic link libraries. (The apigid32.dll project can be found on the CD that comes with this book.)

User-Defined Types

User-defined types are passed to API functions by reference—meaning that a pointer to the structure is passed as a parameter. In most cases, converting a C structure to a Visual Basic user-defined type is straightforward, but there are exceptions. An in-depth explanation of how to handle structures can be found in Tutorial 7, "Classes, Structures, and User-Defined Types."

Variants

The core Win32 API functions do not use variants. However, the OLE subsystem does support variants, and those variants are fully compatible with Visual Basic.

When you use variants in Visual Basic, you see them as a variable like any other. But DLL functions see variants as a 16-byte VARIANT structure.

Unlike user-defined types, you can pass variants by value using the ByVal keyword. This is because Visual Basic knows how to make a copy of a variant.

Variants appear in the C documentation as VARIANT or VARIANTARG structures.

Arrays

You've already seen the secret to handling arrays with Win32 API functions. Remember how a C language string is nothing more than a buffer of characters with a NULL termination, and that a pointer to a string is just a pointer to the first character in the string? API functions use this approach with any type of array. For example, an integer array will usually appear in a C declaration as LPINT or PINT.

For example, let's say you have an API function that expects an array of five shorts. In Visual Basic, you might define the array as follows:

```
Dim myArray(4) As Integer
```

The API function expects a pointer to the array, which means a pointer to the first element in the array. How can you obtain a pointer to the first element of the myArray array? There are two ways, as you saw in Tutorial 5:

- Declare the parameter As Integer and pass the first element of the array as follows:

```
Declare Function MyFunction Lib "mydll.dll" (ArrayPointer As Integer) As Long
Call MyFunction(myArray(0))
```

- Declare the parameter ByVal As Long and pass the address of the first element obtained using the VarPtr operator as follows:

```
Declare Function MyFunction Lib "mydll.dll" (ByVal ArrayPointer As Long) _
As Long
Call MyFunction(VarPtr(myArray(0)))
```

The first option is the one most often used with API functions.

Objects

COM objects (which adhere to the Windows Common Object Model) are fundamental to the operation of Visual Basic and the Windows OLE subsystems. They are not used at all by the core Win32 API functions; however, there may be cases where you will need to pass objects or object pointers to the OLE API functions.

An object is always referenced by an interface. Logically, an interface is a group of functions that are related to each other and can be used to perform operations on the object. An object can expose many interfaces, and each interface has a function, QueryInterface, that can be used to request a different interface to the object.

When you look at the OLE documentation, you'll see that interface names always begin with the letter I. The two most important interfaces you need to know about are IUnknown and IDispatch.

IUnknown is actually a part of every interface. It controls reference counting so objects can track when they are free to delete themselves. It also includes the QueryInterface function that allows programmers to navigate between interfaces. The IUnknown variable type is supported by Visual Basic, though when you set an object into an IUnknown variable, you still cannot access the methods directly from Visual Basic:

```
Dim myObject As IUnknown
Set myObject = any object
```

You'll use the IUnknown type with some OLE API calls in cases where the function retrieves an interface pointer of unknown type.

IDispatch is the interface that supports a technology called Automation (sometimes referred to as OLE Automation or ActiveX automation). When you assign an object into a Visual Basic variable with the type Object, it contains a pointer to the IDispatch interface for the object.

```
Dim myObject As Object
Set myObject = an object that supports the IDispatch interface
```

Internally, an interface is a table of pointers to functions. When an object is passed as a parameter, the actual data passed is a pointer to this table. Both the IUnknown and IDispatch variable types actually store a pointer to an interface, thus they are both 32-bit values. You can use the Visual Basic ObjPtr operator to obtain the value of this pointer, though in fact you will rarely need to do so.

In the C/C++ documentation, you will generally see two types of object parameters:

IUnknown * or LPUNKNOWN   A pointer to an interface. Your Visual Basic declaration for this type should be ByVal As Object. Why? Because the object variable contains the pointer to the object, and you want to pass that pointer as a parameter.

IUnknown **, LPUNKNOWN *   A pointer to a pointer to an interface. The ** may be confusing at first—you know that one * means a pointer. The ** means a pointer to a variable that contains a pointer. The Visual Basic object variable contains a pointer. You can obtain a pointer to that variable using the VarPtr operator or by passing the parameter by reference. Thus, your Visual Basic declaration for this type of parameter will typically be As Object (no ByVal). API functions typically use this type of parameter when they are going to load your variable with a new interface to an object.

COM is one of those technologies that are quite simple once you understand them, but getting to understand them can be very difficult. A complete discussion of COM and object technology is beyond the scope of this tutorial.[5]

This concludes our introduction to translating C header files to Visual Basic. It's a subject that will be covered further in the puzzles and in the tutorials that follow.

---

5. The subject is covered at length in my book *Dan Appleman's Developing COM Components with Visual Basic 6.0: A Guide to the Perplexed*.

Classes, Structures, and User-Defined Types

FROM THE VIEWPOINT OF A VISUAL Basic programmer, there is no difference between C language classes, structs, and Visual Basic user-defined types. They all represent a way to group variables together in memory so they can be handled as a unit—a single structure in memory. Many Win32 API functions take structures as parameters. The individual variables within a structure are sometimes called the "fields" of the structure.

The C language is able to pass structures by value, in which case all of the structure data is placed on the stack. Visual Basic is not able to pass structures by value, but fortunately this will rarely be a problem. Most Win32 API functions expect structures to be passed by reference. In other words, they expect to see a pointer to a structure as a stack parameter.

The one case where a structure is passed by value under Win32 is the POINT structure.

Handling Points

The POINT structure is defined in C and Visual Basic as follows:

C/C++	VISUAL BASIC
```typedef struct tagPOINT```	```Type POINTAPI```
```{```	``` x As Long```
``` LONG x;```	``` y As Long```
``` LONG y;```	```End Type```
```} POINT, *PPOINT, NEAR *NPPOINT, FAR *LPPOINT;```	

You will notice that the Visual Basic structure is not called POINT. This is necessary because "Point" is a Visual Basic reserved word. An error occurs if you try to create a user-defined type with the same name as a reserved word.

The POINT structure shows another form of the typedef statement. The official name of the structure is tagPOINT, but if you use tagPOINT in your C code it must always be preceded by the word "struct," as follows:

```
struct tagPOINT myStruct;
```

By using the typedef version, you can declare a structure variable as follows:

```
POINT myStruct.
```

PPOINT, NPPOINT, and LPPOINT are all pointers to POINT structures.

Another common structure you will use is the RECT structure, which is defined in Visual Basic as follows:

```
Type RECT
        Left As Long
        Top As Long
        Right As Long
        Bottom As Long
End Type
```

The RECT structure describes the points of a rectangle.

Now consider the declaration of the PtInRect function shown below, which can be used to determine if a particular POINT is within a specified rectangle:

```
PtInRect(CONST RECT *lprc, POINT pt);
```

The first parameter is easy to understand. The CONST can be ignored by VB programmers—it just means that the function will not be modifying the contents of the RECT structure passed as a parameter. The RECT * indicates that lprc is a pointer to a RECT structure. The Visual Basic equivalent will be to pass the RECT structure by reference.

But what about the POINT parameter? There is no pointer indication, so it looks like the entire structure needs to be passed by value. Visual Basic cannot pass structures by value, so we have a problem.

To see the solution, take a look at the stack frame in Figure T7-1. The organization of data within structures always places the first fields in the lowest memory. Since the stack grows toward lower memory, a structure passed by value will be organized as shown in the figure, with the X field appearing at a higher location (lower memory address) than the Y field. If the idea of a stack growing toward lower memory is confusing, you might want to review Tutorial 4, "How DLL Calls Work: Inside a Stack Frame."

Now the problem of passing a POINT structure has been simplified. All you need to do is ask what kind of Visual Basic declaration can create this stack frame. The answer is

```
Private Declare Function PtInRect Lib
"user32" (lpRect As RECT, _
ByVal ptx As Long, ByVal pty As Long)
As Long
```

Remember (from Tutorial 4) that parameters are pushed onto the stack in reverse order. Because we want the actual values of the X and Y fields on the stack, we pass the X and Y fields separately by value. The RECT structure is passed by reference.

The following sample code from the Struct.vbp project (on the CD that comes with this book) demonstrates use of the PtInRect function in Visual Basic:

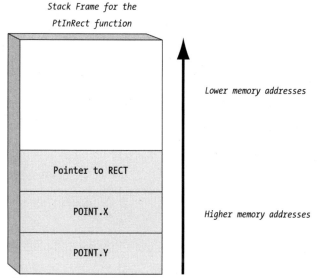

Figure T7-1: Stack frame showing a POINT structure passed by value

```
Private Sub cmdPtInRect_Click()
    Dim r As RECT
    Dim pt As POINTAPI
    r.Right = 100
    r.Bottom = 100
    pt.x = 50
    pt.y = 50
    Debug.Print PtInRect(r, pt.x, pt.y)
    pt.x = 150
    Debug.Print PtInRect(r, pt.x, pt.y)
End Sub
```

Visual Basic's inability to pass structures by value does require you to pass the fields of the structure individually, but at least the function can be called.

The good news is that the POINT and SIZE structures (which are identical except for different field names) are the only structures I know of that are passed by value to Win32 API functions.

Structures and DLL Calls

Before continuing further, we must consider one important fact. The vast majority of Visual Basic programmers will never run into the kinds of problems that are discussed through the rest of this tutorial. For most Visual Basic programmers, handling structures will be as easy as the following example, which illustrates the use of the GetClientRect API to retrieve the dimensions of a window's client area:

```
Type RECT
        Left As Long
        Top As Long
        Right As Long
        Bottom As Long
End Type

Declare Function GetClientRect Lib "user32" _
(ByVal hwnd As Long, lpRect As RECT) As Long

Dim rc As RECT
Call GetClientRect(myHwnd, rc)
```

Structure parameters (except for the cases noted earlier) are always passed by reference. This causes the address of the start of the structure to be passed to the DLL function.

Unfortunately, there are situations where handling structures becomes very complex. So complex that many of the puzzles in this book relate directly to structure declarations and parameters. The problem areas generally fall into the categories of string handling, variable alignment, and combinations of structures (structures within structures and arrays of structures).

The Most Important Thing to Remember

Your ultimate goal when dealing with structures is to cause Visual Basic to pass as a parameter a pointer to a block of memory that corresponds exactly to the format the DLL function expects to see.

From this you can draw two obvious conclusions:

- The most important thing to learn in order to handle structures correctly is how structures are stored in memory and how they are manipulated during the process of a DLL call.

Bringing the world together in music.

Another brilliant line up with world class music at the **Clare World Music Festival.**

Intimate settings in beautiful historic surroundings and a safe family environment with supervised children's activities.

All day bar with real ale. Vegetarian and ethnic food. Free parking and very clean toilets!

With a bigger line up and more major acts you must get there early or you'll miss out. With eleven hours of non-stop music, there is something for everyone.

Tickets are available from a number of sources.

1. From **Cornflowers, Ship Stores** and **DMS/Arthouse** of Clare.
2. Credit card hotline **01440 714140**
3. Festival info line **01787 277000**
4. By post using form below.

Return slip and payment to CWMF Box Office, High Barn, Clifton's Farm Drive, Clare,Suffollk.
Please do not send cash)

Mr/Mrs/Miss/Ms ------ First Name ------------- Surname ------------------

Address --

-- Post Code ------------

Daytime Telephone no. --

Please send ☐ Adult tickets @ **£20** each

☐ Accompanied Under 14's @ **£7** each

☐ Family tickets(2 adult + 2 under 14) @ **£45** each

I enclose a stamped addressed envelope and a cheque for the amount of | £ [ ]
made payable to 'Clare World Music Festival Ltd'

Special 'Early Bird' Booking Price

Adult tickets @ **£15** each   Family tickets(2 adult + 2 under 14) @ **£35** each.
(Offer applies to orders received by post before May 31st 2004)

CWMF PRESENTS

THE COMMITMENTS

with

John Otway Big Band
Roberto Pla & His Latin Ensemble
Ezio
Christine Collister
Swindle
Terrafolk
Fuzzface
Crabs

Clare '04

Advanced Bookings
Adult £20   Child (under 14) £7
Family (2 adult & 2 Children) £45
On the Gate
Adult £25   Child £7   Family £55
Ticket Outlets
Ship Stores, Cornflowers and
DMS/Arthouse all in Clare.
Also at Haverhill Arts Centre.
Credit Card bookings
01440 714140
Online bookings
www.clare-music-festival.co.uk

'Early Birds'
Special Offer
Adult £15
Family £35
(When you book by
31st May 2004)

Saturday July 3rd

Clare Castle Country Park, Clare, Suffolk
12 noon-11pm
subject to licenses

www.clare-music-festival.co.uk

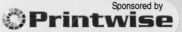

Sponsored by
Printwise

Childrens activities by
Kids Klub

Promoted by Clare World Music Festival Ltd. co reg. no:3935225 A not for profit making company limited by guarantee.
© Clare World Music Festival Ltd. Prepared by dletherington@onetel.net.uk

- It is ultimately possible to handle any structure, no matter what type of data it contains. At the very worst, you can allocate your own memory buffer and copy data into the buffer in the format required.

Strings in Structures

The first issue to consider with regard to strings inside structures follows from the fact that Visual Basic uses Unicode characters internally. Strings inside structures are stored within Visual Basic in Unicode format.

The Struct.vbp project can be used to help understand what is going on within Visual Basic during a DLL call. The project defines the following structure:

```
Private Type Struct1
    a As Integer
    b As Integer
    c As String * 4
    d As String
End Type
```

The project contains the function ShowMemory, which takes a memory address as a parameter and prints the contents of a specified number of bytes in hexadecimal format. We'll be using this function to analyze the contents of memory buffers for the structure.

```
' Display the bytes of memory at the address specified in
' hexadecimal format.
Private Sub ShowMemory(ByVal Address As Long, ByVal bytes As Integer)
    Dim b As Byte
    Dim x As Integer
    ' Print the address
    Debug.Print Hex$(Address) & ": ";
    ' Copy each byte in the buffer one byte at a time into
    ' a temporary variable 'b'
    For x = 0 To bytes - 1
        Call RtlMoveMemory(b, ByVal Address + x, 1)
        ' Display the hex value of byte 'b'
        Debug.Print Hex$(b) & " ";
    Next x
    Debug.Print
End Sub
```

The cmdStruct1_Click function can be used to examine this structure both as it is stored within Visual Basic and as it is passed during a DLL function call. The 'a' and 'b' fields of the structure are set to hex values &H1234 and &H5678, respectively. These numbers are arbitrary and will be easily recognized. Both strings are set to "ABCD" as follows:

```
Private Sub cmdStruct1_Click()
    Dim s As Struct1
    Dim b(40) As Byte
    s.a = &H1234
    s.b = &H5678
    s.c = "ABCD"
    s.d = "ABCD"
    Debug.Print "Structure contains on API call: "
    RtlMoveMemory b(0), s, Len(s)
    ShowMemory VarPtr(b(0)), Len(s)
    ' Why can't we look at the string data?
    ' Answer - temporary buffers!
    Debug.Print "In VB it contains: "
    ShowMemory VarPtr(s), LenB(s)
End Sub
```

The only reliable way to see what a structure looks like during an API call is to make an API call. In this case, we call the ever-useful RtlMoveMemory function. The destination parameter is the first byte of a byte array. The source parameter is the structure. Visual Basic will pass a pointer to that structure. The RtlMoveMemory function will copy the structure data into the byte array so we can display its contents. The resulting display is as follows:

```
Structure contains on API call:
17B168: 34 12 78 56 41 42 43 44 F4 2E 18 0
```

The first two bytes are &H34 and &H12. As you may recall from Tutorial 2, "Memory, Where It All Begins," this corresponds to the 16-bit value &H1234. The bytes only appear swapped because the lower byte of the value appears in lower memory, which is displayed first in the memory buffer dump.

The second integer is &H5678 and appears immediately after the first.

Next, you can see four characters, &H41, &H42, &H43, and &H44. These are the ASCII codes for the letters "ABCD"—the fixed string variable 'c'. The final four bytes are the pointer &H182EF4 (which almost certainly will have a different value on your system). This is a BSTR pointer to an ANSI string created temporarily during the calling process. We'll talk more about dynamic strings inside structures later.

The second part of the function uses the VarPtr function to obtain the address of the structure in Visual Basic's memory. The LenB function retrieves the size of a structure as it is stored within Visual Basic. A dump of the structure within Visual Basic appears as follows:

```
In VB it contains:
12F5E8: 34 12 78 56 41 0 42 0 43 0 44 0 CC 9A 17 0
```

The only difference is the fixed-length string portion of the structure. The string appears here as the characters 41 00 42 00 43 00 44 00—the same "ABCD" string except that each character is 2 bytes—Unicode.

Two facts are apparent from this demonstration:

- Fixed-length strings are stored within a structure, whereas only a 4-byte BSTR pointer is stored in the structure for dynamic strings.

- Strings within a structure are stored as Unicode within Visual Basic and as ANSI when passed to a DLL call.

Tutorial 5, "The ByVal Keyword: The Solution to 90 Percent of All API Problems," discusses how string parameters are either Unicode or ANSI depending on whether you use the ANSI or Unicode entry point for a function. The same situation often applies to structures that contain strings. For example, the LOGFONT structure (which describes a logical font) contains a fixed-length string that holds the name of the font's typeface. If you look in the C header files (on the CD that comes with this book), you will find that there are actually two separate structure definitions, LOGFONTA and LOGFONTW. The LOGFONTA structure defines the string as an array of single byte characters, and the LOGFONTW structure defines the string as an array of wide characters.

Don't assume that this will always be the case. Some functions always use ANSI strings, others always use Unicode characters. You'll have to refer to the documentation of the structure to know which one to use.

Dynamic Strings Inside Structures

A dynamic string is stored in a VB structure as a 32-bit pointer to the string data. There are a number of DLL structures in Windows that contain pointers to strings. You can use a dynamic string in some cases, but you should use caution. The dynamic string pointer in the structure is a BSTR pointer—it points to a block of memory that is managed by the OLE subsystem. If the DLL were to overwrite that pointer value, it could cause a memory leak or lead to a memory exception. This suggests the following rules for using dynamic strings inside structures.

It is safe to use dynamic strings when

- The function you are calling expects a BSTR pointer in the structure (likely only with OLE DLL calls).

or when

- You add a NULL character to the end of the string to be sure it is NULL-terminated.

And if the DLL function modifies the string data, you initialize the string to the necessary length.

It is not safe to use dynamic strings when:

- The DLL function modifies the value of the pointer inside the structure and is not using the OLE subsystem. This is typically the case if the pointer is anything other than BSTR *. Keep in mind that, outside the OLE subsystem, most API functions do not use BSTR variables, so you will rarely use dynamic strings inside structures used by the Win32 API.

Alignment Issues

The Struct.vbp project defines the following structure, which is extremely similar to the one shown in the previous section:

```
Private Type Struct2
    a As Integer
    b As Long
    c As String * 4
    d As String
End Type
```

The cmdStruct2_Click function is almost identical to the cmdStruct1_Click function. The only difference is that the second structure field 'b' is set to &H56789ABC (since it's a 32-bit variable) and that the initial RtlMoveMemory call copies an extra 2 bytes into the temporary byte array (2 bytes beyond the length returned by the Len function). The reason for these 2 extra bytes will become apparent later.

```
Private Sub cmdStruct2_Click()
    Dim s As Struct2
    Dim b(40) As Byte
    s.a = &H1234
    s.b = &H56789ABC
    s.c = "ABCD"
    s.d = "ABCD"
    Debug.Print "Structure contains on API call: "
    ' Alignment screws up byte count on Len command
    RtlMoveMemory b(0), s, Len(s) + 2
    ShowMemory VarPtr(b(0)), Len(s) + 2
    ' Why can't we look at the string data?
    ' Answer - temporary buffers!
    Debug.Print "In VB it contains: "
    ShowMemory VarPtr(s), LenB(s)
End Sub
```

The first ShowMemory call shows the contents of the structure that is passed as a DLL parameter:

```
Structure contains on API call:
187D98: 34 12 0 0 BC 9A 78 56 41 42 43 44 C 5B 16 0
```

Curiously enough, the first field 'a' has two null bytes between it and the 'b' field. The rest of the data is just as before. Where do these two extra bytes come from?

Let's take a look at the contents of the structure as stored in Visual Basic:

```
12F5E4: 34 12 0 0 BC 9A 78 56 41 0 42 0 43 0 44 0 F4 2E 18 0
```

The string is in Unicode as before, and the two extra bytes are still there.

The extra bytes exist because the individual fields within structures are stored within Visual Basic according to certain alignment rules. These rules require that every field begin on its natural boundary. In other words, the address of the first byte in the field must start at an address that is divisible by the length of the field. This means that single-byte fields can begin anywhere, 16-bit numeric fields must begin at an even address (2-byte boundary), and 32-bit long variables or pointers must begin at an address that is a multiple of 4 (4-byte boundary).

Visual Basic uses natural alignment internally and during DLL function calls. This leads to a problem in some cases, because most API functions use single-byte alignment, where all of the fields are packed against each other. This is illustrated in Figure T7-2, which shows how the struct2 structure is stored three different ways.

The first example shows how the structure is stored internally, with the 2 bytes of padding caused by the alignment and the strings in Unicode. The length of the structure as it is stored internally can be determined using the LenB function. The second example shows how the structure is stored in memory when passed as a DLL call. The string is converted to ANSI, but natural alignment rules still apply. The lower example shows how the structure would be stored in a file if written using the VB Put function. As you can see, all of the fields are packed together with no padding (single-byte alignment). The length of the structure with single-byte alignment can be determined using the Len function. How can you determine the length of a structure when passed as a DLL parameter? You have to figure it out for yourself—there is no function available to perform the calculation for you.

What if a structure used by a DLL function requires single-byte alignment? This is actually the default for virtually all Win32 API structures, so you might think this poses a serious problem. Fortunately, the programmers who developed

```
As stored in Visual Basic                    Length=LenB()
34 12 00 00 BC 9A 78 56 41 00 42 00 43 00 44 00 F4 2E 18 00


As passed in a DLL call                      Length=Unknown
34 12 00 00 BC 9A 78 56 41 42 43 44 0C 5B 16 00


As stored in a file (single byte packing)    Length=Len()
34 12 BC 9A 78 56 41 42 43 44 0C 5B 16 00
```

Figure T7-2: The struct2 structure in three forms

Windows were usually careful to define structures so that they are laid out identically in memory with both single and natural alignment. That's why you'll occasionally see reserved bytes in Win32 API structures. They are, in effect, adding the padding bytes explicitly.

For example, you could do this for the struct2 structure by defining it as follows:

```
Private Type Struct2
    a As Integer
    reserved as Integer
    b As Long
    c As String * 4
    d As String
End Type
```

This structure will appear identically in memory under both single-byte and natural-byte alignment (feel free to modify the Struct.vbp project and try it).

The bad news is that, in a number of cases, Microsoft blew it and the structures do not follow the natural alignment rules. There are several ways to deal with these situations. You can redefine the Visual Basic type to deal with the alignment issues—for example, dividing a long variable into two integers. You can temporarily copy the structure into a memory buffer such as a byte array, explicitly copying parts of the structure into the locations where they need to be. You can use a third-party product such as Desaware's SpyWorks, which includes byte-packing functions that automatically perform single-byte packing and unpacking for you.

This concludes our introduction to handling user-defined types. You'll find that many of the puzzles in this book deal with applications relating to this subject, including dealing with pointers to strings and other user-defined types, alignment issues, and working with arrays of structures.

Porting C Header Files

PUZZLE 29, "WHAT DO YOU DO When It Mega Hurts?" demonstrates how to handle DLL functions that return structures, using the example of the cpuspeed function from Intel's cpuinf32.dll dynamic link library. This library allows you to retrieve all sorts of interesting information about the processors on your PC (at least if you're using Intel processors).

This book provides the DLL (on the CD) and sufficient information to demonstrate how to use it in the puzzle. You can obtain the latest version of the DLL and the complete source code for both the DLL and several test programs written in C++ from Intel's Web site at *http://developer.intel.com/design/perftool/cpuid/*. (Note, I obviously can't guarantee that this file will continue to be available in the future or will remain at the location shown above. Check *http://www.desaware.com/* for the latest information in case of changes.)

In this tutorial, you'll see how the original C header files were converted into Visual Basic for use by the cputest application.

Don't worry, reading this tutorial will not spoil the puzzle.

Step 1: Load the Header File into a Visual Basic Module

Consider for a moment the type of information you are likely to find in a Visual Basic standard module:

- Global variable declarations

- Definitions of user-defined types (called "structures" in the C/C++ world)

- Global functions and subroutines

- Comments explaining the various elements of the module

The most important of these are the structure definitions and the function declarations. You can't really access global variables from dynamic link libraries. And although comments are critical for understanding how the module works, there is no functional difference between a comment in VB and one in C/C++.

Just as Visual Basic projects use several types of files (module, form, class, etc.), projects written in C or C++ use different types of files as well. The most important file type when it comes to understanding a DLL is the header file, which typically has the extension .h. A header file usually contains the same information as a standard module except that it rarely contains large blocks of code. Instead, it will contain a declaration for each function that is contained in the actual source file (which will have a .C or .CPP extension, depending on whether the program is written in C or C++).

Now, this is a simplification; C++ header files can contain a great deal of additional information, but you will rarely need it to access the DLL from Visual Basic. Complex DLLs may use dozens of separate header files and source files. But the only header files you need are the ones that include structure definitions and function declarations that are used by outside applications. You can ignore those header files that are only used within the DLL. Once you find these key header files, all you need to do is convert them to Visual Basic, and you'll be able to access the DLL functions. And teaching you to perform these conversions correctly is one of the major goals of this book.

Why worry about learning how to handle C/C++ header files? Why not just rely on the DLL's documentation?

There are two main answers to this question.

First, many DLLs don't bother including actual structure definitions and function declarations in their documentation. Why? Because DLLs are traditionally intended to be called from other C/C++ programs anyway. It is far easier to just tell a programmer to include a header file that comes with the DLL in their own project.[1]

That way, the programmer can call the DLL functions directly in their own applications with no further effort on their part. This is one advantage that C/C++ programmers have over VB programmers—everybody provides C/C++ headers for their DLLs. Not everyone includes a Visual Basic module with the correct declarations and structure definitions.

The second answer applies to the Win32 API as well. Because the header files are primarily intended to be used by applications rather than read by programmers, they are almost always correct. If they weren't correct, the programs that used them wouldn't work. Incorrect documentation may cause nervous breakdowns among programmers, but it has little other effect.

Intel's cpuinf32.dll library includes two header files, speed.h and cpuid.h. The first step in converting these files is to copy them into Visual Basic modules.

---

1. C programs can "include" header files using a command called #include. This command causes a header file to be inserted into a program during compilation. There is, unfortunately, no Visual Basic equivalent to this operation at this time.

Step 2: Eliminate Unnecessary Information

A header file may include information that is used only when building the DLL as well as information needed by those using the DLL. This is the case with both the cpuid.h and speed.h header files. Deleting the private information is a good first step, as it will save you the effort of converting code that will never be used. The cpuid.bas file only comments out unnecessary code rather than deleting it outright in order to illustrate the process more clearly. How do you spot unnecessary code?

Look for Private Functions

One way to spot a private function is to look at the comments within the header file itself. The cpuid.h file makes it easy. Halfway through the file is the following line:

```
// Private Function Declarations ///////////////////////////////'
```

This line suggests that everything that follows is private, which turns out to be the case. Everything after this line is commented out and can be deleted.

You can also use the dumpinfo.exe utility (on the CD provided with this book) to see what functions the DLL actually exports. Any function that does not appear in the export list is private by definition.

Check for Code Excluded via Conditional Compilation

Visual Basic supports conditional compilation using the #if, #else, and #endif constructs. C and C++ support these and a few other conditional compilation terms. At the start of many C/C++ header files, you'll see code such as this near the top of the file:

```
#ifndef cpuid_h
#define cpuid_h
```

followed by the following line near the end of the file:

```
#endif cpuid_h
```

The #ifndef directive means "compile the following lines if the following variable is not defined." The #ifdef directive is similar, except that it compiles the code only if the variable is defined. You see, unlike Visual Basic, it is possible for a C project to include a particular header file more than once. Including a file in C is accomplished by using the command #include <filename> in the source file. This tells the compiler to scan the specified file during compilation. Let's say you have two header files, myfile1.h and myfile2.h, and a single source file mysource-file.cpp. Next, assume that mysourcefile.cpp includes both of the header files, meaning that when it is compiled, the compiler will first scan the two headers, treating them as if they were part of the source file. Finally, assume that myfile2.h also includes myfile1.h. When the compiler tries to build mysoucefile.cpp, it will see the command #include "myfile1.h" and immediately scan that header file. Next, it will see the command #include "myfile2.h" and try to scan it. But while scanning this file, it will see another include of myfile1.h, causing the file to be effectively scanned twice. This can lead to problems, as the C/C++ language does not allow declaring certain elements more than once.

The conditional compilation lines in this example prevent the cpuid.h file from being scanned more than once during a given compilation. The first time the file is scanned, the #ifndef cpuid_h line succeeds—the variable cpuid_h is not yet defined. The constant is then defined using the #define statement (though it is not given a value). The next time the file is scanned, the #ifndef cpuid_h line fails because the variable is defined, and all of the rest of the code in the header file is ignored.

What does all of this mean to you as a Visual Basic programmer? Very little, because the concept of scanning a file more than once during compile time does not exist in VB. So all code of this type can be deleted.

Discard Unneeded Function Declarations

There may be function declarations that you simply don't need for your application. It doesn't make sense to port them unless you expect to need them in the future. There are also exported functions that are used only by the operating system, which you are unlikely to ever call from Visual Basic. These include:

- **DllMain.** The DLL initialization routine is called from the operating system, never directly.

- **DllCanUnloadNow.** This routine is called by the operating system to determine if an ActiveX server can be unloaded.

- **DllGetClassObject.** This routine is called by the operating system to create an ActiveX server object.

- **DllRegisterServer.** This routine is called by applications or the operating system to register an ActiveX DLL server.

- **DllUnregisterServer.** This routine is called by applications or the operating system to unregister an ActiveX DLL server.

If you find declarations for these functions in your header file, go ahead and delete them.

Step 3: Port the Comments

Porting comments is probably the easiest part of the conversion process. Comments in C and C++ are indicated in two ways. The start of larger comment blocks is indicated by the character sequence /* and terminated by the character sequence */. Comments in this form can span multiple lines. Examples of valid comments are:

```
/* comment */
/* first comment line
second comment line
* another comment line

The comment ends here */
```

Single-line comments are indicated by the character sequence //, which can appear anywhere in a line. This sequence works just like the Visual Basic single quote (') comment character. Examples of valid comments are:

```
// A complete comment line here.
#define myconstant 0x55 // Comment starts at the // characters.
```

Converting comments is slightly tedious, but very easy with judicious use of the editor's Replace command. The // sequence can be replaced directly with the single quote (') comment character. Multiline block comments are typically handled manually.

Step 4: Port the Constants

Constant conversions can range from trivial to complex. Constant declarations take the following form:

```
#define constantname value_expression
```

The value_expression term can be an expression made up of one or more other constants (including previously defined constants). Standard arithmetic operations can be used, as can the | operator (bitwise OR) and & operator (bitwise AND). You may also see the >> and << operators (shift right and shift left, which shift the individual bits in the expression by the number of positions specified by the operator).

Hex values in C/C++ are prefixed with the sequence 0x or 0X instead of &H. Constants may have an L suffix, indicating that they are a Long value. Expressions are not limited to numeric values—they may consist of strings or generic text as well. The entire value_expression term is substituted in place of the constantname term when the program is compiled, so any text that would be allowed in that position is allowed.

Declarations are converted into the following generic Visual Basic form:

```
Public Const constantname = constant_value
```

You can use the same constant name, but you must calculate out the value of the constant based on the header file. Here's an example from the cpuid.h file:

```
#define VERSION 0x0101   // Must be 2 bytes in length.
Public Const VERSION = &H0101    ' Must be 2 bytes in length.
```

Here's a hint: You can typically do a global search and replace the term "#define" with "Public Const" to make the porting effort easier. In most cases, all that will remain is to add the equal signs that are needed by Visual Basic. One of the nice things about this part of the porting process is that the Visual Basic compiler will catch most of your errors (such as forgetting the equal sign or forgetting to change the 0x hex indicator to &H).

Step 5: Comment Out the typedef Declarations

The C typedef command is used to describe one type of variable in terms of another type. Its generic form is:

```
typedef variable_type new_type
```

where variable_type is a currently defined C/C++ data type and new_type is a new name for that type. Consider this example from speed.h:

```
typedef unsigned short ushort;
```

This means that, from this point on in the program, the data type ushort refers to an unsigned short variable. A typedef statement doesn't really do anything, it just allows you to create new names for common data types.[2]

Why should you comment these lines out instead of just deleting them? Because they provide crucial hints about what data type you will actually use for variables within structures and function parameters. If you see a parameter in a function in speed.h that is declared as a ushort, the typedef statement lets you know that it is, in fact, an unsigned short variable and thus will be a 16-bit Visual Basic integer in the VB declaration.

Step 6: Port the Structures and Functions

I won't go into further details here on this process other than to refer you to the puzzles in Part I (after all, this whole book is about coming up with declarations for structures and functions). The only challenging function here is the cpuspeed function, which is discussed in Puzzle 29.

---

2. Purists and most C/C++ programmers will immediately protest that the typedef command is, in fact, a very important statement that does quite a lot, specifically concerning enforcing type checking. But that fact is completely irrelevant to Visual Basic programmers, at least with regard to the porting process. So you see, I haven't completely taken leave of my senses.

TUTORIAL 9

Inside a DLL File: Exploring the DumpInfo Program

ONE OF THE MOST COMMON PROBLEMS you will face when using API functions is figuring out which DLL exports a function that you want to use. The reason this is challenging is that the Microsoft documentation does not actually list the DLL name for a function, only the import library that C programs would use to import the function. Unfortunately, the import library name does not always match the DLL name. Not only that, but it is sometimes difficult to know for sure if a function has separate ANSI and Unicode entry points.

Microsoft does provide a program named DumpBin with Visual Studio, which allows you to obtain a list of exported functions for a DLL, but it can take a long time to search through all of the DLLs for a particular function.

Even before starting on this book, I wanted to provide an automatic search utility that would take a function name and search through all of the DLLs in your system directory for the function, optionally checking for both the ANSI and Unicode variations of the function name. Ultimately I ended up writing a program that could read the export table for a DLL file. This involved understanding the specification for the Portable Executable file format (the file format used for DLLs), interpreting the structures and constants that are used with this file format, and converting them to Visual Basic. These are exactly the kinds of tasks that this book is designed to teach VB programmers to accomplish on their own, so it seemed that this utility could actually perform double service, both as a utility and as a case history.

Using DumpInfo

The DumpInfo program performs two distinct functions. First, it has the ability to list all of the exported functions for a specified DLL. The Exports command button on the main form brings up a dialog box that allows you to select a single DLL to examine. The exports for that DLL are displayed in the list box, as shown

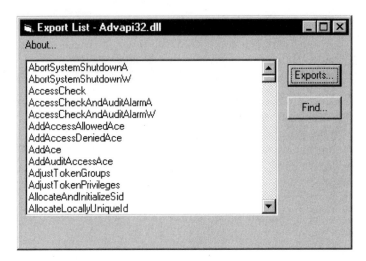

Figure T9-1: Export list for advapi32.dll

in Figure T9-1, which shows the export list for the advapi32.dll dynamic link library.

The Find command button brings up the form shown in Figure T9-2. Enter the name of the function that you want to search for in the text box. The three checkboxes offer the following options:

- **Ignore Case.** Check this box to ignore case during the search.

- **Check A&W Suffixes.** This option searches for the function name you specify and for variations that result in adding either an A or a W suffix to the name. This allows you to detect ANSI and Unicode entry points if they exist for a given function name.

- **Search All DLLs.** When checked, the DumpInfo program will search all of the DLLs in your system directory, even after the functions are found in a particular DLL. Otherwise the program will stop searching once it has found the functions. This option is useful if you think a particular function might be exported by more than one DLL.

A search operation can be aborted while it's in progress by clicking on the Stop button (which appears only during a search). After a search operation has finished, you will see a list of the functions that match your search criteria, such as that shown for the GetWindowText function in Figure T9-3.

Before you read farther, I must stress that this is an expert-level tutorial. To gain full benefit of this tutorial, you should first obtain a copy of the Microsoft Portable Executable File specification (available on MSDN and the Visual Studio

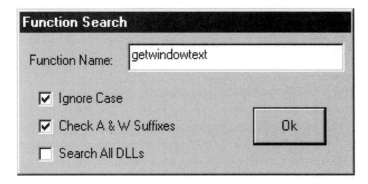

Figure T9-2: Export function search entry form

Figure T9-3: Results of search operation for the GetWindowText function

online documentation). This tutorial does not attempt to explain the executable file format—only to demonstrate how that format can be parsed by a Visual Basic program. You do not need to read or understand this tutorial in order to move on to the tutorials that follow, so I encourage you to skip this one if you find it frustrating or confusing.

The Exports Class

Even though the DumpInfo program performs two distinct functions, it should be clear one follows naturally from the other. The ability to search for a function in a directory full of DLLs is relatively simple, once you have the ability to list all of the exported functions in a single DLL. In fact, it's so simple that this tutorial will not even discuss the process—you'll have to look at the sample program to see how it is implemented. Instead, this tutorial will focus on the more difficult task of obtaining that list of exported functions in the first place.

Because obtaining a list of exported functions is a well-defined task that lends itself to reuse, it makes sense to implement it in a class. The Exports class takes the form of a private collection class that can be loaded with the list of exported functions for a single DLL. Those functions can then be read using a number of collection-like properties. The Exports class implements the following public methods and properties:

- **Sub Load(FileName as String).** Loads the Exports class with a list of exported functions for the specified file name.

- **Function Count() As Long.** Returns the number of exported functions in the collection.

- **Function Ordinal(FunctionNumber As Long) As Long.** Returns the ordinal number of the exported function at the specified index in the collection.[1]

- **Function Name(FunctionNumber As Long) As String.** Returns the name of the exported function at the specified index in the collection.

Now the problem is reduced to scanning a DLL file for exported functions and loading an internal array with the names and ordinal numbers of those functions.

The PE Executable Format

There are two good sources for information on the portable executable (PE) file format, which is the name of the file format used for every Win32 executable and dynamic link library. The first source is the format specification that can be found in the MSDN or Visual Studio library under the Specification-Platforms section of the library, where you should look for a book titled *The Microsoft Portable Executable and Common Object File Format*. The second source will be winnt.h, the header file that contains the C type definitions and constant declarations used by the PE file format.

Our job will be to figure out the contents of the file well enough to find and read the export function information. Fortunately, this does not demand an in-

---

1. Every exported function can also have a number associated with it called an ordinal number. Functions can be found and loaded more quickly by ordinal number than by name. Despite this, ordinal numbers are rarely used.

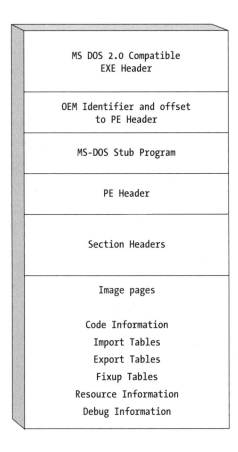

MS DOS 2.0 Compatible
EXE Header

OEM Identifier and offset
to PE Header

MS-DOS Stub Program

PE Header

Section Headers

Image pages

Code Information
Import Tables
Export Tables
Fixup Tables
Resource Information
Debug Information

Figure T9-4: Architecture of a portable executable file

depth understanding of all aspects of the file format—just those portions that are necessary to find and interpret the export function information.

The overall architecture of a PE file is shown in Figure T9-4, which is derived from the specification.

The curious thing about a portable executable file is that it begins with the same kind of header that has been used by executables since the early days of MS-DOS. That header is followed by an MS-DOS stub program. The existence of this header and stub is the reason that you can run any Windows executable under MS-DOS and see the message "This Program Requires Microsoft Windows." The message is generated by the stub program.

The Win32-specific information starts with the PE header. This means that the first step performed by the scanning program will be to scan past the MS-DOS header and stub program to find the PE header.

The DOS header is defined by the following structure from winnt.h:

```
typedef struct _IMAGE_DOS_HEADER {      // DOS .EXE header
    WORD    e_magic;                    // Magic number
    WORD    e_cblp;                     // Bytes on last page of file
    WORD    e_cp;                       // Pages in file
    WORD    e_crlc;                     // Relocations
    WORD    e_cparhdr;                  // Size of header in paragraphs
    WORD    e_minalloc;                 // Minimum extra paragraphs needed
    WORD    e_maxalloc;                 // Maximum extra paragraphs needed
    WORD    e_ss;                       // Initial (relative) SS value
    WORD    e_sp;                       // Initial SP value
    WORD    e_csum;                     // Checksum
    WORD    e_ip;                       // Initial IP value
    WORD    e_cs;                       // Initial (relative) CS value
    WORD    e_lfarlc;                   // File address of relocation table
    WORD    e_ovno;                     // Overlay number
    WORD    e_res[4];                   // Reserved words
    WORD    e_oemid;                    // OEM identifier (for e_oeminfo)
    WORD    e_oeminfo;                  // OEM information; e_oemid specific
    WORD    e_res2[10];                 // Reserved words
    LONG    e_lfanew;                   // File address of new exe header
  } IMAGE_DOS_HEADER, *PIMAGE_DOS_HEADER;
```

This translates into the following Visual Basic structure. Note that the Visual Basic array indexes are one less than those seen in the C declaration. C language array definitions specify the size of the array, whereas Visual Basic array definitions specify the highest index and the default lower base is 0.

```
Public Type IMAGE_DOS_HEADER
   e_magic As Integer
   e_cblp As Integer
   e_cp As Integer
   e_crlc As Integer
   e_cparhdr As Integer
   e_minalloc As Integer
   e_maxalloc As Integer
   e_ss As Integer
   e_sp As Integer
   e_csum As Integer
   e_ip As Integer
   e_cs As Integer
   e_lfarlc As Integer
   e_ovno As Integer
   e_res(3) As Integer
```

```
    e_oemid As Integer
    e_oeminfo As Integer
    e_res2(9) As Integer
    e_lfanew As Long
End Type
```

The e_lfanew field specifies the offset in the file to the start of the PE Header structure. The PE Header structure is defined by an IMAGE_NT_HEADERS structure, which contains a signature that identifies the file as a PE format file and two additional structures: an IMAGE_FILE_HEADER structure and an IMAGE_OPTIONAL_HEADER structure. These structures are as follows:

```
typedef struct _IMAGE_NT_HEADERS {
    DWORD Signature;
    IMAGE_FILE_HEADER FileHeader;
    IMAGE_OPTIONAL_HEADER OptionalHeader;
} IMAGE_NT_HEADERS, *PIMAGE_NT_HEADERS;

typedef struct _IMAGE_FILE_HEADER {
    WORD    Machine;
    WORD    NumberOfSections;
    DWORD   TimeDateStamp;
    DWORD   PointerToSymbolTable;
    DWORD   NumberOfSymbols;
    WORD    SizeOfOptionalHeader;
    WORD    Characteristics;
} IMAGE_FILE_HEADER, *PIMAGE_FILE_HEADER;

typedef struct _IMAGE_OPTIONAL_HEADER {
    //
    // Standard fields.
    //

    WORD    Magic;
    BYTE    MajorLinkerVersion;
    BYTE    MinorLinkerVersion;
    DWORD   SizeOfCode;
    DWORD   SizeOfInitializedData;
    DWORD   SizeOfUninitializedData;
    DWORD   AddressOfEntryPoint;
    DWORD   BaseOfCode;
    DWORD   BaseOfData;
```

```
            //
            // NT additional fields.
            //

            DWORD    ImageBase;
            DWORD    SectionAlignment;
            DWORD    FileAlignment;
            WORD     MajorOperatingSystemVersion;
            WORD     MinorOperatingSystemVersion;
            WORD     MajorImageVersion;
            WORD     MinorImageVersion;
            WORD     MajorSubsystemVersion;
            WORD     MinorSubsystemVersion;
            DWORD    Win32VersionValue;
            DWORD    SizeOfImage;
            DWORD    SizeOfHeaders;
            DWORD    CheckSum;
            WORD     Subsystem;
            WORD     DllCharacteristics;
            DWORD    SizeOfStackReserve;
            DWORD    SizeOfStackCommit;
            DWORD    SizeOfHeapReserve;
            DWORD    SizeOfHeapCommit;
            DWORD    LoaderFlags;
            DWORD    NumberOfRvaAndSizes;
            IMAGE_DATA_DIRECTORY DataDirectory[IMAGE_NUMBEROF_DIRECTORY_ENTRIES];
        } IMAGE_OPTIONAL_HEADER, *PIMAGE_OPTIONAL_HEADER;

        typedef struct _IMAGE_DATA_DIRECTORY {
            DWORD    VirtualAddress;
            DWORD    Size;
        } IMAGE_DATA_DIRECTORY, *PIMAGE_DATA_DIRECTORY;


        Private DosHeader As IMAGE_DOS_HEADER
        Private PEHeader As IMAGE_NT_HEADERS
        Private PEHeaderOffset As Long
        Private ExportDirectory As IMAGE_EXPORT_DIRECTORY

        Public Type IMAGE_NT_HEADERS
           Signature As Long
           FileHeader As IMAGE_FILE_HEADER
           OptionalHeader As IMAGE_OPTIONAL_HEADER
```

```
End Type

Public Type IMAGE_FILE_HEADER
    Machine As Integer
    NumberOfSections As Integer
    TimeDateStamp As Long
    PointerToSymbolTable As Long
    NumberOfSymbols As Long
    SizeOfOptionalHeader As Integer
    Characteristics As Integer
End Type

Public Type IMAGE_DATA_DIRECTORY
    VirtualAddress As Long
    Size As Long
End Type

Public Type IMAGE_OPTIONAL_HEADER
    Magic As Integer
    MajorLinkerVersion As Byte
    MinorLinkerVersion As Byte
    SizeOfCode As Long
    SizeOfInitializedData As Long
    SizeOfUninitializedData As Long
    AddressOfEntryPoint As Long
    BaseOfCode As Long
    BaseOfData As Long
    ImageBase As Long
    SectionAlignment As Long
    FileAlignment As Long
    MajorOperatingSystemVersion As Integer
    MinorOperatingSystemVersion As Integer
    MajorImageVersion As Integer
    MinorImageVersion As Integer
    MajorSubsystemVersion As Integer
    MinorSubsystemVersion As Integer
    Win32VersionValue As Long
    SizeOfImage As Long
    SizeOfHeaders As Long
    CheckSum As Long
    Subsystem As Integer
    DllCharacteristics As Integer
    SizeOfStackReserve As Long
```

```
      SizeOfStackCommit As Long
      SizeOfHeapReserve As Long
      SizeOfHeapCommit As Long
      LoaderFlags As Long
      NumberOfRvaAndSizes As Long
      DataDirectory(15) As IMAGE_DATA_DIRECTORY
End Type
```

Detailed explanations of the IMAGE_NT_HEADERS, IMAGE_FILE_HEADER, IMAGE_DATA_DIRECTORY, and IMAGE_OPTIONAL_HEADER structures can be found in the PE file format specification. In this tutorial, I'll only define those fields that are actually used by the program. The main function used within the Exports class to load the file information is the LoadInfo function shown here:

```
Private Function LoadInfo(FileName As String) As Integer
   Dim x%
   FileHandle = FreeFile()

   On Error GoTo BadLoad
   Open FileName For Binary Access Read As #FileHandle
   On Error GoTo BadBuild
   ' Get the DOS header
   Get #FileHandle, , DosHeader

   ' Calculate the offset to the NT header
   PEHeaderOffset = DosHeader.e_lfanew
   ' Get the NT header
   Get #FileHandle, PEHeaderOffset + 1, PEHeader

   SectionCount = PEHeader.FileHeader.NumberOfSections
   ReDim Sections(SectionCount - 1)
   SectionsOffset = Seek(FileHandle)
   For x = 0 To SectionCount - 1
      Get #FileHandle, , Sections(x)
   Next x

   FindExportBase

   Get #FileHandle, ExportBase + 1, ExportDirectory

   LoadExportInfo

   Close #FileHandle
```

```
   Exit Function
BadLoad:
   LoadInfo = -1
   Exit Function
BadBuild:
   LoadInfo = -1
   Close #FileHandle
End Function
```

The function first loads the IMAGE_DOS_HEADER structure into the variable DosHeader. The e_lfanew field of the structure contains the offset to the start of the PE Header, which is defined by the IMAGE_NT_HEADERS structure. The PEHeader variable is loaded with this information using the following Get statement:

```
Get #FileHandle, PEHeaderOffset + 1, PEHeader
```

Why do you have to add 1 to the offset? Because the offset is based on the assumption that the first byte in the file is at location 0, whereas the Get statement assumes that the first byte in the file is at location 1.

The section table appears immediately after the PE header. The NumberOfSections field in the IMAGE_FILE_HEADER structure allows you to determine the number of sections in the file. Each section is defined using the IMAGE_SECTION_HEADER structure, which is defined as follows:

```
#define IMAGE_SIZEOF_SHORT_NAME                 8

typedef struct _IMAGE_SECTION_HEADER {
    BYTE      Name[IMAGE_SIZEOF_SHORT_NAME];
    union {
            DWORD    PhysicalAddress;
            DWORD    VirtualSize;
    } Misc;
    DWORD    VirtualAddress;
    DWORD    SizeOfRawData;
    DWORD    PointerToRawData;
    DWORD    PointerToRelocations;
    DWORD    PointerToLinenumbers;
    WORD     NumberOfRelocations;
    WORD     NumberOfLinenumbers;
    DWORD    Characteristics;
} IMAGE_SECTION_HEADER, *PIMAGE_SECTION_HEADER;
```

```
Public Type IMAGE_SECTION_HEADER
    ShortName(7) As Byte

    VirtualSize As Long
    VirtualAddress As Long
    SizeOfRawData As Long
    PointerToRawData As Long
    PointerToRelocations As Long
    PointerToLinenumbers As Long
    NumberOfRelocations As Integer
    NumberOfLinenumbers As Integer
    Characteristics As Long
End Type
```

The SectionsOffset variable is loaded with the current offset into the file (which is the location immediately after the PE Header information). The following code loads the Sections array:

```
SectionsOffset = Seek(FileHandle)
    For x = 0 To SectionCount - 1
        Get #FileHandle, , Sections(x)
    Next x
```

The section table includes information on the sections that appear in the image data area. There are three fields that are of interest to us. The VirtualAddress represents the address in memory where the section will start once it is loaded into memory. The PointerToRawData field contains the location of the section in the image file. The SizeOfRawData field contains the size of the section in the image file. Figure T9-5 illustrates the relationship of section tables to sections. As you can see, the export table appears as part of one of the sections.

Finding the Export Table

So far the program has loaded the PE file header, any optional headers, and the file's section table. We'll be looking for the section that contains the export table for the file. The FindExportBase function loads the ExportBase variable with the base to the export table:

```
Private Sub FindExportBase()
    Dim secnum%
    ExportDirectoryOffset = _
    PEHeader.OptionalHeader.DataDirectory(0).VirtualAddress
```

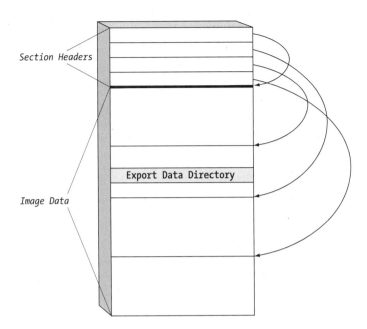

Section Headers

Export Data Directory

Image Data

Figure T9-5: Organization of sections in an image file

```
ExportSection = SectionCount - 1
For secnum = 0 To SectionCount - 1
    If Sections(secnum).VirtualAddress > ExportDirectoryOffset Then
        ExportSection = secnum - 1
        Exit For
    End If
Next secnum
' We now know the section number, calculate the file offset
ExportSectionOffset = Sections(ExportSection).VirtualAddress - _
Sections(ExportSection).PointerToRawData
ExportBase = ExportDirectoryOffset - ExportSectionOffset
End Sub
```

If you look in the IMAGE_OPTIONAL_HEADER structure, you'll see at the end a list of sixteen IMAGE_DATA_DIRECTORY structures. Each of these contains an offset to a particular type of data along with the size of that data. The first of these data directory entries refers to the export function table. How do I know this? From the PE file format specification.

The virtual address for the export table is loaded into the ExportDirectoryOffset variable. The virtual address describes the offset to a particular block of data once the image is loaded into memory, but we need the location of the export information in the file itself. The FindExportBase function scans through the sections to find the first section whose virtual address is greater than this ExportDirectoryOffset value. The section before this must contain the export table itself.

So now we have the virtual address of the export table, the virtual address of the section that contains the export table, and the location of that section in the image file.

The following expression can be used to calculate the location of the export table in the image file:

```
ExportBase = ExportDirectoryOffset -
Sections(ExportSection).VirtualAddress +
Sections(ExportSection).PointerToRawData
```

It takes the offset of the export table from the start of the section and adds it to the location of the start of the section. But this does not match the code in the FindExportBase function. Why is this?

The code in the FindExportBase function does perform the same calculation, but rearranges the terms to first calculate a variable called ExportSectionOffset. The ExportSectionOffset variable now contains a value that can be subtracted from any virtual address in the specified section to find the corresponding location in the file. We'll be using this variable later, as many of the entries in the export table use virtual addresses as well.

```
ExportSectionOffset = Sections(ExportSection).VirtualAddress - _
    Sections(ExportSection).PointerToRawData
ExportBase = ExportDirectoryOffset - ExportSectionOffset
```

The ExportBase variable now contains the file offset to the start of the export data.

Loading the Export Table

The export data begins with an export data directory that is defined by a structure of type IMAGE_EXPORT_DIRECTORY. This structure is defined in C as follows:

```
typedef struct _IMAGE_EXPORT_DIRECTORY {
    DWORD   Characteristics;
    DWORD   TimeDateStamp;
    WORD    MajorVersion;
    WORD    MinorVersion;
    DWORD   Name;
    DWORD   Base;
```

```
    DWORD    NumberOfFunctions;
    DWORD    NumberOfNames;
    PDWORD   *AddressOfFunctions;
    PDWORD   *AddressOfNames;
    PWORD    *AddressOfNameOrdinals;
} IMAGE_EXPORT_DIRECTORY, *PIMAGE_EXPORT_DIRECTORY;
```

The structure looks a bit tricky—how do you handle data types defined as a
PDWORD *? In fact, creating the VB declaration is straightforward. Pointers, and
even pointers to pointers, are always 32 bits and thus declared As Long.

```
Public Type IMAGE_EXPORT_DIRECTORY
    Characteristics As Long
    TimeDateStamp As Long
    MajorVersion As Integer
    MinorVersion As Integer
    Name As Long
    Base As Long
    NumberOfFunctions As Long   ' May not be used
    NumberOfNames As Long
    AddressOfFunctions As Long
    AddressOfNames As Long
    AddressOfNameOrdinals As Long
End Type
```

The IMAGE_EXPORT_DIRECTORY structure is loaded into the ExportDirectory
variable in the LoadInfo function using the ExportBase offset calculated earlier
with this line of code:

```
Get #FileHandle, ExportBase + 1, ExportDirectory
LoadExportInfo
```

The LoadExportInfo function does the real work, as shown here:

```
Private Sub LoadExportInfo()
    Dim idx&
    Dim startaddresses() As Long
    Dim ExportsBuffer() As Byte
    Dim tempstr As String
    Dim stringlen As Long
    Dim sourceloc As Long

    NameCount = ExportDirectory.NumberOfNames
```

```
      ReDim startaddresses(NameCount - 1)
      ReDim Ordinals(NameCount - 1)
      ReDim Names(NameCount)


      ' Load an array with all the ordinals
      sourceloc = ExportDirectory.AddressOfNameOrdinals - ExportSectionOffset + 1
      Get #FileHandle, sourceloc, Ordinals()
      For idx = 0 To NameCount-1
         Ordinals(idx) = Ordinals(idx) + ExportDirectory.Base
      Next idx

      ' Make a copy of all the start addresses
      sourceloc = ExportDirectory.AddressOfNames - ExportSectionOffset + 1
      Get #FileHandle, sourceloc, startaddresses()

      ' Preload the entire section for speed
      ReDim ExportsBuffer(Sections(ExportSection).SizeOfRawData)
      Get #FileHandle, Sections(ExportSection).PointerToRawData + 1, _
      ExportsBuffer()

      ' Extract each start array
      For idx = 0 To NameCount - 1
         sourceloc = startaddresses(idx) - ExportSectionOffset -
   Sections(ExportSection).PointerToRawData
         ' Preinitialize the string
         ' Calculate the length of the string
         'Debug.Print sourceloc
         If sourceloc > 0 Then
            stringlen = lstrlenFromPtr(VarPtr(ExportsBuffer(sourceloc)))
            tempstr = String$(stringlen + 1, 0)
            Call lstrcpyFromPtr(tempstr, VarPtr(ExportsBuffer(sourceloc)))
            Names(idx + 1) = Left$(tempstr, stringlen)
         End If
         'Debug.Print tempstr
      Next idx
   End Sub
```

The function begins by determining the number of exported functions and dimensioning three arrays: one for a temporary address for each function, one for the ordinal value, and one for the function name.

```
NameCount = ExportDirectory.NumberOfNames
ReDim startaddresses(NameCount - 1)
ReDim Ordinals(NameCount - 1)
ReDim Names(NameCount)
```

What is the AddressOfNameOrdinals field? The ordinal values appear in memory and in the file as a list of integer values. The AddressOfNameOrdinals field points to the location of the start of this list.

The location specified by the AddressOfNameOrdinals field is a virtual address, and we earlier calculated the ExportSectionOffset variable, which can be subtracted from any virtual address in a section to obtain a location in a file.

```
' Load an array with all the ordinals
sourceloc = ExportDirectory.AddressOfNameOrdinals - _
ExportSectionOffset + 1
Get #FileHandle, sourceloc, Ordinals()
For idx = 0 To NameCount-1
   Ordinals(idx) = Ordinals(idx) + ExportDirectory.Base
Next idx
```

The ordinal array is loaded as a block. The PE file format specification indicates that the values have to be incremented by the ordinal base value, which can be found in the Base field of the export directory.

Retrieving the function names is a trickier process. Unlike numbers, variable length strings cannot be loaded in an array. Instead, the file contains an array of virtual addresses to each of the function names. Those addresses are loaded into the startaddresses array in the same way as the Ordinals array was loaded earlier.

```
' Make a copy of all the start addresses
sourceloc = ExportDirectory.AddressOfNames - ExportSectionOffset + 1
Get #FileHandle, sourceloc, startaddresses()
```

Rather than loading each string individually from the file, the entire section that contains the string data is preloaded into a byte array named ExportsBuffer using the following code:

```
' Preload the entire section for speed
ReDim ExportsBuffer(Sections(ExportSection).SizeOfRawData)
Get #FileHandle, Sections(ExportSection).PointerToRawData _
+ 1, ExportsBuffer()
```

The location of each string in the file can be calculated using the following term:

```
startaddresses(idx) - ExportSectionOffset
```

Subtracting off the start of the section in the file gives you the offset of the string in the ExportsBuffer table. This offset is stored in the sourceloc variable.

The lstrlenFromPtr function is an alias of the lstrlen function, which obtains the length of a string given a pointer. The lstrcpyFromPtr function uses the lstrcpy function to copy the string into an initialized string buffer. Finally, the Names array is loaded with the string up to the NULL terminating character.

```
' Extract each start array
  For idx = 0 To NameCount - 1
     sourceloc = startaddresses(idx) - ExportSectionOffset _
     - Sections(ExportSection).PointerToRawData
     ' Preinitialize the string
     ' Calculate the length of the string
     If sourceloc > 0 Then
        stringlen = lstrlenFromPtr(VarPtr(ExportsBuffer(sourceloc)))
        tempstr = String$(stringlen + 1, 0)
        Call lstrcpyFromPtr(tempstr, VarPtr(ExportsBuffer(sourceloc)))
        Names(idx + 1) = Left$(tempstr, stringlen)
     End If
  Next idx
```

Conclusion

Interpreting file specifications is not easy, and this tutorial gave you only a taste of what it is like. To gain full advantage of this tutorial, you should obtain a copy of the Portable Executable file specification from either of the two sources given at the beginning of the tutorial and read it yourself. Then step through the DumpInfo program as it performs its work, referring to this tutorial to understand how the information in the specification and header files is translated into Visual Basic.

A Case Study: The Service API

The following article was originally published in my column in Pinnacle's Visual Basic Developer Newsletter. It is such a perfect case study for this book that I decided to reprint it here, even though some of you may have read it in the original form. This tutorial requires Windows NT.

API FUNCTIONS RARELY STAND ALONE.

This book has focused almost entirely on how you can work with individual API functions using Visual Basic. The problem of figuring out how the various API functions work and what you can do with them is largely left up to you. Between my book *Visual Basic Programmer's Guide to the Win32 API* for the core API functions and the Microsoft documentation for everything else, you have a rich set of documentation to draw on. I will concede that the Microsoft documentation sometimes does border on the inscrutable, but for many situations, it is all that is available.

This tutorial presents a case study of how you might approach the Microsoft documentation to solve a specific task that requires use of multiple API functions across an entire subsystem. I'll begin with a discussion of a real problem I faced, then walk you through the entire process, including the implementation of a complete solution.

ASP—A Step Pastward

Okay, I know there is no such word as "pastward," but Microsoft's acronym for Active Server Pages is ASP, not ASB, so I couldn't use "A Step Backward," which is a much more fitting heading. I could, of course, have just selectively capitalized a heading such as "A Step into the Past," but making up a new word seemed much more fun. Besides, if Microsoft's acronym labs can continue to spew forth new acronyms and buzz words at the rate that they do, the least I can do is invent a new word now and then.

But I digress.

Active Server Pages are a special kind of Web page hosted on Microsoft's Internet Information Server. Even though they have the extension .ASP, they are really just text files that contain HTML. What makes them special is their ability to mix in two types of code—code that will run on the server and code that will run on the client (interpreted by the Web browser). To read the trade press, you would think that ASP is a huge advance in programming and that Web sites should immediately convert entirely from plain, static HTML pages to ASP.

Now, I won't try to tell you that ASP isn't powerful. It is. Microsoft uses it extensively on their site. Their commerce server package is little more than a wizard that creates ASP pages for you. But from a computer science point of view, it seems to me to be a huge step backward. Why? Because although ASP pages can and do use objects, the code is not particularly object-oriented. Actually, a complex ASP page almost approaches the unreadability of an APL program. (APL being a language of such elegance that it is said that any program can be written in a single line of code. APL also requires a special keyboard to handle all of the new characters required for its commands.) Server- and client-side code are mixed indiscriminately, and you can spend half your time trying to figure out where your code will actually run. Worse yet, the code is all VBScript or JavaScript and is thus slow and interpreted.

Now, if that isn't a step pastward, I don't know what is.

Of course, this is coming from a person who considers HTML a step backward as well. Think about it—after spending years developing sophisticated and powerful text formats such as RTF, the whole world took a massive step back to a format that was so primitive that we've spent the past few years waiting for new tags and editors to let us do what a good word processor could handle easily. Worse yet, we still can't get pages to look the same under different browsers.

But I digress again.

The point is that ASP, although powerful, is slow, complex, and difficult to support.

The good news is that ASP pages let you easily call dynamic link libraries that can do everything an ASP script can do and then some. These DLLs can be written in any language, including Visual Basic. They run in-process, so they are fast. And they make it easy to distinguish between server-side code (which is the code that makes up the DLL) and client-side code (which is any code that you write out as part of the HTML text generated by the DLL).

Personally, every ASP page I've ever written has done nothing but load an ActiveX object from a DLL and invoke methods on the object. There are some quirks, however, in the way ASP handles these DLLs that can make debugging complicated in some cases.

Let My Object Go!

When an ASP page requires an object from a DLL, the Internet Information Server (IIS) loads the DLL into memory. Once the object is no longer needed, the DLL is released. Maybe. Sometimes.

When does IIS actually unload the DLL? It depends on how you have ASP configured. If you are running the object within the IIS process, it can take some time. That can make life difficult when you need to modify, recompile, and test your code.

What happens when you try to compile a DLL that is loaded by IIS? The compilation fails—Visual Basic cannot write the DLL file because it is locked by IIS.

In these situations, in order to successfully compile the application you must stop the IIS services, do the compilation, then restart the services.

Now, stopping and restarting services is not hard to do. It may be possible to do it through the Internet Control Manager. However, the IIS4 Internet Control Manager does not make it obvious how this can be accomplished (it was much easier with IIS3). Sure, it's easy to stop or start individual Web sites, but stopping the overall service and the administration service as well is not intuitive.

An easier approach is to use the service manager from the Control Panel. You need to stop both the World Wide Web service and the IIS administration service. It's easy, but annoying, because the service manager only allows you to start or stop one service at a time. And since it takes several seconds for each one, the whole process of starting or stopping a service takes about five or six seconds, sometimes more depending on the system configuration.

It seemed to me that it would be very useful to have a utility that could start or stop any selection of services in one operation and quickly toggle them back to their original state.

The Design

I'm a big believer in the importance of good design, even when dealing with relatively simple utilities. You never know when that simple utility is going to become one of those pieces of code that lingers on forever, and a small investment in design ahead of time can mean the difference between something that evolves into a buggy kludge and something that becomes a permanent (and reusable) part of your code library.

Let's start by considering the tasks we need to perform:

- Obtain a list of services.

- Obtain the current running state of a service.

- Start a service.

- Stop a service.

The list of services is necessary to allow the user to select which services to start or stop. Sure, you can hard-code those services needed for IIS 4.0 (the current version of Internet Information Server), but then you would have to recode the utility for future versions of IIS if Microsoft changes the name or selection of services it uses.

You must be able to obtain the running state of a service, both to determine when the operation you have requested is complete and to obtain the initial service state in order to support a restore operation.

Before looking at the actual API functions available to work with services, you need to know a little bit about how services are managed.

There are two types of objects we are concerned with.[1] The first object is called the Service Control Manager. The Service Control Manager is a part of the operating system that manages the services on a system and maintains the internal service database for the system.

The other object is that of the service itself. You must use the Service Control Manager to obtain a handle to a service.

Service Control Manager Functions

The OpenSCManager function is used to open the Service Control Manager. It is defined in C as follows:

```
SC_HANDLE OpenSCManager(
    LPCTSTR lpMachineName,      // pointer to machine name string
    LPCTSTR lpDatabaseName,     // pointer to database name string
    DWORD dwDesiredAccess       // type of access
    );
```

The return value is a 32-bit Long that contains a handle to the Service Control Manager object. Note that it is possible to open the Service Control Manager on a remote system. The lpDatabaseName parameter is always set to NULL or the constant SERVICES_ACTIVE_DATABASE, both of which cause the function to use the current active database. It looks like the designers had the idea of supporting multiple service databases at some point, but that capability has not yet shown up.

---

1. Note that the term "object" here means a Win32 object, not a COM/ActiveX object. As with other Win32 objects, you can expect to find an API function to create or open the object and then return an object handle—a 32-bit Long value that identifies the object. You can also expect to find another API function to close the object when you are finished with it.

The dwDesiredAccess constant allows you to specify a number of constants that define the type of access you wish. Whether you get that access depends on the permission available to the account you are using. Our sample will assume that the user is running as a system administrator, because anyone creating ASP pages and associated components is probably running as an administrator anyway.

When you are finished with the Service Control Manager, you must close it using the CloseServiceHandle function, which is defined as follows:

```
BOOL CloseServiceHandle(
    SC_HANDLE hSCObject   // handle to service or service control manager database
);
```

The CloseServiceHandle function is also used to close a service.

The Service Control Manager is also used to open services using the following function:

```
SC_HANDLE OpenService(
    SC_HANDLE hSCManager,         // handle to service control manager database
    LPCTSTR lpServiceName,        // pointer to name of service to start
    DWORD dwDesiredAccess         // type of access to service
);
```

The function returns a handle to a service. The dwDesiredAccess parameter allows you to specify which operations you wish to perform on the service. The service name is not the name displayed in the Control Panel's service control applet. That name is the "display name"—a version that is designed to be easily understood. The actual service name can be obtained by enumerating the services using the EnumServicesStatus function, which follows:

```
BOOL EnumServicesStatus(
    SC_HANDLE hSCManager,                  // handle to service control manager
                                           //   database
    DWORD dwServiceType,                   // type of services to enumerate
    DWORD dwServiceState,                  // state of services to enumerate
    LPENUM_SERVICE_STATUS lpServices,      // pointer to service status buffer
    DWORD cbBufSize,                       // size of service status buffer
    LPDWORD pcbBytesNeeded,                // pointer to variable for bytes needed
    LPDWORD lpServicesReturned,            // pointer to variable for number returned
    LPDWORD lpResumeHandle                 // pointer to variable for next entry
);
```

This function loads a structure called an ENUM_SERVICE_STATUS structure, which is defined as follows:

```
typedef struct _ENUM_SERVICE_STATUS { // ess
    LPTSTR lpServiceName;
    LPTSTR lpDisplayName;
    SERVICE_STATUS ServiceStatus;
} ENUM_SERVICE_STATUS, *LPENUM_SERVICE_STATUS;

typedef struct _SERVICE_STATUS { // ss
    DWORD dwServiceType;
    DWORD dwCurrentState;
    DWORD dwControlsAccepted;
    DWORD dwWin32ExitCode;
    DWORD dwServiceSpecificExitCode;
    DWORD dwCheckPoint;
    DWORD dwWaitHint;
} SERVICE_STATUS, *LPSERVICE_STATUS;
```

The lpServiceName string in the ENUM_SERVICE_STATUS structure contains the service name. The lpDisplayname string contains the name displayed to users.

The Service Control Manager supports other functions, but they aren't necessary for the task at hand.

Service Functions

Once you've opened a service, there are a number of operations you can perform on the service using API functions. For our purposes, you only need to be concerned with three of these functions.

1. The StartService function is used to start a service and is defined as follows:

```
BOOL StartService(
    SC_HANDLE hService,              // handle of service
    DWORD dwNumServiceArgs,          // number of arguments
    LPCTSTR *lpServiceArgVectors     // address of array of argument
                                     // string pointers
    );
```

The function allows you to pass arguments to the service, but most services don't take arguments when starting—certainly not the services that concern us. So the dwNumServiceArgs and lpServiceArgVectors parameters can both be set to NULL.

2. A service is stopped using the ControlService function, which is defined
    as follows:

```
BOOL ControlService(
    SC_HANDLE hService,                // handle to service
    DWORD dwControl,                   // control code
    LPSERVICE_STATUS lpServiceStatus   // pointer to service status structure
);
```

The dwControl parameter takes a constant value defined with the prefix SERVICE_
CONTROL_*. For our purposes, you will use the SERVICE_CONTROL_STOP constant to stop the service. The function also loads a SERVICE_STATUS structure.

3. The final service function you will need is the QueryServiceStatus func-
    tion, which is defined as follows:

```
BOOL QueryServiceStatus(
    SC_HANDLE hService,                // handle of service
    LPSERVICE_STATUS lpServiceStatus   // address of service status structure
);
```

This function can be used to query the status of a service. You'll use it to find out
when a requested operation is complete.

Choosing Objects

We've now completed the first step in the design process—gaining familiarity
with the underlying objects, data structures, and functions. The order in which I
listed items in that sentence is significant. An important part of object-oriented
programming is choosing the objects for your design. How do you choose
objects? First, there is a good chance that you will have an object that corresponds to objects in the underlying system. We've identified two system objects:
the Service Control Manager and the service itself. This suggests two classes, one
we'll call ServiceManager, which corresponds to the Service Control Manager,
and another called ServiceObject, which corresponds to the service. Each of
these classes will contain a private variable to hold the handle to the corresponding system object.

Next, you may have objects that correspond to the data structures you are
working with. We've identified two objects, the ENUM_SERVICE_STATUS structure and the SERVICE_STATUS structure. You could create one object for each,
but the ENUM_SERVICE_STATUS structure contains the SERVICE_STATUS
structure, so this would result in a potentially complex object hierarchy. While

certainly feasible, it's overkill for this situation. The ServiceStatus class will correspond to the ENUM_SERVICE_STATUS structure and also handle the SERVICE_STATUS structure.

Now it's a relatively simple matter to decide how to allocate methods to the classes.

The ServiceManager class will include the following methods and properties:

OpenSCManager function. Used to initialize the ServiceManager function. Unfortunately, VB doesn't support parameterized constructors[2] (as is possible with C++), so you just have to remember to call this method after creating the class.

EnumServicesStatus. Used to enumerate services, this function returns a collection containing a ServiceStatus object for each service.

OpenService. Used to open a service, this function returns a ServiceObject object.

The ServiceObject class will include the following methods and properties:

Initialize. A Friend method used by the ServiceManager class to initialize a newly created object.

ServiceName. A read-only property used to get the name of the service.

QueryServiceStatus. A function that returns a ServiceStatus object that defines the current state of the service.

ServiceControl. A function that corresponds to the ServiceControl API function.

StartService. A function that corresponds to the StartService API function.

---

2. When a Visual Basic class is created, its Initialize event is called. This event is called a "constructor" in C++ objects—though the mechanism by which they are called is very different. In C++, it is possible for the function creating an object to pass parameters to the object's constructor. In fact, an object can have more than one constructor function, each with a different set of parameters.

The ServiceStatus class will include
the following methods and properties:

Name. A read-only property that is used to get the service name.

DisplayName. A read-only property that is used to get the service display name.

CurrentState. A read-only property that is used to get the current running state of the service.

There will also be two Friend functions used internally to initialize the class.

Almost Ready to Code

Think back for a moment at the original requirements for this project:

- Obtain a list of services.

- Obtain the current running state of a service.

- Start a service.

- Stop a service.

Clearly the three classes here provide the desired functionality. Two things remain. Now that we have the object infrastructure for performing the operations, we need a high-level design for exactly how the utility program will work. Next, we need to figure out the Visual Basic declarations and code needed to actually implement these classes.

The Service Classes

The design of this class follows the philosophy I used when designing Desaware's API class library (which is part of SpyWorks)—that the methods should correspond as closely as possible to the underlying API functions. The advantage of this approach is that it allows you to use the same knowledge for both. The last thing anyone needs is yet another unfamiliar set of commands.

One of the first things you might notice when looking at the service API functions is that they make extensive use of constants. There are two ways to deal with constants: One is to create a .BAS module that contains public constants; the other is to use the Enum operator to expose the constants as part of the object's type library. Using a type library is an obvious approach—it allows you to use the Enum list as a data type, making it easy for people using the object to select values for parameters. The Enum list will appear in the object browser and screen tips while you are coding. The constant approach is reasonable for classes that are designed to be incorporated directly into applications instead of deployed as components.

You might think that Enums have such an overwhelming advantage that you should always use them as constants. In theory, this is true, but I've found that public Enums tend to destabilize components in ways that are not particularly reproducible. Every time I've run into a program that spontaneously crashes even with correct code, or for which I cannot maintain binary compatibility, it's always turned out that the way to solve the problem involved eliminating the public Enums—or at least not use them as parameters or return values for methods or properties.

For that reason, I tend to avoid using them as data types, but in this particular sample program the classes are intended to be incorporated directly into applications, so I took the preferred approach in the hope that VB6 is more stable in the way it handles these data types. The ServiceControlRights Enum shown here specifies the type of rights that are requested for use with the Service Control Manager. The ServiceAccessRights Enum specifies the types of rights that are requested for the service object itself. The ServiceControlConstants Enum specifies the operations that are available when using the ServiceControl API function. The ServiceStateConstants Enum contains constants describing the running state of a service.

```
' Service Control Manager Class
' Copyright © 1998 by Desaware Inc. All Rights Reserved


Option Explicit


' Service constants exposed via typelib

Public Enum ServiceControlRights
    SC_MANAGER_CONNECT = 1
    SC_MANAGER_CREATE_SERVICE = 2
    SC_MANAGER_ENUMERATE_SERVICE = 4
    SC_MANAGER_LOCK = 8
    SC_MANAGER_QUERY_LOCK_STATUS = &H10
    SC_MANAGER_MODIFY_BOOT_CONFIG = &H20
    SC_MANAGER_ALL_ACCESS = &H3F Or STANDARD_RIGHTS_REQUIRED
End Enum
```

```
Public Enum ServiceAccessRights
    SERVICE_QUERY_CONFIG = 1
    SERVICE_CHANGE_CONFIG = 2
    SERVICE_QUERY_STATUS = 4
    SERVICE_ENUMERATE_DEPENDENTS = 8
    SERVICE_START = &H10
    SERVICE_STOP = &H20
    SERVICE_PAUSE_CONTINUE = &H40
    SERVICE_INTERROGATE = &H80
    SERVICE_USER_DEFINED_CONTROL = &H100
    SERVICE_ALL_ACCESS = &H1FF Or STANDARD_RIGHTS_REQUIRED
End Enum


Public Enum ServiceControlConstants
    SERVICE_CONTROL_STOP = 1
    SERVICE_CONTROL_PAUSE = 2
    SERVICE_CONTROL_CONTINUE = 3
    SERVICE_CONTROL_INTERROGATE = 4
    SERVICE_CONTROL_SHUTDOWN = 5
End Enum

Public Enum ServiceStateConstants
    SERVICE_STOPPED = 1
    SERVICE_START_PENDING = 2
    SERVICE_STOP_PENDING = 3
    SERVICE_RUNNING = 4
    SERVICE_CONTINUE_PENDING = 5
    SERVICE_PAUSE_PENDING = 6
    SERVICE_PAUSED = 7
End Enum
```

Let's look at the Service Manager function declarations one by one.

OpenSCManager

This function was declared as follows in the Win32 API documentation:

```
SC_HANDLE OpenSCManager(
    LPCTSTR lpMachineName,     // pointer to machine name string
    LPCTSTR lpDatabaseName,    // pointer to database name string
    DWORD dwDesiredAccess      // type of access
    );
```

What is the function name in the DLL? Because the function uses string parameters, you know that there are two possibilities. If the function only supports Unicode parameters, the name in the DLL will be OpenSCManager. If it supports both ANSI and Unicode parameters, the ANSI entry point will be called OpenSCManagerA, and the Unicode entry pointer will be OpenSCManagerW. Use the DumpInfo utility (on the CD provided with this book) to search the system directory for both OpenSCManager and OpenSCManagerA. You'll find OpenSCManagerA in advapi32.dll.

You can guess that, like most Win32 API functions, this will be a function that returns a Long value. The parameter type returned is an SC_HANDLE, and since you know that almost every handle is a 32-bit Long, you can now be virtually certain that the return type will be a Long. Further proof can be found in the header files provided with the Win32 SDK, where, in file winsvc.h, you'll find the following line:

```
typedef HANDLE SC_HANDLE;
```

The machine name and database name are of the LPCTSTR data type. The data type LPCTSTR can be decoded as follows:

LP indicates a long (32-bit) pointer parameter

C indicates that the parameter is a constant (the data passed to the function will not be changed by the function)

T indicates that the data is ANSI when called from an ANSI entry point, Unicode when called from a Unicode entry point

STR indicates that the data is a NULL-terminated string

Conclusion: These are pointers to NULL-terminated ANSI strings that are not modified by the function.

The dwDesiredAccess function is easy—it's a Long value passed ByVal. The declaration is as follows:

```
' Service functions
Public Declare Function intOpenSCManager Lib "advapi32" Alias _
"OpenSCManagerA" (ByVal lpMachineName As String, ByVal _
lpDatabaseName As String, ByVal dwDesiredAccess As Long) As Long
```

Why did I give the declaration the name intOpenSCManager instead of OpenSCManager? The Alias portion of the declaration uses OpenSCManagerA, the name of the function as it is exported by the DLL. The function name is used by Visual Basic. By using a different name for the declaration, it becomes possible to use OpenSCManager as the name of a public method for the class itself. This does mean that you have to be careful when writing the class to distinguish between the two names. But clients using the class will be able to use the more familiar name—they won't have access to the name used in the API declaration.

The CloseServiceHandle function is trivial by comparison. It takes an SC_HANDLE parameter, which is simply a 32-bit Long passed ByVal as follows:

```
Public Declare Function CloseServiceHandle Lib "advapi32" (ByVal _
schandle As Long) As Long
```

The EnumServicesStatus function is a bit trickier. The first thing to notice is that you must distinguish between the parameters that are specified as DWORD parameters and those specified as LPDWORD. The DWORD parameters are long values and are thus defined as Long parameters that are passed ByVal. The LPDWORD parameters are pointers to DWORD (long) values and are thus defined as Long parameters that are passed ByRef. The lpServices parameter is defined for now as a Long passed ByVal. Why? Because we'll be calculating the pointer in code and passing that pointer value to the function:

```
BOOL EnumServicesStatus(
    SC_HANDLE hSCManager, // handle to service control manager database
    DWORD dwServiceType, // type of services to enumerate
    DWORD dwServiceState, // state of services to enumerate
    LPENUM_SERVICE_STATUS lpServices,      // pointer to service status buffer
    DWORD cbBufSize,      // size of service status buffer
    LPDWORD pcbBytesNeeded,        // pointer to variable for bytes needed
    LPDWORD lpServicesReturned,    // pointer to variable for number returned
    LPDWORD lpResumeHandle         // pointer to variable for next entry
    );
```

The resulting declaration is as follows:

```
Public Declare Function intEnumServicesStatus Lib "advapi32" _
Alias "EnumServicesStatusA" _
    (ByVal hSCManager As Long, _
    ByVal dwServiceType As Long, _
    ByVal dwServiceState As Long, _
    ByVal lpServices As Long, _
    ByVal cbBufSize As Long, _
    pcbBytesNeeded As Long, _
    lpServicesReturned As Long, _
    lpResumeHandle As Long) As Long
```

The OpenService function is quite simple as well. Each of the parameters have been seen in the preceding declarations. The function declaration is shown here:

```
Public Declare Function intOpenService Lib "advapi32" _
Alias "OpenServiceA" (ByVal hSCManager As Long, _
    ByVal lpServiceName As String, _
    ByVal dwDesiredAccess As Long) As Long
```

The ServiceManager object must be initialized after it is created to open the system's service manager. The OpenSCManager method corresponds to the Win32 API OpenSCManager function. The only interesting trick here is the conversion of the Machine and Database string variables to NULL strings from empty strings. If you leave it as an empty string, the API function will receive a pointer to a NULL character, rather than the required NULL value.

The function stores the API handle in a private variable called schandle and returns the value. You aren't actually expected to do anything with the value; the fact that it is non-zero indicates that the function succeeded. This handle is closed during the object's Terminate event. The OpenSCManager method and terminate event follow:

```
' Open the service control manager
' Returns non-zero on success
Public Function OpenSCManager(ByVal Machine As String, ByVal Database _
As String, rights As ServiceControlRights) As Long
    ' Close, then open if necessary
    If schandle <> 0 Then Call CloseServiceHandle(schandle)

    ' Machine and Database must be valid or NULL, not empty
    If Machine = "" Then Machine = vbNullString
    If Database = "" Then Database = vbNullString
    schandle = intOpenSCManager(Machine, Database, rights)
    OpenSCManager = schandle
End Function

Private Sub Class_Terminate()
    If schandle <> 0 Then Call CloseServiceHandle(schandle)
End Sub
```

The OpenService function creates and initializes a ServiceObject object. The function first verifies that the ServiceManager object has been initialized by checking the value of the schandle variable. It then calls the OpenService API function to open the service. If the service is opened successfully, it calls the Initialize method of the ServiceObject object. This method is a Friend function. If you convert these classes into a component, the function will not be accessible to those using the object. In an ideal world, you would be able to specify that only the ServiceManager class could call the Initialize method, but in Visual Basic, using a Friend function is the best we can do. Because the classes are incorporated directly into the utility in this example, the use of a Friend attribute is no different than using a Public attribute, since Friend allows the function to be visible to the entire project. However, Friend is used here in case you decide to place the class in a component and to emphasize to the programmer that access to the function should be limited. The OpenService method is shown here:

```
' Open a service and return the service object
Public Function OpenService(Svc As ServiceStatus, rights As _
ServiceAccessRights) As ServiceObject
    Dim hnd&
    Dim newservice As New ServiceObject

    ' Service manager must be open to perform this operation
    If schandle = 0 Then Exit Function
    hnd = intOpenService(schandle, Svc.Name, rights Or SERVICE_QUERY_STATUS)
    If hnd <> 0 Then
        ' Initialize the service via a Friend function
        Call newservice.Initialize(hnd, Svc.Name, Svc.DisplayName)
        Set OpenService = newservice
    End If
End Function
```

The EnumServicesStatus function is the trickiest one of the lot. The lpServices parameter described earlier takes a pointer to a memory buffer to load with a bunch of ENUM_SERVICES_STATUS structures. Let's take a quick look at this structure and how it will be defined in Visual Basic. The C declarations are as follows:

```
typedef struct _ENUM_SERVICE_STATUS { // ess
    LPTSTR lpServiceName;
    LPTSTR lpDisplayName;
    SERVICE_STATUS ServiceStatus;
} ENUM_SERVICE_STATUS, *LPENUM_SERVICE_STATUS;

typedef struct _SERVICE_STATUS { // ss
    DWORD dwServiceType;
    DWORD dwCurrentState;
    DWORD dwControlsAccepted;
    DWORD dwWin32ExitCode;
```

```
    DWORD dwServiceSpecificExitCode;
    DWORD dwCheckPoint;
    DWORD dwWaitHint;
} SERVICE_STATUS, *LPSERVICE_STATUS;
```

The first two fields of the ENUM_SERVICE_STATUS structures are strings. But if your first reaction is to assume that these will translate into Visual Basic strings, stop reading and go back immediately to Tutorial 7, "Classes, Structures, and User-Defined Types," to find out why that is a sure road to disaster. These fields must be defined as Long variables, as shown in these type declarations:

```
Public Type ENUM_SERVICE_STATUS
    lpServiceName As Long
    lpDisplayName As Long
    Status As SERVICE_STATUS
End Type


' Service structures
Public Type SERVICE_STATUS
    dwServiceType As Long
    dwCurrentState As Long
    dwControlsAccepted As Long
    dwWin32ExitCode As Long
    dwServiceSpecificExitCode As Long
    dwCheckPoint As Long
    dwWaitHint As Long
End Type
```

These structures contain pointers to strings. But where are the strings?

The buffer that is loaded with ENUM_SERVICE_STATUS structures contains the strings as well. Figure T10-1 illustrates a typical buffer that has been loaded by two of these structures.

The buffer is loaded with one or more ENUM_SERVICE_STATUS structures. The buffer also contains any strings that are pointed to by the structure fields. The buffer is initially set to 512, an arbitrary number. On return, the EnumServicesStatus API will

1. Load the buffer with as many ENUM_SERVICES_STATUS structures as will fit,

2. Set the ServicesReturned parameter to the number of services returned,

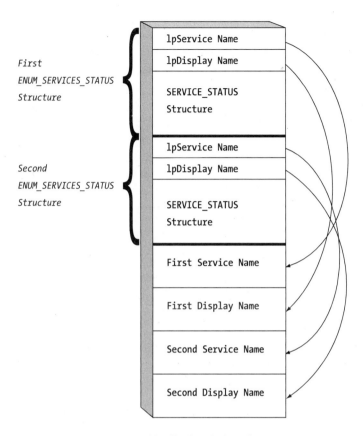

Figure T10-1: Format of buffer loaded with ENUM_SERVICE_STATUS structures

3. Set the BytesNeeded parameter to the size of buffer needed to hold the remaining services, and

4. Set the ResumeHandle parameter to a value used internally to tell the system which service to load first during the next call.

These parameter values can be changed because they were passed by reference (see how the pieces begin to fall together?). The function returns a value of 0 and sets the Err.LastDllError property to the constant ERROR_MORE_DATA if there are more services to read.

For each service, the routine creates a ServiceStatus object. It then passes the buffer along with an offset to the object's ParseServiceInfo method. This method scans the buffer and extracts the service's status information, as you will see shortly.

```
' Retrieve a collection containing ServiceStatus objects
Public Function EnumServicesStatus() As Collection
    Dim res&
    Dim lpServices As Long
    Dim BytesNeeded As Long
    Dim ServicesReturned As Long
    Dim ResumeHandle As Long
    Dim Buffer() As Byte
    ReDim Buffer(512)
    Dim x&
    Dim CurrentOffset&
    Dim c As New Collection
    Dim s As ServiceStatus
    Dim continue As Boolean

    Do
        ' Load the buffer with as many services as possible
        ' We exclude driver services for now
        res = intEnumServicesStatus(schandle, &H30, 3, VarPtr(Buffer(0)), _
        UBound(Buffer()), BytesNeeded, ServicesReturned, ResumeHandle)
        If res = 0 And Err.LastDllError = ERROR_MORE_DATA Then
            ' Buffer couldn't hold all the services
            continue = True
        Else
            continue = False
        End If
        For x = 1 To ServicesReturned
            Set s = New ServiceStatus
            ' The ServiceStatus buffer does the actual extraction
            Call s.ParseServiceInfo(Buffer(), CurrentOffset)
            c.Add s
            ' 36 is the size of the ENUM_SERVICE_STATUS structure
            CurrentOffset = CurrentOffset + 36
        Next x
        If continue Then
            ' Prepare for the next call
            CurrentOffset = 0
            ReDim Buffer(BytesNeeded)
        End If
    Loop While continue
    Set EnumServicesStatus = c
End Function
```

The ServiceStatus class contains the following code. The most recent status is stored in a private SERVICE_STATUS structure called Status. The service name and display name are stored as well.

There are two ways to initialize a ServiceStatus object. One is by parsing a buffer created by the EnumServicesStatus function. The other is by setting the private information directly using the InternalInitialize function. This function is called by the ServiceObject class when a client requests updated status information.

```
' Holds the latest value of each
Private Status As SERVICE_STATUS
Private SvcName As String
Private intDisplayName As String


' Used by the internal objects to initialize a new ServiceStatus object
' that is not created via an enumeration.
Friend Sub InternalInitialize(pName As String, pDisplay As String, _
stat As SERVICE_STATUS)
    intDisplayName = pDisplay
    SvcName = pName
    LSet Status = stat
End Sub
```

The ParseServiceInfo function first copies the part of the buffer that contains the information for this service into a private ENUM_SERVICE_STATUS structure. The first two fields of this structure contain pointers to the service name and display name. These pointers need to be converted into Visual Basic strings using the GetVBStringFromAddress function, which can be found in the modSCMgr module and should be quite familiar to you by now.

```
' Extracts the private information from the buffer. Data is assumed
' to start at the specified offset
' Always returns 0
Friend Function ParseServiceInfo(Buffer() As Byte, ByVal Offset As Long) _
As Long
    Dim svcstat As ENUM_SERVICE_STATUS
    ' Copy the service structure
    Call RtlMoveMemory(VarPtr(svcstat), VarPtr(Buffer(Offset)), Len(svcstat))
    ' Extract the names
    SvcName = GetVBStringFromAddress(svcstat.lpServiceName)
    intDisplayName = GetVBStringFromAddress(svcstat.lpDisplayName)
    ' Store the SERVICE_STATUS portion only
    LSet Status = svcstat.Status
```

```
End Function

' Get a VB string from an address
Public Function GetVBStringFromAddress(ByVal addr&) As String
    Dim uselen&
    Dim res$
    If addr = 0 Then Exit Function
    uselen = lstrlen(addr)
    res$ = String$(uselen + 1, 0)
    Call lstrcpy(res, addr)
    GetVBStringFromAddress = Left$(res$, uselen)
End Function
```

The ServiceStatus class also has properties to read the name, display name, and current running state of the service.

The ServiceObject class is relatively straightforward. It stores the service handle internally, along with the name and display name of the service. It has methods to stop, start, and obtain status for a service. These methods basically call the corresponding API function.

```
' Service Object Class
' Copyright © 1998 by Desaware Inc. All Rights Reserved

' This object represents an open service

Option Explicit

Private intServiceHandle As Long
Private intServiceName As String
Private intDisplayName As String

' For convenience, this object is initialized by the ServiceManager
' with both the name and display name
Friend Sub Initialize(ByVal hnd As Long, Name As String, _
DisplayName As String)
    intServiceHandle = hnd
    intServiceName = Name
    intDisplayName = DisplayName
End Sub

' Get the short name
Property Get ServiceName() As String
    ServiceName = intServiceName
```

```
End Property

' Get the current status
Property Get QueryServiceStatus() As ServiceStatus
    Dim stat As SERVICE_STATUS
    Dim res&
    Dim sres As New ServiceStatus
    res = intQueryServiceStatus(intServiceHandle, stat)
    If res <> 0 Then
        ' Another way to get a ServiceStatus object
        Call sres.InternalInitialize(intServiceName, intDisplayName, stat)
        Set QueryServiceStatus = sres
    End If
End Property

' Perform Stop, Pause, Continue and Interrogate
Public Function ServiceControl(Operation As ServiceControlConstants) As Long
    Dim stat As SERVICE_STATUS
    Dim res&
    res = intControlService(intServiceHandle, Operation, stat)
    ServiceControl = res
End Function

' Perform start
Public Function StartService()
    Dim res&
    res = intStartService(intServiceHandle, 0, 0)
    StartService = res
End Function

' Close the handle on termination
Private Sub Class_Terminate()
    If intServiceHandle <> 0 Then
        Call CloseServiceHandle(intServiceHandle)
    End If
End Sub
```

The Utility Itself—Using the Object Model

The original goal of this exercise was to create a utility that would make it easy to stop and then restart the Internet Information Services so that a DLL called by an Active Server Page could be replaced. I wanted to leave it flexible enough to

415

serve as a general tool for starting and stopping services. So I came up with the
following features:

- A list box to display the name and display names of each service. The list
  box allows multiple selection so that more than one service can be con-
  trolled at a time.

- Buttons to start and stop one or more services.

- A button to restore all services to their original state (as they were when
  the program launched).

- A way to keep track of changes so the utility can prompt whether to
  restore the services to their original state when the program is closed.

- A button to select the IIS services.

Figure T10-2 shows the user interface for the utility.

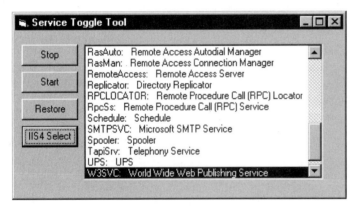

Figure T10-2: The user interface for the SCToggle application

The program defines a set of variables. The sc variable holds the single
ServiceManager object used by the
program. The OriginalStates collection
holds a group of ServiceStatus objects
that are loaded with the original states
of the services. The ServiceCollection
collection holds a group of
ServiceStatus objects reflecting the
current state of the services (though
it's not always kept up to date, as you'll
see). The ChangesInProgress collection
holds ServiceObject objects that are in
the process of being changed. The
Changed variable indicates that you've
changed the state of one or more ser-
vices. The TargetState variable indicates whether you are stopping or starting the
services that are being changed or restoring them to their original state:

```
Dim sc As New ServiceManager

Dim ServiceCollection As Collection ' Hold current states
Dim OriginalStates As Collection    ' Record original states
```

```
' Collection of ServiceObject objects that are currently
' being changed
Dim ChangesInProgress As Collection

Dim Changed As Boolean   ' Mark true if any state change has been caused
Dim unloadpending As Boolean    ' Mark true if final restore operation

' 0 to restore
Dim TargetState As ServiceStateConstants
```

The ServiceManager object is initialized when the main form loads. At that time, the OriginalStates collection is loaded with the original running state of each service:

```
Private Sub Form_Load()
    Dim res&
    ' Open the ServiceManager
    res = sc.OpenSCManager("", "", SC_MANAGER_ENUMERATE_SERVICE _
    Or SC_MANAGER_CONNECT)
    ' Update the ServiceCollection and display the services
    LoadList True
    Set OriginalStates = ServiceCollection
    ' We don't want to hold two references to the collection
    Set ServiceCollection = Nothing
End Sub
```

The ServiceCollection collection is loaded using the LoadList function. This function makes use of the ServiceManger object's EnumServicesStatus method to obtain the names and status of the available services. The ServiceManager object (referenced by the sc variable) is initialized when the form loads:

```
' Loads the ServiceCollection collection with a list of all services
' Optionally displays them
Private Sub LoadList(bDisplay As Boolean)
    Dim res&
    Dim svcstat As ServiceStatus
    lstServices.Refresh
    Set ServiceCollection = sc.EnumServicesStatus()
    If bDisplay Then
        For Each svcstat In ServiceCollection
            lstServices.AddItem svcstat.Name & ":    " & svcstat.DisplayName
        Next
    End If
```

```
End Sub
```

The program has two possible states: The normal state is the idle state during which the user interface is enabled; the execution state is entered when you start a service state change. It can take a while for services to start or stop, so a timer, which waits until each service has entered the requested state, runs during the execution state. The EnablePanel function is used to disable the user interface while the program is in the execution state and re-enable it when the program returns to the idle state. It also controls the timer and the cursor display.

```
' Enables or disables the user interface of the application.
' Also controls the mouse pointer and timer.
' The UI must be disabled while service start or stop is in progress
Private Function EnablePanel(ByVal bEnabled As Boolean)
    cmdStop.Enabled = bEnabled
    cmdStart.Enabled = bEnabled
    cmdRestore.Enabled = bEnabled
    lstServices.Enabled = bEnabled
    If Not bEnabled Then
        Screen.MousePointer = vbHourglass
        Timer1.Enabled = True
    Else
        Screen.MousePointer = vbNormal
        Timer1.Enabled = False
    End If

End Function
```

The first step toward performing a start or stop operation is to obtain a list of services to operate on. The OpenSelectedServices object builds a collection of the services that are selected on the list box. It does this by first loading the ServiceCollection collection with the available services and their current status. The function then compares the names in the list with the available services and adds those that match into the ChangesInProgress collection.

```
' Loads the ChangesInProgress collection with the
' ServiceObject objects for the selected services
Private Function OpenSelectedServices()
    Dim index&
    Dim currententry$
    Dim svcstat As ServiceStatus
    Call LoadList(False)
    Set ChangesInProgress = New Collection
```

```
    For index = 0 To lstServices.ListCount - 1
        If lstServices.Selected(index) Then
            currententry = lstServices.List(index)
            For Each svcstat In ServiceCollection
                ' Match based on the service name
                If InStr(currententry, svcstat.Name & ":") = 1 Then
                    ChangesInProgress.Add sc.OpenService(svcstat, _
                    SERVICE_START Or SERVICE_STOP), svcstat.Name
                    Exit For
                End If
            Next
        End If
    Next index
End Function
```

The codes to stop, start, and restore services are very similar to each other. After obtaining a list of selected services, they query the service for its current state and remove any services from the ChangesInProgress collection that are already in the requested state. The ServiceControl or StartService method is used to stop or start the service if necessary. If any services remain in the ChangesInProgress collection, the EnablePanel function is called to enter the Execution state.

```
' Stops the selected services
Private Sub cmdStop_Click()
    Dim so As ServiceObject
    Dim stat As ServiceStatus
    Dim starttimer As Boolean
    Dim RemoveThis As Boolean
    Dim res&
    Call OpenSelectedServices
    For Each so In ChangesInProgress
        Set stat = so.QueryServiceStatus
        If stat.CurrentState <> SERVICE_STOPPED Then
            res = so.ServiceControl(SERVICE_CONTROL_STOP)
            If res <> 0 Then
                starttimer = True
            Else
                RemoveThis = True
            End If
        Else
            RemoveThis = True
        End If
        If RemoveThis Then ChangesInProgress.Remove stat.Name
```

```
                RemoveThis = False
        Next so
        If starttimer Then
            EnablePanel False
            TargetState = SERVICE_STOPPED
            Changed = True
        Else
            Set ChangesInProgress = Nothing
        End If
    End Sub


    ' Starts the selected services
    Private Sub cmdStart_Click()
        Dim so As ServiceObject
        Dim stat As ServiceStatus
        Dim starttimer As Boolean
        Dim RemoveThis As Boolean
        Dim res&
        Call OpenSelectedServices
        For Each so In ChangesInProgress
            Set stat = so.QueryServiceStatus
            If stat.CurrentState <> SERVICE_RUNNING Then
                res = so.StartService
                If res <> 0 Then
                    starttimer = True
                Else
                    RemoveThis = True
                End If
            Else
                RemoveThis = True
            End If
            If RemoveThis Then ChangesInProgress.Remove stat.Name
            RemoveThis = False
        Next so
        If starttimer Then
            EnablePanel False
            TargetState = SERVICE_RUNNING
            Changed = True
        Else
            Set ChangesInProgress = Nothing
        End If
    End Sub
```

```
' Restores services to their original state
Private Sub cmdRestore_Click()
    Dim so As ServiceObject
    Dim stat As ServiceStatus
    Dim starttimer As Boolean
    Dim orig As ServiceStateConstants
    Dim res&
    Call LoadList(False)
    Set ChangesInProgress = New Collection
    For Each stat In ServiceCollection
        If stat.CurrentState <> OriginalState(stat.Name) Then
            ChangesInProgress.Add sc.OpenService(stat, SERVICE_START _
            Or SERVICE_STOP), stat.Name
        End If
    Next
    For Each so In ChangesInProgress
        orig = OriginalState(so.ServiceName)
        If orig = SERVICE_RUNNING Then
            res = so.StartService
        Else
            res = so.ServiceControl(SERVICE_CONTROL_STOP)
        End If
        If res <> 0 Then
            starttimer = True
        Else
ChangesInProgress.Remove so.ServiceName
        End If
    Next so
    If starttimer Then
        EnablePanel False
        TargetState = 0
        Changed = True
    Else
        Set ChangesInProgress = Nothing
    End If
End Sub
```

When you close the application, you are given the opportunity to restore the services to their original state if any of the services have been changed by this application. If you decide to restore the services, the unload is suspended until after the restore operation is complete, and the unloadpending flag is set to True so the application will know to terminate when the services are restored to their original state.

```
Private Sub Form_Unload(Cancel As Integer)
    Dim res&
    If Changed Then
        ' If any change has been made, give the user
        ' the option to restore
        res = MsgBox("Changes have been made - Restore service states?", _
        vbYesNo, "Exit confirmation")
        If res = vbYes Then
            unloadpending = True
            Me.Hide ' Hide the form - no reason to clutter the screen
            cmdRestore_Click
            Cancel = -1
            Changed = False
            Exit Sub
        End If
    End If

    Set ServiceCollection = Nothing
    Set OriginalStates = Nothing
    Set ChangesInProgress = Nothing
    Set sc = Nothing
End Sub
```

The timer routine checks the status of each of the services in the
ChangesInProgress collection. If the service has entered the desired state, its
object is removed from the collection. Once the collection is empty, the user
interface is re-enabled and the program re-enters the idle state.

```
' Poll for the completion of the operation in progress
Private Sub Timer1_Timer()
    Dim so As ServiceObject
    Dim stat As ServiceStatus
    Dim target As Long
    For Each so In ChangesInProgress
        Set stat = so.QueryServiceStatus
        ' Zero is the restore condition
        If TargetState = 0 Then
            target = OriginalState(stat.Name)
        Else
            target = TargetState
        End If

        If stat.CurrentState = target Then
```

```
            ' Done with this one
            ChangesInProgress.Remove stat.Name
        End If
    Next so
    If ChangesInProgress.count = 0 Then
        ' Once all changes are done, reenable the app
Set ChangesInProgress = Nothing
        Call EnablePanel(True)
        If TargetState = 0 Then Changed = False
    End If
    ' If this was the final restore on close, close the form
    If unloadpending Then Unload Me
End Sub
```

What's Left to Do?

If you look at the sample code closely, you may get the feeling that the code is somehow not quite complete. You are absolutely correct. The code shown here is a long way from what I would consider commercial-quality code. What's missing?

- **Error checking.** Whereas some of the functions do return values indicating whether an error occurred, they do not provide detailed information on the error. The functions that return objects return Nothing if a failure occurs and also neglect to provide detailed information. There are several approaches you could take to fix this:

  - Add an error parameter that is passed by reference that can be set by the called function when an error occurs

  - Create a class level "LastError" style property that can be read to retrieve information about the most recent error

  - Raise errors using VB's error-handling mechanism

- **Timeouts.** The utility as it stands will hang in an infinite loop should a service fail to start or stop as requested. The best way to handle this is to provide some sort of timeout. The SERVICE_STATUS structure provides additional information to help you detect if a service start or stop operation error has occurred.

- **Missing functions.** If you review the service API functions, you'll see that quite a few functions were left out. These include API functions for adding and deleting services, configuring services, determining their dependencies, and setting service security. A fully implemented set of classes would include these features.

- **Interaction with other tools.** The utility creates a reference list of the current state of each service when it loads. If you start or stop a service using another tool, such as the Control Panel, the utility will not see that change or update its internal list. This means that, if you restore the original values using the utility, the values will not reflect changes made after the application loaded.

- **Reentrant version.** The current version of the utility disables all user input while it is trying to start or stop a service. This is necessary to prevent reentrancy problems—for example, an attempt to stop a service while it is being started. A more sophisticated program could manage multiple start and restore operations, preventing such conflicts through a smarter algorithm. Whether it is worth the effort to develop that functionality is up to you.

Good-bye, ASP?

Isn't that the way it always works out? You go to the trouble of creating a useful little utility and it's obsolete before you even use it! Actually, it will continue to be useful for those of you using Active Server Pages and for other applications where you wish to start or stop services. And there is a lot to learn from the example. As for me—I'm going to be writing Web classes using Visual Basic 6.

Reading the Event Log

*The following article was originally published in my column in
Pinnacle's Visual Basic Developer Newsletter. It is such a perfect
case study for this book that I decided to reprint it here, even
though some of you may have read it in the original form. This
tutorial requires Windows NT.*

YOU MAY HAVE NOTICED THAT MANY of my columns are inspired by questions that
arrive relating to either Desaware's products or my books. One of the reasons for
this is that any time I need inspiration for a column, I turn to my e-mail in-box
for inspiration. Many of these questions never get answered because, although I
would like to provide technical support for my Win32 API book (*Dan Appleman's
Visual Basic Programmer's Guide to the Win32 API*), it's simply not economically
feasible to do so. I try to offer quick answers to those questions I can answer easily, but those that take substantial effort often get short shrift—unless, of course,
I base an article on them.

Today's inspiration came from the following question:

*I am trying to call the ReadEventLog function with VB. I have tons of exam-
ples with VC++ but nothing for VB. The part that's killing me is the C type
casting of a pointer. This is the code I am trying to convert. Any help would be
greatly appreciated.*

```
EVENTLOGRECORD *pevlr;
BYTE bBuffer[BUFFER_SIZE];
DWORD dwRead, dwNeeded, cRecords, dwThisRecord = 0;

h = OpenEventLog(NULL,"Application");
if (h == NULL) ErrorExit("could not open Application event log");

pevlr = (EVENTLOGRECORD *) &bBuffer;

while (ReadEventLog(h, EVENTLOG_FORWARDS_READ |
EVENTLOG_SEQUENTIAL_READ, 0, pevlr, BUFFER_SIZE,  &dwRead, &dwNeeded))
   while (dwRead > 0) {
      printf("%02d  Event ID: 0x%08X ", dwThisRecord++, pevlr->EventID);
      printf("EventType: %d Source: %s\n", pevlr->EventType, (LPSTR)((LPBYTE)
```

```
        pevlr + sizeof(EVENTLOGRECORD)));
            dwRead -= pevlr->Length;
            pevlr = (EVENTLOGRECORD *) ((LPBYTE) pevlr + pevlr->Length);
            }
        pevlr = (EVENTLOGRECORD *) &bBuffer;
        }
    CloseEventLog(h);
```

Learning how to translate C language code is an essential task for advanced VB programmers. I tried to cover most of the core Win32 API in my book, but with new API functions being defined daily, it is impossible for any book to cover everything that every VB programmer may need to know. That's why I spent two chapters in my API book discussing how to convert C API declarations to Visual Basic.

Still, practice makes perfect, and the event log question posed here is an interesting exercise indeed.

A first step is to define the EVENTLOGRECORD structure. This can be found in the following api32.txt file, which comes with my Win32 API book:

```
Type EVENTLOGRECORD
        Length as Long        '  Length of full record
        Reserved as Long       '  Used by the service
        RecordNumber as Long    '  Absolute record number
        TimeGenerated as Long    '  Seconds since 1-1-1970
        TimeWritten as Long     'Seconds since 1-1-1970
        EventID as Long
        EventType as Integer
        NumStrings as Integer
        EventCategory as Integer
        ReservedFlags as Integer    '  For use with paired events
        ClosingRecordNumber as Long    'For use with paired events
        StringOffset as Long     '  Offset from beginning of record
        UserSidLength as Long
        UserSidOffset as Long
        DataLength as Long
        DataOffset as Long       '  Offset from beginning of record
End Type
```

The conversion of this structure from the C type declaration is trivial since it only contains DWORD and WORD types. DWORDs translate into VB Long variables, WORDs into VB integers.

Next, let's take a look at the API functions we'll be using:

```
HANDLE OpenEventLog(LPCTSTR lpUNCServerName, LPCTSTR lpSourceName );
```

```
BOOL ReadEventLog(HANDLE hEventLog, DWORD dwReadFlags, DWORD dwRecordOffset,
LPVOID lpBuffer, DWORD nNumberOfBytesToRead, DWORD *pnBytesRead, DWORD
*pnMinNumberOfBytesNeeded );
```

```
BOOL CloseEventLog(HANDLE hEventLog);
```

The Visual Basic equivalents are also found in the api32.txt file. The conversion here is routine. In the OpenEventLog function, the LPCTSTR parameters are string pointers to standard NULL-terminated C strings. Because the function has a string, you can expect it to have two separate entry points: OpenEventLogA, which will use ANSI strings, and OpenEventLogW, which will use Unicode strings. The T in LPCTSTR indicates that the string is Unicode or ANSI depending on which entry point you use. Since we'll be using the ANSI entry point for now, the declaration is as follows:

```
Declare Function OpenEventLog Lib "advapi32.dll" Alias "OpenEventLogA" _
(ByVal lpUNCServerName As String, ByVal lpSourceName As String) As Long
```

The ReadEventLog function is somewhat more complex. The HANDLE and DWORD parameters are 32-bit values that are passed by value and are thus defined as Longs. The DWORD * parameters are pointers to 32-bit parameters. This means that they are also Longs, but are passed by reference—thus the VB declaration leaves out the ByVal for those cases. The lpBuffer parameter is defined in api32.txt as an EVENTLOGRECORD structure, but has been redefined here as a byte that is passed by reference. You'll see why this is necessary shortly. The CloseEventLog function simply passes the Long handle parameter by value.

```
Declare Function ReadEventLog Lib "advapi32.dll" Alias "ReadEventLogA" _
(ByVal hEventLog As Long, ByVal dwReadFlags As Long, ByVal dwRecordOffset _
As Long, lpBuffer As Byte, ByVal nNumberOfBytesToRead As Long, pnBytesRead _
As Long, pnMinNumberOfBytesNeeded As Long) As Long
```

```
Declare Function CloseEventLog Lib "advapi32.dll" _
(ByVal hEventLog As Long) As Long
```

Building Code Step by Step

I've found that the easiest way to convert unfamiliar C code to Visual Basic is to do it step by step, verifying the code along the way. The Event sample has a command button that will run the code and a list box to display results. The first cut contains the following code:

```
Private Sub Command1_Click()
    Dim h As Long
    h = OpenEventLog(vbNullString, "Application")
    Debug.Print h
    if h<>0 Then Call CloseEventLog(h)
End Sub
```

The only difference between this code and the C code is using vbNullString to pass a NULL value to the string parameter. You can't use an empty string ("") because this will pass a pointer to a NULL-terminated string to the function instead of 0. It is important to always include the CloseEventLog function as well. If you fail to close the event log, it will remain open for the life of the process, which in this case is Visual Basic. Not only are open handles wasteful, but they may prevent you from opening the event log when you run the program a second time. When you run this program and click the command button, you'll see a non-zero value displayed in the immediate window. This proves that the event log was opened successfully.

C—A Language Designed to Confuse

The author of the original question was perplexed by the casting of pointers. Frankly, I can't blame him. C may be one of the most cryptic languages ever created. In fact, there was once a book called something along the lines of *The C Puzzle Book* that consisted of nothing but convoluted C code examples that challenged the reader to figure out what they actually did. It was fun, but also a little bit irrelevant—no good programmer would ever use that kind of code in a real application. Professional-quality code should be readable.[1]

Let's take another look at the loop in the C code, but this time I'm going to eliminate some of the parameters and replace them with a description of what is actually going on.

```
while ( The function ReadEventLog(As many EVENTLOGRECORD structures as will fit
entirely in a buffer) reads one or more structures) {
    while (The number of bytes actually read from the event log > 0) {
        Display information from this record
        dwRead -= pevlr->Length; Subtract the size of this record
        And change the pointer to point to the next record in the buffer
        pevlr = (EVENTLOGRECORD *) ((LPBYTE) pevlr + pevlr->Length);
```

1. This book was inspired by *The C Puzzle Book*. However, I tried to create puzzles that were relevant to the needs of real VB programmers, while keeping the element of fun that made the original so unique.

```
    }
    Set the EVENTLOGRECORD pointer to the start of the buffer
    pevlr = (EVENTLOGRECORD *) &bBuffer;
}
```

The pevlr variable is a pointer variable that initially points to the start of an arbitrarily sized buffer. This example reads as many records as possible into the buffer. It then scans through each entry in the buffer.

It's important to take the time to understand exactly what the code is doing rather than try to mimic it line by line in Visual Basic. The best way to do this, if you are not a C programmer, is to back up and read the documentation for the function before trying to figure out the C code. Once you realize that the ReadEventLog function is capable of reading multiple event log records, the code here begins to make sense.

You may wonder why you should read multiple records in a double loop as shown here. Why use a byte array instead of reading one or more EVENTLOGRECORD structures directly?

The trick is in the structure itself. As you can see from the structure declaration, some of the variables in the structure are actually offsets to strings and other variable-length data. The question arises: Where can this additional data be found? The answer is that the data is placed in the buffer along with and immediately after the EVENTLOGRECORD structure. More information can be found in the Win32 SDK documentation for the structure. After the last field in the structure, it shows the following fields:

```
// TCHAR SourceName[]
// TCHAR Computername[]
// SID   UserSid
// TCHAR Strings[]
// BYTE  Data[]
// CHAR  Pad[]
// DWORD Length;
```

These fields can't be defined in the structure itself because they are of variable length. So we need to allocate a buffer that will hold not only the EVENTLOGRECORD structure, but all of the data for the event as well. The Length field contains the total length of the structure and includes the length of the variable length fields. It is stored both at the beginning and end of the structure to make it easier to scan forward or backward through the buffer. The following variables correspond exactly to those in the C example:

```
Private Const BUFFER_SIZE = 8192  ' Arbitrary number
Dim bBuffer(BUFFER_SIZE) As Byte
```

```
Dim dwRead As Long
Dim dwNeeded As Long
Dim cRecords As Long
Dim dwThisRecord As Long
```

Now, the catch is this: Once we load a buffer with one or more of these structure-plus-data combinations, how do we extract the information using Visual Basic?

Well, the first step is to get access to the structure data. The easiest way to do this is to define a temporary EVENTLOGRECORD structure to hold the data. We'll load it from the buffer using the following memory copy routine:

```
Private Declare Sub RtlMoveMemory Lib "kernel32" (dest As Any, _
source As Any, ByVal bytes As Long)
```

See those As Any parameters? They imply that the function can handle any type of parameter. Because the purpose of this function is to copy a block of memory from one location to another, this makes the function extremely dangerous. Any mistake is likely to corrupt memory or raise a memory exception. We also need a pointer variable. Because Visual Basic does not support pointers directly, we'll use a Long variable. This implies two variables:

```
Dim ev As EVENTLOGRECORD
Dim pevlr As Long
```

The C language allows you to access data using pointers and to convert pointers from one type to another using a technique called "casting." We'll fake this process in Visual Basic by copying data into a user-defined type, as follows:

```
pevlr = VarPtr(bBuffer(0))
RtlMoveMemory ev, ByVal pevlr, Len(EVENTLOGRECORD)
```

The VarPtr operator is an undocumented operator built into Visual Basic to obtain the address of a variable. We actually obtain the address of the first byte, because it appears (by definition) at the start of the buffer. Note how it must be passed by value to the RtlMoveMemory function. If you passed it by reference, you would pass the address of the pevlr variable, not the address of the bBuffer array.

Now that we've copied the data into the temporary ev structure, you can access the event data. But how do we get the string data that follows the EVENT-LOGRECORD structure in the buffer? To do this, we'll need two more API functions, lstrlen and lstrcpy, which are declared as follows:

```
Declare Function lstrlenptr Lib "kernel32" Alias "lstrlenA" _
```

```
(ByVal lpString As Long) As Long
Declare Function lstrcpyfromptr Lib "kernel32" Alias "lstrcpyA" _
(ByVal lpString1 As String, ByVal lpString2 As Long) As Long
```

The lstrlenptr function uses the lstrlen API function to obtain the length of a
string. Note, however, that we've declared the function to use a Long variable.
This is because we are going to pass it a pointer value rather than a string. The
same technique is used in the lstrcpyfromptr function, which copies a string
from a location in memory to a Visual Basic string. To make things easier, you
can use the following VB function, which takes a memory address, obtains the
length of the string, allocates a Visual Basic string, and loads it from the memory
address:

```
Private Function LoadStringFromPtr(ByVal ptrval&) As String
    Dim slen&
    Dim resstring$
    If ptrval = 0 Then Exit Function
    slen = lstrlenptr(ptrval)
    resstring = String$(slen + 1, 0)
    Call lstrcpyfromptr(resstring, ptrval)
    LoadStringFromPtr = Left$(resstring, slen)
End Function
```

The resstring variable is initially defined with one extra byte. This is because the
lstrcpyfromptr function will copy a terminating NULL character along with the
string data. The final step is to use the Left$ function to strip off the NULL char-
acter, which is not needed in a Visual Basic string.

Bringing It All Together

Going back to the event log, the first string to appear after the EVENTLOGRECORD
structure in the buffer is a string describing the source of the event. The location
of this string will be at pevlr + Len(ev). This is the final piece of the Visual Basic
routine for reading events. The routine corresponds closely to the C example
shown earlier:

```
Private Sub Command1_Click()
    Dim h As Long
    Dim ev As EVENTLOGRECORD
    Dim pevlr As Long
    h = OpenEventLog(vbNullString, "Application")
    List1.Clear
    If h <> 0 Then
```

```
            pevlr = VarPtr(bBuffer(0))
            While (ReadEventLog(h, EVENTLOG_FORWARDS_READ Or _
                EVENTLOG_SEQUENTIAL_READ, _
                0, bBuffer(0), BUFFER_SIZE, dwRead, dwNeeded) <> 0)
              While dwRead > 0
                ' Copy the data into the ev structure.
                RtlMoveMemory ev, ByVal pevlr, Len(ev)
                List1.AddItem " Event Type: " & Hex$(ev.EventType) & _
                                " Source: " & LoadStringFromPtr(pevlr + _
                                Len(ev))
                dwRead = dwRead - ev.Length
                pevlr = pevlr + ev.Length
              Wend
              ' Reset the pointer to the start of the buffer
              pevlr = VarPtr(bBuffer(0))
            Wend
            Call CloseEventLog(h)
        End If
    End Sub
```

Here's one last challenge: Immediately after the event source string in the buffer, you'll find the computer name. Can you figure out how to retrieve it? The answer is in the actual sample program.

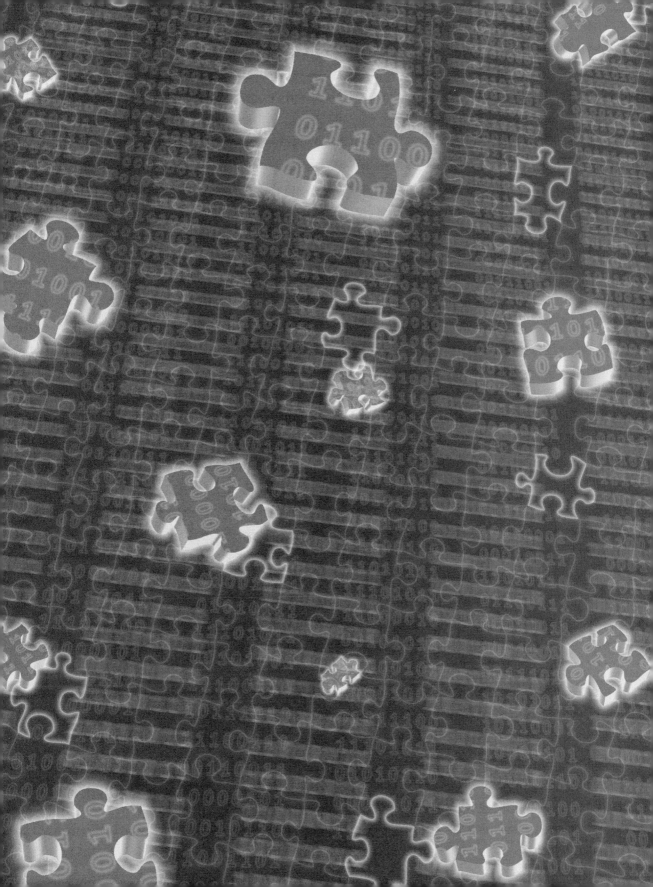

Hints

THE BEST HINT I CAN OFFER for any puzzle is to first apply the "Ten Commandments for Safe API Programming" (from this book's Introduction) to each puzzle. There are few problems that do not relate in one way or another to these commandments.

Puzzle 1

- See my book *Visual Basic Programmer's Guide to the Win32 API*, Chapter 5.

- See Tutorial 1, "Finding Functions," in Part III of this book.

- See API Commandment VIII.

Puzzle 2

- Under Windows, many standard values have descriptive constant names. Thus message &H10 has the constant name WM_CLOSE, as shown in this example.

Puzzle 3

- There are some obvious problems with this program. There are others that—how shall I put it?—are not quite as obvious.

- See API Commandment I.

- See API Commandment IX.

- Consider the ScaleMode property.

Puzzle 4

- Don't give up after you solve the first problem.

- See API Commandment IV.

- See Tutorial 6, "C++ Variables Meet Visual Basic," in Part III of this book.

Puzzle 5

- See API Commandment IV.

Puzzle 6

- See API Commandment 9.

- See Tutorial 6, "C++ Variables Meet Visual Basic," in Part III of this book.

Puzzle 7

- The math is correct.

- So is the program logic.

Puzzle 8

- Once you've solved the obvious problem and still can't get the function to work, read the description of the GetVersionEx function in the Win32 online documentation or in my book *Visual Basic Programmer's Guide to the Win32 API*.

Puzzle 9

- The function declaration is correct.

Puzzle 10

- The api32.txt file (on the CD included with this book) uses the following declaration for GetEnvironmentStrings:

```
Declare Function GetEnvironmentStrings Lib "kernel32" Alias
"GetEnvironmentStringsA" () As Long
```

- See Tutorial 6, "C++ Variables Meet Visual Basic," in Part III of this book.

Puzzle 11

- If you find yourself spending more than five minutes on this problem, take a break, then come back to it, keeping in mind that sometimes the most obvious problems are the most difficult to solve.

Puzzle 12

- The revised version of the GetKeyInfo function can be implemented in a single line of code.

- Oh, by the way, the version of GetKeyInfo shown here doesn't quite work. You might want to fix it first.

- All the information that you need to figure out the problem can be found in this puzzle.

Puzzle 13

- There are two bugs in this code.

- Sometimes fixing one bug will actually seem to make things worse.

Puzzle 14

- Try making a list of declarations that you would use for various data types.

Puzzle 15

- Did you know that it is possible to assign a byte array directly to a string?

Puzzle 16

- Just because the puzzles in this section are more advanced doesn't mean I can't sneak a simple one in now and again.

Puzzle 17

- Changing the declaration to the one shown in api32.txt (on the CD included with this book) is not enough to solve the problem.

- You may need more information than shown in the puzzle to figure this one out—that means going to the documentation for the function.

- See my book *Visual Basic Programmer's Guide to the Win32 API*, Chapter 12 (listing for the DocumentProperties function).

- See the Win32 SDK or MSDN, DocumentProperties reference.

- After you look at one or both of the above two references, read them again *carefully*!

- See Tutorial 4, "How DLL Calls Work: Inside a Stack Frame," in Part III of this book.

Puzzle 18

- See Tutorial 7, "Classes, Structures, and User-Defined Types," in Part III of this book.

- What happens when the first element of an array of structures is passed as a parameter to an API function?

Puzzle 19

- Don't forget the alignment rules.

- Did you know that Visual Basic supports conditional compilation?

- What happens when you assign a short string to a larger fixed-length string?

Puzzle 20

- You might want to become familiar with the Visual Basic Enum keyword.

Puzzle 21

- There are at least two solutions to this problem—can you find both?

- Don't forget the value of experimentation.

Puzzle 22

- The declaration from the win32api.txt provided with Visual Basic should never be assumed to be correct.

- What happens when you step through the code?

- See Tutorial 7, "Classes, Structures, and User-Defined Types," in Part III of this book.

Puzzle 23

- See Tutorial 2, "Memory, Where It All Begins," in Part III of this book, and read up on signed and unsigned variables.

- How many bytes is 168 bits?

Puzzle 24

- What does a Visual Basic function expect to see when a parameter is declared ByVal As String? Is it the same as what an API function would receive in the same circumstances?

- You may also want to look up the EnumSystemLocales function in the Win32 online documentation or in my book *Visual Basic Programmer's Guide to the Win32 API*, but it is not necessary to solve the problem.

Puzzle 25

- Tutorial 8, "Porting C Header Files," in Part III of this book, may be helpful.

Puzzle 26

- Try uncommenting the Err.Raise statement in the GUIDObject class.

- Be sure you've reviewed Puzzle 25, "Universal Identifiers, Part 1," before you try to solve this puzzle.

Puzzle 27

- An OLE string is a BSTR, not an OLESTR.

- Every string must exist somewhere in memory.

Puzzle 28

- Consider: What exactly is an object variable?

- Think about the object relationships involved in the use of ActiveX controls.

- Have you ever wondered how Visual Basic knows you are ready to print a page?

Puzzle 29

- You'll probably run into two types of memory exceptions during your experimentation. The "Privileged Instruction" exception typically will turn up under Windows NT if you set the clocks parameter of the cpuspeed function to anything other than 0, so be sure to use 0 for this parameter. The other exception will be a regular memory exception error.

- See Tutorial 2, "Memory, Where It All Begins," in Part III of this book.

Puzzle 30

- There's a reason this puzzle is in the part of the book titled "Rocket Science."

Puzzle 31

- The Windows documentation clearly indicates that this function is supported on both Windows 95 and Windows NT.

APPENDIX B

Frequently Asked Questions

THIS APPENDIX IS BASED ON QUESTIONS I have received that have inspired the content in this book. As more questions arrive, you'll be able to find additional FAQ content on the book's Web site at *http://www.desaware.com/*. Note that when a puzzle is listed it refers to both the puzzle and solution. In most cases, the answer will actually be found in the solution for the puzzle.

The Basics

How do I find which DLL contains a function?

- See Puzzle 1, "Where, oh, Where Is That API Call?" in Part I of this book.

- See Tutorial 1, "Finding Functions," in Part III of this book.

Are function names case-sensitive?

- See Puzzle 1, "Where, oh, Where Is That API Call?" in Part I of this book.

How do I obtain detailed error information for API functions?

- See Puzzle 2, "The Last Error," in Part I of this book.

- See my book *Visual Basic Programmer's Guide to the Win32 API*, Chapter 3.

What is the LastError value and how do I use it?

- See Puzzle 2, "The Last Error," in Part I of this book.

- See my book *Visual Basic Programmer's Guide to the Win32 API*, Chapters 3 and 6.

What causes the "Bad DLL Calling Convention Error"?

- See Tutorial 4, "How DLL Calls Work: Inside a Stack Frame," in Part III of this book.

How are parameters passed to API functions?

- See Tutorial 4, "How DLL Calls Work: Inside a Stack Frame," in Part III of this book.

When should I use ByVal in a declaration or function call?

- See Tutorial 5, "The ByVal Keyword: The Solution to 90 Percent of All API Problems," in Part III of this book.

How do I pass handles to API functions?

- See Puzzle 3, "Poly Want a Cracker?" in Part I of this book.

How do I handle signed and unsigned numbers?

- See Tutorial 2, "Memory, Where It All Begins," in Part III of this book.

- See Tutorial 6, "C++ Variables Meet Visual Basic."

How are variables stored in memory?

See Tutorial 1, "Finding Functions," in Part III of this book.

How do I handle API functions that return Boolean values?

- See Tutorial 3, "A Bool and Its Bitfields Are Soon Parted," in Part III of this book.

How do I combine constants for use with API calls?

- See Tutorial 3, "A Bool and Its Bitfields Are Soon Parted," in Part III of this book.

How do I set or clear the individual bits?

- See Tutorial 3, "A Bool and Its Bitfields Are Soon Parted," in Part III of this book.

What is the VarPtr operator?

- See Tutorial 5, "The ByVal Keyword: The Solution to 90 Percent of All API Problems," in Part III of this book.

Finding Information About Functions and C Language Tricks

How do I find constant values?

- See Puzzle 23, "There Is a Question in There Somewhere," in Part I of this book.

- Look in the api32.txt file included on the CD that comes with this book.

- Search through the C header files included on the CD.

How do I read C header files?

- See Puzzle 6, "Icon Fix this One," in Part I of this book.

- See Puzzle 19, "The RASDIALPARAMS Structure."

- See Puzzle 25, "Universal Identifiers, Part 1."

- See Tutorial 6, "C++ Variables Meet Visual Basic," in Part III of this book.

- See Tutorial 8, "Porting C Header Files."

What is a C++ "cast" operation?

- See Puzzle 23, "There Is a Question in There Somewhere," in Part I of this book.

- See Puzzle 6, "ICON Fix this One."

How do I handle C language bitfields?

- See Tutorial 3, "A Bool and Its Bitfields Are Soon Parted," in Part III of this book.

How do I call a DLL function that uses the C calling convention instead of the normal stdcall calling convention?

- See Puzzle 29, "What Do You Do When It Mega Hurts?" in Part I of this book.

General Questions About Parameters

How do I handle parameters that can be defined as more than one data type?

- See Puzzle 6, "Icon Fix this One," in Part I of this book.

- See Puzzle 14, "Registry Games, Part 4."

What do I do with API parameters marked as reserved?

- See Puzzle 12, "Registry Games, Part 2," in Part I of this book.

How do I define a callback function?

- See Puzzle 20, "Making Connections," in Part I of this book.

All About Strings

What is a NULL string?

- See Puzzle 2, "The Last Error," in Part I of this book.

How do I pass strings to API functions?

- See Puzzle 4, "It's All in the Name," in Part I of this book.

- See Puzzle 5, "Finding the Executable Name."

- See Puzzle 16, "Serially Speaking."

- See Tutorial 5, "The ByVal Keyword: The Solution to 90 Percent of All API Problems," in Part III of this book.

How do I get rid of the NULL terminating character in a string?

- See Puzzle 1, "Where, oh, Where Is That API Call?" in Part I of this book.

- See Puzzle 4, "It's All in the Name."

- See Puzzle 5, "Finding the Executable Name."

- See Puzzle 16, "Serially Speaking."

How do the VarPtr and StrPtr operators differ?

- See Puzzle 26, "Universal Identifiers, Part 2," in Part I of this book.

- See Tutorial 5, "The ByVal Keyword: The Solution to 90 Percent of All API Problems," in Part III of this book.

How do I handle API functions that return strings?

- See Puzzle 10, "Environmentally Speaking," in Part I of this book.

What is a double NULL-terminated string and how do I work with it?

- See Puzzle 10, "Environmentally Speaking," in Part I of this book.

How can an API callback function pass a string to a VB function?

- See Puzzle 24, "Callback That String," in Part I of this book.

All About Strings, Arrays, and ANSI-to-Unicode Conversions

How do I convert an array containing Unicode characters into a Visual Basic string?

- See Puzzle 15, "What Time Zone Is It?" in Part I of this book.

How do I load a VB string given a pointer to a Unicode string?

- See Puzzle 27, "Universal Identifiers, Part 3," in Part I of this book.

Given a VB string, how do I obtain and load a byte array with the equivalent ANSI string ?

- See Puzzle 22, "What Is That Mapped Drive? Part 2," in Part I of this book.

How do I convert a pointer to an ANSI string into a VB string?

- See Puzzle 22, "What Is That Mapped Drive? Part 2," in Part I of this book.

How do I obtain a pointer to a Unicode string?

- See Puzzle 23, "There Is a Question in There Somewhere," in Part I of this book.

- See Puzzle 26, "Universal Identifiers, Part 2."

- See Tutorial 5, "The ByVal Keyword: The Solution to 90 Percent of All API Problems," in Part III of this book.

What are ANSI and Unicode entry points and how do I use them?

- See Tutorial 5, "The ByVal Keyword: The Solution to 90 Percent of All API Problems," in Part III of this book.

How do I pass Unicode strings to API functions?

- See Tutorial 5, "The ByVal Keyword: The Solution to 90 Percent of All API Problems," in Part III of this book.

All About Arrays

How do I pass arrays to API functions?

- See Puzzle 3, "Poly Want a Cracker?" in Part I of this book.

- See Puzzle 7, "Supercharged Graphics."

How do I set or retrieve individual bits in a byte array?

- See Puzzle 23, "There Is a Question in There Somewhere," in Part I of this book.

All About Structures

Why do some structures require that I specify the size of the structure before passing it as a parameter to an API function?

- See Puzzle 8, "Playing Leapfrog," in Part I of this book.

- See Puzzle 18, "DT, Phone Home."

How do I handle variable length structures?

- See Puzzle 17, "The DEVMODE Is in the Details," in Part I of this book.

What are structure alignment issues?

- See Puzzle 18, "DT, Phone Home," in Part I of this book.

- See Puzzle 30, "File Operations, Part 1."

- See Tutorial 7, "Classes, Structures, and User-Defined Types," in Part III of this book.

How do I handle a C++ "enum" structure?

- See Puzzle 20, "Making Connections," in Part I of this book.

How do I handle API or DLL functions that return structures as a result?

- See Puzzle 29, "What Do You Do When It Mega Hurts?" in Part I of this book.

All About Strange Permutations of Strings, Arrays, and Structures

How do I define arrays inside of structures?

- See Puzzle 9, "Translating DEVMODE," in Part I of this book.

- See Puzzle 15, "What Time Zone Is It?"

How do I handle strings inside of structures?

- See Puzzle 9, "Translating DEVMODE," in Part I of this book.

- See Puzzle 18, "DT, Phone Home."

- See Puzzle 22, "What Is That Mapped Drive? Part 2."

- See Puzzle 30, "File Operations, Part 1."

- See Tutorial 7, "Classes, Structures, and User-Defined Types," in Part III of this book.

How do I handle arrays of structures containing strings?

- See Puzzle 18, "DT, Phone Home," in Part I of this book.

- See Puzzle 19, "The RASDIALPARAMS Structure."

How do I determine the size of a buffer needed by an API function?

- See Puzzle 21, "What Is That Mapped Drive? Part 1," in Part I of this book.

How do I obtain a pointer to an ANSI string for use in structures being passed to API functions?

- See Puzzle 22, "What Is That Mapped Drive? Part 2," in Part I of this book.

How do I handle Unicode strings inside of structures?

- See Puzzle 23, "There Is a Question in There Somewhere," in Part I of this book.

A Little Bit of OLE

How do I pass GUID, IID, or CLSID information to an OLE API function?

- See Puzzle 25, "Universal Identifiers, Part 1," in Part I of this book.

Who is responsible for allocating and freeing OLE API parameters?

- See Puzzle 27, "Universal Identifiers, Part 4," in Part I of this book.

What is an HRESULT?

- See Puzzle 26, "Universal Identifiers, Part 2," in Part I of this book.

How do I free a string allocated by the OLE subsystem?

- See Puzzle 27, "Universal Identifiers, Part 3," in Part I of this book.

How do I pass object references to OLE API functions?

- See Puzzle 28, "Drawing OLE Objects," in Part I of this book.

- See Tutorial 6, "C++ Variables Meet Visual Basic," in Part III of this book.

How do I pass a custom control as a parameter to an OLE API function?

- See Puzzle 28, "Drawing OLE Objects," in Part I of this book.

Learning More About Windows

How do I learn more about Windows?

My book *Visual Basic Programmer's Guide to the Win32 API* is designed to teach Visual Basic programmers about the Windows operating systems by building on what you already know from Visual Basic.

There are many other books on Windows (including the online Microsoft documentation), but most of them are designed for C and C++ programmers.

How do I determine the operating system version?

- See Puzzle 8, "Playing Leapfrog," in Part I of this book.

Where can I find out more about system locales?

- See Puzzle 1, "Where, oh, Where Is That API Call?" in Part I of this book.

- See Puzzle 24, "Callback That String."

- See my book *Visual Basic Programmer's Guide to the Win32 API*, Chapter 6.

Where can I find out more about Windows and the FindWindow function?

- See Puzzle 2, "The Last Error," in Part I of this book.

- See my book *Visual Basic Programmer's Guide to the Win32 API*, Chapter 5.

Where can I find out more about device contexts and API drawing functions?

- See Puzzle 3, "Poly Want a Cracker?" in Part I of this book.

- See my book *Visual Basic Programmer's Guide to the Win32 API*, Chapters 7 and 8.

What is a module handle? And what is the difference between module handles and process handles?

- See Puzzle 5, "Finding the Executable Name," in Part I of this book.

- See my book *Visual Basic Programmer's Guide to the Win32 API*, Chapter 14.

What are Windows resources and how do I use them?

- See Puzzle 6, "Icon Fix This One," in Part I of this book.

- See my book *Visual Basic Programmer's Guide to the Win32 API*, Chapter 15.

How do I work with icons and bitmaps using the Win32 API?

- See Puzzle 6, "Icon Fix This One," in Part I of this book.

- See my book *Visual Basic Programmer's Guide to the Win32 API*, Chapter 9.

How do I work with the system registry?

- See Puzzles 11–14, "Registry Games, Parts 1–4," in Part I of this book.

- See my book *Visual Basic Programmer's Guide to the Win32 API*, Chapter 13.

How do I use a DEVMODE structure to retrieve or set printer information?

- See Puzzle 17, "The DEVMODE Is in the Details," in Part I of this book.

- See my book *Visual Basic Programmer's Guide to the Win32 API*, Chapter 12.

How do I use RAS (remote access services) from Visual Basic?

- See Puzzle 18, "DT, Phone Home," in Part I of this book.

- See Puzzle 19, "The RASDIALPARAMS Structure."

- See Puzzle 20, "Making Connections."

How do I determine network drive mappings?

- See Puzzle 21, "What Is That Mapped Drive? Part 1," in Part I of this book.

- See my book *Visual Basic Programmer's Guide to the Win32 API*, Chapter 22 (CD-ROM edition only).

How can I create a new account under Windows NT?

- See Puzzle 23, "There Is a Question in There Somewhere," in Part I of this book.

How can I use the shell API to copy files?

- See Puzzle 30, "File Operations, Part 1," in Part I of this book.

The APIGID32.DLL Library

THE FUNCTIONS DESCRIBED IN THIS APPENDIX are part of the apigid32.dll dynamic link library. This DLL, provided by Desaware, contains a number of routines that should prove useful when working with API functions. The source code for this library is included on the CD that comes with this book. You may distribute the DLL with your compiled Visual Basic applications. However, Desaware does not provide free support for this DLL.

Numeric Functions

The following functions operate on numeric variables, providing features that are difficult to implement in Visual Basic due to its lack of unsigned data types.

agDWORDto2Integers

```
Declare Function agDWORDto2Integers Lib "apigid32.dll" (ByVal l As Long, lw As _
Integer,
```

Many Windows API functions return a long variable that contains two integers. This function provides an efficient way to separate the two integers. The value passed in parameter l is divided, with the low 16 bits loaded into the lw parameter and the high 16 bits loaded into the lh parameter.

agPOINTStoLong

```
Declare Function agPOINTStoLong Lib "apigid32.dll" (pt As POINTS) As Long
```

Converts a POINTS structure into a Long, placing the X field in the low 16 bits of the result and the Y field in the high 16 bits of the result. This function is convenient for Windows API functions that expect POINTS structures to be passed as Long parameters.

agSwapBytes, agSwapWords

```
Declare Function agSwapBytes Lib "apigid32.dll" (ByVal src As Integer) As Integer
Declare Function agSwapWords Lib "apigid32.dll" (ByVal src As Long) As Long
```

In rare situations, you may need to swap the order of bytes in an integer or the integers in a long. This will typically occur when working with file formats defined originally for non-Intel processors. This function provides an easy way to accomplish this task.

Pointer and Buffer Routines

These functions can be helpful when handling certain types of string and buffer operations. The operation of these functions can be implemented using Visual Basic alone, however, these functions can be more efficient and are easier to use.

agCopyData, agCopyDataBynum

```
Declare Sub agCopyData Lib "apigid32.dll" (source As Any, dest As Any, ByVal _
nCount As Long)
Declare Sub agCopyDataBynum Lib "apigid32.dll" Alias "agCopyData" (ByVal _
source As Long, ByVal dest As Long, ByVal nCount As Long)
```

This function is provided to copy data from one object to another. Two forms of this function are provided. The first accepts any type of object. If the two objects were of the same type, you could simply use the Visual Basic LSet function; however, this function can be used for copying only the specified part of the object.

The second form accepts Long parameters. It is typically used to copy data between Visual Basic structures and string buffers or memory blocks.

The source parameter specifies the address of the start of a block of memory to copy.

The dest parameter specifies the destination address for the data.

The nCount parameter specifies the number of bytes to copy.

The RtlMoveMemory function performs the same task and is used extensively in this book. Note, however, that the order of source and destination parameters is reversed in the two functions.

Be careful that the parameters for this function are valid and that the entire range specified by nCount is also valid.

agGetAddressForObject, agGetAddressForInteger, agGetAddressForLong, agGetAddressForLPSTR, agGetAddressForVBString

```
Declare Function agGetAddressForObject Lib "apigid32.dll" (object As Any) As Long
Declare Function agGetAddressForInteger Lib "apigid32.dll" Alias _
"agGetAddressForObject" (intnum As Integer) As Long
Declare Function agGetAddressForLong Lib "apigid32.dll" Alias _
"agGetAddressForObject" (intnum As Long) As Long
Declare Function agGetAddressForVBString Lib "apigid32.dll" Alias _
"agGetAddressForObject" (vbstring As String) As Long
```

All of these aliases call a very simple function that returns as a Long value the parameter that was passed. It can be useful in determining the value placed on the top of a stack for different parameters. It can also be used to retrieve the address of a variable when it is passed by reference, a task that is more frequently handled now using the VarPtr operator.

agGetStringFrom2NullBuffer

```
Declare Function agGetStringFrom2NullBuffer Lib "apigid32.dll" (ByVal ptr As _
Long) As String
```

There are a number of API functions that load a buffer with a series of strings, where each string is separated from the next by a NULL character and the final string is followed by two NULL characters. Loading a buffer of this type into a Visual Basic string is possible using VB and API functions alone, but it is a complex task that includes using API functions to calculate the length of each string and to copy each string individually. This function takes as a parameter a pointer to a memory buffer containing a double NULL-terminated set of strings, and returns a VB string with all of the strings in a single string (still separated by NULL characters with a double NULL termination at the end). You can then parse the individual strings easily using the VB Instr and Mid$ functions.

agGetStringFromPointer

```
Declare Function agGetStringFromPointer Lib "apigid32.dll" Alias _
"agGetStringFromLPSTR" (ByVal ptr As Long) As String
```

This function takes a parameter containing a memory pointer to a NULL-terminated ANSI string and returns a Visual Basic string containing the string (without the NULL terminating character). This function is the easiest way to convert a pointer to a NULL-terminated string into a Visual Basic string.

FileTime Functions

A number of API functions use 64-bit arithmetic to handle very large numeric variables such as dates, times, and sizes of files or disk drives. Visual Basic provides no support for 64-bit arithmetic, and it can be difficult to handle given that VB does not have an unsigned 32-bit data type. The following functions provide 64-bit arithmetic operations using structures that contain two 32-bit values. The FILETIME and LARGE_INTEGER structures are examples of structures that will work with these functions.

agAddFileTimes

```
Declare Sub agAddFileTimes Lib "apigid32.dll" (f1 As Any, f2 As Any, f3 As Any)
```

This function adds the contents of one FILETIME structure to another. It can also be used with LARGE_INTEGER and other 64-bit integer-based structures. The sum of f1 and f2 is loaded into f3.

agConvertDoubleToFileTime

```
Declare Sub agConvertDoubleToFileTime Lib "apigid32.dll" (ByVal d As Double, f1 _
As Any)
```

This function loads the contents of a FILETIME structure from a floating point value. It can also be used with LARGE_INTEGER and other 64-bit integer-based structures.

agConvertFileTimeToDouble

```
Declare Function agConvertFileTimeToDouble Lib "apigid32.dll" (f1 As Any) As Double
```

This function returns the contents of a FILETIME structure as a floating point value. It can also be used with LARGE_INTEGER and other 64-bit integer-based structures.

agNegateFileTimes

```
Declare Sub agNegateFileTime Lib "apigid32.dll" (f1 As Any)
```

This function negates the contents of one FILETIME structure from another. It can also be used with LARGE_INTEGER and other 64-bit integer-based structures. After this call, f1 will be equal to –f1.

agSubtractFileTimes

```
Declare Sub agSubtractFileTimes Lib "apigid32.dll" (f1 As Any, f2 As Any, f3 As Any)
```

This function subtracts the contents of one FILETIME structure from another. It can also be used with LARGE_INTEGER and other 64-bit integer-based structures. After this call, f3 will be equal to f1 – f2.

Miscellaneous

This function doesn't fit into any of the previous categories.

agIsValidName

```
Declare Function agIsValidName Lib "apigid32.dll" (ByVal o As Object, _
ByVal lpname As String) As Long
```

Given an object reference in parameter o, this function will return True (non-zero) if the string in the lpname parameter represents a method or property name for the automation interface of the object.

Index

D

N

O

X

Z

OTHER BOOKS AND SOFTWARE FROM DANIEL APPLEMAN

Why I founded Desaware

Since the days of Visual Basic 1.0, I've strived to provide high quality products to the Visual Basic community – products designed to help VB programmers not only take full advantage of the language, but also of operating system features and the latest COM/ActiveX technology. These products take the form of books, which are published by traditional book publishing companies, and software, which is published by Desaware Inc.

Most people don't realize that Desaware stands for "Daniel S. Appleman software." Desaware is my way of offering advanced tools and information that cannot be economically developed for books, and Desaware provided many of the sample programs and tools that you see in this book.

On these two pages you'll find brief descriptions of these books and products. I'd like to also invite you to explore the pzl1.hlp help file on the CD-ROM for this book. It contains more detailed product information and a video presentation from VBits where I discuss my books and products in the context of the challenges faced by all Visual Basic programmers.

SpyWorks 6.0

You CAN do it in Visual Basic. SpyWorks 6.0 is Desaware's flagship product, allowing Visual Basic programmers to do virtually anything in Visual Basic that can be done in C++. Available in both a subscription–based professional edition and standard edition, SpyWorks is the indispensible tool for thousands of Visual Basic programmers.

NEW - ATL Based Controls
Lightweight, with new features and no dependencies

Advanced Subclassing
In-process and cross-task, with efficient low level filtering

WINSOCK
VB source code, HTTP & FTP

Common Dialogs
Gain total control over Windows common dialogs

ActiveX Extensions

Call or Implement any Interface - Any method, any interface, no type library needed

Function Exports - Export functions from VB DLLs

Form Customization
Scrollbars, Virtual forms, MouseEnter/MouseExit, Tiny Captions and Rollups

Windows Hooks
Intercept messages and keys for any window or the entire system

API Class Library with source

Control Panel Applets - in VB

Lots of Source Code
Professional Edition
Subscription edition with three updates, additional controls & source

The Desaware ActiveX Gallimaufry

Now that Visual Basic supports the creation of ActiveX controls, more and more VB programmers are taking advantage of that technology. But it's a big step between creating a simple control and one that meets professional standards. Desaware's ActiveX Gallimaufry can help you bridge that gap.

The Desaware ActiveX Gallimaufry includes a collection of useful, entertaining and educational ActiveX controls that come with complete Visual Basic 5.0 source code. Among them are an MDI Taskbar Control, Hex Edit Control, Rotate Picture control, SpiralBox Control, Banner Control, PerspectiveList Control, and a Common Dialog Component. These components are worthwhile for the educational value alone. Includes 32–bit controls for Visual Basic 5.0 and 6.0 and other COM/ActiveX containers.

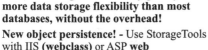
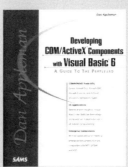

Apress™
License Agreement (Single-User Products)

THIS IS A LEGAL AGREEMENT BETWEEN YOU, THE END USER AND APRESS. BY OPENING THIS SEALED DISK PACKAGE, YOU ARE AGREEING TO BE BOUND BY THE TERMS OF THIS AGREEMENT. IF YOU DO NOT AGREE TO THE TERMS OF THIS AGREEMENT, PROMPTLY RETURN THE UNOPENED DISK PACKAGE AND THE ACCOMPANYING ITEMS (INCLUDING WRITTEN MATERIALS AND BINDERS OR OTHER CONTAINERS) TO THE PLACE YOU OBTAINED THEM FOR A FULL REFUND.

APRESS SOFTWARE LICENSE

1. GRANT OF LICENSE. APress grants to you the right to use one copy of the enclosed APress software program (the "SOFT-WARE") on a single terminal connected to a single computer (i.e., with a single CPU). You may not network the SOFTWARE or otherwise use it on more than one computer or computer terminal at the same time.

2. COPYRIGHT. The SOFTWARE copyright is owned by APress or its suppliers and is protected by United States copyright laws and international treaty provisions. Therefore, you must treat the SOFTWARE like any other copyrighted material (e.g., a book or musical recording) except that you may either (a) make one copy of the SOFTWARE solely for backup or archival purposes, or (b) transfer the SOFTWARE to a single hard disk provided you keep the original solely for backup or archival purposes. You may not copy the written material accompanying the SOFTWARE.

3. OTHER RESTRICTIONS. You may not rent or lease the SOFTWARE, but you may transfer the SOFTWARE and accompanying written materials on a permanent basis provided you retain no copies and the recipient agrees to the terms of this Agreement. You may not reverse engineer, decompile, or disassemble the SOFTWARE. If SOFTWARE is an update, any transfer must include the update and all prior versions.

4. DUAL MEDIA SOFTWARE. If the SOFTWARE package contains both 3.5" AND 5.25" disks, then you may use only the disks appropriate for your single-user computer. You may not use the other disks on another computer or loan, rent, lease, or transfer them to another user except as part of the permanent transfer (as provided above) of all SOFTWARE and written materials.

LIMITED WARRANTY

LIMITED WARRANTY. APress warrants that the SOFTWARE will perform substantially in accordance with the accompanying written material for a period of 90 days from the receipt. Any implied warranties on the SOFTWARE are limited to 90 days. Some states do not allow limitations on duration of an implied warranty, so the above limitation may not apply to you.

CUSTOMER REMEDIES. APress' entire liability and your exclusive remedy shall be, at APress' option, either (a) return of the price paid or (b) repair or replacement of the SOFTWARE that does not meet APress' Limited Warranty and which is returned to APress with a copy of your receipt. This limited warranty is void if failure of the software has resulted from accident, abuse, or misapplication. Any replacement SOFTWARE will be warranted for the remainder of the original warranty period or 30 days, whichever is longer. These remedies are not available outside of the United States of America.

NO OTHER WARRANTIES. APress disclaims all other warratnites, either express or implied, including but not limited to implied warranties of mechantability and finess for a particular purpose, with respect to the SOFTWARE and the accompanying written materials. This limited warranty gives you specific rights. You may have others, which vary from state to state.

NO LIABILITIES FOR CONSEQUENTIAL DAMAGES. In no event shall APress or its suppliers be liable for any damages whatso-ever (including, without limitation, damages for loss of business profits, business interruption, loss of business information, or other pecuniary loss) arising out of the use of or inability to use this APress product, even if APress has been advised of the possibility of such damages. Because some states do not allow the exclusion or limitation of liability for consequential or incidental damages, the above limitation may not apply to you.

U.S. GOVERNMENT RESTRICTED RIGHTS

The SOFTWARE and documentation are provided with RESTRICTED RIGHTS. Use, duplication, or disclosure by the Government is subject to restriction as set forth in subparagraph (c)(1)(ii) of The Rights in Technical Data and Computer Software clause at 52.227-7013. Contractor/manufacturer is APress, 555 De Haro Street, Suite 250, San Francisco, CA 94107.

This Agreement is governed by the laws of the State of California.

Should you have any questions concerning this Agreement, or if you wish to contact APress for any reason, please write to APress, 555 De Haro Street, Suite 250, San Francisco, CA 94107.